Manual

of Structural Design

Structural Principles – Suitable Spans – Inspiring Works

Eberhard Möller

Edition **DETAIL**

Authors

Prof. Dr.-Ing. Eberhard Möller
Karlsruhe University of Applied Sciences (DE)
Faculty of Architecture and Civil Engineering

With specialist contributions from:

Prof. Sigrid Adriaenssens, PhD
Princeton University, New Jersey (US)
Civil and Environmental Engineering

Prof. Dr.-Ing. Jan Akkermann
Karlsruhe University of Applied Sciences (DE)
Faculty of Architecture and Civil Engineering

Jun.-Prof. Dr.-Ing. M.Eng. Arch. Hanaa Dahy
University of Stuttgart (DE)
Faculty of Architecture and Urban Planning

Prof. Maria E. Moreyra Garlock, P.E., Ph.D., F.SEI
Princeton University, New Jersey (US)
Civil and Environmental Engineering

Dr.-Ing. Christian Kayser
Kayser + Böttges, Barthel + Maus, Ingenieure und Architekten
GmbH, Munich (DE)

Prof. Dr.-Ing. Werner Lang and
Dipl.-Ing. Patricia Schneider-Marin
Technical University of Munich (DE) Department of Civil,
Geo and Environmental Engineering

Prof. Dr.-Ing. Lars Schiemann
Munich University of Applied Sciences (DE)
Department of Structural and Building Design

Jonas Schikore, MSc
Academic Advisor
Technical University of Munich (DE), Department of Architecture

Editorial Services

Editing, copy editing (German edition):
Steffi Lenzen (Project Manager),
Jana Rackwitz (theory sections), Daniel Reisch (built examples);
Carola Jacob-Ritz (Proofreading)
Charlotte Petereit (Editorial Assistant)

Drawings:
Ralph Donhauser, Daniel Reisch, Lisa Hurler, Marion Griese

Translation into English:
Susanne Hauger, New York (US)

Copy editing (English edition):
Stefan Widdess, Berlin (DE)

Proofreading (English edition):
Meriel Clemett, Bromborough (GB)

Cover design based on a concept by:
Wiegand von Hartmann GbR, Munich (DE)

Production and DTP:
Simone Soesters

Reproduction:
ludwig:media, Zell am See (AT)

Printing and binding:
Grafisches Centrum Cuno GmbH & Co. KG, Calbe (DE)

© 2022 English translation of the 1st German edition
"Atlas Tragwerke" (ISBN: 978-3-95553-525-4)

Paper:
Les Naturals Olivine (cover),
Magno Volume (content)

Publisher:
Detail Business Information GmbH, Munich (DE)
detail-online.com

ISBN: 978-3-95553-565-0 (printed edition)
ISBN: 978-3-95553-566-7 (e-book)

Bibliographic information published by the German National
Library. The German National Library lists this publication
in the German National Bibliography (Deutsche National-
bibliografie); detailed bibliographic data is available on the
Internet at
http://dnb.d-nb.de.

This textbook uses terms applicable at the time of writing
and is based on the current state of the art, to the best of
the authors' and editors' knowledge and belief. All drawings
in this book were made specifically by the publisher. No
legal claims can be derived from the contents of this book.

Contents

Design and Construction of Structures

Eberhard Möller

"Equilibrium is at its most beautiful right before it collapses." [1]
Peter Fischli and David Weiss

Structures form the backbone of architecture and built infrastructure. They provide stability, serviceability and durability to buildings and constructions. Even if the structure of a building is not explicitly visible at first glance, it is nevertheless always there. The actions of gravity, wind, traffic and other causes make a load-bearing structure necessary for any building project, whether it be a garden shed, a skyscraper or a suspension bridge. The structure brings all forces acting on a built edifice into equilibrium with its own reaction forces.

Ideally, architects and engineers will develop the structure together. However, in practice things often look different. In the 1930s, in his *Architekturlehre,* Bruno Taut describes a situation that may sound quite familiar to some even today:

*"Then, in an architect's practice the following case occurs frequently: he is perhaps tasked with the design of an office building or a warehouse. The footprint is solved; but the architectural solution is still an open question. He turns to an engineer to learn which struc-*tural system is the most suitable, in the hopes that he will be able to use this system to extract the critical elements for his formal solution. They discuss the different options of iron or concrete skeletons, whether certain components should be incorporated into the system of cantilevering or even suspension and so on. Very often such conversations end with the engineer declaring, 'You can do it this way or that, however you want; it all presents no difficulties.' The architect had assumed that there must be a structure that was definitively the best, and from which he could develop his architecture. But in this regard he learns practically nothing from the engineer." [2]
Bruno Taut

This disappointment more urgently raises the question of who is ultimately responsible for the structure. Most of the numerical analyses of stability and usability are supplied by engineers. However, with regard to idea, concept and design the answer to the question is far less unequivocal.

Numerous experienced and famous designers – engineers as well as architects – have expressed their thoughts and presented their personal points of view on the critical aspects surrounding the design

1 Sydney Opera House, Sydney (AU) 1973 (construction begun in 1959), Jørn Utzon, Ove Arup
2 Estação do Oriente railway station, Lisbon (PT) 1998, Santiago Calatrava Architects & Engineers
3 Temporary pavilion at the Serpentine Gallery, London (GB) 2002, Toyo Ito & Associates, Arup, Cecil Balmond

2

and building of structures – the main subject of this book. In the following paragraphs, presented in alphabetical order, they have their say.

"Engineering is not a science. Science studies particular events to find general laws. Engineering design makes use of these laws to solve particular practical problems. In this it is more closely related to art or craft; as in art, its problems are underdefined, there are many solutions, good, bad and indifferent. The art is, by a synthesis of ends and means, to arrive at a good solution. This is a creative activity, involving imagination, intuition and deliberate choice, for possible solutions often vary in ways which cannot be directly compared by quantitative methods." [3]
Ove Arup

*"Structure is architecture.
The elements of structure punctuate space – they create episodes. They initiate movements to the eye.
The placing of structure and its elements creates rhythms.
Regular beats or shifting syncopation – classical or improvising jazz – each type of reference can be 'locked' into how a work is designed.
Structure is about organisation – loose and relaxed, or rigid and fixed in hard symmetries.
A structural element is not just a beam or a column, it can be a hedge in a landscape, a series of chords in a piece of music, a shaft of light in an installation.
Whatever the reference, the outcome of a work is governed by pattern – a base structure for order and primary equilibrium, and the finer markings of ornament for richer dynamics."* [4]
Cecil Balmond

"It is a common fallacy to believe that by following some laws (gravity, material properties, and so forth) strictly, the engineer will achieve the most artistic result. I have tried to show that none of the best designers believed in such an idea; they all recognised that they had the freedom of personal choice and that conscious aesthetic choice was essential to proper design. At the same time, they sought always to understand better both nature's laws and the properties of their materials. They were well trained in detailed mathematical analysis but as they gained more experience with full-scale works, they used such analysis less and less. Thus, they were disciplined but not controlled by nature's laws." [5]
David P. Billington

"Structural engineering comes from the power of the engineer's imagination and is founded on three ideals: efficiency, economy and elegance." [6]
David P. Billington

"When we speak of architecture, of cities and streets, bridges or houses, what we think about is a space. When we speak of architecture, it is a space that we approach by searching, calculating, building. When we speak of architecture, then it is structures, it is constructions that use light, material and proportions to convey intrinsic value and expression to the space. When we speak of architecture, we mean the structure, first and foremost, its usefulness; we mean the beauty and the message of its forms. No structure without space, therefore; and without space, architecture is not at issue." [7]
Hans-Busso von Busse

3

4

5

"It is a contemporary problem that there are people in the world of architectural critique who develop ethical standards for civil engineering. The laws of statics tell you what you can and cannot do. But the new ethicists say that there are things you should not do." Now Calatrava's question is: *"Why should something not be allowed if it is possible? If you were to ask me, for example, why I have designed columns in the form of my hand, I would tell you, because it is possible. That, for me, is civil engineering: the art of the possible."* [8]
Santiago Calatrava

"I suspect that Maillart himself did not consider himself an artist, but felt like Picasso did when he said 'je ne cherche pas, je trouve'." (I do not seek, I find.) [9]
Félix Candela

"Today, when nearly everything is possible, hardly anyone cares anymore about what is sensible or economical. But practising builders with a sense of responsibility should care." [10]
Félix Candela

"Construction, too, is not just reason. The attitude that drove the past century to deepen its knowledge of matter to such an extent that the result was a previously inconceivable mastery is as much an expression of instinctual drive as it is some artistic symbol.
They say that art sends out feelers, but if one is convinced that life's process is indivisible, one must add: industry sends out feelers, too, as does technology, as does construction." [11]
Sigfried Giedion

"Structure – architecture's subconscience. It would be a mistake to view modern engineering structures only through the eyes of an engineer, or to see in them only an effective fulfilment of useful purposes." [12]
Sigfried Giedion

"I almost believe that there is something out there like weightlessness. I really believe that buildings fly. I know they don't, but I believe it – except when I meet with my engineers." [13]
Zaha Hadid

"My way of thinking is a bit different than that of the classical European, who takes a rational view of things. That is how most architects are after all, they deal with what is clear and predictable. I belong to a tradition in which intuition and logic are more closely connected." [14]
Zaha Hadid

"At the same time it happens that there is not necessarily just one solution to a problem. One has only to turn to nature to see this. How many species of beetle have been discovered so far? I think it is about 350,000. Fantastic, they all crawl around and have six legs [...]" [15]
Thomas Herzog

"Structural honesty seems to me one of the bugaboos that we should free ourselves from very quickly." [16]
Philip Johnson

"[Heinrich Klotz]: In other words, there are two main elements that distinguish a room: the structure and the light.
[Louis I. Kahn]: The stucture that contributes light." [17]
Louis I. Kahn (and Heinrich Klotz)

"The main features of creative construction are timeless. They had and have little to do with science." [18]
Werner Lorenz

"I spent years trying to understand how to design a clear and honest structure. My whole life has been a single voyage in this direction." [19]
Ludwig Mies van der Rohe

"Nevertheless, in my opinion the greatest damage arising from the scientific illusion of engineering is the associated impoverishment of the imagination, of the freedom to prepare, develop and improve upon structural intuition, which are the only things that can create a beautiful, economical and stable building." [20]
Pier Luigi Nervi

"At the very least I had to create the designs so that it would be possible even to build them in such a short time. Well, in order to manage that, I decided to emphasise primarily the structures of the buildings. The details weren't so important, what counted was the supporting structure. The architecture was created along with the technology, and as I said, the reinforced concrete allowed me to make everything different, more beautiful and more varied." [21]
Oscar Niemeyer

"But when we realise: 'The form of many structures – such as towers, bridges, roofs – in which the building material is optimally employed is unknown', that surprises laypersons and even many engineers.
Once many years ago, a world-famous engineer wrote to us, 'Of course it is known, there are hundreds of scientific treatises about it. Ultimately all designing and building is nothing other than finding the optimum.'
But after intensive research we came to the conclusion that not even the form of a simple compression-stressed support with the least possible material usage is known, to say nothing of bending-stressed girders or beams." [22]
Frei Otto

"Structure is the mother tongue of the architect. The architect is a poet whose every thought and word is structure." [23]
Auguste Perret

"The architectural profession is an adventurous activity: a profession balanced on the border between art and science, on the knife's edge between invention and memory, between the courage toward modernity and the regard for tradition. The architect lives dangerously out of necessity. […] The act of building is not and cannot be a purely technical exercise, since it is charged with symbolic meaning." [24]
Renzo Piano

"I was on a search for an absolute space without the corset of a shape, for structures without weight, in other words, for an elegance without architecture. The topic of lightness was a game in the real sense of the word: a search that was supported to a great degree by instinct. I felt like I was part of the great 'circus' of construction. Fragile, yes, 'impossible' structures were for me like the exercises of the tightrope artist, developed without the safety net of what had already been seen, had already been done." [25]
Renzo Piano

4   Crown Prince Bridge, Berlin (DE) 1996, Santiago Calatrava Architects & Engineers, PSP
5   World Trade Center Transportation Hub, New York (US) 2016, Santiago Calatrava Architects & Engineers
6   Los Manantiales restaurant, Mexico City (MX) 1958, Félix Candela
7   Library & Learning Center, Vienna University of Economics and Business (AT) 2013, Zaha Hadid Architects
8   Richards Medical Research Laboratories, Philadelphia (US) 1965, Louis I. Kahn, August E. Komendant
9   Gallery, Yale Center for British Art, New Haven (US) 1977, Louis I. Kahn

7

8

9

10

"'Designing' means deciding. However, science does not decide, it affirms. Therefore, the science of structural analysis can merely contribute a few benchmarks toward the overall design process; it serves to verify decisions and to provide dimensions in the context of decisions that have already been made, that is to say, it delivers 'confirmation'. But to design something we need PREFIRMATION, and sadly, structural analysis cannot help us there. So we must also ask whether the study of structural analysis – in the form in which it is currently offered – is at all useful to design or to the training for the ability to design. Just so I am not misinterpreted: I do not question structural analysis, but the way it is taught, not just to architects, in fact, but also to structural engineers." [26]
Stefan Polónyi

"At the outset, the structure is never in the foreground, but it becomes very important in the implementation of the project, in the transformation of the thought into reality. […] In reality our structural engineer is the deconstructivist; he disassembles the complicated and complex systems into individual components so that he can do his calculations." [27]
Wolf D. Prix

"I am a child of my period just as everybody else is, and therefore I am enthusiastic about these same principles – function, structure, and being part of our time." [28]
Eero Saarinen

"It is not the functional but the meaningful that touches us deeply, because structure and form are revealed to us only when seen through this lens." [29]
Hans Scharoun

"Emotion as an integral factor in the design of a building is present in the purely technical realm, as well. One cannot assign emotion to the architect and rationality to the engineer. Each requires both." [30]
Jörg Schlaich

"Let us therefore remember the old piece of wisdom, that a good structure is characterised by the fact that one cannot remove anything from it and one does not have to add anything to it. Accountability in the face of dwindling resources and the constraints of economic efficiency are welcome taskmasters to the responsible engineer, because efficient structures that have been pared down to their essentials and feature clean, clear details are naturally beautiful." [31]
Jörg Schlaich

"The hope remains that in the process of designing, engineers and architects can pass on what we discover in ourselves over and over in 'real life': that self-discipline and a liberal environment do more in the long run to promote individual responsibility and creativity than defending against external constraints. For that reason we must also fight back against the flood of regulations, against the mindless 'that's the way it's done'. The worst obstacle to creative and innovative designs is that these days we spend too much time on doing nothing wrong instead of doing the right thing, recalling the quote by Hegel, ... that the fear of erring is itself the very error." [32]
Jörg Schlaich

"In Germany, the term 'Ingenieur' is poorly substantiated. There is no noun, no verb for what we do. What does an engineer do? Sometimes I answer with the English word: engineering. The English language is better suited: He or she 'engineers' something. This expression is more encompassing in its meaning than the characterless terms 'structural planner' or 'structural designer'. Actually, the [German] word – a noun and a verb – that precisely describes the work engineers do has not yet been devised." [33]
Werner Sobek

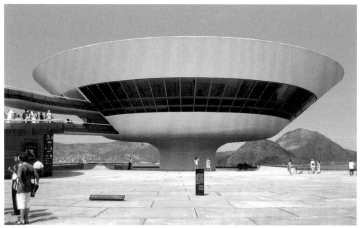

"Engineers have an extremely big responsibility. What they lend their names to can – if incorrectly calculated – lead to catastrophic, irreparable damage, yes, even to the collapse of a building. One must therefore train people to adopt very high precision. This requires concentration and is internal, extremely introverted work. In the process of designing, these very same people must be taught to move away from this high degree of precision, and to sketch out and discuss things that are only about fifty, sixty per cent certain. Many find that very difficult." [34]
Werner Sobek

"It is a mistake to believe that semi-skilled knowledge, as encompassing as it may be, enables one to find a suitable solution to a given structural problem. There is a big difference between sketching a structure and verifying its strength on the one hand, and finding the optimal solution and design with the complete incisive accuracy of a master on the other. One can achieve the latter only through years of work and specialisation, the intensive execution of which requires a strong will. Of course it also requires intelligence for making choices, memory for the development of an informative archive of creative intuition, and more than anything else, a lot of good old common sense.
A creative imagination is also necessary, and though it is cultivated in the course of daily work, it must be to some degree innate. One must have a gift for observation, in order to become aware of all useful details. A keen eye and a discriminating mind are two excellent weapons to forge the way for one's own creative abilities." [35]
Eduardo Torroja Miret

"Construction is the art of forming a meaningful whole from many individual pieces. Buildings are testaments to the human ability to construct concrete things. For me, the act of building contains the actual kernel of every architectural undertaking. Here, where tangible materials are joined and erected, architectural ideas become part of the real world." [36]
Peter Zumthor

According to many experienced engineers and architects, the building of structures can be compared to natural evolutionary processes. Similarly to these, many development and design processes in the realm of construction rely on the two elements of variation and selection. In the formation of variants, chance plays an important role. Without it, hardly anything new is created. Outdated conventions, thought control and other arbitrary restrictions, on the other hand, diminish the chances of substantive developmental improvements. As with mutations in nature, it is frequently the small, random changes that lead to significant new potentials. Often, however, by the time the improvements have prevailed against the familiar status quo to become the new standard, much time has passed. Sometimes it takes generations.

Therefore it is advisable to attempt to accelerate this process through active, rational and attentive selection. A conscious analysis of different construction possibilities on the basis of logical, reproducible criteria has been shown to better facilitate the identification and selection of advantageous variants in large available numbers.
Many designers assume that, in addition to such evolution-like development processes, targeted optimisation is also possible. Especially for complex problems, however, fulfiling this hope hardly seems attainable. Though nowadays most single-parameter optimisations can be performed without difficulty, multi-parameter optimisa-

10 Crown Hall, IIT, Chicago (US) 1956, Ludwig Mies van der Rohe
11 Museu de Arte Contemporânea de Niterói (MAC), Niterói (BR) 1996, Oscar Niemeyer
12 Keramion, Frechen (DE) 1971, Peter Neufert, Stefan Polónyi
13 Palazzetto dello Sport, Rome (IT) 1957, Pier Luigi Nervi

14

tions rarely deliver the definitively best results. Yet what construction – in architecture, especially – can possibly be designed on the basis of a single objective? As a built reflection of life, architecture is much more diverse. Ultimately it is barely calculable.

Diversity and optimisation are fundamentally incompatible. If a complex task had many equally good solutions, none of them would be the best. Nature relies more on diversification than on optimisation in its facilitation of life over the long term. Optimisation always requires a goal. But for nature and for life, no such goal is defined. The proliferation of species is evidence for the fact that optimisation for complex systems is at best a subordinated tool. This recognition is in line with a contem-

porary paradigm shift: science and research are nowadays less reliant on the search for absolute truths. The physics-informed world view of the 20th century is changing into a biology-inspired concept of diverse interconnection, interaction and chance.

"Biological diversity is in the process of taking the top spot away from physical unity." [37]
Eberhard Möller

The practical knowledge that is needed for building is correspondingly diverse. Designers must draw from different sources, of which the scientific one is not necessarily the foremost. If one is to believe the famous designers cited here, then they rely more on experience-nurtured intuition and hard-won creativity for designing and building, in

other words, more on artistic than purely scientific expertise.

However, intuition becomes a useful tool only when it is founded on current scientific knowledge as well as a thorough analysis of built examples. It is the goal of this publication to make precisely these two qualifications accessible to the reader, in order to provide support in the development and building of structures.

The Manual of Structural Design lays a foundation for discussions between the disciplines of architecture and structural engineering and the building clients. Classical masterpieces as well as extraordinary contemporary projects are used to illustrate the real-world stylistic, constructive, structural and even economical potential solutions for many different building assignments. The logical applications for various structural systems are enumerated, as are their limitations. Good examples aid in the rapid assessment of options and facilitate focused discussions. Essential relationships are graphically illustrated and thoroughly explained. Numerous best-practice examples demonstrate the wide range of practical possibilities.

Clearly presented, easily compared structural principles, combined with built examples and technical background information, help to provide enduring support for structural quality through cooperative processes in the building industry. *The Manual of Structural Design* offers a foundation for interdisciplinary communication in the building culture of tomorrow.

14 Tanzbrunnen and canopies, National Garden Show, Cologne (DE) 1957 and 1971, Frei Otto
15 Olympic Stadium, Munich (DE) 1972, Behnisch & Partner, Frei Otto, Leonhardt und Andrä
16 Ice hockey arena, David S. Ingalls Rink (The Whale), Yale University, New Haven (US) 1958, Eero Saarinen, Fred Severud

Notes:

[1] Fischli, Peter; Weiss, David: *Stiller Nachmittag.* Basel 1985

[2] Taut, Bruno: *Architekturlehre* (published 1938: Mimarî Bilgisi). In: ARCH+ 194, 2009, p. 96–98

[3] Arup, Ove: "The World of the Structural Engineer." Maitland Lecture to the Institution of Structural Engineers. In: The Structural Engineer 47, 1, 1969, p. 3f.

[4] Balmond, Cecil: "Definition." In: Balmond, Cecil; Tsukui, Noriko (eds.): Cecil Balmond. a+u – Architecture + Urbanism. Special issue, Tokyo 2006, p. 131

[5] Billington, David P.: *The Tower and the Bridge. The New Art of Structural Engineering.* Princeton 1983, p. 266f.

[6] Billington, David P.; Maillart, Robert: *Robert Maillart und die Kunst des Stahlbetonbaus.* Zurich, Munich 1990. p. 116

[7] Busse, Hans-Busso von: "Wenn Wissenschaft zur Poesie aufsteigt [...] Stefan Polónyi, dem Freund der Baukunst zugeschrieben [...]." In: Walochnik, Wolfgang (ed.): *Bauwerksplanung.* Commemorative publication Polónyi. Cologne 1990, p. 365

[8] Calatrava, Santiago; Lyall, Sutherland (eds.): *Santiago Calatrava: Dynamische Gleichgewichte, neue Projekte / Dynamic Equilibrium, Recent Projects.* 3rd expanded edition, Zurich 1993

[9] Candela, Félix: "Mein Weg – und was ich Maillart verdanke." In: Tragende Häute, archithese 6, 1973, p. 18–22

[10] Candela, Félix: "Schalenbau – gestern und morgen." In: Tragende Häute, archithese 6, 1973, p. 23–29

[11] Giedion, Sigfried: *Bauen in Frankreich, Bauen in Eisen – Bauen in Eisenbeton.* 1928. Reprint Berlin 2000, p. 3

[12] Giedion, Sigfried: *Raum, Zeit, Architektur. Die Entstehung einer neuen Tradition.* 5th Ed., Zurich 1992, p. 46

[13] Hadid, Zaha: "Häuser können fliegen." Zaha Hadid interview by Alvin Boyarski. In: ARCH+ 86, 1986, p. 28–33

[14] Hadid, Zaha: "Ich will die ganze Welt ergreifen. Schwebende Häuser, unbequeme Sofas und die große Lust am Schreien – ein Gespräch mit der Architektin Zaha Hadid über ihren erstaunlichen Weg zum Erfolg." Zaha Hadid interview by Hanno Rauterberg. In: Zeit, 14.06.2006. zeit.de/2006/25/Hadid-Interv__xml (accessed 20.02.2021)

[15] Herzog, Thomas: "Kunst und Technik zur Entsprechung bringen." Thomas Herzog interview by Petra Hagen Hodgson and Rolf Toyka. In: Architecture, Biology, Techniques, archithese 2, 2002, p. 27

[16] Johnson, Philip: Letter to Dr. Jürgen Joedicke dated 6 December 1961 In: Johnson, Philip; Scully, Vincent; Eisenman, Peter; Stern, Robert A. M. (eds.): *Texte zur Architektur.* Stuttgart 1982, p. 63

[17] Klotz, Heinrich; Cook, John W. (ed.): "Louis Kahn." In: *Architektur im Widerspruch. Bauen in den USA*

von Mies van der Rohe bis Andy Warhol. Zurich 1974, p. 247

[18] Lorenz, Werner: *Konstruktion als Kunstwerk. Bauen mit Eisen in Berlin und Potsdam 1797–1850.* Dissertation, TU Berlin 1995, p. 106

[19] Mies van der Rohe, Ludwig: "Ein Moderner Klassiker" Katherine Kuh interviews Mies von der Rohe in Chicago, 1964. In: Mies van der Rohe, Ludwig (ed): *Die neue Zeit ist eine Tatsache.* Berlin 1986, p. 9–15

[20] Nervi, Pier Luigi: "Scienzia o arte dell'ingegnere?" From *L'ingegnere,* trade journal of the Italian National Fascist Union of Engineers, 7, 1931. In: Greco, Claudio (ed.): *Pier Luigi Nervi. Von den ersten Patenten bis zur Ausstellungshalle in Turin 1917–1948.* Lucerne 2008, p. 282

[21] Niemeyer, Oscar: "Viel wichtiger als die Architektur ist für mich das Leben, sind Freunde und Familie." In: Rauterberg, Hanno: *Worauf wir bauen. Begegnungen mit Architekten.* Munich 2008, p. 127

[22] Otto, Frei: Preface. In: *Form – Kraft – Masse 1, Grundlagen / Form – Force – Mass 1, Basics. Mit einem Beitrag und einer Diskussion über das Ästhetische.* Schaur, Eda (ed.), Mitteilungen des Instituts für leichte Flächentragwerke (IL), University of Stuttgart. Stuttgart 1979, p. 4

[23] Perret, Auguste: "Doctrine de l'architecture." In: Techniques et Architecture, 9, 1-2, 1949, p. 108f.; German transl. by Stefan Barmann. In: Lampugnani, Vittorio Magnago; Hanisch, Ruth; Schumann, Ulrich M. (eds.): *Architekturtheorie 20. Jahrhundert. Positionen, Programme, Manifeste.* Ostfildern-Ruit 2004, p. 186ff.

[24] Piano, Renzo: *Renzo Piano, Mein Architektur-Logbuch.* In connection with the exhibition *Out of the Blue.* Renzo Piano Building Workshop 31 January –

6 April 1997 in the Kunst- und Ausstellungshalle in Bonn. Ostfildern-Ruit 1997, p. 10

[25] *ibid.,* p. 22

[26] Polónyi, Stefan: "Der Tragwerksentwurf." In: Polónyi, Stefan (ed.): *...mit zaghafter Konsequenz. Aufsätze und Vorträge zum Tragwerksentwurf 1961–1987.* Braunschweig/Wiesbaden 1987 (Bauwelt-Fundamente Tragwerkslehre, Statik, Architektur 81), p. 106

[27] Prix, Wolf D.: "On the Edge." In: Noever, Peter (ed.): *Architektur im AufBruch. Neun Positionen zum Dekonstruktivismus.* Munich 1991, p. 23

[28] Saarinen, Eero: Selected Writings. Pelkonen, Eeva-Liisa; Albrecht, Donald (eds.): *Eero Saarinen. Shaping the future.* New Haven 2006, p. 349

[29] Scharoun, Hans: "Struktur in Raum und Zeit." In: Jaspert, Reinhard (ed.): *Handbuch moderner Architektur.* Berlin 1957, p. 21

[30] Schlaich, Jörg: *Bauen mit Seilen.* Lecture notes. Institut für Konstruktion und Entwurf II, University of Stuttgart 2000, p. 1–6

[31] Schlaich, Jörg: "Vom Sinn des Details." In: Detail 8/2000, p. 1432

[32] Schlaich, Jörg: "Ingenieur und Architekt." In: Detail 12/2005, p. 1398

[33] Sobek, Werner: "Sobeks Sensor." Werner Sobek interview by Nikolaus Kuhnert and Angelika Schnell. In: ARCH+ 157, 2001, p. 28

[34] Sobek, Werner: "Integrale Planung – ein Gespräch mit Werner Sobek." In: Detail 12/2005, p. 1417

[35] Torroja Miret, Eduardo: *Logik der Form.* Munich 1961, p. 288

[36] Zumthor, Peter: *Architektur Denken.* Basel 1999, p. 11

[37] Möller, Eberhard: *Die Konstruktion in der Architekturtheorie. Positionen und Entwicklungen von 1950 bis 2010.* Munich 2011, p. 181

Part A   Fundamentals

City library, Schweinfurt (DE) 2007, Bruno Fioretti
Marquez

Fundamentals

Eberhard Möller

The Role of Structures

The connected load-bearing and reinforcing components of a building or civil engineering construction are considered the structure. Structures fulfil specific functions. It is their job to safely, permanently and without significant deformations accommodate essentially all the forces acting on them. They should allow for economically viable, hazard-free utilisation of buildings. Thus, the main goals for the design of structures may be summarised as follows:
· Stability
· Serviceability
· Durability
· Economic viability

Apart from these considerations, in the case of a fire, a structure should be flame-resistant and should maintain its bearing capabilities for a given period of time to allow for escape and evacuation. The appropriate mandated fire resistance rating depends primarily on the building's purpose. Even extraordinary events such as impacts, explosions or human error should not result in disproportionately significant damage. In order to meet the most important goal, stability, and thus to ensure the protection of life and limb for a building's users, the forces acting on its structure may not exceed its load resistance capability. A basic requirement is therefore:
Acting forces F < Resistance R

To that end, appropriate building materials, suitable constructions, sensible structural detailing and proven inspection processes must be chosen for the structure's design, manufacture, execution and use. In most countries, detailed guidelines exist in the form of laws, building ordinances, technical building regulations and standards. Equivalent European Standards (EN) apply uniformly over large parts of Europe. Apart from stability, building regulations often also cover other subjects such as fire resistance, heat insulation, acoustic protection and building protection as well as environmental protection and health-related safety. While the above-mentioned goals are timeless, the ways and means employed to reach the goals are subject to significant historical changes.

Historical and Scientific Background

Fairly early in their evolutionary history, human beings began to use tools to erect buildings. At first they used naturally occurring building materials such as clay, wood, reeds, animal skins, natural stones and fibres (Fig. A 1.2). The constructions were inspired in part by examples in nature, or resulted from the difficult and occasionally risky principle of trial and error. Bit by bit, humans expanded their catalogue of building materials to include technically sourced, manufactured and processed materials such as fired bricks, adhesives, products of various ores, glass and cement as well as artificial stone, plastics, synthetic fibres and resins.

Science
During the Enlightenment, the age of reason and rational thought that manifested itself especially in science and research, architects, master builders and members of the relatively new engineering profession began to try their hand at new building technologies for civilian construction projects to supplement traditional techniques. Building on insights gained during the Renaissance (Fig. A 1.1), it was now possible through experimentation and calculation to estimate and predict the behaviour of materials and constructions with ever greater accuracy. Today, sciences such as physics, chemistry, geology and meteorology deliver important findings for construction in general and

A 1.1 Research into the relationship between loading and deformation, Codex Madrid I.2, Fol. 54v f137r, ca. 1492–1495, Leonardo da Vinci
A 1.2 Reeds, a natural building material with a long-standing tradition
A 1.3 Bust of Sir Isaac Newton, Library, Trinity College, Dublin (IE)

for load-bearing structures in particular. While biology studies, among other things, the necessary conditions for life, physical, chemical and geological research provides the foundations for understanding the behaviour of constructions, building materials and subsoils under many different environmental conditions, two of which are climate and weather.

Despite the fact that science aspires to generate well-founded knowledge, the history of mankind is replete with occasions on which widely accepted theories were later proven to be inaccurate or even inapplicable. For this reason, the current state of science and technology should likewise be viewed as a time-dependent snapshot and subject to continual development. It is worth remembering that highly decorated scientists such as Albert Einstein (1879–1955) did not exclude random chance as a fundamental possibility. Werner Heisenberg (1901–1976), for example, demonstrated the natural limits of our knowledge with his Uncertainty Principle.

Physics, mechanics, statics

Physics, of "natural things", deals with the basic phenomena and laws of the environment. On the basis of accumulated findings, it enables us to explain and accurately predict many natural phenomena. It is divided into five main branches: optics, electricity and magnetism, thermodynamics, nuclear physics and mechanics. For construction, the last and oldest of these branches, mechanics, is of the greatest significance. It is itself subdivided into subjects such as kinematics and dynamics (English: "power"). Acoustics, the study of sound and its propagation, is also a part of mechanics. While kinematics describes the motions of bodies, dynamics studies the actions of forces. Within dynamics there is yet another distinction between statics on the one hand – the unmoving or resting state, in which forces are in equilibrium

and objects are at rest – and kinetics on the other, in which forces change the motion of objects. Statics can thus be seen as a special case in which motion equals zero.

Force F – Parameters

The term force describes a reciprocating action that can accelerate or deform objects. Forces are hard to visualise quantities, unseen and recognised only by their effects. They invariably act reciprocally between two or more objects. The forces existing between two objects are always equal in magnitude and opposite in direction. A force is a physical quantity that is uniquely determined by line of action, direction, application point and a magnitude with an associated unit.

The unit of force F is named after the English physicist Isaac Newton (1643–1727) (Fig. A 1.3). One Newton (1 N) is the force required to give an object of mass m = 1 kg an acceleration of a = 1 m/s^2 (F = m · a). Forces can be represented as vectors.
force F [N] = mass m [kg] · acceleration a [m/s^2]

Several forces can be combined through vector addition to yield a resultant force R. Often it is helpful to break up a force vector F into a horizontal component F_H and a vertical component F_V, as these are the most common orientations of building components (Fig. A 1.4, p. 16).

Gravity

Though physicists are working on unifying theories, at present four fundamental forces are generally recognised. These four fundamental forces of physics are the gravitational, weak, electromagnetic and strong forces. By far the weakest of these is gravity, or gravitational force, an attractive force occurring between all objects with mass. It has an infinite range, though it decreases with distance, and it cannot be shielded against.

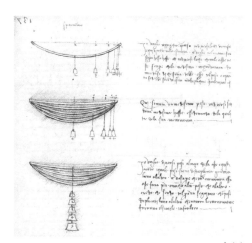

A 1.1

A 1.2

A 1.3

The attractive force of the earth represents the bulk of the gravitational force that determines our lives. It is responsible for the fact that we generally remain on the ground and do not "fall" into space. For construction, gravity is of the utmost importance. It attracts every mass toward the centre of the earth, that is, orthogonally to the earth's surface, and makes our body mass perceptible.

The so-called weak nuclear force and the electromagnetic force are much stronger. In recent years some physicists have preferred to combine these into an electroweak force. Finally, the strong force, also known as the strong nuclear force, is responsible among other things for the internal cohesion of neutrons and protons within the atomic nucleus; these would otherwise repel one another due to the electromagnetic force.

Weight

The acceleration experienced by an object on earth due to the mass and radius of the earth depends on location and has a magnitude of about $g = 9.81$ m/s^2 (local factor g). Therefore, near the earth's surface there is a mutual compression force due to gravity at the contact area between an object with a mass of 100 kg and the surface on which

it lies; its magnitude is approximately $F = 100$ kg $\cdot$ 9.81 m/s^2 = 981 kg m/s^2 = 981 N, or just under 1000 N or 1 kN. To put it simply, in earth's gravitational field, a person with a mass of around m = 100 kg will have a weight of 1 kN – or, more simply yet: 1 person ~ 1 kN

Forces, Loads and Other Actions

Since weights often act as loads, they are commonly also referred to as loads. The same is true in construction, where weights that are to be supported are regularly called loads. Buildings are also subject to numerous additional external forces, which also fall under the term loads. They can be subdivided using different criteria. Frequently used classifications refer to the sources of the forces, to the direction of action, to the duration of the action or to the distribution geometry.

Surface loads, line loads, point loads

Depending on the geometrical distribution of the action areas of loads on the ground, engineers distinguish between surface loads, line loads and point loads. Of course, point (or concentrated) loads as well as line

loads are idealisations, since forces are always distributed over areas, even though these areas are sometimes quite small. The terms point or concentrated load are used when the action area of the load is very small in comparison to the entire surface area. The forces transferred by columns at their bases are often idealised as concentrated loads, whilst a ground slab discharges its load into the ground as a surface load spread over its entire area. The load of a floor slab is simplified as a line load directed into a wall or a girder.

Engineers usually use a capital letter such as F (force), N (normal force), W (weight) or Q (variable force) to indicate concentrated loads. The unit commonly used is the kilonewton (kN). For surface and line loads, lower-case letters are more commonly employed, e.g. g (self-weight), q (live load), p (traffic), s (snow) or w (wind). The unit generally applied for line loads is the kN/m; for surface loads it is the kN/m^2. To simplify calculations, surface loads may be combined to resultant line or point loads.

Vertical and horizontal loads

Another way to categorise loads is by their direction of action. The main cause of so-called vertical loads, which act orthogonal to the earth's surface toward the centre of the earth, is gravity. Examples of vertical loads are the self-weight of constructions, as well as the weight of users and mobile objects.

Horizontal loads, on the other hand, are generated from the motions of more or less solid objects as in the case of impacts, the pressure of the ground on basement walls or earthquakes, for example. Liquids also create horizontal loads by way of hydrostatic pressure or tides, as do gasses in the case of wind or as gauge pressure in containers.

Loads in all three dimensions, the vertical loads in addition to the horizontal loads in the longitudinal as well as transverse build-

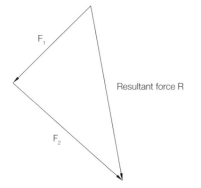

Adding forces to find the resultant force

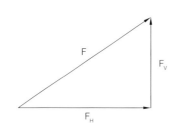

Separating a force F into components F_H and F_V

A 1.4

ing directions, must be absorbed by the structure and redirected into the ground in order to prevent or at least minimise the movement of buildings or engineering structures. For the transfer of horizontal loads, therefore, reinforcing building components along both the longitudinal and transverse building directions are generally required. Load transfer in both horizontal directions, often also referred to as the x and y directions, must be considered and verified separately.

Constant, varying and extraordinary loads

On the basis of duration, structural engineers distinguish between constant, varying and extraordinary loads. Constant loads include the self-weights of a construction and any fixed installations. These values can be determined fairly exactly. The characteristic self-weight G in [kN] of every building component can be calculated from the volume V [m³] and the specific weight γ of the given material [kN/m³] (Fig. A 1.5, Fig. A 1.6):

self-weight G [kN] = volume V [m³] · specific weight γ [kN/m³]

The projection of locally or temporally varying loads such as live loads, traffic, wind or snow loads is much less exact. In calculations, the values usually assigned to these are likely to be exceeded only rarely or not at all over the expected service lifetime of the structure. Values extracted from experience and observation as well as past weather data yield characteristic assumed loads for such acting forces, which are documented in regulations and standards such as Eurocode 1 (EC1 EN 1991 "Actions on Structures"). Standards commissions primarily monitor these applied values to ensure that there is a 98 % probability of their not being exceeded within a year. Statistically speaking, this means that, for the typical 50-year service lifetime of a building, the value is likely to be met or exceeded only once. Though extraordinary loads such as impacts, fire, explosions or earthquakes occur very rarely, they nevertheless should not result in excessive damage. Consequently, even these types of loads must be considered in the design if there is a sufficient probability of their occurring during the service lifetime of an engineering structure or building.

The characteristic values of constant, variable and extraordinary loads must be separately identified, since they are subject to different partial safety factors γ prior to the verification of a building's stability. For safety reasons, therefore, constructions must be capable of supporting far greater loads than are statistically likely to act on them. Nevertheless, it is impossible to rule out the possibility that even the increased assumed load values incorporating the margin of safety will be exceeded through statistically unforeseen events such as extreme weather phenomena, aeroplane crashes or meteor strikes.

Forces on Structures, Assumed Loads

The forces that act on structures have very different sources. In addition, the values of these acting forces vary strongly according to current usage or weather. In order to enable planners to assume realistic magnitudes and to design structures accordingly, standards offer statistically determined assumed loads primarily for the following types of forces.

A 1.4 Adding forces to find the resultant R, separating a force F into F_H und F_V
A 1.5 The specific weights γ of common building materials [kN/m³]
A 1.6 Timber and concrete – building materials with very different specific weights

Specific weights γ of common building materials [kN/m³]

Insulating materials	0.2 … 10.0 kN/m³
Softwood	3.5 … 5.0 kN/m³
Hardwood, depending on strength	6.4 … 10.8 kN/m³
Derived timber products	3.7 … 12.0 kN/m³
Water	10 kN/m³
Brick masonry	8.0 … 20.0 kN/m³
Sand-lime brick masonry	12.0 … 20.0 kN/m³
Natural stone	20.0 … 31.0 kN/m³
Glass panes	25.0 kN/m³
Lightweight concrete	9.0 … 20.0 kN/m³
Normal concrete	24.0 kN/m³
Reinforced concrete	25.0 kN/m³
Heavyweight concrete	> 28.0 kN/m³
Asphalt	18.0 … 25.0 kN/m³
Magnesium	18.5 kN/m³
Aluminium	27.0 kN/m³
Cast iron	72.5 kN/m³
Steel	78.5 kN/m³
Copper	89.0 kN/m³
Lead	114.0 kN/m³

A 1.5

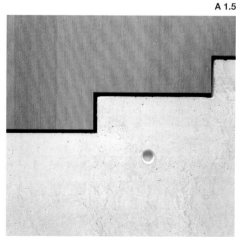

A 1.6

Examples of roof constructions	Self-weight [kN/m²]
Rafter roof with tile shingles	
Roofing tiles, battens, counter battens	0.60 kN/m²
25 mm sheathing, roofing sheet	0.16 kN/m²
10/24 cm rafters, e = 0.80 m	0.20 kN/m²
20 cm thermal insulation,	0.20 kN/m²
vapour barrier	
12.5 mm plasterboard panel	0.14 kN/m²
Total	**g_k = 1.30 kN/m²**
Flat timber roof	
Roof covering	0.20 kN/m²
25 mm sheathing	0.16 kN/m²
Roofing sheet	
10/24 cm timber beams, e = 0.80 m	0.20 kN/m²
24 cm thermal insulation	0.30 kN/m²
Vapour barrier	
12.5 mm plasterboard panel	0.14 kN/m²
Total	**g_k = 1.00 kN/m²**
Flat steel roof	
Roof covering	0.20 kN/m²
24 cm thermal insulation	0.30 kN/m²
Vapour barrier	
Trapezoidal sheet	0.20 kN/m²
Steel beam, e.g. HEB 200,	0.30 kN/m²
e = 3.00 m	
Total	**g_k = 1.00 kN/m²**
Flat reinforced concrete roof	
5 cm gravel fill	1.00 kN/m²
Waterproofing	0.20 kN/m²
24 cm thermal insulation	0.30 kN/m²
Vapour barrier	
Reinforced concrete slab, d = 22 cm	5.50 kN/m²
Total	**g_k = 7.00 kN/m²**

Examples of floor constructions	Self-weight [kN/m²]
Lightweight timber beam floor (old building)	
Floor covering	0.20 kN/m²
25 mm floor boards	0.16 kN/m²
12/20 cm timber beams, e = 0.80 m	0.20 kN/m²
Acoustic fill	0.80 kN/m²
12.5 mm plasterboard panel	0.14 kN/m²
Total	**g_k = 1.50 kN/m²**
Timber beam floor, residential construction	
Floor covering	0.20 kN/m²
Screed, impact sound insulation, sheathing	2.00 kN/m²
12/20 cm timber beams, e = 0.80 m	0.20 kN/m²
2 × 12.5 mm plasterboard panels	0.30 kN/m²
Total	**g_k = 2.70 kN/m²**
Reinforced concrete floor, residential construction, approx. 5 m span	
Floor covering	0.20 kN/m²
Screed, impact sound insulation	1.50 kN/m²
Reinforced concrete slab, d = 18 cm	4.50 kN/m²
15 mm interior plaster	0.30 kN/m²
Total	**g_k = 6.50 kN/m²**
Reinforced concrete floor, public areas, approx. 8 m span	
Floor covering	0.20 kN/m²
Screed, impact sound insulation	1.50 kN/m²
Reinforced concrete slab, d = 28 cm	7.00 kN/m²
Drop ceiling, plumbing	1.30 kN/m²
Total	**g_k = 10.00 kN/m²**

A 1.7

Forces due to self-weight

The loads due to self-weight, which must be applied for every individual building component, are counted among the constant and fixed-location forces. They can be determined from the dimensions of the components and the specific weights of the materials, and are typically expressed as surface loads g [kN/m²]. Sample values for frequently used roof and floor constructions are given in Fig. A 1.7.

Live loads

Loads generated during the use of buildings or engineering structures by people, furniture, movable fixtures or vehicles, for example, usually change with time and should be regarded as quasi-static loads (Fig. A 1.8). If the forces result in significant acceleration of the structure, however, they must be considered in the context of dynamic calculations. In the case of oscillations or repeated changes in loading, the fatiguing of building components must also be studied. In general, in the certification of load-bearing capacity, the worst-case loading situation should be assumed. Live loads can often be estimated in the form of uniformly distributed surface, line or concentrated loads.

Frequently occurring live loads are subdivided into categories such as residential housing (A), office spaces (B), spaces with congregations of people (C), sales floors (D) or areas for industrial use and storage (E). Sample values for the associated orthogonal live loads for floors, stairs and balconies are given in Fig. A 1.9.

A comparison of the values for live loads with the values for self-weight in floor constructions shows that about 50 % of the force on a timber beam floor in an old residential building is from its self-weight and about 50 % from live loading. For a reinforced concrete floor, on the other hand, the self-weight alone already accounts for over 80 % of the load, while the live loads make

A 1.7 Sample self-weights of typical roof constructions
A 1.8 Estimates of live loads for stands should be relatively high.
A 1.9 Sample values of perpendicular live loads for floors, stairs and balconies according to DIN EN 1991-1-1/NA:2010-12 (excerpt)

A 1.8

up less than 20 %. Thus, with regard to its load-bearing characteristics, a reinforced concrete floor yields a very low degree of efficiency.

Impact of fire on structures

Fire is considered one of the extraordinary loading situations. In order to estimate the consequences of a possible fire on structures, the temperature changes in building components and the response of the structure to fire stresses are studied for different fire scenarios based on a fire risk assessment.

In general, it is advisable to take measures to prevent fires from occurring in the first place or, at the very least, to keep them from spreading quickly. Cladding, coatings or over-dimensioning of building components at risk of fire exposure may help to ensure their load-bearing capability remains at safe levels.

Snow and ice loads

Snow and ice loads are among the variable loads. Snow is usually distributed over the full surface (Fig. A 1.12, p. 21). However, winds or snowslides can cause it to accumulate locally. The expected loads on buildings as a result of snowfalls can be estimated on the basis of weather observations made over many years. While snow at lower elevations typically melts quickly, at the higher elevations of average and high-altitude mountains, snow cover builds up successively over longer periods of the winter and can reach thicknesses of several metres. For many countries there are maps in which different zones indicate the associated expected snow accumulations (Fig. A 1.10).

The characteristic values for snow loads s_k [kN/m²] on the ground (ground snow loads) may then be determined by formula or via graphs as a function of height above sea level. For Germany, the appropriate curve for each given zone is shown in Fig. A 1.11.

Usage areas	Examples	Live load q_k [kN/m²]
Attics without standing height	Accessible attic spaces unsuited for habitation with up to 1.80 m clear height	1.0
Living and communal spaces	Floors with sufficient transverse load distribution, rooms and hallways in residential buildings, patient rooms in hospitals, hotel rooms, including any associated kitchens and bathrooms	1.5
	As above, but lacking sufficient transverse load distribution	2.0
Office spaces, work areas, hallways	Offices, hallways in office buildings, medical practices without heavy equipment, nurses' stations, recreation rooms including hallways	2.0
	Kitchens and hallways in hospitals, hotels and old people's homes, corridors in boarding schools, etc., treatment rooms in hospitals including operating rooms without heavy equipment, cellar rooms in residential buildings	3.0
	Examples as listed above, but with heavy equipment	5.0
Rooms, meeting rooms and areas that could serve as gathering places for people	Areas with tables, e.g. nursery schools, day care centres, school rooms, cafés, restaurants, dining halls, reading rooms, reception rooms, staff rooms, etc.	3.0
	Areas with fixed seating, e.g. churches, theatres, cinemas, convention halls, auditoriums, waiting rooms, etc.	4.0
	Freely accessible areas, e.g. museum areas, exhibition areas, entrance halls in public buildings, hotels, courtyard cellar roofs closed to motorised traffic, as well as hallways belonging to this and the two previous categories	5.0
	Sports and recreation areas, e.g. sports halls, gymnastics and weight-lifting areas, dance halls, stages	5.0
	Areas for large congregations of people, e.g. in entrance areas, concert halls, on terraces or in stands with fixed seating	5.0
	Areas used regularly by substantial crowds, stands without fixed seating	7.5
Sales floors	Sales floor areas of up to 50 m² in residential, office or similar buildings	2.0
	Areas in retail stores and department stores	5.0
Warehouses, factories, stables, storage rooms and accesses	Areas in factories or workshops with modest operations, areas in large-animal stables	5.0
	General storage areas including libraries	at least 6.0
	Areas in factories and workshops with moderate to heavy operations	at least 7.5
Stairs, stairway landings	Stairs and stairway landings in residential buildings, office buildings and medical practices without heavy equipment	3.0
	Stairs and stairway landings that cannot be assigned to one of the other stair categories	5.0
	Accesses and stairs to stands without fixed seating which serve as escape routes	7.5
Entrances, balconies and such	Arbours, roof terraces, loggias, balconies, exit landings, etc.	4.0

A 1.9

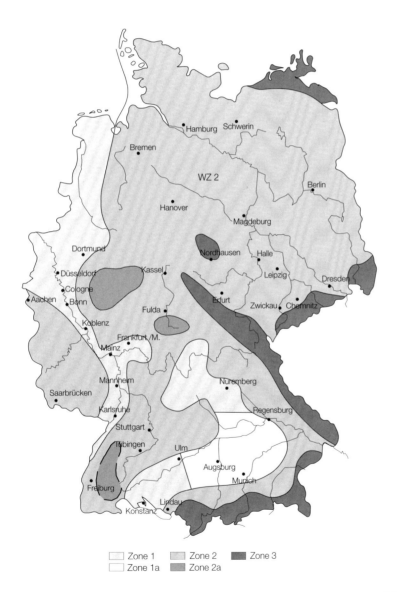

☐ Zone 1	☐ Zone 2	■ Zone 3
☐ Zone 1a	☐ Zone 2a	

A 1.10

The characteristic values for zones 1a and 2a are arrived at by increasing the zone 1 and 2 values, respectively, by a factor of 1.25. The minimum values for the characteristic ground snow load s_k are given by the following base quantities:
Zone 1: $s_k = 0.65$ kN/m^2 (up to 400 m AMSL)
Zone 2: $s_k = 0.85$ kN/m^2 (up to 285 m AMSL)
Zone 3: $s_k = 1.10$ kN/m^2 (up to 255 m AMSL)

Depending on the region, the altitude of the property, the building form, the wind exposure and the heat transmission of snow-covered building components, standards specify how to determine estimates for roof surface snow loads. Since balconies and roof terraces must be designed with live load assumptions, it is not generally necessary in these cases to calculate additional snow loads, since these two load types do not typically attain high values simultaneously. The snow load s [kN/m^2] that should be assumed for roofs is calculated as follows:
snow load s [kN/m^2] = $\mu_i \cdot C_e \cdot C_t \cdot s_k$ where
μ_i is the shape coefficient ($\mu_i = 0 \dots 0.8 \dots$ 2.0, depending on roof shape);
C_e is the exposure coefficient ($C_e = 0.8 \dots$ 1.0 $\dots$ 1.2 for windswept, normal, sheltered topography, respectively);
C_t is the thermal coefficient ($C_t = 1.0$ for insulated roofs); and
s_k is the characteristic ground snow load at the relevant building site [kN/m^2]

For simple double or mono-pitched roofs and a roof slope α between 0° and 30°, the shape coefficient is given by $\mu_1 = 0.8$. If the slope α lies between 30° and 60°, the shape coefficient is calculated via the formula $\mu_1 = 0.8 (60 - \alpha)/30$. For simple roofs that are steeper than $\alpha = 60°$, the snow usually slides off. In this case snow loads need not be assessed. However, local effects at the eaves due to snow guards or resulting from snowdrifts against walls and installations must be considered. Especially in the troughs of saw-tooth and barrel roofs, phys-

ical obstacles can lead to significant snow accumulations. Snow overhang at the roof eaves should also be taken into account. The applicable snow load on an insulated ridged roof with a 45° slope in Karlsruhe (115 m AMSL) is thus given by
$s = \mu_i \cdot C_e \cdot C_t \cdot s_k =$
$0.8 \; (60°\text{-}45°)/30° \cdot 1.0 \cdot 1.0 \cdot 0.65 \text{ kN/m}^2 =$
0.26 kN/m^2.
The applicable snow load for an insulated shed roof with a 20° slope in Garmisch-Partenkirchen (700 m AMSL), on the other hand, is given by $s = \mu_i \cdot C_e \cdot C_t \cdot s_k = 0.8 \cdot 1.0 \cdot 1.0 \cdot 3.85 \text{ kN/m}^2 = 3.1 \text{ kN/m}^2$, and is therefore more than ten times the value in Karlsruhe.
In cases of sleet, freezing fog or rime, building components may ice over to varying degrees depending on the temperature and humidity. The loads from such ice crusts are determined by the thickness of the ice. The specific weight of ice is about $5-9 \text{ kN/m}^3$. Added to this is the fact that ice accretion on filigree building components increases their effective wind exposure. Zoned maps similar to those for snow loads exist for ice loads, as well. They show by region what kind of ice loads are to be expected.

Wind loads

Since 1906, wind has been classified by its speed into thirteen wind force categories according to the Beaufort scale (Bft) (Fig. A 1.14, p. 22), named after the British hydrographer Sir Francis Beaufort (1774–1857). On this scale, any wind speeds in excess of 118 km/h are considered to be hurricane-force winds. Because cyclonic storms such as hurricanes, typhoons or

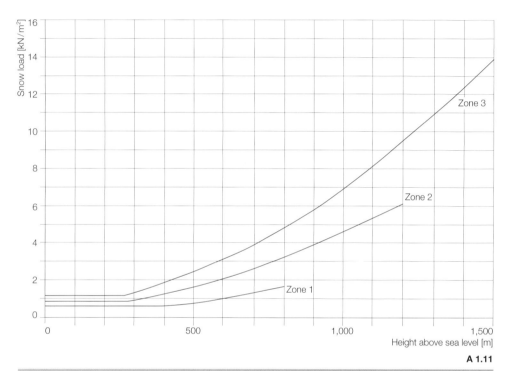

A 1.11

A 1.12

A 1.10 Map of snow load zones for Germany according to DIN EN 1991-1-3/NA:2010-12
A 1.11 Characteristic value of ground snow load s_k in Germany according to DIN EN 1991-1-3/NA:2010-12
A 1.12 Snow and ice can exert loads on structures

A 1.13

tornadoes can generate wind speeds of
up to around 300 km/h, however, there are
additional scales that address classifications beyond the upper range of the Beaufort scale.
While wind at high altitudes and over level
surfaces such as oceans, other bodies
of water or treeless, undeveloped plains
encounters little to check its speed (Fig. A
1.13), it is slowed by friction near ground
level in hilly, forested or built-up regions.
Therefore, much as with snow loads, one

can also differentiate among wind zones
with varying wind loads (Fig. A 1.16).
When gas molecules strike building components with some speed, they exert pressure
on them. On the sides where the molecules
flow past, as well as on the leeward side,
wind suction forces are generated. For a
given air density ρ, every wind speed v can
be assigned a velocity (or dynamic) pressure q. This is given by:
velocity pressure q [kN/m²] = wind speed
squared v² [m²/s²] · air density ρ [kg/m³]/2

At the average air pressure of 1,013 hPa and
an air temperature of 10 °C, the air density
at sea level is ρ = 1.25 kg/m³. For buildings
up to 25 m tall, Fig. A 1.15 gives simplified
reference values for the velocity pressure q_p
that may be taken to be constant over the
entire height of the building.
Given the reference height z_e, the velocity
pressure q and the external pressure
coefficient c_{pe} for each surface segment,
a vertical or horizontal exterior surface of
a building is subject to the following wind
pressure w_e:
wind pressure w_e [kN/m²] = c_{pe} · q (z_e)

The aerodynamic external pressure coefficients c_{pe} for buildings and building components depend in part on wind direction and
on the size of the respective surface segment. The values for typical building shapes
and different tributary load areas can be
taken from standardised tables. The values
of the aerodynamic external pressure coefficient c_{pe} generally lie between -2.9 for wind
suction forces and +1.0 for wind pressures.
Wind-exposed sharp building corners and
edges such as eaves or bargeboards are
subject to the greatest suction loads. Wind
suction values there can reach 3.8 kN/m²
or more. Therefore, it is important to ensure
that all building components at those locations are well anchored. In complex situations, engineers determine the expected
loads from wind on vertical surfaces like
facades as well as on horizontal and sloped
roof surfaces by experimenting with models
in wind tunnel facilities.
Wind can also cause buildings or structures
to oscillate. A now-famous example of this
occurred at the Tacoma Narrows Bridge in
the US state of Washington on 7 November,
1940, when the bridge collapsed in gale-
force (category 8) winds after only four
months of operation. As a result, in the construction of large bridges or towers since,
not only the static but also the dynamic
effects of wind forces are now studied.

Wind force [Bft]	Description	Wind speed [knots]	Wind speed [km/h]	Effects
0	calm	0–< 1	0–1	Smoke rises vertically
1	light air	1–< 4	1–5	Smoke drifts slightly
2	light breeze	4–< 7	6–11	Leaves rustle
3	gentle breeze	7–< 11	12–19	Small twigs in motion
4	moderate breeze	11–< 16	20–28	Small branches in motion
5	fresh breeze	16–< 22	29–38	Small trees in motion
6	strong breeze	22–< 28	39–49	Large branches in motion
7	near gale	28–< 34	50–61	Whole trees sway
8	gale	34–< 41	62–74	Twigs break off trees
9	strong gale	41–< 48	75–88	Slight damage to houses
10	storm	48–< 56	89–102	Trees uprooted
11	violent storm	56–< 64	103–117	Severe damage to forests
12	hurricane	≥ 64	≥ 118	Extreme storm damage

A 1.14

Wind zone		Dynamic pressure q_p in kN/m² at a building height h in the range h ≤ 10 m	10 m < h ≤ 18 m	18 m < h ≤ 25 m
1	Inland	0.5	0.65	0.75
2	Inland	0.65	0.80	0.90
	Coast and islands of the Baltic Sea	0.85	1.00	1.10
3	Inland	0.80	0.95	1.10
	Coast and islands of the Baltic Sea	1.05	1.20	1.30
4	Inland	0.95	1.15	1.30
	Coast of the North and Baltic Seas and Baltic Sea islands	1.25	1.40	1.55
	North Sea islands	1.40	–	–

A 1.15

Temperature effects

Thermal influences such as sun exposure or air temperature change the dimensions of building components. Heat causes components to expand, whilst cold makes them contract. Every material can be assigned what is known as a temperature coefficient α_T (Fig. A 1.17).

Especially in statically overdetermined structural systems, changes in shape can lead to constraints and can therefore cause internal stresses or deformations that could endanger the stability or serviceability of the structure. For this reason, the consequences of temperature-induced forces must be carefully considered in the certification of building components in uninsulated areas or in bridges. Structures that are not subjected to daily or seasonal climatic or user-dependent temperature variations, on the other hand, need not be studied further with regard to temperature-induced forces.

Forces acting during construction

In the course of construction, loads are often transferred differently than in the finished building, since not all components are in place at the outset. Accordingly, internally generated documentation of stability is frequently required for different construction stages. Aside from the loads already discussed, i.e. self-weight, wind or snow, other forces such as those stemming

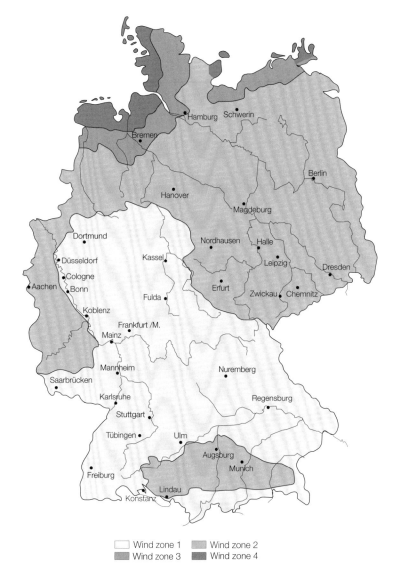

Wind zone 1   Wind zone 2
Wind zone 3   Wind zone 4

a

A 1.13   Using the force of the wind in front of the Boston skyline
A 1.14   Wind force categories according to the Beaufort scale
A 1.15   Simplified dynamic pressures q_p for building heights of up to 25 m according to DIN EN 1991-1-4/NA:2010-12
A 1.16   Wind zone map for Germany according to DIN EN 1991-1-4/NA:2010-12
    a   Wind zone map
    b   Wind speeds and associated dynamic pressures
A 1.17   Thermal coefficients αT of various building materials

Wind zone	Wind speed $v_{b,0}$ [m/s]	Dynamic pressure $q_{b,0}$ [kN/m²]
WZ 1	22.5	0.32
WZ 2	25.0	0.39
WZ 3	27.5	0.47
WZ 4	30.0	0.56

b   A 1.16

Building material	Temperature coefficient α_T
Wood along the fibre	$5 \cdot 10^{-6}/°C$
Wood across the fibre	$30 \ldots 70 \cdot 10^{-6}/°C$
Normal concrete	$10 \cdot 10^{-6}/°C$
Structural steel	$12 \cdot 10^{-6}/°C$
Stainless steel	$16 \cdot 10^{-6}/°C$
Aluminium	$24 \cdot 10^{-6}/°C$

A 1.17

from movement of the ground, earth pressure, prestressing, pre-deformation, hydration, shrinkage, moisture or earthquakes must also be taken into consideration wherever applicable. Added to these are the loads from the construction work itself, exerted by workers, vehicles, materials storage, machines and waste products. Appropriate assessments should be planned for the whole structure, individual building components and the partially built structure, as well as for auxiliary constructions and pieces of equipment, so as to accommodate the requirements of every individual situation.

Traffic loads on bridges

In addition to the loads covered thus far, roadway, pedestrian and railway bridges are subject primarily to variable and extraordinary loads due to traffic. Added to these are forces stemming from road

and bridge maintenance construction activities. Forces from road traffic (cars, trucks and special-purpose vehicles) represent vertical and horizontal, static and dynamic loads (Fig. A 1.18). Associated standards contain the appropriate, comprehensive calculation models for the verification of the stability and usability of bridges. The constantly varying loads from traffic flow often lead to a stress spectrum that can result in the fatiguing of building components.
In many engineering structures, not only is the stability documented before erection, but it also undergoes regular inspections throughout its lifetime. In Germany, in addition to an annual visual inspection, every six years a major test of the stability, traffic safety and projected longevity is scheduled to be performed by experts.
All relevant data pertaining to such structures is now digitally documented in the so-called structural record. The results of

the regular inspections are likewise added to this record, making them trackable over the long term.

Forces due to cranes and machines

Heavy movable equipment such as cranes or machinery represents special challenges to structures. Under typical operational circumstances, cranes produce temporally and locally varying forces. These include gravitational forces and hoisting loads, inertial forces from acceleration and braking and damping forces, as well as forces, deformations and oscillations from dynamic effects. Added to these are the constant forces. Examples of these are the self-weight of all rigid and moveable components as well as static effects from operations. Machines produce forces from the self-weight of casings or rotors, from capacitors, from drive torques, from friction at the bearings, from thermal expansion and similar sources.

Forces on silos and tanks containing fluids

Bulk materials and liquids generate vertical as well as horizontal loads in tanks, silos and swimming pools. In addition, the filling or emptying of such vessels in particular produces forces of considerable magnitude.

Seismic forces

Earthquakes cause mainly horizontal and vertical accelerations of the building substrate and therefore of the buildings themselves, which can have significant effects on the structure. In seismically active regions, therefore, structures are required to be able to withstand typical earthquake magnitudes without partial or comprehensive failure. In addition, appropriate planning is supposed to ensure that possible damage is kept at a minimum. To ensure this, relevant construction principles apply. Simple and direct load transfer pathways are just as important as

A 1.18

Building component	Typical total vertical load for pre-dimensioning
Hall roofs (timber/steel)	~1.5 ... 3 kN/m²
Timber beam floors	~4 ... 6 kN/m²
Solid roofs	~7 ... 11 kN/m²
Solid floors	~10 ... 13 kN/m²

A 1.19

A 1.20

the regular spacing of load-bearing elements in the building's ground plan and elevation. Reinforced building components with similar stiffness in both main directions as well as sufficient torsional rigidity are also advantageous (Fig. A 1.21).

Handling extraordinary loads – Robust structures

There are various available strategies for curtailing the negative consequences of extraordinary loads. First, robust structures, sensible safety measures and appropriate dimensioning are used in an effort to minimise damage from explosions or impacts. Second, possible damage is expected to be confined to a limited area, so that entire structures or buildings are not destroyed. In this regard, redundancies – that is, a safety backup in the form of additional components – are important, as are structural regulations regarding cohesion and ductility.

Robust structures are characterised by their insensitivity to errors or imperfections, by load-bearing and system reserves, by the redundancy of critical building components as well as by constructions that signal an impending component or system failure in an obvious way, for example through deformations. Statically determinate structures without back-up systems, structures with brittle deformation behaviour or prefabricated constructions without redundant connections are considered unfavourable and of lesser robustness.

A better alternative is found in statically indeterminate constructions with back-up systems as well as compressible-ductile structural behaviour. Constructions with extensive system redundancy and large flexible system reserves are considered very robust. Examples of robust structures are in many cases statically indeterminate systems such as multi-span single and multi-storey frame constructions, cable-stayed constructions and covered arch structures.

Load combinations

Not all of the above-named forces are present in every engineering structure or building. In addition, it is virtually impossible for all the generally possible loads on a structure to occur simultaneously at full strength. Thus, a pure sum of the potential assessed values can often be reduced according to the appropriate combination rules with the relevant combination factors ψ. Depending on the duration of the action, a distinction is made between combination factors ψ_0 for rare loads, ψ_1 for frequent loads and ψ_2 for near-constant loads. The assumption for high-rises, for example, is that not all storeys will be subjected to the maximal loads at the same time.

Structural Design, Load Transfer

The structure ensures that any acting forces, no matter their origin or direction, are channelled into the highly load-resistant building substrate and brought into equilibrium. At the same time, it seeks to supply a safe, sheltered living area or a useful function within the space between the incident forces and the ground.

In a figurative sense, the structure helps to transfer the acting loads down into the foundations and from there into the subsoil. For this, it is usually necessary to ensure that the various load-bearing and stiffening elements, such as floors, walls, columns, beams, frames and cross braces, are logically arranged and interconnected.

Stiffening building components include, among others, components that also transfer horizontal loads such as wind and impact forces. Therefore, apart from the horizontal elements such as floor slabs, every storey must feature at least three vertical building components that cannot all be arranged parallel to one another. In addition, the lines of action of these members cannot con-

verge on a single point. Stiffening components include wall panels, frames, cross braces and fixed columns (Fig. A 1.20). As is the case for any planning process, the design and development process for structures passes through various phases or steps from the conceptual search to the preliminary and developed design stages to the detailed design. The careful compilation of the functional specifications and wishes, as well as the financial, target date, legal, technical, local and climatic conditions, form the critical planning groundwork. A well-founded and inspiring overview of high-quality built reference objects helps to foster and stimulate creativity (Fig. A 1.22, p. 26).

In each design phase, a thoughtful analytical selection process should follow a creative compilation of all feasible options in order to separate the good solutions from less suitable alternatives.

A 1.18 Both static and dynamic loads act on bridges. Brooklyn Bridge, New York (US) 1883, John A. Roebling
A 1.19 Assumed loads for pre-dimensioning (typical total vertical load)
A 1.20 Bracing of the Kunsthal (art museum), Rotterdam (NL) 1993, Rem Koolhaas
A 1.21 Springs and dampers for decoupling a high-rise from ground movements during earthquakes

A 1.21

Analysis of structural behaviour

In the design process, the structural behaviour of the planned bearing elements must be studied. How large is the anticipated load for each individual element as a result of potential forces? Which dimensions should the designer choose for the element that are appropriate to its loading? In order to make reasonable estimates for such values, analyses must be performed for both the entire system and for all individual parts.

Computability through abstraction and modelling

Simply the act of compiling all the forces acting on structures makes it clear that reality is too complex to be precisely predictable and calculable in each particular. Often, statistically determined, extrapolated probable values are used in place of actually existing loads in order to make computations and comparisons possible. But such simplifications of complex situations do not only apply for loads. For the load-bearing

construction, too, there are helpful abstractions, idealisations and models that come sufficiently close to reality on the one hand, while remaining somewhat manageable with an acceptable degree of difficulty on the other. Thus, it is common to separate complex, three-dimensional systems into level, two-dimensional partial systems. Such static systems are represented in abstract line and symbol drawings. The overarching rule for these is that static systems are at rest as long as all forces and moments remain in equilibrium with one another.

Moment M

The moment M of a force F describes the rotating, bending or twisting action that the force exerts on an object. Depending on the action, the terms torque, bending moment or torsional moment are also used. The magnitude of such a moment M [kNm] is given by the product of the force F [kN] that acts at right angles to a lever arm, and the lever arm's length h [m]:

Moment M [kNm] =
force F [kN] · lever arm h [m]

In addition to the magnitude of the moment, it can often be important to specify the pivot point or rotational axis as well as the sense of rotation. Moments turning an object counter-clockwise about the pivot are often given a plus sign.

Degrees of freedom f

Every rigid object in three-dimensional space can be moved in six different, mutually independent ways which are known as degrees of freedom f. The object can be translated in the x direction without changing its position along the y or z axis. The same reasoning applies to translations along the y and z directions. In addition, rotations of the object in the xy, the xz or the yz plane are possible without an associated translation of the object.
In a two-dimensional, planar partial system, only three of the six degrees of freedom f remain. For analysis purposes, structural engineers often use xz planes placed orthogonal to the earth's surface, in which the x coordinates represent horizontal values H and the z coordinates stand for vertical values V. In such a system, mutually independent horizontal and vertical translations as well as rotations in the xz plane are possible.
In order to prevent the motion of structures or building components, these degrees of freedom must be matched with at least the same number of connections. Such connections can be created through supports or through linkages with adjacent, immobile building components.

Supports and joints

In general, the supports of structures can be sorted into three different categories, depending on how many connections they make available. Three-force fixed supports offer three connections. They prevent trans-

A 1.22

lations along both axes as well as rotation (Fig A 1.23). Two-force jointed but non-displaceable supports allow for rotation but prevent both translations (Figs. A 1.24 and A 1.25). Single-force jointed and one-axis translatable supports only prevent displacement in a single direction, but do not prevent either orthogonal displacements or rotations. Such single-force supports allow the constraint-free thermal expansion of large bridges.

A three-force support is sufficient to prohibit the freedom of motion of a building component. Alternatively, the element may be fixed, for example, by supporting it at one end by a two-force and at the other by a single-force support. If the number of degrees of freedom (f) of a component is equal to zero (taking into account all of its support connections (a)), the system is said to be statically determinate:

Degrees of freedom $f = 3 - a$
a   number of support connections
$f = 0$ rigid, statically determinate
$f > 0$ unstable, moveable, statically under-determined
$f < 0$ rigid, statically overdetermined (or indeterminate)

For a statically determinate system, $f = 0$ is a necessary but not sufficient condition. When three single-force supports are arranged in parallel, $f = 0$, but the system is nevertheless translatable. In addition to $f = 0$, it is therefore important to ensure that the lines of action of all supports are neither parallel nor converge on a single point.

In multipart, planar structures, every additional component raises the number of degrees of freedom by three. Accordingly, additional connections are needed. Often, these are provided by hinged joints (Fig. A 1.26; Fig. A 1.27, p. 28). They prevent both translations between the building components but allow for rotation. They are therefore two-force joints. The following equation can be used to determine the degrees of freedom of a multicomponent system:

Degrees of freedom $f = 3 \cdot n - (a + z)$
n   number of elements
a   number of support connections
z   number of joints

Equilibrium

Buildings or building components are in a motionless resting state when all acting forces are in equilibrium. The forces acting on components must therefore be opposed by reaction forces. These reactions are generally not visible in building construction. Furthermore, they can only be measured once the component has been separated from its supports. Once this is done, exactly one support reaction can be determined for each support connection. The support reaction will then manifest in such a way as to establish an exact static equilibrium with the corresponding acting forces. If the supports can provide these reaction forces, the building component will maintain its resting state.

Every static equilibrium can be expressed as a mathematical equation. Equilibrium exists when two forces are of equal magnitude and acting in opposite directions.

A 1.22   Barcelona Pavilion (ES) 1929, Ludwig Mies van der Rohe
A 1.23   Three-force fixed support of columns, Neue Nationalgalerie, Berlin (DE) 1968, Ludwig Mies van der Rohe
A 1.24   Two-force hinged but non-displaceable support, Fondation Louis Vuitton, Paris (FR) 2014, Gehry Partners, Setec Bâtiment, RFR + T/E/S/S
A 1.25   Two-force hinged but non-displaceable support, Galerie des Machines, Paris (FR) 1889, Charles Louis, Ferdinand Dutert, Victor Contamin
A 1.26   Various types of joint connections, Fondation Louis Vuitton, Paris (FR) 2014, Gehry Partners, Setec Bâtiment, RFR + T/E/S/S

Three-force support (fixed)

Support connections s = 3

Possible support reactions: S_V, S_H, M_S

Degrees of freedom f = 0 (no translations, no rotation)

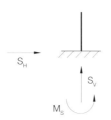

Two-force support (hinged, non-displaceable)

Support connections s = 2

Possible support reactions: S_V, S_H

Degrees of freedom f = 1 (no translations, but rotation is possible)

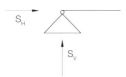

Single-force support (hinged, displaceable in one direction)

Support connections s = 1

Possible support reactions: S_V or S_H (here: S_V)

Degrees of freedom f = 2 (one translation and rotation possible)

Intermediate joint (hinged, non-displaceable)

Joint connections z = 2

Possible joint reactions: J_V, J_H

Degrees of freedom f = 1 (no translations, but rotation is possible)

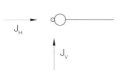

Equilibrium of two forces:
$$F_{action} = - F_{reaction}$$
or
$$F_{action} + F_{reaction} = 0$$

In general, equilibrium exists when the sum of all forces equals zero:
Overall equilibrium: $\Sigma F = 0$

Equilibrium conditions
In three-dimensional space, therefore, for the six degrees of freedom, six associated equilibrium conditions must be met to ensure a system at rest:

$\Sigma F_x = 0$	$\Sigma F_y = 0$	$\Sigma F_z = 0$
$\Sigma M_x = 0$	$\Sigma M_y = 0$	$\Sigma M_z = 0$

In the case of a planar subsystem in the vertical xz plane, placed on the surface of the earth and perpendicular to it, the x coordinate is usually referred to as the horizontal H and the z coordinate as the vertical V. Here, static equilibrium can be expressed as three independent equations, since in principle three independent motions are possible in the xz plane. In such a planar subsystem, in order for the system to be at rest – i.e. for all forces and moments to be in equilibrium – the following three equilibrium conditions must be met simultaneously:
· Sum of all horizontal forces:
  ΣF_H [kN] = 0
· Sum of all vertical forces:
  ΣF_V [kN] = 0
· Sum of all moments about any arbitrarily chosen point:
  ΣM [kNm] = 0

Support reactions
Through the use of these three equilibrium conditions, the reaction forces at supports can be determined. First, sign conventions for the different directions must be established. Often, forces that act upward or to the right are given a plus sign, while those

A 1.27 Supports and intermediate joints: symbols and
explanations
A 1.28 Support reactions in a statically determinate
beam system
a with point load F
b under uniformly distributed load q
c overhanging and under uniformly distributed
load q

that act downward or to the left are given a minus sign. Fig. A 1.28 a shows the calculation of the support reactions for a statistically determinate simple beam that is subjected to a point load F, while Fig. 1.28 b demonstrates the calculation of the support reactions for a statically determinate simple beam under a uniformly distributed load q. In symmetrical systems, symmetrical loads produce symmetrical reaction forces. Fig. A 1.28 c illustrates the calculation of the support reactions for a statically determinate simple beam with an overhang subjected to uniformly distributed load q.

Joint reactions

The reaction forces at joints can be determined according to the same procedure by breaking down the system into subsystems at the joints, labelling the joint reactions and then calculating them for each subsystem by means of the three equilibrium conditions.

External Loads – Internal Forces: Stresses

Every external force acting on a structure generates internal forces within the structural building components. One such internal force effect within structural elements is often referred to in mechanics as the stress σ. This term can best be visualised using the example of the bow and arrow. When nocking an arrow and drawing the bow, the string stretches in response to the tensile stress σ_N and the bow bends in response to the bending stress σ_B or σ_M. If the stresses become too great, the bow may break or the string snap. A stress that acts perpendicularly (or normal) to the cross-sectional area of a member or cable is called the normal or axial stress σ_N. If it stretches the member, it is known as a tensile stress; if it compresses the member, it is a compressive stress. The magnitude of

$$\Sigma F_H = 0 \quad A_H = 0$$
$$\Sigma M_A = 0 \quad -F \cdot l_1 + B_v \cdot (l_1 + l_2) = 0 \qquad \rightarrow B_v = F \cdot l_1 / (l_1 + l_2)$$
$$\Sigma M_B = 0 \quad F \cdot l_2 - A_v \cdot (l_1 + l_2) = 0 \qquad \rightarrow A_v = F \cdot l_2 / (l_1 + l_2)$$

a

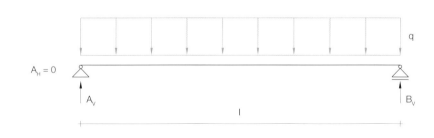

$$\Sigma F_H = 0 \quad A_H = 0$$
$$\Sigma M_A = 0 \quad -q \cdot l \cdot l/2 + B_v \cdot l = 0 \qquad \rightarrow B_v = q \cdot l/2$$
$$\Sigma M_B = 0 \quad q \cdot l \cdot l/2 - A_v \cdot l = 0 \qquad \rightarrow A_v = q \cdot l/2$$

b

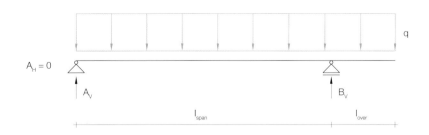

$$\Sigma F_H = 0 \quad A_H = 0$$
$$\Sigma M_A = 0 \quad -q \cdot (l_{span} + l_{over})^2/2 + B_v \cdot l_{span} = 0 \qquad \rightarrow B_v = q \, (l_{span} + l_{over})^2/2 \, l_{span}$$
$$\Sigma F_V = 0 \quad A_v - q \, (l_{span} + l_{over}) + B_v = 0 \qquad \rightarrow A_v = q \, (l_{span} + l_{over}) - B_v$$

c

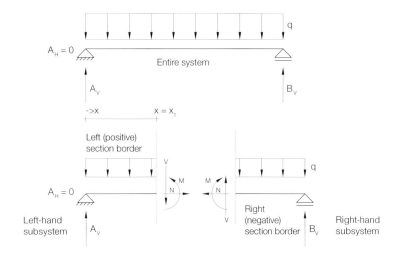

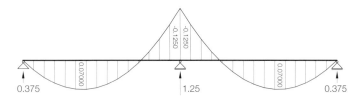

A 1.29

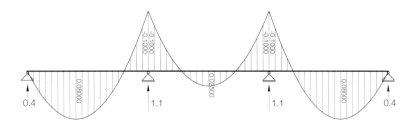

Coefficients k for a continuous double-span beam (total length 2l)

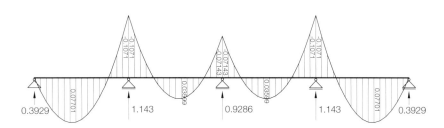

Coefficients k for a continuous triple-span beam (total length 3l)

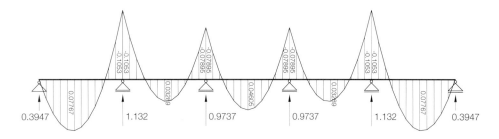

Coefficients k for a continuous four-span beam (total length 4l)

Coefficients k for a continuous five-span beam (total length 5l)

such a normal stress σ_N is given by the external normal force N acting along the member direction divided by the cross-sectional area A of the member:
normal stress σ_N [kN/cm^2] = normal force N [kN]/cross-sectional area A [cm^2]

Aside from normal stresses, depending on the loads acting on an element, shear, torsional or bending stresses may also occur as a result of internal forces. The immediate consequences of stresses are changes in shape, though in construction, for reasons of building serviceability, these are kept so small that – unlike in the example of the bow and arrow – they are barely perceptible. Tensile stresses cause stretching, while compressive stresses cause shortening, buckling or bulging, torsional stresses cause twisting, and bending stresses cause warping, flexural buckling and lateral torsional buckling.

Section Forces
The magnitudes of internal stresses can be calculated by sectioning the structural system at the point which is to be examined and drawing up diagrams of the two resulting subsystems. At the cut margins on these diagrams, the three reaction forces are entered that eliminate the three degrees of freedom of the sectioned element at the point of the cut. On the left-hand subsystem, the normal force N acts along the member direction and along the x axis, while the transverse force V acts at right angles to it downward along the z axis. The third sectional quantity is the bending moment M, which in the left-hand subsystem must be applied anticlockwise. On the cut margin on the right-hand subsystem, the sectioned-off reaction forces are applied in the opposite direction. In the static resting state, the forces on both margins of the cut are equally large exactly opposed. When looking at the entire system, therefore, they

A 1.30

balance each other out perfectly (Fig. A 1.29).

The cut margin forces N, V and M can now be calculated for each of the two subsystems from the equilibrium conditions $\Sigma F_H = 0$, $\Sigma F_V = 0$ and $\Sigma M = 0$, after the support reactions have first been determined from the full system diagram. For the left-hand subsystem, a cut at the position $x = x_1$ yields the following equations:

$\Sigma FH = 0$:
$S_H + N = 0 \rightarrow N = - S_H = 0$

$\Sigma F_V = 0$:
$S_V - q \cdot x_1 - V = 0 \rightarrow V = S_V - q \cdot x_1 = ql/2 - qx_1$

$\Sigma M_A = 0$:
$- q \cdot x_1 \cdot x_1/2 - V \cdot x_1 + M = 0$
$\rightarrow M = q \cdot x_1^2/2 + V \cdot x_1$

Mathematically, the relationships shown in Fig. A 1.31 between the load q, the transverse force V and the bending moment M apply. In statically overdetermined systems, the calculation of support reactions and section forces is usually more difficult than in statically determinate systems. For this reason, for multi-span (continuous) beams that traverse one or several intermediate supports, values taken from tables or mathematical programmes are often employed. In many cases, however, simple computation aids are enough for pre-dimensioning. Figure A 1.30 shows the coefficients k that are used to determine the support reactions as well as extreme values for bending moments in continuous beams with supports placed at several equal or approximately equal intervals l and subjected to a uniform distributed load q. The unknown forces and moments can then be calculated using these two equations:
Reaction forces $R = k \cdot q \cdot l$
Bending moments $M = k \cdot q \cdot l^2$

The sectional quantities – the normal force N, the transverse force V and the bending moment M – are always quantities resulting from the associated internal stresses. In reality, instead of these resulting sectional quantities, actual stresses such as the normal stress σ_N (see p. 45), the shear stress τ (see p. 57) or the bending stress σ_M (see p. 56) are distributed over the full surface of the cross section. To prevent damage to structural elements, the stresses in the component must not be allowed to become too large.

Safety Concept

A critically important principle of safe construction is that the sum of forces F acting on a building component cannot exceed its capacity to withstand them, i.e. its load resistance R. In Europe, a concept incorporating coefficients known as partial safety factors has been agreed upon in order to achieve this. Since loads are not assigned with exact, real-time values but with probable values, and in order to improve the overall level of stability, the values used to populate

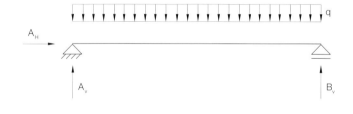

Transverse force $V(x)$ [kN] $= - \int q \, dx = - q \, x + C_1$
where $C_1 = A_v = ql/2$

Graphic representation of the transverse force V [kN] along the beam axis

Bending moment $M(x)$ [kNm] $= - \iint q \, dx \, dx = - qx^2/2 + C_1 x + C_2$
where $C_1 = ql/2$; $C_2 = 0$

Graphic representation of the bending moment M [kNm] along the beam axis

A 1.31

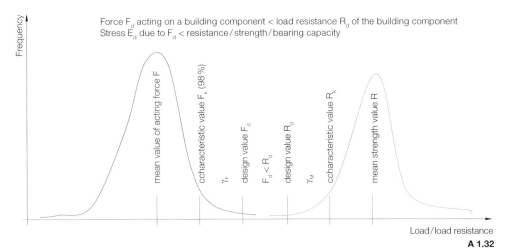

Force F_d acting on a building component < load resistance R_d of the building component
Stress E_d due to F_d < resistance / strength / bearing capacity

Frequency

mean value of acting force F

ccharacteristic value F_k (98 %)

γ_F

design value F_d

$F_d < R_d$

design value R_d

γ_M

ccharacteristic value R_k

mean strength value R

Load / load resistance

A 1.32

the acting forces F are calculated values that have been increased by a partial safety factor γ_F. The design value of a force F_d is therefore given by the product of the characteristic value of that force F_k and the partial safety factor γ_F:

design value of a force $F_d = F_k \cdot \gamma_F$
subscript d: design value
subscript k: characteristic value (without additional safety)

While the partial safety factor γ_G for constant loads, depending on the design situation, is usually 1.35, the partial safety factor γ_Q for unfavourable, varying loads is 1.5. Structures must therefore be capable of supporting 50 % more varying loads than are statistically likely to occur or be exceeded only once during a 50-year lifetime. In order to raise the safety level even further, there is an additional partial safety factor γ_M that comes in on the resistance or material side. The design value of the load resistance R_d of a building component is arrived at by dividing the characteristic value of the resistance R_k by the partial safety factor γ_M:

design value of the load resistance
$R_d = R_k / \gamma_M$

The resistance of a building material is largely determined by its properties. That is why the partial safety factor γ_M depends on the type of material (Fig. A 1.35). Natural building materials such as timber exhibit a greater scatter in their material properties and therefore require a higher partial safety factor than the industrially manufactured material steel. Brittle materials such as glass have higher associated safety factors than do ductile, elastic materials.
The incorporation of partial safety factors on both the load and load resistance sides, while also taking into account issues of economic viability, raises the safety level in the construction industry to such a degree that

collapses of buildings due to structural failures are extremely rare. However, they cannot be fully ruled out either through this nor through any other safety concept. The basic premise that every force should always be smaller than the load resistance may now be more precisely stated in light of safety considerations (Fig. A 1.32):
$F_d = F_k \cdot \gamma_F \; < \; R_d = R_k / \gamma_M$

Building Materials, Properties, Load Resistance

Many different materials are used for structures. Apart from industrially manufactured steel, reinforced concrete and classic masonry, the carbon-sequestering, renewable, traditional raw material timber is once again experiencing growing popularity after having played a very marginalised role during the modern age. In terms of their properties, these materials differ markedly from one another. Among the organic materials are timber, bitumen and plastics, for example. The inorganic materials, on the other hand, include not only the brittle mineral materials such as concrete, glass, mortar or natural stone, but also the ductile metallic materials such as steel, aluminium or copper, which show signs of an imminent break in advance in contrast to their brittle counterparts.
Materials can be classified by their microstructure into crystalline, amorphous or fibrous types. While metal, brick and glass materials feature largely homogeneous internal structures, those of timber, concrete or reinforced concrete are rather more inhomogeneous.

Strength f of a building material
For the load-bearing capacity of a building material, its ability to support the largest possible mechanical loads is of great importance. The elastic limit or yield limit $f_{y,k}$ indicates the point at which the deformation

due to a load switches from a reversible elastic to a permanent plastic deformation. The ultimate strength f shows when a break or failure of the building material is to be expected. For every building material, the strengths f [kN/cm² (= 10 N/mm²)] for the various types of stresses such as tension, compression, bending, shear or torsion, can be determined. These strengths f are expressed as maximum allowable stresses σ_{all} where $\sigma_{all} = f$ [kN/cm²].

Elastic modulus E of a building material
The stretching behaviour that a material exhibits under tension in the linear-elastic region is described by its elastic modulus E [kN/cm² (= 10 N/mm²)]. This E-modulus describes the relationship between the normal (or axial) tensile stress σ_N and the axial strain ε. The strain ε is the ratio of the change in length $\triangle l$ and the unstretched length l_0 of an element under tensile stress. Elastic modulus E [kN/cm²] $= \sigma_N / \varepsilon = \sigma_N / (\triangle l / l_0)$

Soft materials have a small E-modulus, stiff ones like steel a large one.

Stiffness of a building component
The axial stiffness EA [kN] and the bending stiffness EI [kNcm²], as well as the shear and torsional stiffness values, depend on both the material and geometry of a given building component and indicate the component's resistance to the respective loads. While the material dependence is reflected in the elastic modulus E or the shear modulus G, the component geometry usually comes into the stiffness value via the cross-sectional area A or the second moment of area I, also known as the area moment of inertia.

Timber
Viewed through a microscope, wood resembles a bundle of very fine tubes through which the tree transports water

out of the ground and into the leaves (Fig. A 1.33). Cellulose chains ($C_{12}H2_0O_{10}$) form the quite tear-resistant fibrous structures that perform the load-bearing functions in the walls of these capillaries. Given this context, it is apparent why wood exhibits very different properties in the direction of the fibres than transverse to them. For this reason it is called an anisotropic material. Both the tensile and compressive strength are significantly higher in the fibre direction than across. The fibre direction should therefore always be chosen for the main load-bearing effect.

Given its low self-weight, the natural material timber features relatively high strength and low thermal conductivity. Timber is easy to process. The larger or more complex building components can be prefabricated at the factory and installed dry. Of course, wood is flammable and therefore requires the appropriate fire safety measures. Moisture can also lead to problems such as swelling, weathering and fungal or insect infestations. It is thus important to avoid moisture in general, to drain it away or to evaporate it quickly via ventilation if needed. The typical timber used in construction is softwood of strength class C 24 (coniferous = bearing cones, bending strength $f_{m,k}$ = 24 N/mm²). Less frequently employed is the more expensive hardwood in strength classes D 18 and D 70 (deciduous = shedding leaves, bending strength $f_{m,k}$ = 18 … 70 N/mm²). To manufacture large building components, boards are bonded together to create glulam (glued laminated timber). Glulam comes in strength classes up to GL36h (bending strength $f_{m,k}$ = 36 N/mm², homogeneous).

In addition to solid wood, veneer, chipped wood or fibreboard timber composites are also available. First, this makes it possible to use qualitatively less valuable timber species, offcuts and wood waste as materials in the construction industry. Secondly, it allows for the manufacture of products with properties that natural timber does not offer. Plywood, cross-laminated timber and blockboard, for example, exhibit high strength in two directions as opposed to just one.

Timber and timber composites achieve higher strength values for short-duration loads than for longer-acting loads. For this reason, distinctions are made between five different load duration classes (KLED). They range from "very short" for wind gusts to "average" for traffic loads to "constant" for self-weight. Climatic conditions in the vicinity of timber building components also affect their properties. In general, dry timber has greater strength than moist timber. The European standards differentiate among three use classes (EC5 DIN EN 1995):
- Use class 1 (~20°, 65 % relative humidity → average wood moisture content < 12 %), primarily in fully enclosed and heated buildings
- Use class 2 (~85 % relative humidity → average wood moisture content < 20 %), primarily in covered open structures
- Use class 3 (other), primarily for constructions exposed to the weather (Fig. A 1.34)

Taking into consideration the corresponding use class and load duration class yields modification factors k_{mod} for the strength of timber building products. The value of these factors lies between k_{mod} = 0.20 for chipboard in use class 2 subject to constant

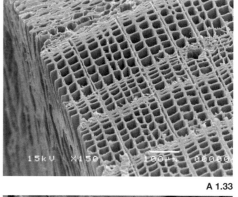

A 1.33

A 1.34

A 1.32 Fundamental safety concept for structures. To prevent damage, the stresses E_d resulting from the acting forces F_d may not exceed the load resistance R_d of a building component: $E_d < R_d$
red: frequency distribution of acting forces F
blue: frequency distribution of the load resistances R of building components/materials
A 1.33 Spruce under the microscope
A 1.34 Roofed timber structure of the approx. 300-year old Komma Bridge near Hittisau, Vorarlberg (AT)
A 1.35 Partial safety factors γ_M for various building materials

Building material	Partial safety factor γ_M
Timber and timber products	γ_M = 1.3
Steel	γ_M = 1.00 … 1.10 … 1.25
Masonry	γ_M = 1.3 … 1.5
Concrete	γ_C = 1.30 … 1.50
Reinforced concrete	γ_S = 1.00 … 1.15
Glass	γ_M = 1,5 … 1,8

A 1.35

loads to k_{mod} = 1.10 for solid wood in use class 1 or 2 and exposed to very short load durations. For pre-dimensioning, k_{mod} = 0.80 is often used, which is valid for traffic loads in use classes 1 or 2. The design value for the load resistance R_d of timber is therefore given by:

resistance $R_d = k_{mod} \cdot R_k / \gamma_M$

The following reference values have proven useful in the pre-dimensioning of structural timber components in the typical strength class C 24:
· C 24 tensile strength $f_{t,0,d} = k_{mod} \cdot f_{t,0,k} / \gamma_M = 0.8 \cdot 14$ N/mm^2/1.3 = 0.9 kN/cm^2
· C 24 compressive strength $f_{c,0,d} = k_{mod} \cdot f_{c,0,k} / \gamma_M = 0.8 \cdot 21$ N/mm^2/1.3 = 1.3 kN/cm^2
· C 24 bending strength $f_{m,d} = k_{mod} \cdot f_{m,k} / \gamma_M = 0.8 \cdot 24$ N/mm^2/1.3 = 1.5 kN/cm^2
· C 24 elastic modulus (along the fibre) $E_{0,mean} = 11$ N/mm^2 = 1,100 kN/cm^2

Steel

The industrial building material steel is an alloy that consists mostly of iron. Added to the iron is up to 2 % carbon, as well as sulphur and phosphorus impurities. In order to achieve special properties such as resistance to rust, further chemical elements such as chromium are added. Steel is a homogeneous, isotropic, ductile material with high strength that can be shaped either cold or warm. Its manufacture is enormously energy-intensive; on the other hand, it is highly recyclable. Its drawbacks include considerable self-weight, significant loss of strength when heated, fatiguing and susceptibility to oscillations and corrosion. Steel exhibits peculiar stress-strain behaviour. Typical structural steel of the type S 235 stretches elastically up to its elastic or yield limit of $f_{y,k}$ = 23.5 kN/cm^2. Without a significant increase in stress it first continues to expand plastically before it reaches the ultimate limit of its stress tolerance at about $f_{u,k}$ = 36.0 kN/cm^2. After that, even a decreasing stress is enough to cause further lasting expansion until the steel finally fractures at a breaking strain of about 20 to 25 % (Fig. A 1.37).

In addition to S 235, structural steel types S 275 and S 355, as well as fine-grained structural steel types S 420 and S 460, are also available. Though these have higher strength values $f_{y,k}$ and $f_{u,k}$ as indicated by their labelling, within the elastic region they all have the same elastic modulus E = 21,000 kN/cm^2. For purposes of pre-dimensioning it is a good idea to use S 325. That way, if it becomes necessary further along in the design process, it is possible to fall back on the higher strength types to improve load-bearing capacity without having to change the component dimensions.

Thin, flat steel building components are usually contoured as corrugated or trapezoidal steel in order to achieve greater stiffness. Structural elements under compressive or bending stresses are often shaped as round or square hollow profiles or in the shapes corresponding to the capital letters I, H or U, in order to supply material where the stresses are high and save it where they are low (Fig. A 1.36).

The following reference values have proven useful in the pre-dimensioning of structural steel components of the common strength class S 325:
· S 235 tensile strength $f_{y,d} = f_{y,k} / \gamma_{M0}$ = 235 N/mm^2/1.0 = 23.5 kN/cm^2
· S 235 compressive/bending strength $f_{y,d} = f_{y,k} / \gamma_{M1}$ = 235 N/mm^2/1.1 = 21.4 kN/cm^2
· S 235 elastic modulus E = 210,000 N/mm^2 = 21,000 kN/cm^2

Since first, these strength values lie close together, and second, they refer to the elastic yield limit instead of the significantly higher breaking limit, back-of-the-envelope calculations are frequently done using a standard strength value of $f_{y,d}$ = 24 kN/cm^2/1.1 = 21.8 kN/cm^2.

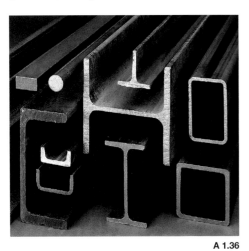

A 1.36

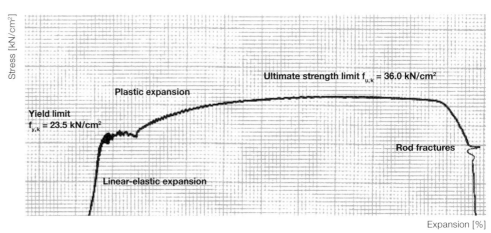

Stress [kN/cm^2]

Ultimate strength limit $f_{u,k}$ = 36.0 kN/cm^2

Plastic expansion

Yield limit
$f_{y,k}$ = 23.5 kN/cm^2

Rod fractures

Linear-elastic expansion

Expansion [%]

A 1.37

Reinforced concrete

The man-made material reinforced concrete is a construction material that is currently used in extremely high quantities throughout the industrialised world (Fig. A 1.39). As a composite material, reinforced concrete makes use of the fire and corrosion-resistant properties, the free formability and the compressive strength of the synthetic stone concrete. The comparatively low tensile strength is addressed by the targeted incorporation of ribbed or contoured steel bars (rebar), particularly in the areas of the reinforced concrete building components that are under tension. The applications of reinforced concrete range from foundations to columns, wall panels, floor and ceiling slabs, large-span roofs and bridges all the way to enormous dam walls. The drawbacks of this building material include the very high climate-damaging energy expenditure required for the cement and steel production, its thermal conductivity, its high self-weight-to-live-load ratio as well as its modest upgradability or reusability. Concrete consists of the hydraulic binding material cement, added water, rock aggregates such as sand or gravel and often additional chemical additives that serve to control the properties of the freshly mixed or the eventual hardened concrete. When these ingredients are cured, the result is a brittle, mineral material.

In construction, concrete commonly used is of strength classes C 25/30 or C 30/37. The characteristic compressive strength of concrete C 30/37 is $f_{ck,cyl} = 30$ N/mm². The design value for the compressive strength should take into account not only the partial safety factor $\gamma_C = 1.50$, but also the factor $\alpha_{cc} = 0.85$, since concrete, too, exhibits lower strength under constant loads than under short-duration trials:

- C 30/37 compressive strength $f_{cd} = \alpha_{cc} \cdot 30$ N/mm²$/\gamma_C = 0.85 \cdot 3.0$ kN/cm²$/1.5 = 1.7$ kN/cm²
- C 30/37 elastic modulus $E_{cm} = 33{,}000$ N/mm² $= 3{,}300$ kN/cm²

For the reinforcement of concrete building components, ribbed steel rods or steel mats of strength class B 500, with diameters of between 6 and 40 mm and lengths of up to 18 m, are used (Fig. A 1.38). The design value of its tensile strength is calculated as follows:
B 500 tensile strength $f_{yd} = f_{yk}/\gamma_S = 500$ N/mm²$/1.15 = 43.5$ kN/cm²

The load-bearing behaviour of reinforced concrete components is complex, thanks to their very different constituents. The pre-dimensioning of components is often predicated on the serviceability requirements. To estimate the component height h of a reinforced concrete ceiling as a function of its span length l and the coefficient k appropriate to the static system in question, the following formula, based on experimental values, can be used:
Component height of a reinforced concrete ceiling h [m] $\geq$ l / (k $\cdot$ 35) + 0.04 m

For enhanced requirements that limit deformations of the ceiling in order to prevent

A 1.36 A sampling of steel profiles
A 1.37 Log of a tensile strength experiment on a steel rod
A 1.38 Reinforcing steel (rebar)
A 1.39 Exposed concrete, Fukutake Hall, University of Tokyo (JP) 2008, Tadao Ando

A 1.40

A 1.41

A 1.42

damage to adjacent building components, experiment has shown:
Component height for enhanced requirements h [m] $\geq$ l^2 / (k$^2 \cdot$ 150) + 0.04 m

The coefficient k varies between k = 0.4 for cantilevers like freely projecting balconies, k = 1.0 for flexibly laid simple slabs and k = 1.5 for the interstitial areas of a continuous panel that extends over multiple supports. For reasons of fire and acoustic protection, the minimum thickness of a floor slab in a high-rise building is usually h $\geq$ 16 cm.
Lightweight or ultralightweight concrete can be employed to decrease thermal conductivity. For highly stressed building components, on the other hand, high-strength or ultrahigh-strength concretes are used that achieve characteristic compressive strengths of $f_{ck,cyl}$ = 100 N/mm^2 or more. Steel, polymer or special glass fibres may be incorporated into the concrete to raise its tensile and bending-tensile strengths.

Masonry

The term masonry describes not so much a building material as a joining technique for a range of completely different materials, such as dried or fired bricks, natural stone, concrete or cinder blocks or sand-lime bricks (Fig. A 1.40). Similarly to concrete, masonry generally exhibits a relatively high compressive strength, but is very weak under tension. The individual stones or bricks are arranged in a bond, that is to say, they are placed in an interlocking pattern. Mortar, a mixture of sand, water and binding agents such as lime or cement, is most commonly used as a bed for the stones and to fill joints (Fig. A 1.41).
The main application for masonry is load-bearing or reinforcing walls, the thickness of which is a function of height and must be between 11.5 and 30 cm or more. The nominal strengths of masonry walls depend on bulk density and material and lie between

2 and 28 MN/m^2. This is equivalent to 0.2–2.8 kN/cm^2. There is a structural regulation for masonry that states that computational proof of bearing capacity is not required if the chosen wall thickness is manifestly sufficient (DIN EN 1996-1-1/NA, NCI for 8.1.2). This rule should be understood within the context of the fact that masonry was erected over millennia of building history without ever having been subject to computational proof. Nowadays, however, this regulation should not be used without appropriate experience.
As for concrete, the use of reinforcement can increase the tensile strength of masonry, as well. Particularly in regions prone to earthquakes, this can improve structural stability.

Other building materials

Other materials and composites than the materials described thus far are used in load-bearing applications, albeit more rarely.
Aluminium has a very low specific weight and can be shaped more easily than steel. Extruded aluminium profiles are very frequently used to frame glass panes in post & beam or element facades.
Glass panes in such facades must be capable of withstanding wind loads. In cases where glazing is subjected to foot traffic or suspended overhead, the self-weight of the glass as well as some other loads must also be taken into account. For these applications, laminated safety glass (LSG) composed of multiple bonded panes of glass is available. In very rare cases, glass is even employed to support the loads from other building components (Fig. A 1.42).
Clay is an environmentally friendly building material and is available in large quantities nearly all over the world. It can be produced without great energy expenditure, it is non-flammable, recyclable and structurally advantageous. Clay high-rises in Yemen that are almost 400 years old attest to its

load-bearing capacity. In half-timbered houses, it is used as infill for the timber framework. Clay has great potential for sustainable construction.

Fibre-reinforced plastics (FRP) use glass (GFRP) or carbon fibres (CFRP) incorporated into synthetic resins to achieve high tensile strengths combined with low self-weight. This rather cumbersome building technique has thus far become prevalent especially in the construction of pleasure craft. In building construction, slats of FRP have primarily found use in the reinforcement of existing building components. Laminated textile membranes and synthetic films allow large areas to be roofed over at relatively modest cost. Such thin sheets are particularly suited to accommodating tensile stresses. In order to support loads without significant deformation, they must be mechanically or pneumatically prestressed. Membranes are used not only for small tents but also as roof coverings for large sports arenas all over the world (Fig. A 1.43).

The particular characteristics of all building materials with respect to their bearing capacity must be taken into account in the design of the relevant structures. If no applicable standards exist, the use of a given material must be assessed on an individual basis and coordinated with the appropriate building supervisory authority.

A 1.40 Historical masonry from the 10th century, Glendalough Cathedral (IE)
A 1.41 Modern masonry, European Hansemuseum (DE) 2015, Andreas Heller Architects & Designers, Kröger & Steinchen
A 1.42 The glass facade supports the roof of the Main Gate of the Novartis Campus, Basel (CH) 2006, Marco Serra, EBP
A 1.43 Inflated ETFE film panels form the roof and facade of the Allianz Arena, Munich (DE) 2005, Herzog & de Meuron in collaboration with Arup, Sailer Stepan und Partner (ssp)

A 1.43

Part B   Structural Elements

Tensegrity, tension and compression-stressed elements
in equilibrium, Needle Tower II in the sculpture garden
of the Kröller Müller Museum, Otterlo near Arnhem (NL)
1969, Kenneth Snelson

Structural Elements

Eberhard Möller

Structures are usually composed of individual structural elements. The most important of these basic elements can be classified into three categories according to their predominant internal stresses:
- structural elements under tension
- structural elements under compression
- bending-stressed structural elements

In the following sections, prominent examples and important variations of the above-mentioned categories will be introduced. Indications of typical applications, simple rules of thumb, current analysis methods, typical stress resultants or additional pre-dimensioning methods offer information about the use of such structural elements.

Structural elements often fulfil other roles in addition to their load-bearing function. As walls or ceilings they serve as spatial enclosures and provide protection from view, sounds, fire, wind, moisture and temperature extremes. Given the broad range of their functions, such building components often comprise multiple layers in order to meet all requirements to the greatest extent possible..

Structural Elements Under Tension

Structural elements under tension include tension members (tie rods), cables and membranes. The building material steel, from which elements subject to tensile stresses are often made nowadays, is comparatively new. Even newer are some of the construction methods that push the potential of this material to its limits. During the age of industrialisation it became possible to make sufficient quantities of the novel material while simultaneously producing work pieces of reasonable size. Thus, while construction methods using structural elements under tension have not existed for very long, many relevant buildings with impressive dimensions already exist.

Tension elements in civil engineering
Tension elements are frequently used in bridges with long spans. With lengths of several thousand metres, ropes and cables are among the longest structural elements available in construction.

Suspension bridges
Large suspension bridges such as the Golden Gate Bridge in San Francisco, built in 1937 with a main span of 1,280 metres, or the Akashi Kaikyō Bridge in Japan with its span of 1,991 m, could not have been built without steel cables (Fig. B 1.1). Apart from the main suspension cables, which run over the tops of the high pylons, the vertical hangers, to which the deck of the bridge is attached, are also under tension.

Cable-stayed bridges
In cable-stayed bridges, the load-bearing cables run directly from the bridge deck to the pylons like the strings of a harp. For the Erasmus Bridge in Rotterdam, completed in 1996, the designers Ben van Berkel and Caroline Bos made use of structural elements under tension. A little imagination allows the viewer to recognise the kneeling

B 1.1 Suspension bridge, Akashi Kaikyō Bridge, Kobe (JP) 1998, Honshu Shikoku Bridge Authority
B 1.2 Suspension bridge, Millennium Bridge, London (GB) 2000/2002, Norman Foster, Arup
B 1.3 Cable-stayed swing bridge, St. Saviour's Dock Footbridge, London (GB) 1996, Nicholas Lacey, Whitby & Bird
B 1.4 Cable-stayed bridge, Erasmus Bridge, Rotterdam (NL) 1996, van Berkel & Bos, Gemeentewerken Rotterdam

B 1.1

Erasmus, whose fanned-out, spidery arms hold up the road over the Nieuwe Maas.

Hybrid cable-stayed/suspension bridges

An early juxtaposition of the two construction principles – suspension and cable-stayed bridges – can be seen in the Brooklyn Bridge in New York (Fig. A 1.18, p. 24). It was designed by John A. Roebling (1806–1869). After his death, his son took over the construction management; when he in turn became ill, Roebling's daughter-in-law Emily Warren Roebling assumed the task. The bridge was opened in 1883 by US President Chester Alan Arthur on horseback. With

its span of 486 m, it was at that time by far the longest bridge in the world. The French bridge construction engineer Michel Virlogeux adopted the idea of a combination cable-stayed and suspension bridge for the third bridge over the Bosphorus (Fig. D 2.14, p. 115). On this bridge, opened in 2016, stays lend rigidity to the bridge sections near the pylons while the more flexible vertical hangers support the central portion of the bridge.

Pedestrian bridges

Pedestrian bridges also employ filigree tensile elements in order to overcome

large spans with relatively little material. There are pedestrian bridges of both the suspension type, such as the Millennium Bridge in London by Norman Foster and Arup (Fig. B 1.2), and of cable-stayed construction, like the swing footbridge at St. Saviour's Dock (Fig. B 1.3).

Tension elements in architecture

In addition to their uses in civil engineering, tensile structural elements are also found in architecture. Here, it is primarily the large-span constructions in which such building components are used.

B 1.2

B 1.3

B 1.4

B 1.5

B 1.6

Saddle-shaped suspension roofs

The J.S. Dorton Arena (formerly State Fair Arena) in Raleigh (Fig. B 1.5) represents a milestone in the development of suspended, primarily tensile-stressed roofs. Its Polish-born architect Matthew Nowicki (1910–1950) conceived the novel structure. After his tragic death in a plane crash in 1950, the New York structural engineer Fred Severud helped make the project reality. While the cables suspended between the upper portions of the two arches support the self-weight, the tensile elements stretched across them between the lower points of the arches prevent wind suction from lifting off the lightweight roof. Because of the form of such roof constructions, surfaces with analogously opposing curvatures are often called saddle surfaces.

A short time later, in the 1950s, Norwegian-born Fred Severud, together with Finnish architect Eero Saarinen (1910–1961), designed an ice hockey arena for Yale University in New Haven. Here, the cables are stretched between three arches, a central upright arch and two lateral arches lying on their sides. Thanks to the resulting sweeping form, complete with an illuminated tail fin at the entrance, the David S. Ingalls Rink is also known by the nickname "The Yale Whale" (Fig. B 1.6).

Inspired by these buildings, Kenzo Tange, Yoshikatsu Tsuboi and Mamoru Kawaguchi decided to give the halls for the 1964 Olympic Games in Tokyo similar suspension roofs (Fig. B 1.7).

Spoked wheel constructions

The spokes of bicycle wheels have similarly slender forms as the structural cables in suspension bridges or roofs. In 1958, the US Pavilion at the World's Fair in Brussels demonstrated the concept of using the spoked wheel construction horizontally as a large roof structure. In this case, Edward Durell Stone arranged the structural tensile elements radially. A second tier of tensioned cables above the structural cables helped stiffen the construction and prevent wind suction from carrying off the roof. Both sets of cables were anchored on the outside at the compression ring and internally at a shared wheel hub several metres tall.

The Russian-born engineer Lev Zetlin used the same principle in 1959 for the roof of the Utica Memorial Auditorium in New York state (Fig. B 1.8). Unlike the temporary pavilion in Brussels, this building has been in continuous operation as a multifunctional hall ever since.

For the World's Fair in 1964, in collaboration with Philip Johnson and Richard Foster,

Lev Zetlin also designed the New York State pavilion, the so-called Tent of Tomorrow (Fig. B 1.9). In contrast to Utica and Brussels, the suspension cables here are situated above the bracing cables. The compression-stressed outer rim had to be built correspondingly tall. Here, too, the filigree spokes are suspended within a massive compression ring supported by colossal concrete columns. The structure of the pavilion still stands as a sculpture in Flushing Meadows Park in the New York borough of Queens.

Spoked wheel constructions have been used frequently since the 1990s as roof coverings for the stands in stadiums and arenas. Aside from their modest weight, such structures have the additional advantage that the horizontal tensile forces from the stressed spokes are short-circuited through the compression ring, and that therefore only the vertical loads from self-weight must be transmitted into the columns and foundations. An exactly circular form of rim and hub is no longer necessary. Examples can be viewed all over the world, including in Stuttgart, Frankfurt, Hanover, Hamburg, Rome, Madrid, Seville, Zaragoza, Warsaw, Bucharest, Kiev, Shenzhen, Brasilia and Rio de Janeiro.

a

b

B 1.7

Weight-stiffened suspended roofs

While the projects mentioned thus far feature bracing cables for stiffening the roof construction in addition to the main support cables, Eero Saarinen instead used the weight of concrete for this purpose in the elegantly curved roof of the terminal building at Dulles International Airport in Washington.(Fig. B 1.11). In this structure, steel cables attached to the outward-slanted solid columns support a slender, yet comparatively heavy reinforced concrete roof.

In Álvaro Siza Vieira's and Cecil Balmond's Pavilhão de Portugal at the 1998 Expo in Lisbon, the self-weight of the concrete skin likewise serves to stiffen the embedded cables (Fig. B 1.10). In 1996 in Exhibition Hall 26 in Hanover, Thomas Herzog used gravel-filled timber elements, complemented by two guy wires with oscillation dampers per main support cable. In the glazed roofing of the railway station forecourts in Ulm in 1993 and Heilbronn in 2001, as well as at the Römertherme (Roman baths) in Baden near Vienna in 1999, the engineers of Schlaich Bergermann Partner (sbp) had only the weight of the glass panes themselves at their disposal.

B 1.5 Structural model of the J. S. Dorton Arena, Raleigh (US) 1953, Matthew Nowicki, Fred Severud

B 1.6 Support cables between arches, structural model of the David S. Ingalls Rink ice hockey arena (The Yale Whale), Yale University, New Haven (US) 1958, Eero Saarinen, Fred Severud

B 1.7 Yoyogi National Gymnasium and Yoyogi 2nd Gymnasium, Tokyo (JP) 1964, Kenzo Tange, Yoshikatsu Tsuboi
    a external view of the Yoyogi National Gymnasium
    b interior of the Yoyogi 2nd Gymnasium

B 1.8 Support cables in spoked wheel construction, Memorial Auditorium, Utica (US) 1959, Gehron Seltzer, Lev Zetlin

B 1.9 New York State Pavilion, New York (US) 1964, Philip Johnson, Richard Foster, Lev Zetlin

B 1.10 Pavilhão de Portugal, Expo 1998, Lisbon (PT) Álvaro Siza Vieira, Cecil Balmond

B 1.11 Main terminal of Dulles International Airport near Washington (US) 1962, Eero Saarinen

B 1.8

B 1.9

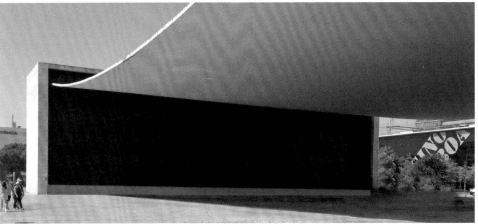

B 1.10

B 1.11

B 1.12

B 1.13

Other types of suspension roof

For the Stuttgart fair in 2007, the engineers at Mayr Ludescher Partner once again opted for bracing cables below and parallel to the support cables in order to prevent large deformations or even a separation of the roof (Fig. B 1.12). The structural and bracing cables are connected via vertical coupling members.

A similar concept was implemented by the designers at gmp and sbp at Exhibition Halls 8/9 in Hanover in 1998. In contrast, the externally placed load-bearing structure for the roof of the Europahalle, built in 1983 in Karlsruhe, is strongly reminiscent of a suspension bridge (Fig. B 1.13).

Suspended timber roofs

Today, through the use of glue, long tensile elements can also be made from engineered timber products. In 1988, for four assembly pavilions at a furniture manufacturer in Bad Münder, Frei Otto used curved timber

tension rods suspended between a glazed ridge frame and the circumferential eaves beam. In 2000, the engineers of Merz Kley Partner (mkp) were able to cover the municipal works yard in Hohenems near Dornbirn with 39-mm thick and 20-m long laminated veneer lumber panels. A suspension roof of timber has spanned an athletic and recreational swimming pool in Surrey, Canada, since 2015.

Vertical tension members

Vertical tension members are also used in smaller dimensions for the suspension of building components. In 1960, Philip Johnson anchored the gallery of the upper storey of the Munson Williams Proctor Arts Institute in Utica on high beams above the plane of the roof (Fig. B 1.14). This allows the level below the gallery to remain free of columns.

In 2017, as a means of acoustically decoupling instrument practice rooms from one

another and thereby minimising sound transmission between them, Steven Hall Architects and Arup used tension rods to hang individual timber cubes from the main structure of the New Music Building of the Lewis Arts Complex at Princeton University (Fig. B 1.18). The full-surface glazing of the facade allows unencumbered views of the individually suspended room modules. In many buildings, tension rods are employed to suspend balconies, galleries, catwalks, canopies, stairs, etc. from above (Fig. B 1.17). However, in practice all of the vertical loads from such tension rods must be transferred by roundabout ways downward and into the ground.

Load-bearing behaviour of structural elements under tension

The bearing behaviour of single-axis elements subjected to tensile stresses is known from everyday experience and is easy to understand. The greater the weight of an object that we carry with our arm hanging straight down, the more the arm is stretched and the greater the pain we feel. In 1638, Galileo Galilei (1564–1642) described his theories on the topic of elements under tension in his famous *Discorsi* ("Discourses and Mathematical Demonstrations Concerning Two New Sciences Relating to Mechanics and Motion"; Fig. B 1.15): "For a closer understanding we imagine a cylinder or a prism AB, made of wood or another material, fastened at the top at A, hanging vertically and with a weight C attached at B. Whatever its strength may be, one can always imagine a weight C that is so great that the body breaks. For if we allow the weight to increase, the body must eventually tear like a rope." [1]

Hooke's law

After Galileo Galilei, Robert Hooke (1635–1703) also studied how elements behave when placed under tension. The law that he developed and that is named after him states that for many materials, the change

B 1.14

B 1.15

in length Δl remains proportional to the acting tension F as long as the force does not exceed a certain magnitude.
Hooke's law
Change in length Δl [cm] ~ Force F [kN]

Experiments show that the deformation or change in length Δl of a rod under tensile stress from a normal force N, that is, a force whose line of action is orthogonal (normal) to the cross-sectional area, is influenced by the following parameters:
- the normal force N [kN] pulling on the rod
- the length l_0 [cm] of the unstressed rod
- the cross-sectional area A [cm²] of the rod
- the material of the rod, expressed through its elastic modulus E [kN/cm²]

Within the elastic region, the value of the change in length Δl [cm] is therefore given by:
Change in length $\Delta l = N \cdot l_0 / (E \cdot A)$

In undergoing a change in length Δl, a stretched rod does not gain additional matter but merely redistributes its own. Therefore, a positive increase in length is associated with a negative change in the transverse dimension. However, in many building materials the changes in length and width are so small that they are barely discernible.

Normal stress σ_N
The internal stress on a rod in response to external loading by a normal force N is called the normal stress σ_N.
Normal stress σ_N [kN/cm²] = normal force N [kN]/cross-sectional area A [cm²]

Strain ε
The ratio of the change in length Δl and the original length l_0 of a rod is known as the strain ε. It is a dimensionless ratio. The strain ε of a tension rod can also be determined using the ratio of the normal stress σ_N and the elastic modulus E of a building material:

Strain $\varepsilon = \Delta l / l_0 = (N/A) / E = \sigma_N / E$

Pre-dimensioning of tension members
The pre-dimensioning of structures is used primarily to establish reasonable component dimensions for structural elements during the design phase. It is done before all the factors affecting the structure are precisely defined and long before the eventual proof of structural stability and serviceability of the structure as well as all its parts is required. The careful pre-dimensioning of load-bearing elements therefore plays an essential role in the responsible development and construction of engineering structures and buildings.

B 1.16

B 1.17

a

b

B 1.18

B 1.12 Fairground Hall 3, Stuttgart (DE) 2007, Wulf Architekten Partner, Mayr Ludescher Partner
B 1.13 Europahalle Karlsruhe (DE) 1983, Schmitt, Kasimir + Partner (SKP), Schlaich Bergermann Partner (sbp)
B 1.14 Munson Williams Proctor Arts Institute, Utica (US) 1960, Philip Johnson
B 1.15 Galileo Galilei: *Discorsi e dimostrazioni matematiche (Discourses)*. Leiden 1638, Fig. 7
B 1.16 Suspended timber roof, assembly pavilion, Bad Münder (DE) 1988, Frei Otto
B 1.17 Suspended catwalk, city library, Landau/ Palatinate (DE) 1998, Lamott.Lamott Architekten
B 1.18 Hanging boxes, New Music Building, Lewis Arts Complex, Princeton (US) 2017, Steven Hall Architects, Arup
   a view of the hanging boxes from outside
   b interior

B 1.19

However, it in no way replaces the necessary certifications that must be performed in accordance with the regulations, standards, construction provisions and laws put forward by building authorities. Extensive literature exists to aid in the application of these regulations [2].

According to empirical evidence, a stretched element will fracture when the normal stress σ_N becomes very large and exceeds certain limiting values. In order to prevent such failure and the damage associated with it, the allowable stress in construction engineering must be capped at a maximum value $\sigma_{N,all}$. This value must be smaller than the respective tensile strength f_t of the material in question.

The basic rule is:

$$\sigma_N = N_{t,d}/A \; < \; f_{t,d} = f_{t,k}/\gamma_M$$

For pre-dimensioning, it has proven helpful to ensure that the tensile stress σ_N resulting from the design value of an acting tensile force $N_{t,d}$ does not exceed the following design values for the strengths $f_{t,d}$:

Timber construction: Tensile strength of C 24
$f_{t,0,d} = k_{mod} \cdot f_{t,0,k}/\gamma_M = 0.8 \cdot 14 \text{ N/mm}^2/1.3$
$= 0.9 \text{ kN/cm}^2$

Steel construction: Tensile strength of S 235
$f_{y,d} = f_{y,k}/\gamma_{M0} = 235 \text{ N/mm}^2/1.0 = 23.5 \text{ kN/cm}^2$

When these strengths $f_{t,d}$ are applied, the required cross-sectional area A_{req} can be determined for every acting force
$N_{t,d} = \gamma_F \cdot N_{t,k}$
Required cross-sectional area A_{req} of a tension member $[\text{cm}^2] = N_{t,d}/\sigma_{N,all} = \gamma_F \cdot N_{t,k}/f_{t,d}$

In the case of solid round sections, the cross-sectional area $A = r^2 \pi = (d/2)^2 \pi$. Thus, the required diameter d of a tension member as a function of the acting tensile force $N_{t,d}$ is given by:
Required diameter d_{req} of a round tension rod:
$2r = 2 \sqrt{(A/\pi)} = 2 (N_{t,d}/f_{t,d}/\pi)^{0.5}$

To support a load of $N_{t,d} = 100$ kN, a round wooden tension rod of the typical strength class C 24 must have a diameter $d_{req} = 2 (N_{t,d}/f_{t,d}/\pi)^{0.5} = 2 (100 \text{ kN}/0.9 \text{ N/mm}^2/\pi)^{0.5} = 12$ cm.

A wooden member of this diameter with original length $l_0 = 5$ m and subjected to a force N = 100 kN would experience an increase in length $\Delta l = N \cdot l_0/(E \cdot A) = 100 \text{ kN} \cdot 500 \text{ cm}/(1{,}100 \text{ kN/cm}^2 \cdot 113 \text{ cm}^2) = 0.4$ cm.

To support the same a load of $N_{t,d} = 100$ kN, a round steel rod of the common steel type S 325 would only need a diameter $d_{req} = 2 (N_{t,d}/f_{t,d}/\pi)^{0.5} = 2 (100 \text{ kN}/23.5 \text{ N/mm}^2/\pi)^{0.5} = 2.4$ cm.

This steel rod with original length $l_0 = 5$ m and subjected to a force N = 100 kN would experience an increase in length given by $\Delta l = N \cdot l_0/(E \cdot A) = 100 \text{ kN} \cdot 500 \text{ cm}/(21{,}000 \text{ kN/cm}^2 \cdot 4.5 \text{ cm}^2) = 0.5$ cm.

It is therefore very easy to determine the required cross section A_{req} $[\text{cm}^2]$ of timber or steel tensile elements for any given load $N_{t,d}$ acting on them. Building materials such as unreinforced concrete or masonry exhibit very low tensile strengths f and are therefore not used in structural elements under tension. In addition to the one-dimensional tensile stresses, membranes

B 1.19 Bränden bus stop, Krumbach, Vorarlberg (AT) 2014, Sou Fujimoto
B 1.20 Carré d'Art, Nîmes (FR) 1993, Norman Foster, Arup
B 1.21 Catenary curve and thrust arch of the dome of the Basilica of St. Peter. Giovanni Poleni, *Memorie istoriche della gran cupola del Tempio Vaticano*. Padua 1748, Fig. XIV
B 1.22 Gateway Arch, St. Louis (US) 1965 (design 1947), Eero Saarinen, Hannskarl Bandel
B 1.23 Pont du Gard, near Nîmes (FR) mid 1st century CE.
B 1.24 Pont d'Arc, naturally formed arch over the Ardèche River (FR)

B 1.20

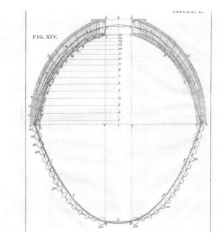

B 1.21

may experience tensile stresses along two axes. Construction methods involving these are covered in the chapter "Membrane and Air-Inflated Structures" (p. 130ff.).

Structural Elements Under Compression

While structural elements under tension are stretched, compression-stressed elements are compacted or compressed. Compressive stresses are commonly found in columns, walls, panels, arches and vaults. Unlike the elongated tension elements, many such compression elements have a long-standing tradition in construction. Structures from ancient and medieval architecture frequently relied on the transfer of loads by way of compression-stressed building components.

Columns and pillars
In Nîmes in the south of France, structural elements of various epochs stand facing each other. The stone columns of the Maison Carrée, a Roman temple from the beginning of the 1st century CE, contrast with the slender steel pillars of the Carré d'Art cultural centre built by Norman Foster and the engineers of Arup on the opposite side of the square in 1993 (Fig. B 1.20). The vertical rods of the bus stop in Vorarlberg by Sou Fujimoto (Fig, B 1.19) likewise appear very slender.

Arches and vaults
Along with columns, pillars and walls, arches and vaults are also among the predominantly compression-stressed structural elements. In aqueducts like the Pont du Gard near Nîmes, Romans made use of the rigorous geometry of circular arches (Fig. B 1.23).
Naturally occurring structures, however, seem to suggest somewhat different, struc-

turally more ingenious forms. The stone arch of the Pont d'Arc over the Ardèche river, for example, is reminiscent of an upright parabola (Fig. B 1.24).

Catenary curves and thrust lines
Gothic arches and vaults come quite close to the geometric form of a parabola. Scientifically speaking, it was probably already known to Galileo Galilei that the inversion of the form of a hanging chain could yield advantageous compression-stressed constructions. But he was unable to find an exact mathematical equation for the catenary curve. In order to investigate damage to the dome of the Basilica of St. Peter in Rome, the mathematician Giovanni Poleni utilised the catenary curve as well as its inverted form, the thrust line. He published his results in 1748 under the title "Memorie istoriche della gran cupola del Tempio Vaticano" (Historic memories about the great dome of the Vatican church). For many, this date represents the birth of modern structural engineering, since it marks the first time that the load-bearing behaviour of a building component was thoroughly scientifically analysed (Fig. B 1.21).
The Catalan architect Antoni Gaudí (1852–1926) made use of such insights in some of his famous projects such as the Sagrada Familia in Barcelona, on which construction began in 1882. With the aid of hanging models he developed arch and vault forms and even entire structures. The Gateway Arch in St. Louis, designed by Eero Saarinen in 1947 and achieved in conjunction with engineer Hannskarl Bandel, is also modelled on the catenary curve (Fig. B 1.22), as are the vaults of the St. Stephen Martyr Church in Washington from 1961 (Fig. B 1.27, p. 48). Frei Otto (1925–2015) worked with hanging chains in the Mannheim Multihalle project, among others, in order to find advantageous forms for large lattice domes (Fig. B 1.25, p. 48). Typical building materials for structural

B 1.22

B 1.23

B 1.24

B 1.25

B 1.26

elements under compression are clay (loam), natural stone, artificial stone such as sand-lime brick, brick and concrete, as well as timber, steel and reinforced concrete.

Air pressure and compressed air

A particularly lightweight compression-stressed "building material" is air. Air pressure not only provides structure in bicycle tyres and bouncy castles, but also in air-inflated domes which can span entire tennis arenas, football pitches or other athletic fields (Fig. B 1.26). A slight internal over-pressure of 1 kN/m² = 1,000 Pa = 10 hPa is usually enough to support not only the

self-weight, but wind and snow loads as well. The internal overpressure creates tensile stresses in the material of the surrounding envelope. People can barely perceive the difference in air pressure between the interior and exterior, since it is less than that between a low pressure area (about 980 hPa) and a high pressure area (about 1,030 hPa). In such domes, the smallest leak will cause the continual escape of air just as in a bicycle tyre. For this reason, blower fans must constantly resupply air and force it into the interior. The internal pressure can be adaptively raised during storms or heavy snowfall, for example.

Load-bearing behaviour of structural elements under compression

In physics, the pressure p is defined as the effect produced by an orthogonal force F acting on an area A. The unit was named after the French scientist Blaise Pascal (1623–1662).

Pressure p [Pa] = force F [N]/area A [m²]

In construction, the more commonly used unit is the kN/m²
(1 kN/m² = 1 kPA = 1,000 Pa) or the kN/cm²
(1 kN/cm² = 10 MPa = 10,000 kPa).

Uniaxial pressure

To determine the compression strength f_c of compact concrete test objects, cubes are often placed between two parallel plates and the plates pushed together with ever-increasing force. In such a compression test, the first thing to appear are fractures on the test object (Fig. B 1.29). This is surprising, since fractures are an immediate consequence of tensile stresses and not compressive stresses. If the object is stressed further, it ruptures, sometimes with a loud bang.

The cause of the fractures are expansions transverse to the compression direction. In other words, the test object is not directly destroyed by the compressive stress, but indirectly through transverse tensile stresses, which develop at right angles to the compression direction as a result of a uniaxial pressure. The tensile strength of rock is fundamentally less than its compressive strength.

Omnidirectional pressure

How test objects react to omnidirectional, so-called hydrostatic pressure as opposed to uniaxial pressure is equally important to investigate, as a failure due to transverse tensile stresses would in this case be impossible. Since all materials except water manifest a greater density in their solid state than in their liquid or gaseous states, solid objects are, unlike gases, hardly compressible. How-

B 1.27

B 1.25   Ceiling construction of the Multihalle Mannheim
(DE) 1975, Carlfried Mutschler, Joachim Langner,
Frei Otto
B 1.26   Temporary air-inflated dome over the football
pitch at Princeton University Stadium, Princeton
(US)
B 1.27   St. Stephen Martyr Church, Washington, DC
(US) 1961, Johnson & Boutin
B 1.28   Slender cast iron columns, Feldafing railway
station (DE) 1865, Georg Dollmann
B 1.29   Compression test of a concrete test cube

B 1.28

ever, high temperatures that arise under pressure could eventually exceed the melting point of the solid object, causing it to liquify. This change in physical state brings with it a simultaneous increase in volume. Correspondingly high temperature and pressure conditions exist in the interior of the earth. The increase in volume that accompanies the melting of rock could be related to volcanic eruptions. In these events, high pressure in the earth's mantle is discharged outward.

Stability
Compression elements used in construction are rarely as compact as the test cubes used in experiments. It is even more rare for them to be subject to pressure from all sides. The compression elements mostly used today are quite slender elements such as pillars or walls (Fig. B 1.28). These generally exhibit a fundamentally different form of failure. When they are stressed beyond a certain limit, they suddenly buckle laterally. Stability is no longer guaranteed. The associated load is often called the critical load F_{cr} or the critical normal force N_{cr}. The term buckling load is also frequently used. Stability failure modes such as the buckling and torsional buckling of compression members, the warping of panels and the lateral torsional buckling of beams occur

without warning signs such as deformations or noises, often long before the greatest allowable compressive stress of the material is reached. The more slender the building component, the sooner this happens.

Buckling load N_{cr}
When the buckling load N_{cr} is reached, the stable equilibrium of a compression-stressed structural element is lost. An equilibrium is stable when it returns to its original state after a perturbation. In the case where the ideal buckling load N_{cr} is applied, the equilibrium is theoretically neutral, a situation which should already be avoided from a practical engineering standpoint. Beyond this load N_{cr}, the system becomes labile and therefore unstable. The smallest perturbation would cause it to fail immediately by lateral buckling.

Experiments show that the critical load N_{cr} for a compression member depends on the constant π, on the material and on various geometrical properties of the member:
Buckling load N_{cr} [kN] $= \pi^2 \, E \, I / L_{cr}^2$
where E [kN/cm^2] is the elastic modulus of the material, I [cm^4] is the area moment of inertia (also called the second moment of area) and L_{cr} is the buckling length or effective length of the member, where $L_{cr} =$ effective length factor $\beta \cdot$ length l

Area moment of inertia I
The area moment of inertia I [cm^4], also known as the second moment of area, is a geometrical quantity of a cross section, in which areas that lie far from the area centroid of the cross section along the direction of the load are weighted more heavily than those close to the centroid. Values for many cross sections and profiles can be found in reference tables (Fig. B 1.31, p. 50). For a simple rectangular cross section of width b and height h, the area moment of inertia I along the height h can be calculated as follows:
area moment of inertia I [cm^4] $=$
$\int z^2 \, dA = b \, h^3 / 12$

Buckling length L_{cr}
The buckling length L_{cr} (also: s_k) depends on the member's length l and its supports. It is also called the effective length and it makes it possible to compare the buckling behaviour of variously supported compression members. Leonhard Euler (1707–1783) had already classified a few such cases based on their supports. For members fixed at both ends, the effective length factor is $\beta = 0.5$; for members hinged at both ends it is $\beta = 1.0$; for cantilevered members fixed at one end it is $\beta = 2.0$. For arches, frames and spring-mounted members, the effective

B 1.29

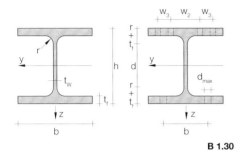

B 1.30

B 1.30 Broad I profile of the HEB series
B 1.31 Cross section values for hot-rolled wide I pro-
files (with parallel flange surfaces) of the
HEB series (as per DIN 1025-2/Wendehorst,
see Note 2)
B 1.32 Critical buckling stress σc_r as a function of
slenderness ratio λ
B 1.33 Cross section values for hot-finished, circular
hollow sections (as per Wendehorst, see
Note 2)

length factor β can reach values of 10
or more.
Buckling or effective length
L_{cr} = effective length factor $\beta \cdot$ member
length l

Buckling stress σ_{cr}
For a given buckling load N_{cr} of a compression member, the associated buckling
stress σ_{cr} can be determined by: buckling
stress $\sigma_{cr} = N_{cr}/A = \pi^2 E I /(L_{cr}^2 \cdot A) = \pi^2 E /$
$(L_{cr}^2 \cdot (\sqrt{(I/A)})^2)$

Radius of gyration i
The two values that describe the cross section of a compression member, the area
moment of inertia I and the cross-sectional
area A, are often combined under the term
radius of gyration i [cm]:

Radius of gyration i [cm] = $\sqrt{(I/A)}$ = $(I/A)^{0.5}$

Like the area moment of inertia I, the radius
of gyration i is also a geometric quantity
that depends on the shape and area of a
cross section. Values for typical steel profiles and other common cross sections can
be found in reference tables. Figures B 1.31
and B 1.33 show sample cross-sectional
values for frequently used sections such as
hot-rolled, wide I-profiles of the HEB series
(Fig. B 1.30) and hot-finished circular hollow
sections.
For square solid cross sections with side
length d, such as those often found in timber
construction, the calculation of the radius of
gyration is straightforward:
Radius of gyration i [cm] = $\sqrt{(I/A)}$ =
$\sqrt{((d \cdot d^3/12)/d^2)}$ = $d/\sqrt{12}$ = 0.289 d

Slenderness ratio λ
Using the descriptive concept of the slenderness ratio λ, the entire geometry of a
compression member with respect to its
buckling risk can be expressed as a single
value. The greater a member's slenderness
ratio, the more readily it will buckle. The
slenderness ratio λ is a dimensionless quantity. It takes into account the mounting and
the length l, as well as the shape I and area
A of the cross section of a compression-
stressed member.
Slenderness ratio $\lambda = L_{cr}/i = \beta \cdot l/\sqrt{(I/A)}$

A compression member with an effective
length L_{cr} = 5.00 m = 500 cm and a square
cross section of side length d = 17.3 cm,
for example, has a slenderness ratio λ =
L_{cr}/i = 500 cm/(0.289 $\cdot$ 17.3 cm) = 100.

Sym-bol	Dimensions [mm]						A [cm²]	A_vy [cm²]	A_vz [cm²]	G [kg/m²]	U [m²/m]	For bending about the y-axis			For bending about the z-axis		
	h [mm]	b [mm]	t_w [mm]	t_f [mm]	r [mm]	d [mm]	A [cm²]	A_{vy} [cm²]	A_{vz} [cm²]	G [kg/m²]	U [m²/m]	I_y [cm⁴]	S_y [cm³]	i_y [cm]	I_z [cm⁴]	S_z [cm³]	i_z [cm]
HEB (IPB)																	
100	100	100	6	10	12	56	26.0	20.0	9.04	20.4	0.567	450	89.9	4.16	167	33.5	2.53
120	120	120	6.5	11	12	74	34.0	26.4	11.0	26.7	0.686	864	144	5.04	318	52.9	3.06
140	140	140	7	12	12	92	43.0	33.6	13.1	33.7	0.805	1,510	216	5.93	550	78.5	3.58
160	160	160	8	13	15	104	54.3	41.6	17.6	42.6	0.918	2,490	312	6.78	889	111	4.05
180	180	180	8.5	14	15	122	65.3	50.4	20.2	51.2	1.04	3,830	426	7.66	1,360	151	4.57
200	200	200	9	15	18	134	78.1	60.0	24.8	61.3	1.15	5,700	570	8.54	2,000	200	5.07
220	220	220	9.5	16	18	152	91.0	70.4	27.9	71.5	1.27	8,090	736	9.43	2,840	258	5.59
240	240	240	10	17	21	164	106	81.6	33.2	83.2	1.38	11,260	938	10.3	3,920	327	6.08
260	260	260	10	17.5	24	177	118	91.0	37.6	93.0	1.50	14,920	1,150	11.2	5,130	395	6.58
280	280	280	10.5	18	24	196	131	101	41.1	103	1.62	19,270	1,380	12.1	6,590	471	7.09
300	300	300	11	19	27	208	149	114	47.4	117	1.73	25,170	1,680	13.0	8,560	571	7.58
320	320	300	11.5	20.5	27	225	161	123	51.8	127	1.77	30,820	1,930	13.8	9,240	616	7.57
340	340	300	12	21.5	27	243	171	129	56.1	134	1.81	36,660	2,160	14.6	9,690	646	7.53
360	360	300	12.5	22.5	27	261	181	135	60.6	142	1.85	43,190	2,400	15.5	10,140	676	7.49
400	400	300	13.5	24	27	298	198	144	70.0	155	1.93	57,680	2,880	17.1	10,820	721	7.40
500	500	300	14.5	28	27	390	239	168	89.8	187	2.12	107200	4,290	21.2	12,620	842	7.27
600	600	300	15.5	30	27	486	270	180	111	212	2.32	171,000	5,700	25.2	13,530	902	7.08
800	800	300	17.5	33	30	674	334	198	162	262	2.71	359,100	8,980	32.8	14,900	994	6.68
1,000	1,000	300	19	36	30	868	400	216	212	314	3.11	644,700	12,890	40.1	16,280	1,090	6.38

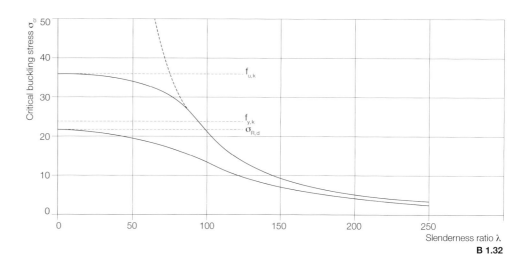

B 1.32

If one substitutes the slenderness ratio λ into the formula for buckling stress σ_{cr}, this equation simplifies to:

Buckling stress $\sigma_{cr} = N_{cr}/A = \pi^2\,E\,I\,/(L_{cr}^2 \cdot A)$
$= \pi^2\,E/(L_{cr}^2 \cdot (\sqrt{(I/A)})^2 = \pi^2\,E/\lambda^2$

Graphing the buckling stress σ_{cr} as a function of slenderness ratio λ yields a hyperbola known as the Euler curve. In construction, only compression members whose compressive stress lies beneath their buckling stress σ_{cr} may be used. At the same time, particularly for less slender members, the compressive strength $f_{c,d}$ may not be exceeded (Fig. B 1.32).

Pre-dimensioning of compression members

The pre-dimensioning of compression members is more complicated than that of tension members, since various different failure modes must be taken into account for compression. In order to prevent every possible failure of compression-stressed members, as well as the damage associated with those failures, the allowable stress in construction must be capped at a maximum value $\sigma_{N,all}$. This value must be smaller than the product of the compressive strength $f_{c,d}$ of the material in question and the buckling coefficient k_c, which is a function of the slenderness ratio λ.

As a general rule,
$\sigma_N = N_{c,d}/A < k_c \cdot f_{c,d} = k_c \cdot f_{c,k}/\gamma_M$

The essential feature distinguishing this from the pre-dimensioning of a tension member is the buckling coefficient k_c. Its value lies between 0 and 1 and, for a given slenderness ratio λ, can be looked up in graphs or tables. The slenderness ratio $\lambda = L_{cr}/(I/A)^{0.5}$, in turn, also depends on the cross-sectional area A. Solving the equation above for A as is done in the pre-dimensioning of tension members therefore proves unsuccessful. It is rather an iterative process involving estimation, testing and

Hot-finished, circular hollow sections, seamless or welded

d [mm]	t [mm]	A [cm²]	G [kg/m²]	U [m²/m]	I [cm⁴]	S_{el} [cm³]	S_{pl} [cm³]	i [cm]	I_T [cm⁴]	$C_t = S_T$
33.7	3.2	3.07	2.41	0.106	3.60	2.14	2.99	1.08	7.21	4.28
	4	3.73	2.93	0.106	4.19	2.49	3.55	1.06	8.38	4.97
48.3	3.2	4.53	3.56	0.152	11.6	4.80	6.52	1.60	23.2	9.59
	5	6.80	5.34	0.152	16.2	6.69	9.42	1.54	32.3	13.4
60.3	3.2	5.74	4.51	0.189	23.5	7.78	10.4	2.02	46.9	15.6
	5	8.69	6.82	0.189	33.5	11.1	15.3	1.96	67.0	22.2
76.1	3.2	7.33	5.75	0.239	48.8	12.8	17.0	2.58	97.6	25.6
	5	11.2	8.77	0.239	70.9	18.6	25.3	2.52	142	37.3
88.9	4	10.7	8.38	0.279	96.3	21.7	28.9	3.00	193	43.3
	6.3	16.3	12.8	0.279	140	31.5	43.1	2.93	280	63.1
101.6	4	12.3	9.63	0.319	146	28.8	38.1	3.45	293	57.6
	10	28.8	22.6	0.319	305	60.1	84.2	3.26	611	120
114.3	4	13.9	10.9	0.359	211	36.9	48.7	3.90	422	73.9
	6.3	21.4	16.8	0.359	313	54.7	73.6	3.82	625	109
	10	32.8	25.7	0.359	450	78.7	109	3.70	899	157
139.7	5	21.2	16.6	0.439	481	68.8	90.8	4.77	961	138
	8	33.1	26.0	0.439	720	103	139	4.66	1,441	206
	12.5	50.0	39.2	0.439	1,020	146	203	4.52	2,040	292
168.3	6.3	32.1	25.2	0.529	1,053	125	165	5.73	2,107	250
	12.5	61.2	48.0	0.529	1,868	222	304	5.53	3,737	444
193.7	6.3	37.1	29.1	0.609	1,630	168	221	6.63	3,260	337
	16	89.3	70.1	0.609	3,554	367	507	6.31	7,109	734
244.5	8	59.4	46.7	0.768	4,160	340	448	8.37	8,321	681
	20	141	111	0.768	8,957	733	1,011	7.97	17,914	1,465
323.9	8	79.4	62.3	1.02	9,910	612	799	11.2	19,820	1,224
	25	235	184	1.02	26,400	1,630	2,239	10.6	52,800	3,260
406.4	10	125	97.8	1.28	24,476	1,205	1,572	14.0	48,952	2,409
	25	300	235	1.28	54,702	2,692	3,642	13.5	109,404	5,384
508.0	12.5	195	153	1.60	59,755	2,353	3,070	17.5	119,511	4,705
	40	588	462	1.60	162,188	6,385	8,782	16.6	324,376	12,771

B 1.33

improved estimation that is needed in order to find a cost-effective profile capable of supporting the necessary loads.
Using a typical slenderness ratio λ, as well as the length l and support-dependent effective length factor β of a member, the required radius of gyration i can be determined:
$i = L_{cr}/\lambda = \beta \cdot l/\lambda$

After this, it must be verified whether the load on the cross section due to the normal stress $\sigma_N = N_{c,d}/A$ is smaller than the load resistance $k_c \cdot f_{c,d}$. If this is not the case, the designer must repeat the same process with progressively smaller slenderness ratios λ, until the load on the compression member is smaller than its load resistance.

Timber compression members
In timber construction, a starting value for the slenderness ratio $\lambda = 100$ has proven useful in pre-dimensioning. For softwood of strength class C 24, tables list the associ-ated buckling coefficient as $k_c = 0.305$. The compressive strength $f_{c,0,d} = 1.3$ kN/cm² may therefore be utilised up to 30.5 % without putting the member at risk of buckling. For such a compression member of C 24 softwood with slenderness ratio $\lambda = 100$, the maximum allowable compressive stress would be $\sigma_{N,all} = k_c \cdot f_{c,0,d} = 0.305 \cdot 1.3$ kN/cm² = 0.4 kN/cm².
A timber pillar with effective length $L_{cr} = 5.00$ m and a square cross section with side length d = 17.3 cm, whose slenderness ratio is therefore given by $\lambda = 100$, can thus support a load of $N_{c,d} = A \cdot k_c \cdot f_{c,0,d} = (17.3 \text{ cm})^2 \cdot 0.305 \cdot 1.3$ kN/cm² = 118 kN. Additional buckling coefficients k_c for timber are shown in Fig. B 1.34.

Steel compression members
Some steel profiles exhibit complex geometries. Calculating pre-dimensioning values for compression-stressed structural steel elements is correspondingly difficult.

To simplify the process, tables have been created for many common steel sections (Fig. B 1.37), from which the load-bearing capacity N_d can be obtained as a function of profile shape and effective length L_{cr}. Conversely, a designer may simply find the necessary profile for a given load and effective length L_{cr}.
For a steel pillar with effective length $L_{cr} = 5.00$ m that is intended to support a load of $N_d = 120$ kN, Fig. B 1.35 shows that, for example, a circular hollow section (CHS) with a diameter of d = 114.3 mm and a wall thickness of t = 4 mm would be suitable. As an alternative, an HEB 120 profile could be used, which at this effective length is capable of supporting up to 180 kN.

Reinforced concrete compression members
The load-bearing behaviour of reinforced concrete as a composite material is complex. It depends on multiple parameters, such as the strengths of the steel and concrete, as well as on the proportion of reinforcement and on its configuration. As a simple rule of thumb, it can be assumed that reinforced concrete columns can bear stresses of about 1 kN/cm². A column with a square cross section of side length d = 20 cm can therefore support about 400 kN. For the total load of $q_d = 10$ kN/m² that is typical for a reinforced concrete structure, there should consequently be a 10-cm² cross section column for every m² of floor area to be supported.

Compression-stressed masonry
Masonry walls and pillars are considered to be load-bearing if they assume vertical or horizontal loads or serve as reinforcement against buckling of load-bearing walls. Their thickness may not fall below a minimum of d = 11.5 cm. Pillars must have a minimal cross section of A = 400 cm². Masonry is also governed by the principle that the design value of the acting normal force N_{Ad}

| Slenderness ratio λ | Strength class (Grade) | | | | | |
	C 18 (S 7)	C 24 (S 10)	C 30 (S 13)	C 40	D 35 (LS 10)	D 60
10	1.000	1.000	1.000	1.000	1.000	1.000
20	0.989	0.991	0.991	0.992	0.966	1.000
30	0.943	0.948	0.947	0.950	0.957	0.964
40	0.878	0.887	0.885	0.890	0.905	0.917
50	0.781	0.796	0.793	0.803	0.830	0.851
60	0.655	0.676	0.671	0.686	0.726	0.759
70	0.531	0.554	0.548	0.564	0.609	0.649
80	0.429	0.450	0.445	0.459	0.502	0.542
90	0.351	0.368	0.364	0.376	0.414	0.450
100	0.290	0.305	0.302	0.312	0.345	0.377
110	0.244	0.256	0.253	0.263	0.291	0.318
120	0.207	0.218	0.216	0.223	0.248	0.272
130	0.178	0.188	0.185	0.192	0.213	0.234
140	0.155	0.163	0.161	0.167	0.186	0.204
150	0.136	0.143	0.141	0.147	0.163	0.179
160	0.120	0.126	0.125	0.130	0.144	0.159
180	0.095	0.101	0.099	0.103	0.115	0.127
200	0.078	0.082	0.081	0.084	0.094	0.103
220	0.065	0.068	0.067	0.070	0.078	0.086
240	0.055	0.058	0.057	0.059	0.066	0.073
250	0.050	0.053	0.053	0.055	0.061	0.067

B 1.34

B 1.34 Buckling coefficients k_c for compression members of softwood(C) and hardwood (D) timber as a function of the slenderness ratio λ according to DIN EN 1995-1-1:2010-12, 6.3.2 (excerpt per Wendehorst, see Note 2, Table 10.101)
B 1.35 Design values in kN of the flexural buckling resistance $N_{b,Rd}$ of compression-stressed, hot-finished CHS sections of S235
B 1.36 Timber columns, city library, Schweinfurt (DE) 2007, Bruno Fioretti Marquez, Ingenieurbüro Dörband
B 1.37 Canteen of the internal revenue office, Munich (DE) 2003, Peck Daam Architekten, Behringer Ingenieure
B 1.38 Reinforced concrete compression members, Netherlands Architecture Institute, Rotterdam (NL) 1993, Jo Coenen

CHS section d [mm]	t [mm]	Effective length L_{cr} [m]							
		1.50	2.00	2.50	3.00	4.00	5.00	6.00	8.00
33.7	3.2	25.2	15.1	9.95	7.02	4.03	2.61	1.82	1.03
	4	29.4	17.6	11.6	8.18	4.69	3.03	2.12	1.20
48.3	3.2	64.5	43.8	30.1	21.6	12.6	8.20	5.76	3.28
	4	77.9	52.5	35.9	25.8	15.0	9.76	6.85	3.90
	5	93.0	62.0	42.3	30.3	17.6	11.5	8.04	4.58
60.3	3.2	98.3	77.1	56.6	41.8	24.8	16.3	11.5	6.58
	4	120	93.5	68.3	50.3	29.9	19.6	13.8	7.90
	5	146	113	81.7	60.0	35.6	23.3	16.4	9.40
76.1	3.2	138	122	101	79.3	49.4	32.9	23.4	13.5
	4	170	150	123	96.5	59.9	39.9	28.3	16.3
	5	209	183	149	117	72.2	48.0	34.1	19.6
88.9	4	208	192	169	142	93.3	63.4	45.4	26.3
	5	257	236	207	173	113	76.7	54.9	31.8
	6.3	318	292	254	210	137	92.7	66.2	38.4
101.6	4	245	232	213	188	133	93.1	67.4	39.4
	5	303	286	262	231	163	113	81.9	47.9
	6.3	376	354	323	283	198	138	99.5	58.1
114.3	4	281	269	253	232	178	129	94.8	56.1
	6.3	433	414	388	354	268	193	141	83.3
	8	540	515	482	438	329	235	172	101
139.7	5	438	425	409	389	334	264	203	124
	8	684	663	637	604	513	402	306	186
	10	841	814	782	740	624	485	368	223
168.3	6.3	673	658	640	620	566	490	401	259
	10	1,042	1,018	990	957	869	744	605	387
	12.5	1,281	1,250	1,215	1,174	1,061	903	730	465
193.7	6.3	785	771	755	737	692	629	547	379
	10	1,220	1,197	1,172	1,143	1,070	968	836	573
	12.5	1,504	1,475	1,443	1,406	1,314	1,184	1,017	693
244.5	8		1,254	1,236	1,216	1,170	1,112	1,036	829
	12.5		1,921	1,891	1,860	1,788	1,695	1,573	1,245
	16		2,419	2,382	2,341	2,248	2,127	1,968	1,544
323.9	8			1,682	1,664	1,624	1,580	1,527	1,385
	12.5			2,588	2,560	2,498	2,428	2,345	2,118
	16			3,274	3,237	3,158	3,068	2,960	2,665
406.4	10				2,644	2,598	2,549	2,494	2,360
	20				5,148	5,056	4,956	4,845	4,570
	25				6,348	6,233	6,107	5,968	5,619
508.0	12.5					4,117	4,060	3,999	3,860
	20					6,483	6,390	6,292	6,068
	30					9,515	9,375	9,227	8,886

B 1.36

B 1.37

B 1.35

B 1.38

B 1.39

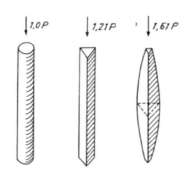

$\downarrow 1.0\,P$ $\downarrow 1.21\,P$ $\downarrow 1.61\,P$

B 1.40

must be smaller than the design value of the normal load resistance N_{Rd}.

$$N_{Ad} = \gamma_G \cdot N_{Gk} + \gamma_Q \cdot N_{Qk}$$
$$= 1.35 \cdot N_{Gk} + 1.50 \cdot N_{Qk} < N_{Rd} = N_{Rk}/\gamma_M$$

The normal load resistance N_{Rk} depends on the compressive strength f_k of the masonry in question, as well as on a reduction factor to allow for buckling risk and loading eccentricities – that is, loads that do not act along the centre-of-mass axis of the building component.

There is a plethora of building materials with a wide range of compressive strengths available for use in masonry, as well as a broad selection of block sizes for different wall thicknesses. Because of this variety and the concomitant lack of simple rules of thumb, it makes sense to base the pre-dimensioning of compression-stressed structural elements of masonry on comparable built examples.

Combinations of stresses

Often, pillars or walls are not subjected purely to compression stresses. The exterior walls of buildings, in particular, are also bending-stressed by wind loads. Deformations, imperfections and eccentrically acting loads can create bending stresses in addition to the compression stresses. In designing such building components subject to multiple stresses, it is important to take care that even the combination of the individual stresses E always remains smaller than the load resistance R.

Design of compression members

Unlike the case of tension members, design plays an important role for slender compression members at risk of buckling (Fig. B 1.40). Since the critical buckling load N_{cr} depends on the area moment of inertia I, it would seem obvious that the material should be concentrated far from the centre of mass of the member cross section. A comparison of the load-bearing capacities of several different solid profiles of uniform section length shows that round bars yield better values than square bars. An equilateral triangle section made with the same amount of material, however, exceeds the load-bearing capacity of solid round bar by another 21%. If the ends of the member are narrowed and the central part is thickened, the bearing capacity can even be raised by 61% in comparison with members of uniform cross section.

A further improvement upon the bearing capacity of solid profiles is exhibited by hollow or open-geometry compression members. For this reason, in steel construction, round or angled tubes are often used as compression members. Tall electricity pylons are frequently built as a framework. Triangular constructs that widen at the centre are common in lightweight construction (Fig. B 1.41). Despite all these improvements and efforts, the optimal form of a compression member has not yet been determined.

Structural Elements Subject to Bending Stresses

Bending-stressed structural elements include, among others, simple and multi-span beams, cantilever beams and panels. Bending occurs when a member is stressed transverse to its axis as opposed to longitudinally along the axis. This happens in floor joists or slabs under self loads or traffic loads as well as in exterior walls and glass facades under wind loads. For a long time, timber was the material from which flexural (bending) members were commonly made. Many roof trusses still feature very old timber beams for this reason (Fig. B 1.39). Today, industrial materials such as steel, reinforced concrete and timber-concrete composite systems offer a broader array of options for bending-stressed structural elements (Fig. B 1.43–B 1.45). Aside from the rod-shaped girders, beams and joists, flat plates of contoured sheet metal as well as slabs of engineered timber, reinforced concrete or combinations of these are used. Bending-stressed structural elements allow for a simpler and more economical stacking of levels than compression-stressed vaults. They are therefore a critical foundation for the multistorey construc-

B 1.41

B 1.42

tion that has characterised our cities since antiquity. In the comparatively new timber-concrete composite construction method, building components of concrete are situated over or (more rarely) underneath those of wood (Fig. B 1.46). Connecting hardware such as timber-concrete composite screws, TCC (timber-concrete composite) shear connectors, reinforced-concrete bonded anchors and flat-steel locks secure the load-bearing function of the hybrid cross section. This raises the bearing capacity and rigidity by a factor of two to five as compared to that of a non-composite timber frame structure.

Load-bearing behaviour of bending-stressed structural elements

The behaviour of building components subject to bending stresses was also studied by Galileo Galilei. He explains his 1638 drawing (Fig. B 1.42) as follows: "Clearly, the prism will break at B, where the wall edge serves as a support, and BC will be the lever arm of the force; the thickness BA of the prism forms the other lever arm on which the resistance that wants to separate the parts of BD from the parts lodged in the wall will act." [3]

The exact observation of the deformation of a structural element, supported at both ends and subject to a transverse load, goes beyond Galileo's insights to provide information about internal stresses, which studies done by Jacob Bernoulli (1654–1705) and Henri Navier (1785–1836) confirm. While compaction and therefore compressive stresses can be identified above the axis of the system, below the axis, stretching and the associated tensile stresses are evident. The axis itself becomes curved, but is neither compressed nor stretched. The most heavily stressed areas of the beam are the top and bottom sides (Fig. B 1.47).

Internal stresses

A load acting at right angles to the axis of a member results in the internal stresses

B 1.43

B 1.44

B 1.45

B 1.46

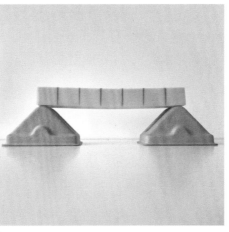

a

b   B 1.47

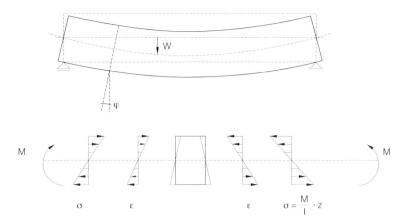

$$\sigma \qquad \varepsilon \qquad \qquad \varepsilon \qquad \sigma = \frac{M}{I} \cdot Z$$

B 1.48

already examined. In the stretched fibres of the member, the tensile stress $\sigma_{t,d}$ may not exceed the tensile strength $f_{t,d}$ of the material, while the compressed fibres must simultaneously remain below its compressive strength $f_{c,d}$. In addition, in order to avoid risk to the bearing capacity of the member, both the buckling of the compressed fibres as well as a lateral torsional buckling of the entire cross section must be prevented. In the ideal elastic region, strain ε and stress σ are proportional to one another.

The above-mentioned stresses are also smaller in the vicinity of the supports than in the area located midway between them. In the centre of the span, the acting load deforms an originally rectangular area in such a way that it resembles a trapezoid. Sections near the supports, on the other hand, remain nearly rectangular even under loading. When comparing these observations with the behaviour of the resulting bending moment M, the relationship is striking. Wherever the bending moment M is large, the aforementioned deformations are also large (Fig. B 1.48).

Stress trajectories
When examining a bending-stressed beam in more detail, the directions of the main stresses can be visualised as curves known as stress trajectories. In this process, the relationships between tensile stress lines and catenary curves become apparent, as does that between compressive stress lines and arch shapes. The trajectories in the centre of the span are primarily horizontal, while near the supports they can be vertical, as well. This matches the behaviour of the two resultants, the bending moment M and the transverse force V. While the bending moment M reaches an extreme value in the middle of the span, the transverse force V at this spot is zero. In the case of a uniform distributed load, the latter increases linearly towards its extreme values at the supports. Correspondingly, the internal compressive stresses there are mainly vertical (Fig. B 1.49).
The internal tensile stresses in the lower half of the beam can be combined to a resultant tension F_{ten}, while the internal compressive stresses in the upper half yield the resultant compression F_{com}. The maximum allowable magnitude of these two forces depends on the maximum allowable stresses $\sigma_{Rd} = f_d$,

which must not be exceeded even in the extreme edge fibres. Thus, the mean stress for a rectangular cross section is at most $1/2 \cdot \sigma_{Rd} = 1/2 \cdot f_d$. The maximum allowable forces are therefore given by:
$$F_{ten} = F_{com} \le (1/2 \cdot R_d) \cdot (b \cdot 1/2 \ h) = 1/4 \cdot \sigma_{Rd} \cdot bh$$

The line of action of the tensile force F_{ten} lies in the geometric centre of mass of the tensile stresses σ_t; that of the compressive force F_{com} in the centre of mass of the compressive stresses σ_c. Between these two forces there exists a lever arm. In a beam with a rectangular section this lever arm is two thirds of the height h of the beam.

Bending stress σ_m
The two forces F_{ten} and F_{com} resulting from the internal stresses, together with their associated lever arm of 2/3 h, correspond exactly to the bending moment M due to the load q.
Bending moment M [kNm] $= F_{ten} \cdot 2/3 \ h = F_{com} \cdot 2/3 \ h \le (1/4 \ \sigma_{Rd} \cdot bh) \cdot 2/3 \ h = \sigma_{Rd} \cdot bh^2/6$

Solving this equation for the stress σ yields the so-called bending stress σ_m in the edge fibre. It must be less than or equal to the design value of the bending strength $f_{m,d}$ of the building material in question.,
Rectangular section beam: Bending stress $\sigma_{m,d}$ [kN/cm²] $= M_d/(bh^2/6) \le f_{m,d} = f_{m,k}/\gamma_M$

Section modulus S
The geometric value (bh²/6) of a rectangular beam of section width b and height h which resists deformation due to an acting bending moment M is called the section modulus S.
Rectangular beam:
Section modulus S [cm³] $= bh^2/6$

For the cross section shapes of common steel profiles, the section modulus S may be found in reference tables (Fig. B 1.53,

q

0.5000

-0.5000

a

b

0.1250

c

b

h

$F_{compression}$

$F_{tension}$

$\sigma \le \sigma_{Rd}$

d

B 1.49

B 1.48 Internal forces of a simple beam
B 1.49 Stresses in a flexural member, stress trajectories
  a Lines of the main stresses (compressive stresses dashed, tensile stresses solid)
  b Qualitative behaviour of the transverse force V due to uniform distributed load q
  c Qualitative behaviour of the bending moment M due to uniform distributed load q
  d Internal tensile and compressive forces
B 1.50 Timber beams as bending-stressed structural elements, community centre in Blons (AT) 2004, Bruno Spagolla
B 1.51 Trapezoidal sheet panels on HEB 200 beams, Wildparkhalle Karlsruhe (DE) 1992, Heinz Kuhlmann, Paul Schuler

p. 58; B 1.31, p. 50). In general terms, the bending stress σ_m represents the ratio of the acting bending moment M and the geometric section modulus S of the stressed structural element:
Bending stress $\sigma_{m,d}$ [kN/cm²] = M_d/S

Shear stress τ

Aside from the bending stresses σ_m corresponding to the bending moment M, bending-stressed structural elements also experience shear stresses τ due to the transverse force V. The shear stress τ is proportional to the transverse force V due to the load, as well as to the static moment of area Q = $\int$ z dA corresponding to the geometry of the beam. For rectangular cross sections, the maximum value of the shear stress τ due to the transverse force V is:
Maximum shear stress τ_{max} [kN/cm²] = V · Q/(I · b) = 3/2 V/(b · h)

The shear stress τ may not exceed the shear strength f_v = V/A [kN/cm²]. However, it is only rarely decisive, e.g. in the case of short, highly stressed beams.

Pre-dimensioning of bending-stressed structural elements

Since the height of a structural beam depends primarily on the span length l, a rule of thumb for a rough estimate is
Beam height h [cm] ~ span length l [cm]/20

A significantly more precise estimate for the beam height h can be made if, in addition to the span length l, data on acting forces and thus on stress resultants are also available. In statically determinate systems such as simple or cantilevered beams and with the load q_d as a starting point, the required design value of the bending moment M_d can be calculated quite easily as described in Part A (p. 30f., see also p. 95). For statically indeterminate systems such as continuous beams, fixed frames and two-hinged arches, computation programs or reference

tables may be used to determine the required design values of the bending moment M_d. Making use of continuity effects over multiple spans instead of stringing together a series of simple beams usually reduces the extreme values of the bending moments.
As a prerequisite for further material-dependent pre-dimensioning steps, one must first determine the required section modulus S as a function of the design value of the bending strength $f_{m,d}$ of the chosen material:
Required section modulus
S [cm³] = M_d/$f_{m,d}$

Bending-stressed structural elements of timber

In timber construction, once the required section modulus S = M_d/$f_{m,d}$ = M_d/1.5 kN/cm² has been identified, the corresponding component dimensions can be determined. For bending-stressed applications, beams with rectangular cross sections are usually used (Fig. B 1.50). Since the height h enters the section modulus S of a beam as a second power, it makes sense to choose an h greater than the width b. Beams with heights h of about twice the width b have been found to be quite advantageous. In this case, the required beam height h may

be calculated as follows:
Required beam height h [cm] = $\sqrt{(6\,S/b)}$ = $(12\,S)^{0.33}$ = $(12\,M_d/f_{m,d})^{0.33}$ = $(12\,M_d/1.5\,\text{kN/cm}^2)^{0.33}$
The corresponding beam width is given by b = h/2.

A floor joist in residential construction, supported as a simple beam of span length l = 5.00 m and with a load q_d = 5.0 kN/m acting on it, experiences a bending moment M_d = q_d · l_2/8 = 5.0 kN/m · (5.00 m)²/8 = 15.6 kNm = 1,560 kNcm. The structural height of the joist in this case would have to be h = $(12\,M_d/1.5\,\text{kN/cm}^2)^{0.33}$ = (12 · 1,560 kNcm/1.5 kN/cm²)$^{0.33}$ = 24 cm and the width b = h/2 = 12 cm.
If flat slabs such as stacked-board or cross-laminated timber panels are used instead of a joist, the 1-m width of the panel can be entered as the beam width b to simplify the calculation. The required height h of a continuous one-way slab can be determined as follows:
Required slab height h [cm] = $\sqrt{(6\,S/b)}$ = $(6\,(M_d/f_{m,d})/100\,\text{cm})^{0.5}$ = $(6\,M_d/150\,\text{kN/cm}^2)^{0.5}$

For the same bending moment M_d = 1,560 kNcm, with regard to the load-bearing capacity, a floor slab

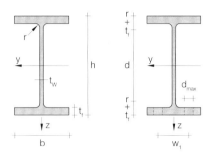

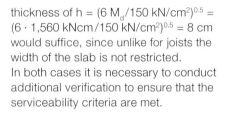

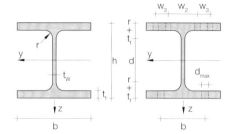

B 1.52

thickness of $h = (6\,M_d/150\,\text{kN/cm}^2)^{0.5} = (6 \cdot 1{,}560\,\text{kNcm}/150\,\text{kN/cm}^2)^{0.5} = 8$ cm would suffice, since unlike for joists the width of the slab is not restricted.

In both cases it is necessary to conduct additional verification to ensure that the serviceability criteria are met.

Bending-stressed structural elements of steel

In steel construction, after the required section modulus $S = M_d/f_{y,d} = M_d/21.4\,\text{kN/cm}^2$ has been found, the appropriate profile dimension for beams may be looked up by section shape in the relevant reference tables (Fig. B 1.53).

Since bending stress σ_m is large in the extreme fibres at the top and bottom of a member but decreases toward its axis, the valuable building material steel is primarily

used where it can contribute substantially to the load-bearing capacity, i.e. in the edge areas, also called the top and bottom flanges. The flanges are connected by a thin web that serves among other things to accommodate shear stresses τ. This structural form resembles the capital letter I in serif font. If the two flanges are wider, as seen in HEB beams, the profile looks like a letter H on its side (Fig. B 1.52).

IPE profiles are very effective for their relatively small weights and correspondingly low costs. To reduce installed heights, profiles of the HEA, HEB and HEM series can be used. However, these bring with them greater self-weights and higher costs. As an alternative, rectangular hollow profiles are also utilised in steel construction.

The steel beam of a lightweight hall roof, mounted as a simple beam and spanning

a length $l = 12.00$ m, is subjected to a load $q_d = 3\,\text{kN/m}^2 \cdot e = 15\,\text{kN/m}$ due to its tributary area $e = 5.00$ m. Its bending moment is then given by $M_d = q_d \cdot l2/8 = 15\,\text{kN/m} \cdot (12.0\,\text{m})^2/8 = 270\,\text{kNm} = 27{,}000\,\text{kNcm}$. A structural steel section must therefore have a section modulus $S = M_d/f_{y,d} = M_d/21.4\,\text{kN/cm}^2 = 1{,}262\,\text{cm}^3$. A suitable choice would be an IPE 450 with $S_y = 1{,}500\,\text{cm}^3$, for example (Fig. B 1.53).

In addition to rod-shaped flexural members, flat structural elements of corrugated or trapezoidal sheet metal are also used. Applications for these contoured, in some cases coated, sheets are base courses, roof coverings and wall elements (Fig. B 1.51, p. 57). The profile descriptions of such metal sheets essentially consist of the profile height h and the rib width b. The bearing capacity depends on the material, the type

Sym-bol	Dimensions											For bending about the y axis			For bending about the z axis		
	h [mm]	b [mm]	t_w [mm]	t_f [mm]	r [mm]	d [mm]	A [cm²]	A_{vy} [cm²]	A_{vz} [cm²]	G [kg/m²]	U [m²/m]	I_y [cm⁴]	S_y [cm³]	i_y [cm]	I_z [cm⁴]	S_z [cm³]	i_z [cm]
IPE																	
80	80	46	3.8	5.2	5	59.6	7.64	4.78	3.58	6.00	0.328	80.1	20.0	3.24	8.49	3.69	1.05
100	100	55	4.1	5.7	7	74.6	10.3	6.27	5.08	8.10	0.400	171	34.2	4.07	15.9	5.79	1.24
120	120	64	4.4	6.3	7	93.4	13.2	8.06	6.31	10.4	0.475	318	53.0	4.90	27.7	8.65	1.45
140	140	73	4.7	6.9	7	112.2	16.4	10.1	7.64	12.9	0.551	541	77.3	5.74	44.9	12.3	1.65
160	160	82	5.0	7.4	9	127.2	20.1	12.1	9.66	15.8	0.623	869	109	6.58	68.3	16.7	1.84
180	180	91	5.3	8.0	9	146.0	23.9	14.6	11.3	18.8	0.698	1,320	146	7.42	101	22.2	2.05
200	200	100	5.6	8.5	12	159.0	28.5	17.0	14.0	22.4	0.768	1,940	194	8.26	142	28.5	2.24
220	220	110	5.9	9.2	12	177.6	33.4	20.2	15.9	26.2	0.848	2,770	252	9.11	205	37.3	2.48
240	240	120	6.2	9.8	15	190.4	39.1	23.5	19.1	30.7	0.922	3,890	324	9.97	284	47.3	2.69
270	260	135	6.6	10.2	15	219.6	45.9	27.5	22.1	36.1	1.04	5,790	429	11.2	420	62.2	3.02
300	280	150	7.1	10.7	15	248.6	53.8	32.1	25.7	42.2	1.16	8,360	557	12.5	604	80.5	3.35
330	300	160	7.5	11.5	18	271.0	62.6	36.8	30.8	49.1	1.25	11,770	713	13.7	788	98.5	3.55
360	320	170	8.0	12.7	18	298.6	72.7	43.2	35.1	57.1	1.35	16,270	904	15.0	1,040	123	3.79
400	340	180	8.6	13.5	21	331.0	84.5	48.6	42.7	66.3	1.47	23,130	1,160	16.5	1,320	146	3.95
450	360	190	9.4	14.6	21	378.8	98.8	55.5	50.8	77.6	1.61	33,740	1,500	18.5	1,680	176	4.12
500	400	200	10.2	16.0	21	426.0	116	64.0	59.9	90.7	1.74	48,200	1,930	20.4	2,140	214	4.31
550	500	210	11.1	17.2	24	467.7	134	72.2	72.3	106	1.88	67,120	2,440	22.3	2,670	254	4.45
600	600	220	12.0	19.0	24	514.0	156	83.6	83.8	122	2.01	92,080	3,070	24.3	3,390	308	4.66

B 1.53

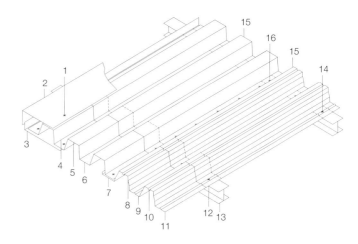

1 Connecting element on longitudinal edge (blind rivet, screw)	4 Web	10 Top chord beading	14 Fastener for support (screw, cartridge-fired pin)
2 Edge reinforcement	5 Top chord	11 Level longitudinal edge	15 Contoured panel
3 Longitudinal edge crimping	6 Bottom chord	12 Transverse joint	16 Connecting element on longitudinal joint (blind rivet, screw)
	7 Longitudinal joint	13 Girder, purlin, tie rod	
	8 Web beading		
	9 Bottom chord beading		

of profile, the profile height h and the sheet thickness t. In extensive tables, manufacturers quote the load-bearing capacity of their profiles as a function of profile cross section, sheet thickness, span, static system and deformation limit. The values shown in Fig. B 1.54 apply to uniformly distributed loads subject purely to bending stresses. Here, too, taking advantage of continuity effects across several spans raises the bearing capacity with respect to single-span applications.

Bending-stressed structural elements of reinforced concrete

As is the case with compression-stressed building components of reinforced concrete, the pre-dimensioning of bending-stressed components of this composite material is not as simple as for timber or steel. Aside from the general rule of thumb regarding beam heights (h ~ l/20), the pre-dimensioning procedures for reinforced concrete described in Part A (p. 35f.) are also applicable here. The use of pre-stressed reinforced concrete elements is expensive, but allows for large spans with comparatively modest overall heights.

Because of the low tensile strength of concrete, reinforcing steel (rebar) must be embedded into bending-stressed reinforced concrete building components in order to provide resistance against tensile stresses. Steel is thus always necessary wherever significant tensile stresses occur in beams, joists or panels. There are proven methods for identifying the required steel cross sections. The compression stresses are accommodated predominantly by the concrete. If necessary, however, the compression zone may also be reinforced through the targeted use of reinforcement. It is also practical to include lightweight hollow bodies in little-stressed regions near the system axis in order to save on self-weight without significantly reducing load-bearing capacity.

Dimensions [mm]	Self-weight g [kN/m²]	Rated sheet thickness d [mm]	Static system	Span [m]										
				1.0	2.0	3.0	4.0	5.0	6.0	7.0	8.0	9.0	10.0	11.0
Trapezoidal section (l/150) in positive position				**Load-bearing capacity q [kN/m²]**										
35/207	0.072	0.75	⊓	8.98	1.74	0.52	0.22	0.11						
	0.096	1.00		14.31	2.63	0.78	0.32	0.17						
	0.144	1.50		26.99	4.15	1.23	0.52	0.27						
		0.75	⊓─⊓	7.55	2.25	1.00	0.54	0.31						
		1.00		12.28	3.59	1.60	0.79	0.40						
		1.50		24.74	6.57	2.92	1.27	0.64						
		0.75	⊓─⊓─⊓	8.36	2.67	1.05	0.50	0.32						
		1.00		13.49	4.33	1.47	0.62	0.31						
		1.50		25.87	7.38	2.34	0.99	0.50						
135/310	0.097	0.75	⊓			2.88	2.13	1.75	1.32	0.96	0.65			
	0.130	1.00				5.37	3.97	2.82	1.92	1.21	0.81			
	0.195	1.50				14.28	7.91	4.79	2.94	1.85	1.24			
		0.75	⊓─⊓			3.18	2.14	1.77	1.35	1.02	0.80			
		1.00				5.36	3.97	2.82	2.21	1.63	1.25			
		1.50				14.26	8.32	5.42	3.89	2.86	2.13			
		0.75	⊓─⊓─⊓			3.60	2.47	1.88	1.39	1.05	0.85			
		1.00				6.10	4.02	2.93	2.23	1.73	1.42			
		1.50				14.28	8.30	5.53	4.00	3.08	2.29			
160/250	0.121	0.75	⊓				3.44	2.54	1.77	1.30	0.96	0.68	0.49	
	0.161	1.00					6.70	4.22	2.93	1.96	1.31	0.93	0.68	
	0.241	1.50					10.18	6.69	4.58	2.98	2.00	1.41	1.04	
		0.75	⊓─⊓				3.45	2.51	1.83	1.39	1.09	0.85	0.59	
		1.00					6.47	4.33	3.12	2.36	1.82	1.41	0.96	
		1.50					9.88	6.91	4.95	3.74	2.86	2.28	1.77	
		0.75	⊓─⊓─⊓				3.45	2.57	1.84	1.41	1.12	0.90	0.73	
		1.00					6.70	4.34	3.11	2.38	1.85	1.47	1.17	
		1.50					10.18	6.90	4.95	3.77	2.90	2.34	2.18	
200/375	0.118	0.75	⊓					2.12	1.76	1.51	1.22	0.96	0.74	0.56
	0.158	1.00						3.69	3.07	2.53	1.93	1.41	1.03	0.77
	0.237	1.50						8.84	6.19	4.55	3.16	2.22	1.62	1.22
		0.75	⊓─⊓					2.12	1.65	1.31	1.06	0.88	0.72	0.61
		1.00						3.77	2.87	2.26	1.82	1.50	1.22	1.04
		1.50						7.38	5.53	4.28	3.41	2.75	2.25	1.89
		0.75	⊓─⊓─⊓					2.12	1.76	1.51	1.22	0.96	0.81	0.69
		1.00						3.92	4.76	2.63	2.02	1.59	1.38	1.17
		1.50						8.82	6.19	4.55	3.48	2.75	2.56	2.16

The specifications apply to uniformly distributed loads q.

B 1.54

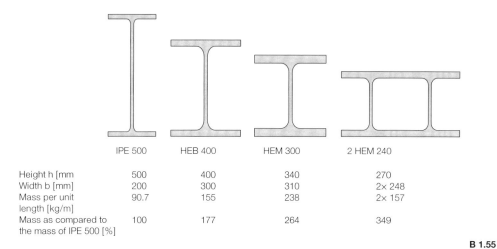

	IPE 500	HEB 400	HEM 300	2 HEM 240
Height h [mm]	500	400	340	270
Width b [mm]	200	300	310	2× 248
Mass per unit length [kg/m]	90.7	155	238	2× 157
Mass as compared to the mass of IPE 500 [%]	100	177	264	349

B 1.55

Bending-stressed structural elements of other materials

In addition to the frequently used materials timber, steel and reinforced concrete, other building materials or composite systems such as aluminium, glass, sandwich panels, steel and reinforced concrete composite construction or timber-concrete composite systems are also employed. In cases for which no simple procedures for pre-dimensioning or proven rules of thumb exist, it is generally advisable to seek out as many built reference structures as possible.

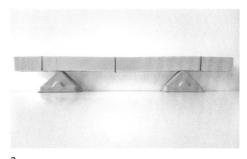

a

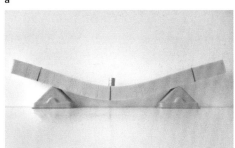

b

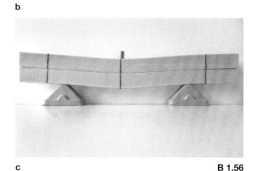

c

B 1.56

Deformation of bending-stressed structural elements

Experiments show that the deformation of a bending-stressed structural element depends on the load q, the span l, the geometry I and the elastic modulus E of the building material. The greater the load q and the span l, the greater the deflection w. A large E-modulus as well as a high area moment of inertia I, on the other hand, tend to decrease the deformation. For a rectangular-section simple beam under uniform distributed load q with $I = bh^3/12$, doubling the beam height will reduce the maximum value of the deflection w to $1/2^3 = 1/8$ of its original value. In other words, the deflection for the double-height beam is 87.5 % smaller than for the regular-height beam (Fig. B 1.56).

Mathematically speaking, the differential equation of the deflection curve derives from the observation of a rod that is bent due to a load q(x) acting at right angles to the rod axis. In this situation the following general relationship exists between the deflection curve and the load q, where EI represents the bending stiffness of the rod due to its material (E-modulus) and geometry (area moment of inertia I) (see p. 32):
$$w^{IV}(x) = q(x)/EI$$

B 1.55 Sections of equal stiffness (same deflection, $I \geq 48,000$ cm⁴)
B 1.56 Bending-stressed structural elements under load q
    a Unstressed beam of height h
    b Large deformation of a beam of height h under load
    c Significantly smaller deformation of beam of height 2h under the same load
B 1.57 Qualitative shape of the bending moment M of a simple beam under uniform distributed load q
B 1.58 Beam shape and bending moment, Campus de Jussieu, Paris (DE) 1968, Édouard Albert
B 1.59 Tapering cantilever of an elevated walkway, reinforced concrete, TWA terminal (now hotel), New York (US) 1962, Eero Saarinen

The load q(x) is therefore proportional to the fourth derivative of the deflection curve $w_{IV}(x)$. Conversely, this means that the EI multiple of the deflection curve can be determined via a quadruple integration of the loading function q(x). In this process, the first integration yields the transverse force V(x), the second the bending moment M(x) and the third the angle of twist ψ (or φ) of the cross section.

For a simple beam under uniformly distributed load q_k, the maximum value of the deflection w_{max} in the centre of the span is computed as follows:

Maximum deflection w_{max} [cm] = $(5/384)\, q_k l^4/EI$

In this context, a comparison among different profile types with approximately the same flexural stiffness EI is informative. Figure B 1.55 shows various beams that respond to the same boundary conditions such as load q or span length l with the same deflection w. This comparison demonstrates that it is possible to nearly halve the overall height by using two HEM 240 profiles instead of an IPE 500 profile. At the same time, however, the weight and the costs increase by a disproportionate factor of 3.5 as compared to IPE 500. The comparison reveals that an appropriate choice of profile can be economically advantageous, and that the broad, heavy and short beams should therefore be employed primarily where reduced height is required, such as in restorations or reinforcements of historical structures with very small storey heights or headroom.

Serviceability of bending-stressed structural elements

In order to secure the practical serviceability of constructions, any deformations as a result of loading must be kept within reasonable limits. In slender compression members subject to normal (axial) forces, deformations due to loading are usually small,

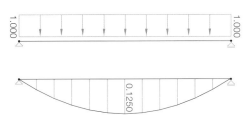

B 1.57

B 1.58

since the actual strength of the material cannot be fully exploited because of the buckling risk. For flexural structural elements loaded to capacity, on the other hand, the static and dynamic deformations can become quite obvious long before the ultimate limit state (ULS) is reached.

Since large deformations and oscillations of structural elements under load are perceived as alarming, and since they can also cause damage to adjacent building components such as glass facades and lightweight partition walls, the serviceability limit state (SLS) should be taken into account along with the ultimate limit state (ULS).

In the case of oscillations, this occurs through the study of the dynamic behaviour by means of measurements and calculations. With regard to the deflection of building components, recommendations exist that provide limiting values of deflection for characteristic loads q_k which should not be exceeded. The regulations recommend that flexural members with span length l comply with the following limiting values of deflection w.

For subordinate building components such as rafters and purlins or in agricultural buildings, these are:
• overhanging: maximum deflection w ≤ l_k/100
• otherwise: maximum deflection w ≤ l/200

For all remaining building components, the recommendations are:
• overhanging: maximum deflection w ≤ l_k/150...l_k/200
• otherwise: maximum deflection w ≤ l/300...l/500

Practice has shown that the criterion of serviceability is often the decisive factor for beam heights, especially for simple beams. Proof of load-bearing capacity alone is thus insufficient for such elements, since beams that have not yet come close to the ultimate limit state can nevertheless exhibit deformations that are unsuitably large. In such

cases it is advisable to utilise a beam with greater height, for which the area moment of inertia I is greater than that of the earlier choice by the ratio of the calculated deflection w to the recommended maximum deflection w_{max}.

To minimise the deflection of bending-stressed structural elements in the final mounted state, cambered beams and slabs can be incorporated. Such elements are positively curved in their unloaded state. After installation and the removal of form work or auxiliary supports, the deformation due to self-weight causes the camber to diminish, allowing the pre-curved arch-like element to adopt an approximately straight form.

Construction of bending-stressed structural elements

In order to make practical use of bending-stressed building components, it helps to consider a few basic principles. They per-

tain to the design of the components as well as to considerations such as the running of cables or provisions to prevent the buckling of chords.

Design

The close relationship between the notional stress resultant, the bending moment M and the bending stress σ_m suggests that bending-stressed beams should be made thicker wherever the bending moment M is large. For a simple beam under a uniform distributed load, for example, it makes sense to design the beam with greater dimensions in the centre of the span than near the supports (Fig. B 1.57, Fig. B 1.58).

As a rule, not all parts of simple beams are equally stressed. In fact, three subsections are subject to particular stresses. The bending or flexural stress σ_m is large in the middle portion of the span, while the shear stress τ is great in the vicinity of the two

B 1.59

B 1.60 Tapered cantilevers on steel pillars support the grandstand roof. Stadium in Bregenz (AT) 1994, Johannes Kaufmann, Bernd Spiegel, Helmut Dietrich, Robert Schedler, Ernst Mader
B 1.61 Options for potential material savings through the appropriate placement of supports and hinges
B 1.62 Art Institute of Chicago, Modern Wing, Chicago (US) 2009, Renzo Piano Building Workshop

B 1.60

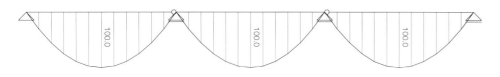

Shape of the resultant bending moment M in three independent simple beams

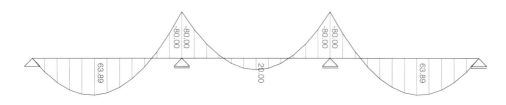

Extreme value of the bending moment M (20 % smaller through use of continuity effect)

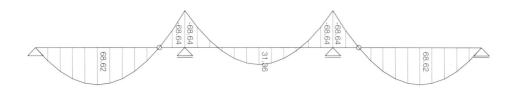

Extreme value of the bending moment M (31.4 % smaller through advantageous placement of hinges)

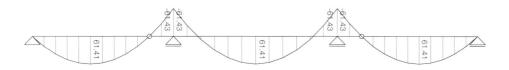

Extreme value of the bending moment M (38.6 % smaller through advantageous placement of supports and hinges)

B 1.61

supports. The situation is different for cantilevered or continuous beams over central supports. In these cases, both types of stress are large near the supports, while they diminish to zero in the direction of a free cantilever. Therefore, one often sees that beam heights are tapered toward the free ends of cantilevers, while they increase toward the supports (Fig. B 1.60). Designers can influence the size of the bending moment M through the reduction of span lengths, the targeted use of statically indeterminate systems and the clever placement of hinges, and can thereby scale down both the height h and the material consumption of structural elements (Fig. B 1.61).

Recesses for cabling

The integration of building services presents a challenge in the development of a structural design. In this context, designers often look for practical ways to run cables at beam level. Given the modest shear stresses in the central portion of the span, openings for installations can be advantageously placed there, whereas they would cause problems in the vicinity of the supports because of the large shear stresses τ present in those locations. Therefore, penetrations through the web of an I or H profile in steel construction are usually possible wherever the transverse force V is small. The same applies to reinforced concrete girders.

Stiffening of compression chords

Compression-stressed areas of flexural members are generally at risk of buckling. In simple beams this affects the upper chords. These beams are often located in the plane of the floor or roof. At these locations, it is quite easy to prevent lateral buckling or lateral torsional buckling by connecting the upper chords with reinforced floor slabs or wind bracing to safeguard against sideways deflections.

Overview of the Pre-Dimensioning of Structural Elements

Requirements for structural elements:
- stability, load-bearing capacity
- serviceability (limitations on deformations and oscillations)
- economic viability
- durability

Note
As a basic principle, before they are built, the stability and the serviceability of designed structural elements must be certified according to the standards and regulations introduced by the relevant building authorities. In many cases, these certifications must be presented for inspection.

Geometric cross-section values
Geometric cross-section values may be taken from profile tables; values for solid rectangular cross-sections of height h and width b are given by:
Cross-section area $A = bh$
Section modulus $S = bh^2/6$
Area moment of inertia $I = bh^3/12$
Radius of gyration $i = \sqrt{(I/A)} = h/\sqrt{12}$
Slenderness ratio $\lambda = L_{cr}/i = \beta \cdot l/i$

Simplified material parameters for pre-dimensioning

Timber (C 24)
$E = 1{,}100\ kN/cm^2$
$f_{t,d} = 0.9\ kN/cm^2$
$f_{c,d} = 1.3\ kN/cm^2$
$f_{m,d} = 1.5\ kN/cm^2$

Steel (S 235)
$E = 21{,}000\ kN/cm^2$
$f_{t,d} = f_{c,d} = f_{m,d} = 21.8\ kN/cm^2$

Stability, load-bearing capacity

Basic principle:
The stresses E_d due to acting forces < load resistance R_d of the material

Tension members:
$\sigma_{N,d} = N_{t,d}/A < f_{t,d}$

Compression members:
$\sigma_{N,d} = N_{c,d}/A < k_c \cdot f_{c,d}$

Flexural members:
$\sigma_{m,d} = M_d/W < f_{m,d}$

Compression + bending:
$(N_{c,d}/A)/(k_c \cdot f_{c,d}) + (M_d/W)/f_{m,d} < 1$

Serviceability (limiting deformations)
Simple beams:
$w_{max} = (5/384)\ q_k l^4/EI < l/300...l/500$
$M_d = q_d l^2/8$

Cantilevered beams:
$w_{max} = (1/8)\ q_k l^4/EI < l_k/150...l_k/200$
$M_d = -q_d l_k^2/2$

Notes
[1] Galileo Galilei: *Unterredungen und mathematische Demonstrationen. Über zwei neue Wissenszweige, die Mechanik und die Fallgesetze betreffend.* Leipzig 1890, p. 98
[2] see e.g. Vismann, Ulrich (ed.): *Wendehorst – Bautechnische Zahlentafeln.* 36th edition, Heidelberg/Berlin 2018
Schneider, Albert: *Bautabellen für Ingenieure.* Munich 2020
Holschemacher, Klaus: *Entwurfs- und Berechnungstafeln für Bauingenieure.* Munich 2019
[3] see note [1]
[4] *ibid.,* p. 98

Part C   Structural Systems

George Washington Bridge Bus Station, New York (US)
1963, Port Authority of New York and New Jersey, Pier
Luigi Nervi

Structural Systems

Eberhard Möller

From Element to System

The structural elements introduced in Part B (p. 38ff.) can be used to assemble entire buildings or engineering structures, but also more limited load-bearing systems for individual building segments. Flat elements such as slabs and panels often form the basic support framework of multistorey buildings, especially in solid construction.

Box frame and cross-wall construction
In solid construction, building techniques such as traditional box frame masonry (Fig. C 1.1) and reinforced concrete cross-wall construction (Fig. C 1.2) are widespread. Alongside these, the use of full-surface stacked timber and cross-laminated timber elements is steadily growing. Because of the high self-weights of solid building components, it is advantageous in these applications to arrange the load-bearing elements of all storeys on top of one another. A special building method using normal force-stressed panels and bending-stressed slabs is seen in folded plate constructions (Fig. C 1.5). The folds produce shear-resistant edges. Through these, the two adjacent areas lend each other mutual rigidity. By folding a piece of paper its load-bearing capacity increases visibly in com-parison to that of an unfolded, flat sheet. Folded plate constructions thus demonstrate in a comprehensible way that not just material, but also form has a decisive impact on the bearing capacity of building components. An industrial application of the folded-plate principle is the trapezoidal sheet that is frequently used in steel construction (Fig. C 1.3, C 1.4).

Skeleton construction
In addition to solid, planar elements and building techniques, skeleton-like frame constructions are also in widespread use. In reference to the natural support structure of living things, structures for engineering works and buildings which consist mainly of rod-shaped elements are called skeletons. Skeleton frameworks are fairly lightweight and therefore represent a counterpart to the relatively heavy solid construction methods. Skeleton-like structures are common in timber construction as well as in the steel and reinforced concrete sector. Mediaeval half-timbered houses, American balloon frame construction, the large glass palaces and railway station halls of the early indus-trial age, the famous *Maison Dom-Ino* by Le Corbusier and many skyscrapers of the modern age are examples of the application of the skeleton construction principle.

C 1.1

C 1.2

C 1.3

C 1.4

While lightweight timber or steel skeleton frames dominate the construction sector in the UK and especially in North America, central and southern Europe have thus far traditionally relied on more energy and mass-intensive reinforced concrete construction. Reinforced concrete structures provide somewhat greater stiffness, but are almost impossible to dismantle into reusable components after their service life.

Systems that function as an integral unit

Especially in big buildings or for large spans, it is useful to develop dedicated load-bearing systems for constructions or parts of buildings by basing them on the known structural elements. In this way, synergy effects that arise from the basic structural systems can be used advantageously, because the integrated effect of the individual systems has greater load-bearing capacity than the sum of their parts would imply.

An analysis of the bearing behaviour of bending-stressed elements has shown that the material used is fully exploited only in the extreme (edge) fibres. The greater the span of the beams is, the greater their height dimension must be. But as a consequence, the proportion of material that is not fully exploited increases, as well. Many of

the structural systems presented in this chapter have been developed based on this finding. Designers have placed members in the strongly stressed edge areas while significantly reducing the material density in the less stressed areas in between. In place of continuous regions or surfaces, in these cases only individual rods are employed to connect the top and bottom chords. The dissolution of structures into skeleton-like structural systems that function as integral units therefore offers not only material, but also environmental and economic advantages (Fig. C 1.6, p. 68).

Structural principles

Some types of structural system are in widespread use in the construction sector. Though they may differ in size, material and building execution, for the most part

they can be traced back to a few essential basic concepts and follow proven structural principles.

The structural systems discussed here comprise previously introduced structural elements. The mechanism of action of structural systems is predominantly based on the mechanisms of action of the basic structural elements such as tension, compression and flexural members (see Part B, p. 38ff.). If the fundamental principles of the structural elements are clearly understood, the structural systems themselves will hardly pose any difficulties.

The structural principles of the following frequently used load-bearing systems will be presented – as was done for the structural elements – along with common applications, building types, up-to-date analytical procedures and computational methods,

C 1.1 Box frame construction, traditional stone houses in Lavertezzo, Ticino (CH)
C 1.2 Cross-wall construction offers generous possibilities for light exposure. Obstbaumwiese building cooperative, Tutzing (DE) 2015, PLAN-Z Architekten, TWP Tragwerkplan
C 1.3 Roof covering of trapezoidal sheet, industrial folded plate
C 1.4 Folded plate construction, bus stop in Unterkrumbach Süd (DE) 2014, de Vylder Vinck Taillieu, gbd
C 1.5 Curved folded plate, Paketposthalle, Munich (DE) 1969, Rudolf Rosenfeld, Herbert Zettel, Ulrich Finsterwalder, Helmut Bomhard, Paul Gollwitzer

C 1.5

C 1.6

C 1.7

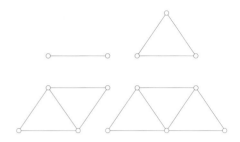

C 1.8

typical stress resultants, rules of thumb and pre-dimensioning information, as well as prominent examples and inspiring variants via images, graphs and text.

Trusses

A frequently used structural system is the truss. The truss system consists of members that are more or less flexibly connected with one another. Acting loads are meant to impact the nodes only, leaving the members to be stressed exclusively by normal forces. The German term *Fachwerk* presumably derives from the Middle High German words *vach* or *fah* for a mesh, or an area subdivided into sections. The formal relationship between trusses (German: *Fachwerkträger*) and half-timbered houses (German: *Fachwerkhäuser*) is obvious. Regarding the bearing behaviour, however, there are similarities – for example, the stiffening effect of triangles – as well as differences.

Applications
Trusses have frequently proven themselves ideally suited for spanning large areas without the need for columns. Such buildings include halls for sports, industrial fairs and railway stations, museum exhibit spaces,

storage and factory areas, airport terminals and hangars (Fig. C 1.7, C 1.9a). Trusses are also often used in bridge structures, high-voltage power line pylons and construction cranes (Fig. C 1.13).
However, they are not used only in the building sector. In many other engineering fields such as vehicle manufacture, aircraft construction and space travel, designers rely on these relatively lightweight, efficient structures (Fig. C 1.10).
Often, in construction as well as in machine production, trusses are concealed behind cladding. Today, computer-assisted analysis techniques such as the Finite Element Method (FEM) make it possible to use multiple statically indeterminate construction types and structural principles that were considered computationally intractable until the mid 20th century. In the mass production of vehicles, these more complex structures have now largely supplanted the analytically simple, statically determinate truss (Fig. C 1.11).

Rules for forming trusses
The fundamental element of the truss is the triangle. In general, planar trusses can be formed in three ways. The basic method is to connect two members to the nodes of a beam or an existing truss such

that a new triangle is formed (Fig. C 1.8). A planar truss may also be built by joining two existing trusses together via a suspension rod and a common hinge or via three suspension rods whose lines of action are neither all parallel nor intersect at a point. A third assembly rule for planar trusses says that the members of an existing truss may be repositioned.

Construction basics
A few basic principles must be taken into account when building structural trusses:
- Trusses must be assembled from straight members.
- Trusses must be joined at the nodes via hinged or at least flexible connections.
- Trusses are supported exclusively at nodes.
- Significant loads should act only at the truss nodes.

If one or more of these points is disregarded, the members of the truss will be subjected to bending stresses in addition to the usual normal stresses. As a result, a major advantage of this structural system will be lost, at least for sections of the truss. This can lead to greater deformations or require larger member cross-sections.

a

b

C 1.9

It is also important to ensure that the compression-stressed chords of trusses are secured against lateral buckling. Often, it is mainly the top chords that are under compression. They can be easily stiffened through horizontal bracing in the roof. Because of their width, the risk of lateral buckling in the so-called three-chord trusses is smaller than in their planar counterparts (Fig. C 1.9 b).

Degrees of freedom in planar trusses
As is true for all multipart structures, simple rules regarding degrees of freedom exist for planar trusses, as well. For every degree of freedom of a building component, at least one joint or support connection must counteract it in order for the truss to remain rigid and immovable and therefore capable of bearing loads. While the outer degrees of freedom f_o correspond to the support connections, the inner degrees of freedom f_i pertain to the connections between the individual truss members. Then:
outer degrees of freedom: $f_o = 3 - a$
inner degrees of freedom: $f_i = 2 \cdot n - (3 + m)$
degrees of freedom of the entire system:
$f = 2 \cdot n - (a + m)$, where
a   is the number of support connections,
n   is the number of nodes, and
m   is the number of members

If the degrees of freedom total f = 0, the truss is typically rigid and statically determinate, as long as none of the three rules for the formation of trusses has been broken. In a statically determinate truss, all the member forces can be graphically or analytically determined in a straightforward way. The truss system depicted in Fig. C 1.12 with n = 14 nodes, a = 3 support connections and m = 25 members has zero outer ($f_o = 3 - a = 0$) as well as zero inner ($f_i = 2 \cdot n - (3 + m) = 0$) degrees of freedom. The overall system likewise has $f = 2 \cdot n - (a + m) = 0$ degrees of freedom and is rigid as well as statically determinate.

C 1.6   Truss, footbridge over the Bolgenach river near Hittisau, Vorarlberg (AT)
C 1.7   Trusses in roof construction and cranes, Allianz Arena, Munich (DE) 2005, Herzog & de Meuron, Arup, Sailer Stepan und Partner (ssp)
C 1.8   Composition of planar trusses
C 1.9   Werner-von-Linde Hall, Munich (DE) 1972, Behnisch & Partner, Richard Schardt
          a Three-chord truss indoors
          b Three-chord truss outdoors
C 1.10 Helicopter from the 1940s, Museum of Modern Art, New York (US)
C 1.11 Chassis of a car from the 1950s
C 1.12 Static system of a truss
C 1.13 Truss with translucent cladding, Krattenbrug bicycle bridge , Rotterdam (NL) 2010, Atelier Kempe Thill

C 1.10

C 1.11

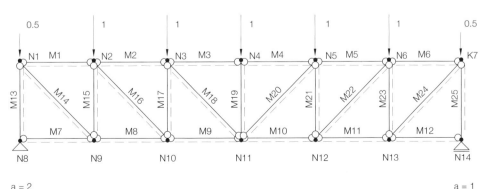

a = 2

a = 1

C 1.12

C 1.13

Types of member forces

In determining the forces in the members, it may be helpful to first gain a qualitative overview. In general, truss members can experience three different kinds of stresses. Depending on the external loading of the truss, some members will be subject to tensile stresses, some to compressive stresses and some perhaps to no stresses at all (Fig. C 1.14).

To identify the tensile or compressive stresses in members, it is often useful to employ display models that have a basic similarity to the truss in question, e.g. in terms of external forces, arrangement of supports etc. These models allow the observer to recognise and understand the types of stresses occurring in many of the members. The deformation due to loading of the display model in Fig. C 1.15 shows tensile stresses on the bottom and compressive stresses at the top of the beam. The stress types of further members may also be derived from the way in which the model deforms.

Members that remain unstressed by external loading are called zero-force members. Under no circumstances, however, can these members be omitted: first, this would break the formation rules, making the truss unstable; second, different loading conditions will produce different member stresses. Many zero-force members can be recognised through simple rules:

- If a node with two members has no external forces such as loads or support reactions acting on it, then both members are zero-force members.
- If a node with two members is acted upon by an external force in the direction of one of the members, then the other member is a zero-force member.
- If a node with three members has no external forces such as loads or support reactions acting on it, and if two of the three members share a common axis, then the third member is a zero-force member.

The two zero-force members in Fig. C 1.14 can be identified on the basis of the second rule.

Magnitudes of member forces

To pre-dimension the individual elements of the truss structure, it is necessary to estimate the magnitudes of the forces in the members. Various methods are available for determining both the qualitative and the quantitative forces in the individual members of a truss due to acting loads. Graphical methods are very illustrative. In these, all loads and member forces are represented as vectors. The foundational principle is the knowledge that, in the static resting state, every node of a truss is in equilibrium. This means that all external forces, reaction forces and member forces at the node balance each other out. The sum of the forces ΣF_i is therefore equal to zero at every node and also for the entire system (Fig. C 1.17 a).

The first step, whenever possible, is to use the three equilibrium conditions $\Sigma M = 0$, $\Sigma V = 0$ and $\Sigma H = 0$ to find the support reactions. Then the forces of the members at the nodes can be graphically constructed

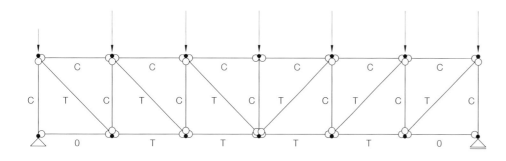

C = compression member, T = tension member, 0 = zero-force member

C 1.14

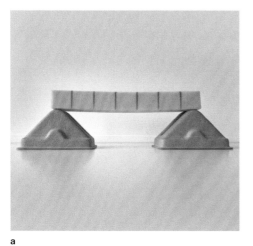

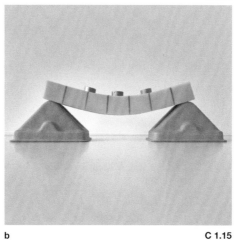

a   b   C 1.15

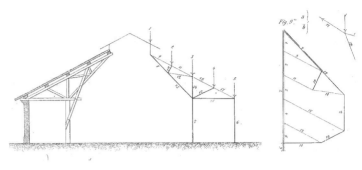

C 1.16

with at most two unknowns. This requires a drawing of the layout of the node (free-body diagram) and, more particularly, a true-to-scale force diagram. The force diagram is begun by drawing the known forces. These may be external forces, calculated support reactions or already-determined member forces. The magnitudes of the two unknown member forces can be constructed by a parallel translation of their action lines into the force diagram. Due to the equilibrium conditions $\Sigma V = 0$ and $\Sigma H = 0$, the vector sum of all the member forces and external forces acting on a node yields a closed polygon in the force diagram. Using the proportionality of the force diagram, the magnitudes of the individual forces may be measured. At node 1, the support reaction $A_V = 10$ kN is known. The two member forces S1 and S2 can therefore be constructed and measured with respect to A_V. This process makes clear that the magnitude of S1 is greater than that of S2, and that both are significantly larger than A_V (Fig. C 1.17 c). At node 3, the external force F = 20 kN is known. Consequently, the forces in members S1 and S3 can be found and measured with respect to F (Fig. C 1.17 d). This shows that S1 and S3 are exactly equal in magnitude and somewhat larger

than the external force F (Fig. C 1.17 b). The graphical approach can be used for individual nodes as well as for entire trusses. For trusses, a connected force diagram produced in this way is named after the Italian mathematician Luigi Cremona (1830–1903) (Fig. C 1.16).
A computational method used to determine member forces, known as Ritter's method of sections after the engineer August Ritter (1826–1908), is based on the principle of

cutting (or sectioning) off unknown forces. In this method, too, the first step, whenever possible, is to use the three equilibrium conditions $\Sigma M = 0$, $\Sigma V = 0$ and $\Sigma H = 0$ to find the support reactions. Then a cut is made through a maximum of three unknown members and the sectioned-off member forces are applied as usual at the section border. The newly created subsystem is also in equilibrium. Once again, the three equilibrium conditions $\Sigma M = 0$, $\Sigma V = 0$ and

C 1.14 Qualitative illustration of member forces as a function of acting loads
C 1.15 Display model for the visualisation of tensile and compressive stresses in a beam
 a unstressed beam
 b deformation of a beam under load
C 1.16 Cremona diagram. Luigi Cremona: *Le figure reciproche nella statica grafica.* Milan 1872
C 1.17 Simple truss with three members and three nodes
 a Example of a graphical determination of the member forces
 b Quantitative illustration of the member forces as a function of the acting load in kN: tension members blue, positive sign, compression members red, negative sign
 c Node 1, free-body and force diagrams
 d Node 3, free-body and force diagrams

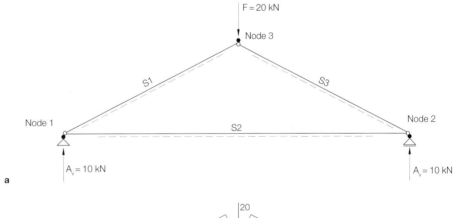

a

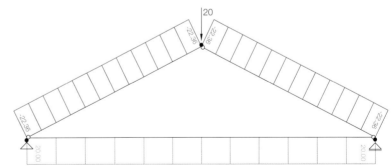

b

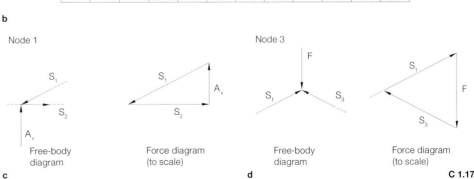

c   d   **C 1.17**

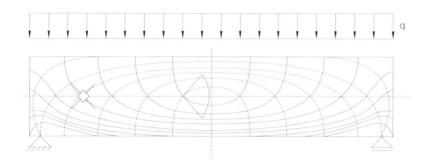

Compressive stresses dashed, tensile stresses solid

C 1.18

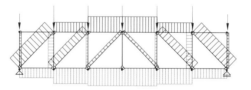

Compressive stresses: red, tensile stresses: blue

C 1.19   C 1.20

C 1.21   C 1.22

$\Sigma H = 0$ apply. Now, the node at which two of the cut members join together is selected as a pivot point. The magnitude of the third unknown member force can then be found using $\Sigma M = 0$ about this node. In the next step, with a different node as a pivot, as well as with the help of the two equilibrium conditions $\Sigma V = 0$ and $\Sigma H = 0$, the remaining two sectioned member forces can be determined. Further cuts can be used progressively to identify all member forces.

Frequently used truss constructions
In general, trusses allow for great freedom in design. A few basic constructions are used very frequently. A look at the different construction types reveals information about the stresses in individual members under typical loading of the truss. Tensile stresses are generally represented in blue, compressive stresses in red. An

C 1.18   Stress trajectories in a flexural member
C 1.19   Truss with tensile-stressed members approximating the lines of hanging cables (two zero-force members)
C 1.20   Truss with compression-stressed members approximating the lines of arches (three zero-force members)
C 1.21   Room-high trusses with slender, tensile-stressed diagonal members
C 1.22   Tensile-stressed members oriented like hanging cables, pedestrian bridge over the A9, Munich (DE) 2003, Ackermann Architekten, Ackermann Ingenieure
C 1.23   Design of a swing bridge, Leonardo da Vinci, circa 1490, Codex Atlanticus, fol. 855r
C 1.24   Truss with only diagonal web members, of which the tensile-stressed members approximate the lines of hanging cables
C 1.24   Truss with only diagonal web members, of which the compression-stressed members approximate the lines of arches
C 1.26   Truss with a catenary-like curve of the bottom chord, also known as the fishbelly truss because of its shape
C 1.27   Truss with a curved top chord, arched or parabolic truss, web members modestly stressed
C 1.28   Truss with diagonal web members, sports centre, Munich (DE)
C 1.29   Truss with a curved top chord, sports hall, Feldafing (DE)

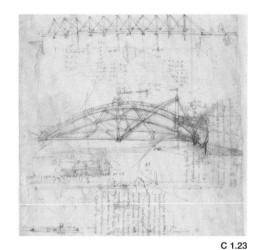

C 1.23

important design consideration for truss girders is that tension members, particularly steel tension members, can be made very slender, especially in comparison to the compression members, which are vulnerable to buckling. For this reason, designers often try to create trusses in which the diagonal members are under tension. This design simultaneously frees many long members of a truss from any buckling risk (Fig. C 1.21).

A very widespread construction type for trusses employs sets of tensile-stressed members whose arrangements resemble hanging cables. In this case, all the diagonal members are under tension and correspondingly understated, while the top chord and the vertical members are under compression (Fig. C 1.19).

A comparative look at the main stresses in a flexural member is instructive. The stress trajectories in the flexural member shown in Fig. C 1.18 can be interpreted as lines along which compressive (dashed) and tensile (solid) stresses run. The similarities to the stresses present in the truss are obvious. In the central region between the two supports, horizontal compressive stresses act at the top, horizontal tensile stresses at the bottom. In the vicinity of the supports, multiple diagonal and vertical stresses are visible.

An easily understood constructive implementation of the cable-like suspension of a series of tensile-stressed members is featured in the pedestrian bridge over the A9 in Munich (Fig. C 1.22). The bottom chord in this case consists of one, two or three parallel beams, depending on the stress condition.

The effect of trusses with sets of compression-stressed members in an upright arch-like conformation is markedly different from that of the cable-like arrangement of tension members. A very early illustration of such a truss in timber construction was published in 1581 by Andrea Palladio in his *I Quattro*

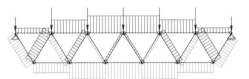

C 1.24

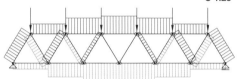

C 1.25

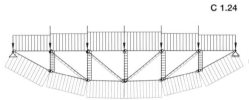

C 1.26

C 1.27

C 1.28

C 1.29

C 1.30 C 1.31

C 1.32

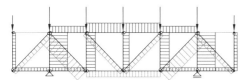
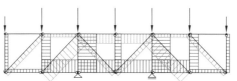

C 1.33 C 1.34

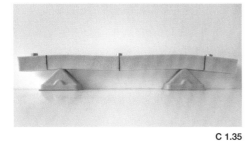
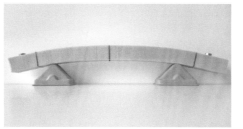

C 1.35 C 1.36

C 1.30 Lenticular truss, also called Laves or Pauli truss
C 1.31 Truss with a gable-roof shaped, sloped top chord
C 1.32 Lenticular truss, Lavesbrücke, Welfengarten, Hanover (DE) 1846, Georg Ludwig Friedrich Laves
C 1.33 Truss with short cantilevers; diagonal members under tension, vertical members under compression, bottom chord under compression near supports, under tension mid-span

C 1.34 Truss with long cantilevers and diagonal members under tension, vertical members under compression
C 1.35 Display model for Fig. C 1.33
C 1.36 Display model for Fig. C 1.34
C 1.37 Comparison of trusses with large and modest heights
C 1.38 Comparison of a bending-stressed simple beam and a truss subject to normal stresses

Libri dell'Architettura. In these truss types, the diagonal members are under compression and appear more dominant because of the buckling risk. The entire bottom chord is under tension (Fig. C 1.20, p. 72). Also commonly found are trusses with purely diagonal web members (Fig. C 1.24, C 1.28, p. 73). In this example, the members that conform to the catenary lines of the truss are tensile-stressed, while those that follow the arch lines are compressed (Fig. C 1.25, p. 73).

Apart from trusses with parallel chords, there are also trusses with curved or slanted chords that are advantageous, for example, with regard to the homogenisation of chord forces or for roof drainage (Fig. C 1.26, C 1.27, p. 73). In appropriately designed truss forms and for symmetrical loads, diagonal members are barely or not at all stressed. The degree to which vertical members are stressed also depends on whether the loads act on the top chord as with roofs or more on the horizontal chord as with bridges. A very early representation of a truss is depicted in Leonardo da Vinci's 1490 design of a swing bridge (Fig. C 1.23, p. 73). Trusses in which both chords are curved are also known as lenticular trusses (Fig. C 1.30, C 1.32). In these, the web members are often very minimally stressed, since the loads are transferred mainly via the combination of upper arch and lower tension beams. Lenticular trusses are also called Laves trusses, after Georg Ludwig Friedrich Laves (1788–1864), or Pauli trusses, after Friedrich August von Pauli (1802–1883).

In trusses with a gable-roof-shaped top chord and diagonal members under tension, the stress conditions of the members diverge from those of the previously presented structural forms (Fig. C 1.31). For example, the stresses in the chords are significantly greater in the vicinity of the supports than in the centre of the span. When trusses overhang their supports or

Tall truss

Resultant normal force N

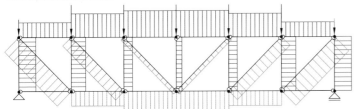

Large heights lead to comparatively low member forces and therefore to low material expenditure for the members

Simple beam (bending-stressed)

Resultant normal force N

No normal stresses, N = 0

Resultant transverse force V

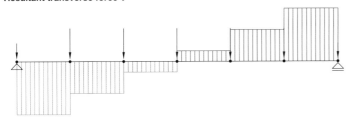

Large transverse force V near supports (see normal stresses in vertical and diagonal members near supports in the truss)

Resultant bending moment M

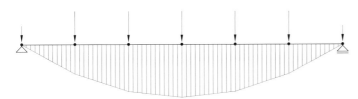

High bending moment M in mid-span (see normal stresses in the middle of the top and bottom chord members in the truss), high material expenditure

Resultant deformation w

Large deformation, strong deflection in mid-span due to the high bending moment M, despite significant material expenditure

Low truss

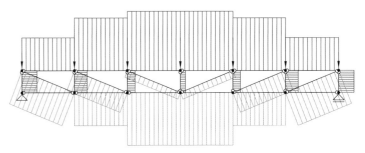

Small heights lead to comparatively high member forces and therefore to high material expenditure for the members

C 1.37

Truss (subject to normal stresses)

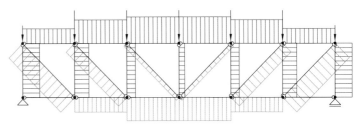

High normal stresses in vertical and diagonal members near the supports (see transverse force V in the simple beam)
Flat diagonal web members → high web member forces
High normal stresses in middle of top and bottom chord members (see bending moment M in the simple beam)
Low height → large chord forces

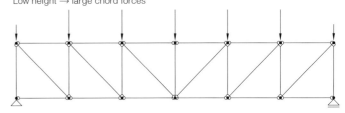

No transverse force, V = 0

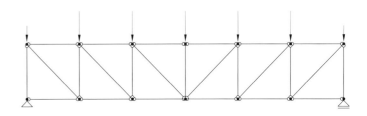

No bending stress, M = 0
Advantageous, since it avoids unfavourable poor exploitation of cross sections and saves on material costs

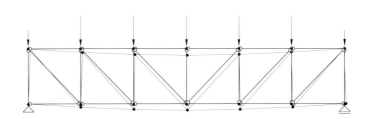

Small deformation, since there is no bending stress (normal stresses more rarely cause large deformations)

C 1.38

C 1.39

C 1.40

C 1.41

extend over several supports, the orientation of the diagonal members at each support must be changed in order to maintain a consistent level of stress in the members (Fig. C 1.33, C 1.35, p. 74). Additionally, the stresses present in the top and bottom chords vary along the length of the truss. Long or heavily loaded cantilevers can cause the typical type of stress present in the chords of non-overhanging trusses to flip. In such cases, it may happen that the top chord is largely tensile-stressed while the bottom chord is entirely under compression (Fig. C 1.34, C 1.36, p. 74).

Comparison of truss girders and flexural members

Figure C 1.37 (p. 75) contrasts a truss with large overall height to one with a small height. Large heights result in comparatively

small member forces and consequently in modest material expenditures for the members, while low overall heights exhibit correspondingly high member forces and high material expenditures.
Figure C 1.38 (p. 75) compares a flexural beam with a truss.

Applications by building material
The manufacture of trusses makes use of different materials such as timber and steel, but also reinforced or prestressed concrete.

Timber trusses
It is fairly rare for a truss to be made entirely from timber (Fig. C 1.39). Even in timber construction, at least the connecting elements are often made of steel. Particularly the joining of tension members causes difficulties

in timber trusses. However, outside of the building material timber, the range of available fastening options is extensive. Options include glue, nails, screws, fitted bolts, bar dowels, specialised fasteners such as dowel rings, tooth plate connectors and drive-in anchors, as well as truss and gusset plates. In timber engineering, the diagonal tension members are frequently steel rods. This reduces the cross section and halves the number of load transfers between the two building materials.
In timber truss applications, and as a rule of thumb for the required height h of the truss as a function of its span length l, the following experimental values are often used:
- The span length l is between 10 and 40 m.
- The truss height h usually lies between l/12 und l/8.

Steel trusses
As is true for the material steel, the spread of the truss as a structural system is closely related to industrialisation. Thus it is understandable why steel is to date the most frequently used material in these systems. The range of possible applications for steel trusses is about as large as that of their different forms. While the bare structure of the Eiffel Tower was supplemented with

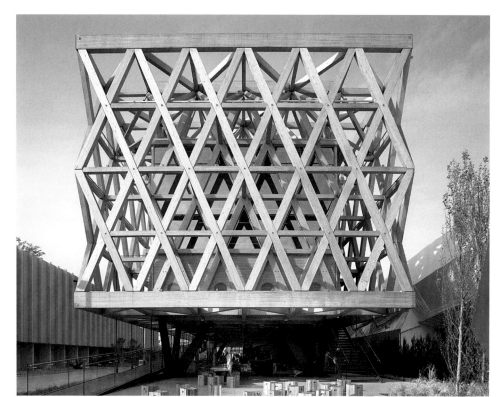

C 1.42

C 1.39 Timber truss with slender diagonal tension members of steel, Exhibition Hall 11, Frankfurt (DE) 2009, Hascher Jehle Architektur
C 1.40 Superposition of various truss types and supplementary embellishment, Eiffel Tower, Paris (FR) 1889, Gustave Eiffel, Maurice Koechlin
C 1.41 Mercat de Colón, Valencia (ES) 1916, Francisco de Mora y Berenguer
C 1.42 Chilean Pavilion, Expo 2015 in Milan (IT) 2015, Undurraga Deves Arquitectos
C 1.43 Trusses as facade pillars, Kunsthal, Rotterdam (NL) 1992, OMA, Arup, Theo Wulffraat & Partners
C 1.44 Recumbent truss, National Museum of African American History and Culture, Washington (US) 2016, Freelon Group, Adjaye Associates, Davis Brody Bond, Guy Nordenson, Silman

C 1.43

C 1.44

technically unnecessary embellishments in response to protests from writers, painters, sculptors and architects, only a short time later, many were paying homage to the clean appearance of technical structures (Fig. C 1.40). Examples of these include the interior of the Parisian church Notre Dame du Travail and the Mercat de Colón market hall in Valencia (Fig. C 1.41).

On a smaller scale, steel trusses serve as vertically or horizontally installed facade beams (Fig. C 1.43, C 1.44). They are often found in roof trusses or in bridges with widely varying spans (Fig. C 1.45). Steel trusses are also concealed behind the cladding of sculpturally shaped architecture (Fig. C 1.47). They are also used to reinforce high-rise buildings (Fig. C 1.48) against horizontal wind or seismic loads.

In steel truss applications, and as a rule of thumb for the required height h of the truss as a function of its span length l, the following experimental values are often used:
- The span length l generally lies between 8 and 80 m.
- The truss height h usually lies between l/15 und l/10.

Examples of the broad spectrum of possible construction applications for steel trusses are shown in Figs. C 1.43–C 1.48.

C 1.45

C 1.46

C 1.47

C 1.48

C 1.45 Simple steel trusses, also called spaghetti trusses because of their thin diagonals
C 1.46 Multistorey truss bridging the platform hall, Hauptbahnhof Berlin (DE) 2006, von Gerkan, Marg und Partner (gmp), Schlaich Bergermann Partner (sbp)
C 1.47 Truss structure on display, Guggenheim Museum Bilbao (ES) 1997, Frank O. Gehry, SOM
C 1.48 Reinforcing truss structure, John Hancock Center, Chicago (US) 1970, Bruce Graham, Fazlur Khan, SOM
C 1.49 School building in Leutschenbach near Zurich (CH) 2009, Christian Kerez, Joseph Schwartz
C 1.50 Bridge with balustrade of truss-like reinforced concrete beams, Milstein Hall, Cornell University, Ithaca, NY (US) 2011, OMA, Silman

C 1.49

C 1.50

C 1.51

Trusses of reinforced and prestressed concrete

On occasion, in addition to timber and steel, reinforced and prestressed concrete are used as materials for trusses. In tensile members, however, the concrete contributes mainly to fire safety and corrosion protection. The tensile stresses are generally borne entirely by the reinforcing steel (rebar). Parts of the reinforcement can be prestressed actively via hydraulic presses or passively through cambering during construction. Trusses of reinforced concrete obviously conform less to the basic concept of lightweight construction than do timber or steel trusses. This is probably the reason

C 1.51 Trussed beam footbridge at the Castelvecchio, Verona (IT) 1964, Carlo Scarpa
C 1.52 Filigree trussed beams in a church in Schönow near Berlin (DE) 1961, Frei Otto, Ewald Bubner
C 1.53 Trussed ceiling, Modern Wing of the Art Institute of Chicago (US) 2009, Renzo Piano Building Workshop, Arup
C 1.54 Composition of the "trussed beam" structural system
    a trussed beam (structural system)
    b bending-stressed continuous beam (subsystem 1)

    c truss subject to normal stresses (subsystem 2)
    d trussed beam with one strut
C 1.55 Two oppositely oriented trussed facades connected with coupling members, extension of the Staatliche Akademie der Bildenden Künste (State Academy of Fine Arts), Stuttgart (DE) 1994, Mahler Gumpp Schuster, Hartmut Fuchs, Armin Günster
C 1.56 Trussed beam with one strut
C 1.57 Trussed ceiling slab, protective structure at the *Villa rustica* near Leutstetten (DE) 2004, a + p Architekten

they are rarely used for simple hall structures, but are more likely to be found as multistorey space-forming frameworks or as bridge girders (Fig. C 1.49, C 1.50, p. 77).

Trussed Beams

If the span of a timber beam or plate girder is very large, it makes sense to place a column somewhere along its length to act as an intermediate support. Whenever such a column would be very obtrusive – in the middle of a sports hall, for example – it could be placed atop a cable underneath the roof. Its load is transferred by

the cable tension to the lateral supports. The method works not only with one, but with multiple pillars. This simple and elegant solution for the support of beams is widespread throughout the construction industry.

Applications

Trussed beams have similar applications as trusses. Particularly for the lightweight roof structures of halls with widely divergent functions, designers often rely on this structural system in which the bottom chord is always under tension and therefore very slender (Fig. C 1.53). The system has also proven suitable for pedestrian and bicycle bridges (Fig. C 1.51). It is often employed in conjunction with large glass facades, as well, since its filigree construction has a visually subtle appearance. For high loads and especially for strongly varying or unevenly distributed loads, however, trusses are often better suited than trussed beams.

Construction basics

Apart from the tensile-stressed stabilisation cable and one or more compression struts, trussed girders comprise a compression and bending-stressed top chord in the form of a continuous beam. In order for the bottom chord to be able to support the load of the strut, it must exhibit a kink at the base of each strut. This is the only way that a closed force triangle and, consequently, a balance of forces can exist between the strut and the adjacent sections of the bottom chord. Because of its compression stresses and its length, the top chord must be secured against buckling (Fig. C 1.52).

For reasons of stability, the top chord should be slightly curved, bent or cambered in opposition to the bottom chord. If it were bent in the same direction as the bottom chord, the latter could avoid the load transfer through lateral displacement. The system would fail.

C 1.52

The underslung cable aids the top chord only for loads that tend to deform the continuous beam in the direction of the cable. The slender, bending-prone bottom chord can do nothing against uplift loads such as wind suction that would tend to pull the top chord away from it. In particular, facade constructions in which the load directions change with wind direction must therefore be trussed both ways (Fig. C 1.55). In these cases, two series of tensile-stressed members with opposing curvature are required.

Mechanism of action

To analyse the load-bearing behaviour of trussed beams, it is helpful to split the structural system into two pieces. The upper piece (subsystem 1) is a statically over-determined continuous (multi-span) beam. When subjected to a load q, it is flexurally stressed. Subsystem 1 transfers its support reactions as loads to a truss (subsystem 2). As a result, the truss experiences normal forces (Fig. C 1.54 a–c).

The "trussed beam" structure is therefore composed of the common structural elements: flexural, compression and tension members (Fig. C 1.56). After the forces in all the elements have been determined, the elements can be pre-dimensioned according to the principles introduced in Part B (p. 38ff.). The usual distributions of the most critical stress resultants, the bending moment M [kNm] and the normal force N [kN], are depicted in Fig. C 1.54 d. Tensioning the bottom chord controls the magnitude of the force that the struts take up from the continuous beam. In the absence of pretensioning, the struts do not act as vertically non-translatable supports but merely furnish the top chord with a springy suspension.

In trussed beam applications, and as a rule of thumb for the required overall height h as a function of span length l, the following experimental values are often used:

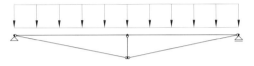

Trussed beam (structural system)

a

=

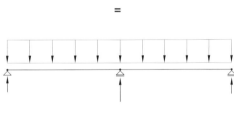
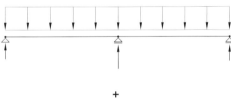

Bending-stressed continuous beam (subsystem 1)

b

+

Truss, subject to normal stresses (subsystem 2)

c

Trussed beam with one strut, bending moment M [kNm]

Trussed beam with one strut, normal force N [kN]

d   C 1.54

C 1.55

C 1.56

C 1.57

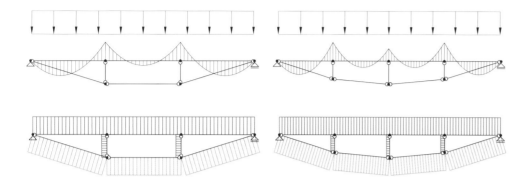

C 1.58   C 1.59

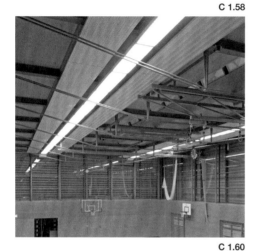

C 1.60

C 1.61

C 1.62

C 1.63

- The span length l generally lies between 6 and 60 m.
- The truss height h usually lies between l/15 and l/8.

Frequently used constructions

There is a large bandwidth of geometric forms available to trussed beam systems. They differ mostly in the number and arrangement of the struts. The larger the span of the beam, the more struts are called for. Apart from vertical compression members, diagonal braces can also be incorporated. In addition, the top of every strut can serve as the point of origin of a further set of tensile members. Flexural panels can be trussed similarly to beams (Fig. C 1.57, p. 79).

Trussed beams with two or more struts

Constructions that are very common are systems with two struts. Their applications range from small bus shelters to riding and sports arenas and factory halls (Fig. C 1.60). To secure slender, tall columns against buckling, they may be trussed in the same manner as large glass facades. Between the two struts, the bottom chord is parallel to the top chord (Fig. C 1.58).
Beyond these there are trussed beams with three or more struts (Fig. C 1.59, C 1.62, C 1.63). Special versions of trussed beams include, among others, the Wiegmann Polonceau truss and the Fink truss.

The Wiegmann Polonceau truss

The Wiegmann Polonceau truss is named after Rudolf Wiegmann (1804–1865) and Jean Barthélémy Camille Polonceau (1813–1859). It is presumed that both developed this system independently in the late 1830s by combining well-known and proven systems in an obvious way. The construction consists of two trussed rafters that meet at the roof ridge and are held together by an additional tension member between the bases of the struts (Fig. C 1.64, C 1.65).

C 1.58   Trussed beam with two struts, bending moment M [kNm] and normal force N [kN]
C 1.59   Trussed beam with three struts, bending moment M [kNm] and normal force N [kN]
C 1.60   Trussed beam with two struts, sports hall, Riesstraße vocational training centre, Munich (DE) 2007, Bauer Kurz Stockburger & Partner, Mayr Ludescher Partner
C 1.61   Trussed beams, riding centre in St. Gerold (AT) 1997, Hermann Kaufmann + Partner, Merz Kley Partner (mkp)
C 1.62   Trussed beams, Exhibition Hall 4, Hanover (DE) 1995, von Gerkan, Marg und Partner (gmp), Schlaich Bergermann Partner (sbp)
C 1.63   Trussed beams, glass pyramid, inner courtyard

of the Louvre, Paris (FR) 1989, Ieoh Ming Pei, NCK Engineering, Franz Knoll
C 1.64   Wiegmann-Polonceau truss, bending moment M [kNm], normal force N [kN]
C 1.65   Wiegmann-Polonceau truss, open hall, Nottingham Anlage (park), Karlsruhe (DE) 1988
C 1.66   Fink truss, bending moment M [kNm], normal force N [kN]
C 1.67   Fink truss, Puente Bolívar (also Puente de Fierro), Arequipa (PE) 1871, Phoenix Iron Co.
C 1.68   Hall with cable beams, conceptual sketch, normal force N [kN]
C 1.69   Upright cable beams for facade reinforcement, Stadttor, Düsseldorf (DE) 1998, Petzinka Pink und Partner, Arup, Lavis

Fink truss

In this truss, developed by Albert Fink (1827–1897) in the mid 19th century, small truss cables are supported at the tops of neighbouring struts (Fig. C 1.66, C 1.67). The individual cables are thus cleverly interlaced. In addition, the taller struts are often connected on at least one side to a support by a set of variously angled tension members. The Bollman truss, patented in 1852 by Wendel Bollman (1814–1884), features similarities to the Fink truss.

Cable Beams

Closely related to the trussed beams are lenticular cable beams. Here, too, the loads are largely transferred to compression-stressed struts and on to the supports via sets of tensile-stressed members or cables. In contrast to the trussed beam, however, the top chord in this case is resistant neither to bending nor to compression, but is itself also a cable. This upper tensioned cable is called a stay. It is often associated with the covering of large areas. The stay also serves to stiffen the very lightweight construction against variable, unevenly distributed or uplift loads. Much like the bottom support cable, the stay must be anchored to the outside. Because of this, the difficulty inherent in the anchoring of cable beams during construction must not be underestimated, though their manufacture requires very little material. Both sets of cables are pretensioned in order to prevent large deformations due to live loads (Fig. C 1.68). Unlike trussed beams, cable beams are well-suited to accommodating forces not only from wind pressure but also from wind suction. Depending on the direction of the load, the suspension cable becomes the stay and the stay the suspension cable. Cable beams are therefore often used as vertically or horizontally integrated structures for withstanding wind loads (Fig. C 1.69).

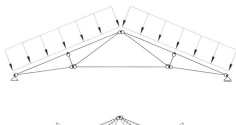

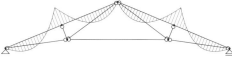

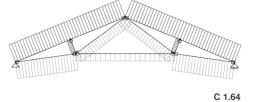

C 1.64

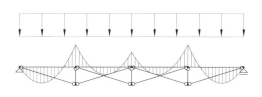

C 1.66

C 1.68

C 1.65

C 1.67

C 1.69

In radially arranged cable beams in roof structures, the horizontal support reactions of the two sets of cables are elegantly short-circuited through an outer compression ring. Such a structure corresponds to the familiar spoked bicycle wheel, which in this case is laid on its side. These types of spoked-wheel constructions are among the most efficient roof structures in the history of building. With little material it is possible to span very large areas (Fig. B 1.8, B 1.9, p. 43). In cable beam applications, and as a rule of thumb for the required overall height h as a function of span length l, the following experimental values are often used:

- The span length l generally lies between 5 and 150 m.
- The beam height h usually lies between l/12 and l/6.

Cable Trusses

In cable trusses (Jawerth trusses), of which David Jawerth (1920–1998) was one of the developers, the suspension and stay cables of the cable beam are reversed. Here, the suspension cable is on top and the stiffening stay cable below. The connections between the two sets of cables are under tension. Unlike for the cable beam, the two pretensioned sets of cables terminate at different heights (Fig. C 1.70).

If these cable trusses are arranged radially, two compression rings placed one above the other are necessary to anchor the suspension cables at the top and the stays at the bottom. The lower of the two compression rings is often placed at the level of the roof covering. This can be observed in the stadium roofs in Stuttgart and Kiev (Fig. C 1.71).

The wind loads acting on large glass facades can also be taken up by cable trusses. Much as for the trussed beams, the cables must be oriented in both directions in order to resist forces of both wind pressure and wind suction. If the two necessary cable sets cross one another as they do in the Tokyo International Forum, it is impossible to categorically assign them to either the cable beam or cable truss system. Near the supports, such a system acts like a cable truss, in mid-span like a cable beam. Interconnecting the two different systems is a clever way to reduce the overall height of the structure (Fig. C 1.72, C 1.73).

In cable truss applications, and as a rule of thumb for the required overall height h as a function of span length l, the following experimental values are often used:
- The span length l is between 20 and 150 m.
- The truss height h usually lies between l/10 and l/5.

Cable-stayed Beams

Long-span beams can be supported not just from below, but may also be stayed from above. Such cable-stayed beams are also known as guyed beams. Tensioned ropes, cables or members supply the flexural beam with intermediate supports and thereby subdivide its free span. Cable-stayed beam systems are often used in

C 1.70

C 1.71

C 1.72

C 1.73

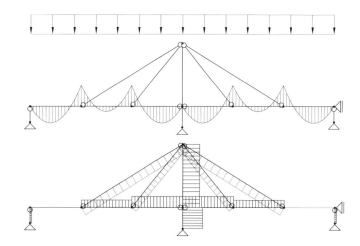

C 1.74

bridges, for example in the Köhlbrand Bridge in Hamburg (Fig. C 1.75) or in the Millau Viaduct in southern France, which was designed by Michel Virlogeux in collaboration with Norman Foster. The main deck of cable-stayed bridges is usually stayed by many cables from one or several tall pylons (Fig. C 1.76). It is practical to arrange the stay cables symmetrically on either side of the pylon so that the horizontal forces remain in equilibrium and the pylon itself is mainly under compression.

The slender stays are under tension. When appropriately dimensioned, each cable forms a barely elastic intermediate support for the flexural beam. The beam therefore becomes a continuous beam. Since the stays are rarely vertical but rather diagonal, they produce not only bending stresses but also normal forces within the stayed beam. The flatter the angle of the stay, the larger the normal forces become. They add up from the outside toward the symmetry axis and are therefore greatest in the vicinity of the pylon. Because of the combination of flexural and compressive stresses in the horizontal beam, the risk of buckling is greatest there, as well.

To analyse the structure, it is helpful as for the trussed beam to partition the system into a continuous beam subsystem and a truss subsystem. The support reactions of the continuous beam are applied to the truss as loads. In this way, all of the decisive stress resultants can be determined (Fig. C 1.74).

Cable-stayed beams are also used in buildings. Designers like to use such structural systems for small as well as monumental canopies. It is also a good way to cover large areas without the need for columns, and is employed in sports and cultural buildings as well as industrial, manufacturing or maintenance halls (Fig. C 1.77 to C 1.80, p. 84).

As in the case of trussed beams, cable stays generally offer no protection against uplift loads such as wind suction. For this

C 1.75

C 1.76

C 1.70 Spatial cable truss with a support cable on top and two stay cables below, pedestrian bridge over Schenkendorfstraße, Munich (DE) 1985, Richard J. Dietrich, Suess + Staller

C 1.71 Radially arranged cable trusses, support cables above, stay cables below, roof of the Olympic stadium, Kiev (UA) 2011, von Gerkan, Marg und Partner (gmp), Schlaich Bergermann Partner (sbp)

C 1.72 Horizontal cable trusses for reinforcement of the glass facade against wind pressure and suction, Custom House Quay (CHQ) Building, Dublin (IE) 2007, RFR Engineers Peter Rice

C 1.73 Vertical cable beams/trusses for reinforcement of the facade, Tokyo International Forum (JP) 1996, Rafael Viñoly Architects, Structural Design Group

C 1.74 Cable-stayed beam, bending moment M [kNm] and normal force N [kN] due to uniformly distributed load q

C 1.75 Cable-stayed beam, Köhlbrand Bridge, Hamburg (DE) 1974, Paul Boué, Egon Jux

C 1.76 Cable-stayed beam, pedestrian and bicycle bridge, Almere (NL) 2004, René van Zuuk Architekten, Ingenieurbüro van de Laar

reason, the two central stay-beams on the Princeton Technology Center are dimensioned so that they can withstand compressive forces (Fig. C 1.80). Together with the two long outer tension members, they form an inverted trussed beam "underslung" cable that reinforces the hall roof against suction loads.

The applications for cable-stayed structures are numerous and range from small canopies to bridges with spans of several hundred metres (Fig. C 1.77 to C 1.80). To arrive at reasonable estimates for component heights, it is often helpful to orient oneself by built systems of comparable size.

Arches

Arch structures are curved structures that are primarily under compression. Depending on how they are built they can be classified as either more of a structural element or more of a structural system. If their cross sections are predominantly acted on by normal forces, arch constructions are very efficient. This is the case for arches where shape and loading correspond to the thrust line. The thrust line is similar to an inverted catenary curve (Fig. C 1.81). Using little material, such arches can support large loads over impressive spans. Vertical loads not only generate compressive stresses in the cross section and vertical support reaction forces, but also horizontal reaction forces. These can be accommodated either by sufficiently load-bearing adjacent building components or by the ground itself. The alternative is to short-circuit them through a tension member that connects the two supports.

Applications

Arch structures were already in widespread use in antiquity. They provided openings in walls, spanned rooms and bridged rivers. In the present day, too, carefully designed arch structures aid in the economical construction of large civil engineering projects such as dams, bridges and tunnels. Arches are used in the roof structures of sports halls, factories, railway stations and exhibition halls (Fig. C 1.85, C 1.86). Suitable building materials are those that are strong in compression, such as bricks, steel, reinforced concrete and glued laminated timber (glulam). In addition to arches of solid masonry, timber, reinforced concrete and various structural steel sections, open arch structures like truss arches can also be used.

C 1.77

C 1.78

C 1.79

C 1.80

C 1.77 Cable-stayed canopy, Café Brauer, Chicago (US) 1908, Dwight H. Perkins
C 1.78 Cable-stayed convertible roof, Boulevard Carnot swimming pool, Paris (FR) 1967, Roger Taillibert, Frei Otto, Stéphane du Chateau
C 1.79 Cable-stayed roof, Olympiastadion, Munich (DE) 1972, Behnisch & Partner, Frei Otto, Leonhardt + Andrä
C 1.80 Cable-stayed roof, PA Technology Center, Princeton (US) 1984, Richard Rogers Partner, Arup, Robert Silman Associates
C 1.81 Catenary curve under uniformly distributed load as a model for a thrust line, normal forces N [kN]
C 1.82 Three-hinged arch with tie, normal forces N [kN]

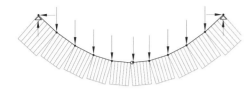

C 1.81

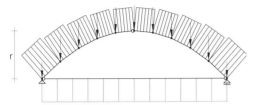

C 1.82

C 1.83

C 1.84

C 1.85

C 1.86

Mechanism of action

A chain under uniformly distributed vertical loading will naturally adopt a parabolic shape. The parabola's height depends on the length of the chain. Therefore, for every load there is an infinite number of inter-related thrust lines. If an arch follows one of these thrust lines, its cross section will manifest only compressive stresses.

The size of the horizontal reaction forces A_H and B_H in this case depends, among other things, on the rise f of the arch. The rise is a measure of the vertical distance between the crown and the supports. The steeper the arch, the smaller the forces (Fig. C 1.87). Since these horizontal reaction forces also act as constant horizontal stresses throughout the entire arch, it stands to reason that they should not be allowed to become too large, so that buckling of the compression-stressed arch is prevented. The rise of an arch r should therefore typically be no less than one eighth of the span l:
rise $r > 1/8\ l$

The horizontal force H in the arch and at the supports due to a vertical, uniformly distributed load q is constant and depends on the span l and the rise r. It is given by
horizontal force $H = A_H = B_H = ql^2/8r$

When connecting the support points with a tie, the same horizontal force H acts within the tie, though in this case it is a tensile force. This cancels out the horizontal support reactions (Fig. C 1.82).

In addition to the horizontal force H, the arch is acted upon by a vertical force V due to its self-weight and a vertical load q. Much like the transverse force V in a flexural beam, V is zero at the crown (midpoint) of the arch and increases toward the supports. There, the vertical component V is equal to the vertical support reactions A_V and B_V. The magnitude of the normal force N resulting from the vector sum of H and V in symmetrical arches under uniform distributed load q is therefore smallest at the crown, where $N_C = H$, and largest at the supports, where $N_S = \sqrt{(H^2 + V^2)} = \sqrt{(A_H^2 + A_V^2)} = \sqrt{((ql^2/8r)^2 + (ql/2)^2)}$. In arches whose shape and loading correspond to a thrust line, this normal force N always acts along the arch axis.

If the shape or loading deviates from that of a thrust line, the force N is not centred in the arch axis. Such an eccentricity e in the arch creates a bending moment $M = N \cdot e$ in addition to the compression force N, which is large wherever the arch line deviates significantly from the thrust line. This leads to deformations in the arch. The action of varying, unevenly distributed loads such as wind, snow and live loads alone can cause the thrust line and arch axis to diverge at least temporarily. It is therefore important to construct arches that are not only strong in compression, but also relatively bending-resistant. This is true even if the arch shape under typical loading essentially coincides with a thrust line.

In historical arches, their form was often reinforced through large, evenly distributed loads such as cover fill or superstructures. The latter are also useful in that they geometrically impede significant changes in the shape of the arch. Today, lightweight

C 1.83 Ponte dei Salti, Valle Verzasca, Ticino (CH) 17th century
C 1.84 Truss arches, Hackerbrücke bridge, Munich (DE) 1894, Maschinenbau-Actiengesellschaft Nürnberg
C 1.85 Steel arch construction, west entry hall of the Leipzig Trade Fair (DE) 1995, von Gerkan, Marg und Partner (gmp), Stefan Polónyi und Partner, Schlaich Bergermann Partner (sbp), Ian Ritchie Architects
C 1.86 Converging arch-like branched steel columns, platform hall, Estação do Oriente railway station, Lisbon (PT) 1998, Santiago Calatrava Architects & Engineers
C 1.87 Steep parabolic arch, St. Bonifatius church, Lübeck (DE) 1952, Emil Steffann

C 1.87

C 1.88 Arch with radial cable stays, Postgalerie shop-
ping centre, Karlsruhe (DE) 2002, Chapman
Taylor
C 1.89 Reinforcing construction to shore up abutments
in danger of giving way, Colosseum, Rome (IT)
80 CE
C 1.90 Three-hinged arch of reinforced concrete,
Salginatobel Bridge (CH) 1930, Robert
Maillart
C 1.91 Parabolically curved steel decks between
parabolic twin arches, railway station in Leuven
(BE) 2006, Samyn and Partners
C 1.92 Steel arch bridge, Streicker Bridge, Princeton
(US) 2010, Christian Menn, HNTB

C 1.93 Strutted frame, bending moment M [kNm] and
normal force N [kN] due to uniformly distributed
load q (members under compression)
C 1.94 Queen-post truss, bending moment M [kNm]
and normal force N [kN] due to uniformly
distributed load q
C 1.95 Historical queen-post truss, Gießenbrücke bridge
over the Bolgenach river, Vorarlberg (AT) 1792
C 1.96 Queen-post truss bridge over the Loisach river,
Eschenlohe (DE) 2006, Richard J. Dietrich
C 1.97 Strutted frame bridge over the A8 in Kirchheim/
Teck (DE) 1992, Schlaich Bergermann Partner
C 1.98 Post truss bridge, Düsseldorf harbour (DE)
1992, Schüßler-Plan

radial or sectional tension wires aid in
securing the shape of slender arches
and thus their load-bearing capacity
(Fig. C 1.88).

Damage to historical masonry arches
often results from the lateral giving way of
abutments due to the horizontal pushing
action of the force H. Large deformations
or even collapses of such arches can
be prevented by buttresses as in Gothic
cathedrals, lateral retaining walls as in
the Roman Colosseum or ties between
the supports (Fig. C 1.89).

Depending on the design of the supports as
well as possible intermediate connections,
and therefore on the degrees of freedom f, it
is possible to distinguish between statically
determinate three-hinged arches, singly
over-determined two-hinged arches and
triply overdetermined fixed arches.

For the large railway station halls of the
19th century, engineers like Johann Wilhelm
Schwedler (1823–1894) often used three-
hinged arches, as seen at Frankfurt Hauptbahnhof and Berlin Ostbahnhof stations.
Nowadays, two-hinged arches are frequently
employed, in order to save the construction costs necessary for the fixed mounting
on the one hand and a third hinge on the
other. While no inner stresses develop in
statically determinate three-hinged arches
as a result of thermal expansion or support
displacements, overdetermined systems
are considered somewhat more robust
and less likely to deform (Figs. C 1.90 to
C 1.92).

In arch applications, and as a rule of thumb
for the required overall height h as a function of span length l, the following experimental values are often used:

• The span length l generally lies between
  5 and 80 m.
• The arch depth h often ranges from l/70
  and l/40.
• Usually, the centre rise r > l/8.
• The effective length factor β lies in the
  range β × 0.5 … 0.625 · arc length.

C 1.88

C 1.89

C 1.90

C 1.91

C 1.92

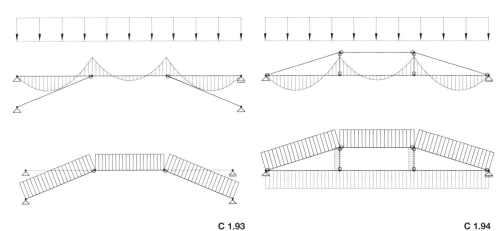

C 1.93   C 1.94

Strutted Frames

Often, especially for bridges, a flexural beam cannot be supported on vertical piers, whether it be because the subsoil in river beds is insufficiently load-bearing or because vehicles pass under the bridge. In such cases, it is often useful to incorporate diagonal struts (Fig. C 1.97). In accordance with the arch-like arrangement of the members, compression develops in the elements involved (Fig. C 1.93). The explosive potential effect of these considerable compression forces lends the strutted frame structure its German name, *Sprengwerk* (exploding framework). The buckling risk in the compressive members must be accounted for. While the origins of strutted frames lie in timber construction, they are mostly used today in the building of re-inforced concrete bridges. For reasonable estimates of span lengths and component heights it is advisable to study built examples of strutted frame construction.

King and Queen-post Trusses

Just like strutted frames, king and queen-post trusses also trace their origins back to historical timber construction (Fig. C 1.95, C 1.96). They were frequently used in large roof frameworks over churches, staterooms or warehouses. Moreover, in his *I Quattro Libri dell'Architettura* (Book III, ch. VII, p. 15), published in 1570, Andrea Palladio presents a design for a queen-post truss bridge.

Similarly to strutted frames, king and queen-post trusses also have an arch-like arrangement of members under compression. Suspended from these load-bearing beams by tension members is a flexural beam located at the usage plane (Fig. C 1.94, C 1.98). The horizontal pressure from the upper beams stretches or pulls the lower beam. In roof frameworks, this bending as well as tensile-stressed

C 1.95

C 1.96

C 1.97

C 1.98

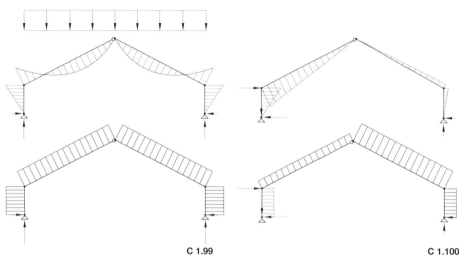

C 1.99   C 1.100

bottom chord is also called the tie beam. A comparison of the normal forces present in the king or queen-post truss and in an equivalent trussed beam reveals that tension and compression are reversed. The post truss can be viewed as an upwardly reflected counterpart to the trussed beam. Today, because of the buckling risk of compression members and the associated high cost of materials, king and queen-post trusses are rarely used. For reasonable estimates of span lengths and component heights it is advisable to orient oneself to the following built examples of king-post and queen-post truss construction.

Frames and Trussed Frames

It is easy to picture how the frame structural system got its name. In a frame, a set of flexural members encompass a space, usually at the top and on both sides. As a rule, the frame consists of a more-or-less horizontal beam with bending-resistant connections to one or both vertical posts (Fig. C.101, Fig. C 1.102, see also Built Example p. 211ff.). The system has advantageous load-bearing characteristics. First, frames can accommodate not only vertical, but also horizontal loads. They therefore have inherent stiffening properties. Second, if appropriate measures are taken,

the material of a frame can be better exploited than that of a beam resting flexibly on two supports; this results in material savings.

Construction principles and mechanisms of action

Depending on the degrees of freedom f, it is possible to distinguish between statically determinate three-hinged frames, singly over-determined two-hinged frames and triply overdetermined fixed frames.

Three-hinged frames

Frames with three hinges have the advantage that support displacements and thermal effects do not produce internal stresses. Two of the hinges are usually located at the bases of the two posts. The third hinge can be placed at various points along the horizontal member. The magnitude distribution of the stress resultants and therefore the stresses in the building components can be controlled by the positioning of this hinge along the horizontal beam. Three-hinged frames can generally be transported to the construction site in two separate pieces. Today, such frames are quite widespread, especially in timber construction.

C 1.101

C 1.102

C 1.99   Three-hinged frame under vertical, uniformly distributed load q, bending moment M [kNm] and normal force N [kN]
C 1.100   Three-hinged frame under concentrated horizontal load H, bending moment M [kNm] and normal force N [kN]
C 1.101   External frame structure, Crown Hall, IIT, Chicago (US) 1956, Ludwig Mies van der Rohe
C 1.102   Frame corners rendered bending-resistant through Y-shaped posts, platform hall of Rotterdam central railway station (NL) 2014, Benthem Crouwel Architects, MVSA Meyer en Van Schooten Architecten, West 8, Arcadis and Gemeentewerken
C 1.103   Three-hinged frame under uniformly distributed vertical load q, hinge at x = 0.1464 l, bending moment M [kNm]

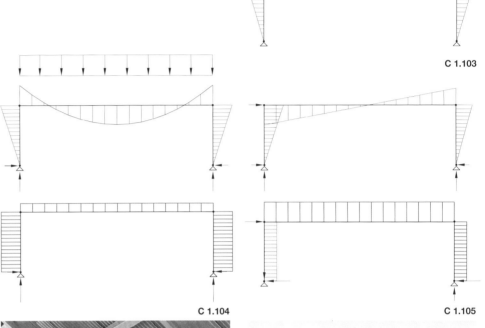

C 1.103

The hinges cannot transmit bending moments. Given the decrease in the bending stresses toward the hinges, the cross sections at those locations can be made smaller. In contrast, the bending-resistant frame corners, where the moment is typically large, require greater cross sections. Particularly in timber construction, a multitude of costly fasteners are needed to join the members at the corners.

Three-hinged frames with a horizontal beam and a central hinge are not very practical. They are therefore rarely used. In order to make better use of the member cross sections, it helps if the frame approximates an arch shape, in which the beam is cut in two and forms a kink at the central hinge (Figs. C 1.106 to C 1.108).

For a horizontal beam subject to a uniformly distributed load q, it is useful to incorporate the hinge at 14.6 % of the beam length l so that the cross section is fully exploited in the centre of the span and at both of the frame corners (Fig. C 1.103). For horizontal loads, this creates asymmetric forces.

If the hinge is placed right at the transition between post and beam, the frame is referred to as an asymmetric three-hinged frame. It has the advantage of being able to resist horizontal loads. Under vertical loads, however, it behaves similarly to a

C 1.104   C 1.105

C 1.106

C 1.107

C 1.104 Two-hinged frame under uniformly distributed vertical load q, bending moment M [kNm] and normal force N [kN]
C 1.105 Two-hinged frame under concentrated horizontal load H, bending moment M [kNm] and normal force N [kN]
C 1.106 Three-hinged timber frame, *Transgenerational House,* pavilion at the MUGAK Architecture Biennial, San Sebastian (ES) 2019, EHAEO/COAVN Gipuzkoa
C 1.107 Asymmetric three-hinged frame, former petrol station, Weil am Rhein (DE) circa 1953, Jean Prouvé, since 2003 Vitra Campus
C 1.108 Frame-like supports, Becton Engineering and Applied Science Center, Yale University, New Haven (US) 1970, Marcel Breuer
C 1.109 Two-hinged steel frame, Highlight Towers, Munich (DE) 2004, Helmut Jahn, Werner Sobek

C 1.108

C 1.109

C 1.110

C 1.111

C 1.112

beam on two supports. The post under the hinge can be made more slender than the one under the flexurally stressed frame corner.

As with arches, many frames from the 19th and early 20th centuries are statically determinate three-hinged systems. This is true for the Galerie des Machines in Paris from 1889 just as for the railway platform hall at Hamburg's central station from 1906.

Two-hinged frames

Today, two-hinged frames are frequently used in economical industrial steel construction, especially for commercially utilised warehouses or factory floors with no representational aspirations. In the simply statically overdetermined two-hinged frame, the degree to which particular building · components are stressed can be controlled through the length and flexural stiffness of posts and beams. The more rigid the posts, the greater the moment at the frame corners. For a very flexurally stiff beam, in contrast, the moment is greater in the centre of the span than at the corners (Fig. C 1.104 – C 1.109, p. 89).

Fixed frames

For fixed frames, deformations are smaller than for similar two or three-hinged frames. However, since it is significantly less expensive to provide the posts with hinged rather than fixed supports, such systems are only rarely used (Fig. C 1.110). They are practical mainly for high halls or in the case of large horizontal loads arising from crane runways.

Support connections

An essential feature of frames is that both supports are at least two-force supports, preventing both vertical and horizontal displacement. As for the arch, vertical loads on frames generate not only vertical but also horizontal support reactions. If one of the

supports was capable of horizontal movement, the system would not constitute a frame, but rather a bent beam.

Similarities between frames and arches

Frames and arches have several things in common. In both cases, the supports are, at a minimum, two-force supports, and horizontal reaction forces also arise in response to vertical loads. Both can withstand vertical and horizontal forces and thus have stiffening properties. A frame can be thought of as an angled special case of the arch. This is made clear in the step-wise transition from curved arch to polygonally arranged members to the rectangular frame. Some structures cannot be uniquely assigned to one or the other system. Significant bending moments are created anywhere where the separation between the load-dependent thrust line and the system axis is large. For rectangular frames, this often occurs at the corners (Fig. C 1.111).

Example applications

Frames find especially varied use in large public or commercial buildings with moderate spans (Fig. C 1.113 – C 1.115).

In frame applications, and as a rule of thumb for the required overall height h as a function of span length l, the following experimental values are often used:
- The span length l generally lies between 5 and 40 m.
- The beam height h usually lies between l/40 and l/20.

In larger structures or buildings, a frame can be broken up into member frameworks, in which the posts and beams of the frame could comprise trusses, for example. If the vertical and horizontal trusses transition directly into one another at the frame corners, the corners will become bending-resistant due to the diagonal members of the system even when the individual members are pin-

C 1.110 Fixed steel frame, Frieder Burda Museum, Baden-Baden (DE) 2004, Richard Meier, Schumer + Kienzle

C 1.111 Between arch and frame, basement level of Stadelhofen railway station, Zurich (CH) 1990, Santiago Calatrava

C 1.112 Between arch and frame, polygonal arrangement of timber members, Shin-toyosu Brillia Running Stadium, Tokyo (JP) 2017, Yukiharu Takematsu & E.P.A

C 1.113 External frames, Munson-Williams-Proctor Arts Institute, Utica (US) 1960, Philip Johnson, Bice & Baird

C 1.114 Clad frames, Philharmonic Hall (now David Geffen Hall), Lincoln Center for the Performing Arts, New York (US) 1962, Max Abramovitz

C 1.115 Reinforced concrete frames, Kraanspoor, Amsterdam (NL) 2009, OTH Ontwerpgroep Trude Hooykaas, Aronsohn Raadgevende Ingenieurs

C 1.116 Lightweight trussed frames, MFO Park, Zurich (CH) 2002, Raderschallpartner AG Landschaftsarchitekten, Burckhardt + Partner

C 1.117 Trussed frame as a bridge pylon, George Washington Bridge, New York (US) 1931, Othmar Ammann

connected. The corner sections of the trussed frame then form part of the beam as well as part of the post.

A further option is to expand only the beam into a truss, while the posts, which are usually shorter, remain as compression and bending-stressed solid wall elements. In order to achieve a stiffening effect in the frame in this case, the top and bottom chords of the truss must be connected by the posts (Fig. C 1.116, C 1.117).

In trussed frame applications, and as a rule of thumb for the required overall height h as a function of span length l, the following experimental values are often used:

- The span length l is between 10 and 60 m.
- The truss height h usually lies between l/20 and l/10.

Rigid Frame Trusses

If several bending-resistant frames are lined up alongside one another, the result is a beam that at first glance looks like a truss. However, it is missing its stiffening diagonal members. For such a structure to bear loads, all elements must be rigidly joined together. In contrast to the truss, in which only normal stresses occur, the building components of the rigid frame truss are thus subjected to occasionally large bending stresses, particularly at the frame corners. Rigid frame trusses, which are also known as Vierendeel trusses after their inventor Arthur Vierendeel (1852–1940), therefore require significantly more material expenditure than standard trusses (Fig. C 1.118, p. 92). However, their openings remain free of diagonal members. Rigid frame trusses can be employed lying flat, but also standing upright like trusses for use in towers or high-rise structures, and they can withstand vertical and horizontal forces simultaneously (Fig. C 1.119, p. 92).

C 1.113

C 1.114

C 1.115

C 1.116

C 1.117

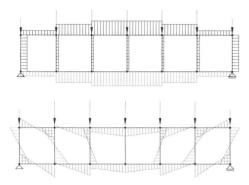

C 1.118

a

b

C 1.119

In rigid frame truss applications, and as a rule of thumb for the required overall height h as a function of span length l, the following experimental values are often used:

- The span length l usually lies between 15 and 65 m.
- The truss height h is generally between l/15 and l/10.

Figures C 1.120 to C 1.123 illustrate further applications.

Girder Grids and Truss Grids

In order to span a rectangular area, it is advisable to arrange the main girders or rafters to lie along the shorter dimension. The span is smaller there, making the material expenditure to bridge it correspondingly less. The distance between the axes of two main girders often lies between 4 m for the shorter spans and 8 m for the longer ones. The secondary beams are run transverse to these as simple beams between the main girders or as continuous beams over the girders' top chords. They are also called purlins. They support the full-surface roof or floor covering, which is often made of engineered wood panels, trapezoidal sheet, steel-reinforced concrete composite slabs or timber-concrete composite systems.

If the area to be spanned is approximately square, it is possible to use load-bearing systems that differentiate little or not at all between main and secondary directions. In girder grids, the girders are arranged along two or more directions, mostly on a single plane. Since neither timber nor steel beams can penetrate one another, these building materials necessitate a significant constructional effort at every single node. In the case of steel, many welding seams are generally

C 1.120

C 1.122

C 1.121

C 1.123

C 1.124

required, while gusset plates or stacked-board methods are useful for timber. Girder grids are comparatively easy to implement using reinforced concrete. However, the work needed to clad the material must not be underestimated.

In order to prevent the centres of the girder grids from deflecting downward, it is useful to manufacture them cambered or trussed. If the aim is a relatively even distribution of stresses throughout all the elements, it is counterproductive to support girder grids at the corners only. A better option is to move the columns under a girder grid inward, much as Ludwig Mies van der Rohe did at the Neue Nationalgalerie in Berlin (Fig. C 1.124). A very effective way to support girder grids is through tree-like branching structures as featured at Stuttgart Airport (Fig. C 1.125), since these provide many support points.

In solid-beam girder grid applications, and as a rule of thumb for the required overall height h as a function of span length l, the following experimental values are often used:

- The span length l usually lies between 15 and 65 m.
- The beam height h generally ranges from l/35 to l/20.

C 1.125

In place of solid-beam girder grids, grids of trusses or rigid frame trusses may also be used. Reinforced concrete is well-suited for grids of Vierendeel trusses, as Louis Kahn and August E. Komendant demonstrated in 1965 at the Richards Medical Research Laboratories in Philadelphia (see Fig. 8, p. 7).

Truss constructions of steel rods are one of the frequently employed building forms for grids (Fig. C 1.127). Here, the nodes at the top and bottom chord levels are relatively easy to implement, in contrast to the costly nodes needed for tall solid beams. In truss grid applications, and as a rule of thumb for the required overall height h as a function of span length l, the following experimental values are often used:

- The span length l usually lies between 25 and 95 m.
- The truss height h usually lies between l/20 and l/15.

Space Frames

Truss grids are, of course, three-dimensional, spatial structures. However, unlike space frames, they are assembled from planar trusses. The basic module of a space

C 1.126

C 1.118 Vierendeel (or rigid frame) truss, normal force N [kN] similar to the standard truss, bending moment M [kNm] shows high stresses at frame corners
C 1.119 Beinecke Library, Yale University, New Haven (US) 1963, SOM, Gordon Bunshaft, Paul Weidlinger
    a stacked Vierendeel trusses, supported by only one column at every building corner, ornamental effect of the bending-resistant frame corners
    b the ornamental effect extends to the interior
C 1.120 Structural facade acting as a Vierendeel truss, Simmons Hall, MIT, Boston (US) 2002, Steven Holl, Guy Nordenson and Associates
C 1.121 Vierendeel truss, Gustav Heinemann Bridge, Berlin (DE) 2005, Max Dudler, Ingenieurbüro Grassl

C 1.122 Reinforcing frame structure in the plane of the facade, Prada store, Tokyo (JP) 2003, Herzog & de Meuron, Takenaka Corporation, WGG Schnetzer Puskas Ingenieure
C 1.123 Vierendeel truss facade pillars, New York Times Building (US) 2007, Renzo Piano Building Workshop, Thornton Tomasetti
C 1.124 Steel girder grid, Neue Nationalgalerie, Berlin (DE) 1968, Ludwig Mies van der Rohe
C 1.125 Truss grid over branching columns, Terminal 1, Stuttgart Airport (DE) 1991, von Gerkan, Marg und Partner (gmp), Schlaich Bergermann Partner (sbp)
C 1.126 Steel girder grid, Expo roof, Exhibition Pavilions 32–35, Hanover (DE) 2000, Thomas Herzog, Julius Natterer
C 1.127 Truss grid, Exhibition Hall 13, Hanover (DE) 1997, Ackermann und Partner, Schlaich Bergermann Partner (sbp)

C 1.127

C 1.128

C 1.129

C 1.130

C 1.131

frame, in contrast, is a tetrahedron, a spatial structure composed of four triangles.
In large space frames, half or whole octahedrons are created in the spaces between tetrahedrons. A half octahedron has the form of a pyramid with a square base. Trusses composed of octahedrons and tetrahedrons are also called octet trusses.

Entrepreneur Alexander Graham Bell (1847–1922), who was able to secure an early patent for the telephone in 1876, built an observation tower from such octet trusses in 1907 (Fig. C 1.129). After this had apparently faded from memory, Richard Buckminster Fuller (1895–1983) received a patent for such a structure under his name in the early 1960s.

The development of a node at which converging rods could be simply connected provided space frames with a plethora of applications in lightweight, large-span structures. Max Mengeringhausen (1903–1988) began building nodes of this kind starting in 1937 (Fig. C 1.128).

As is the case for girder grids, space frames represent a non-directional structure. It is therefore advantageous for a space frame to choose similar span lengths along both directions. Cambering the frame during manufacture is helpful in preventing the structure from sagging under load. As in planar trusses, all members of a space frame are subject only to normal and not to bending forces.

This lightweight and efficient structure makes it possible to build spans over large distances in excess of 100 m as are needed for exhibition halls, airports and sports venues (Fig. C 1.131). In space frame applications, and as a rule of thumb for the required overall height h as a function of span length l, the following experimental values are often used:
- The span length l usually lies between 20 and 120 m.
- The frame height h generally ranges from l/25 to l/15.

Overview of Structural Elements and Systems

Figure C 1.132 (p. 95ff.) provides an overview of the frequently used structural elements and systems, including design help in the dimensioning of building components. The data given is approximate guide values for basic systems in architecture. It is primarily based on static structural reasoning.

Other considerations regarding cost-effectiveness, transport and assembly must also be taken into account. Depending on the weight assigned to these factors, the dimensions arrived at in individual cases may diverge significantly from the values presented here.

C 1.128 Mero node, since 1937, Max Mengeringhausen
C 1.129 Tetrahedral Tower, model reconstruction TU Munich, Beinn Bhreagh (CA) 1907, Alexander Graham Bell
C 1.130 Design for an aeroplane hangar, 1950s, model reconstruction TU Munich, Konrad Wachsmann
C 1.131 Jacob K. Javits Convention Center, New York (US) 1986, Pei Cobb Freed & Partners, Thornton Tomasetti
C 1.132 Frequently used structural elements and systems

Typology		Applications, rules of thumb and typical spans

Simple beam

 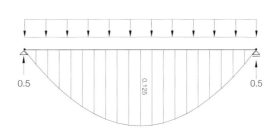

- System example, bending moment M due to uniformly distributed vertical load q
- $A_V = B_V = ql/2 = 0.5\, ql$
- $M_{span} = ql^2/8 = 0.125\, ql^2$
- $w_{max} = (5/384)\, q_k l^4/EI$
- Span length l generally between 3 and 20 m
- Beam height h generally ranges from l/30 to l/12

Simple beam with overhang

 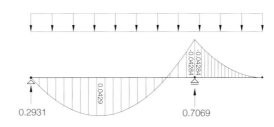

- System example, bending moment M due to uniformly distributed vertical load q
- Advantageous overhang length $l_{over} = l_{span}/2.42 \sim 0.3\, l_{total}$
- Bending moment up to 65 % smaller than for simple beam of same length with no overhang
- A_V and B_V can be determined from equilibrium conditions
- $M_{over} = -q\, l_{over}^2/2$; $M_{span} = A_V^2/2q$
- Span length l generally between 5 and 20 m
- Beam height h generally ranges from l/35 to l/15

Simple beam with double overhang

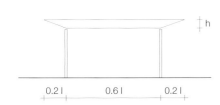 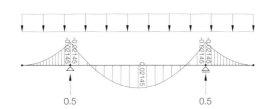

- System example, bending moment M due to uniformly distributed vertical load q
- Advantageous overhang length $l_{over} = l_{span}/2.83 \sim 0.2\, l_{total}$
- Bending moment up to 80 % smaller than for simple beam of same length with no overhangs
- AV and B_V can be determined from equilibrium conditions
- $M_{over} = -q\, l_{over}^2/2$ $M_{span} = q\, l_{span}^2/8 + M_{over}$
- Span length l generally between 5 and 25 m
- Beam height h generally ranges from l/40 to l/20

Continuous beam

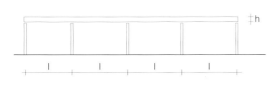 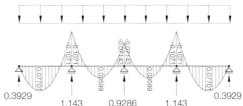

- System example, bending moment M due to uniformly distributed vertical load q
- Statically overdetermined system
- Bending moment M smaller than for series of simple beams
- Reaction forces $R = k \cdot q \cdot l$
- Bending moments $M = k \cdot q \cdot l^2$
- Coefficients k, see also p. 30
- Span length l generally between 3 and 30 m
- Beam height h generally ranges from l/30 to l/20

Hinged beam

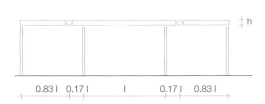 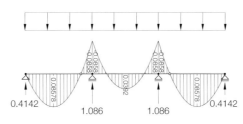

- System example, bending moment M due to uniformly distributed vertical load q
- Statically determinate system
- Bending moment M often smaller than for continuous beam
- Reaction forces R can be determined from equilibrium conditions
- Bending moments can be determined by method of sections
- Span length l generally between 3 and 40 m
- Beam height h generally ranges from l/30 to l/15

Typology	Applications, rules of thumb and typical spans

Truss

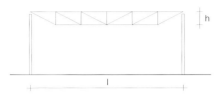

- System example, normal force N due to vertical forces F on nodes
- Multitude of forms and applications
- Efficient load-bearing behaviour, only normal forces N, no bending moments M
- Member forces can be determined through graphical or analytical methods
- Horizontal and vertical applications, used as stiffening system in high-rises
- Span length l generally between 10 and 40 m (timber) and 8 and 80 m (steel)
- Truss height h generally between l/12 and l/8 (timber) and l/15 and l/10 (steel)

Trussed beam

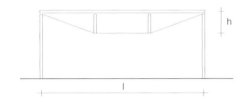

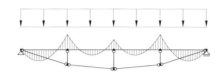

- System example, bending moment M due to uniformly distributed vertical load q
- Continuous beam, supported on lengths of cable via struts
- Top chord bending- and compression-stressed
- Take into account problems occurring from uplift loads
- Span length l generally between 6 and 60 m
- Trussed beam height h generally ranges from l/15 to l/8

Cable beam

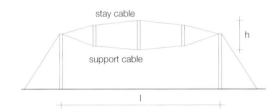

- System example, normal force N due to vertical forces F on nodes
- Large horizontal reaction forces due to vertical loads
- Support cable on bottom, stay cable above, pretensioning required in both
- Horizontal and vertical applications, used as stiffening system in facades
- Span length l generally between 5 and 150 m
- Beam height h generally ranges from l/12 to l/6

Cable truss

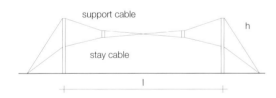

- System example, normal force N due to uniformly distributed vertical load q
- Shape of the cable truss depends on load
- Horizontal reaction forces due to vertical loads
- Stiffened through superimposed load, coupling with stay cables, flexural beams or similar
- $A_V = B_V = ql/2$ $A_H = B_H = ql^2/8r$
- $N_{extreme} = \sqrt{(A_V^2 + A_H^2)}$ $\sigma_{N,d} = N_{t,d}/A < f_{t,d}$
- When pretensioned, larger forces and stresses
- Span length l generally between 20 and 150 m
- Rise r or truss height h generally ranges from l/10 to l/5

Cable-stayed beam

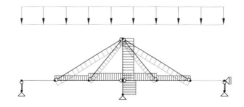

- System example, normal force N due to uniformly distributed vertical load q
- Continuous beam supported via stay cables
- Horizontal chord subject to bending and, in part, normal stresses
- Take into account problems occurring from uplift loads
- Considerable variation in spans and heights

Typology	Applications, rules of thumb and typical spans
Arches 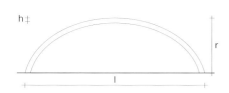 	• System example, normal force N due to uniformly distributed vertical load q • Design following the thrust line is useful, since system is then predominantly compression-stressed • Horizontal reaction forces result from vertical loads; may be short-circuited by tension member • May be stiffened through superimposed loads, bracing, bending resistance, etc. • $A_V = B_V = ql/2$ $A_H = B_H = ql^2/8r$ • $N_{extreme} = -\sqrt{(A_V^2 + A_H^2)}$ $(N_{c,d}/A)/(k_c \cdot f_{c,d}) + (M_d/S)/f_{m,d} < 1$ • Effective length factor $\beta \sim 0.5 \ldots 0.625 \cdot$ arch length • Central rise r often greater than l/8 • Span length l generally between 5 and 80 m • Arch depth h generally ranges from l/70 to l/40
Frame  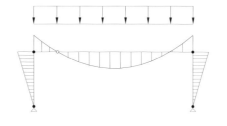	• System example, bending moment M due to uniformly distributed vertical load q • Posts, beam and at least one corner bending-resistant • Takes up vertical and horizontal loads, has stiffening characteristics • Horizontal reaction forces as a result of vertical loads • Effective length factor $\beta \sim 1.0 \ldots 3.5 \cdot$ post height • Span length l generally between 5 and 40 m • Beam height h generally ranges from l/40 to l/20
Rigid frame trusses 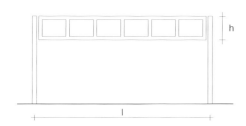 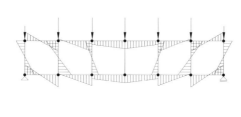	• System example, bending moment M due to uniformly distributed vertical F • No diagonal members, significant flexural stresses • Large material expenditure compared to standard trusses • Horizontal and vertical applications, used as stiffening system in high-rises • Span length l generally between 15 and 65 m • Truss height h generally ranges from l/15 to l/10
Girder grids 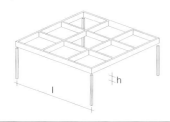	• Similar spans in both grid directions favoured • Cambered manufacture advantageous • Span length l generally between 15 and 65 m • Beam height h generally ranges from l/35 to l/20
Truss grids 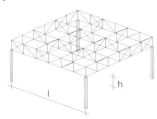	• Similar spans in both grid directions favoured • Cambered manufacture advantageous • Span length l generally between 25 and 95 m • Truss height h generally ranges from l/20 to l/15
Space frames 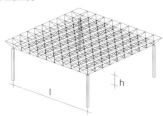	• Similar spans in both member directions favoured • Cambered manufacture advantageous • Span length l generally between 20 and 120 m • Truss height h generally ranges from l/25 to l/15

C 1.132

Part D   Complex Structures

Reinforcing truss, John Hancock Center (now 875 North Michigan Avenue), Chicago (US) 1970, Bruce Graham, Fazlur Khan, SOM

Historical Structures

Christian Kayser

Characteristics of Historical Constructions

The history of construction begins yesterday, and the construction methods of our university days may already be worthy of being listed. Nowadays, the spectrum of historical buildings and structures encompassed within the field of applied cultural resource management is broad, ranging from Roman walls made of *opus caementitium,* a building material similar to concrete, all the way to membrane structures, and thus ultimately encompassing all building typologies and techniques. In a somewhat narrower interpretation, the term "historical structure" primarily implies building types of the pre-industrial age.

Significant differences between these and contemporary structural systems stem firstly from the limitations imposed by the then-available means – with regard to both materials and manpower – and secondly, from the fact that structures were built based on experience and artisanal traditions rather than on a foundation of scientifically grounded rules.

D 1.1 Complex suspension of the roof beam tier through a series of tension members with dowelled tenon joints, late Gothic roof framework of the abbey church in Blaubeuren (DE)

D 1.2 Nave with flying buttresses to accommodate the thrust of the vault; schematic representation of a typical cross section. Augsburg Cathedral (DE)

D 1.3 Typical construction that is still characteristic of the cultural landscape of the Alpine foothills in Bavaria. Block construction with slightly slanted purlin roof and shingle roof covering, Bartlhof in Schnapping, now the Bauernhausmuseum (Farm House Museum) in Amerang (DE)

D 1.4 Fieldstone city wall from the High Middle Ages; hard rock from the Inn Glacier serves as a local source of natural stone, Wasserburg am Inn (DE)

D 1.5 Securing the open margins of the vault with wrought iron tie rods, vestibule of the Rathaus (town hall), Stralsund (DE)

D 1.1

D 1.2

Availability of natural resources

At first, the only building materials available for use were locally occurring natural resources. In heavily forested central Europe, for example, timber was an obvious choice. Throughout the High Middle Ages, thanks to incursions into the virgin forestlands also known as primary forests, it was possible to work with beams of sometimes astonishing dimensions. However, starting in the 14th century, only modest wood cross sections remained available because of the high timber consumption in the growing cities. This necessitated the development of sustainable forest management methods. A striking example of this can be seen, for example, in the active reforestation of the Nuremberg imperial forest, beginning in 1368, by the councilman and entrepreneur Peter Stromer. At the same time, the limited availability of timber also led to the implementation of more lightweight timber constructions. While high-strength flexural beams had still been used in the 12th and 13th centuries to overcome large spans in roof frameworks, the trend now turned increasingly toward strut frames and king and queen-post trusses.

A further example for the influence of available building materials on building types are masonry structures. The brick churches of the northern German Hanseatic cities are the result of significant scarcity. The coastal regions as well as the Alpine foothills lack appreciable natural stone deposits. Before the "rediscovery" of brick firing, which had disappeared from northern Europe with the Roman Empire, monumental buildings such as castles and churches had to be built either from timber or from fieldstones (small boulders) (Fig. D 1.4), both placing limitations on the possible dimensions of the buildings. The use of bricks made possible the dimensional jump to the large "Hanseatic cathedrals" of the 14th and 15th centuries.

Even the locally available roof coverings had an immediate influence on the way structures were built: the inexpensive and readily accessible shingles in Alpine regions could only be installed on gently inclined roofs, thus promoting the development of a landscape characterised by purlin roofs (Fig. D 1.3).

Joining techniques and manufacturing processes

In appraising historical structures, one must take into account not only the resources available at the time of their construction, but also what joining techniques could be executed with the craftsmanship of the day. For a long time, the creation of connections with a high tensile strength was particularly difficult. Typical timber construction details such as mortises and scarf joints possess only limited tensile resistance; to withstand large forces, complicated connections had to be built, such as dowelled tenon joints at the bases of king and queen-post trusses (Fig. D 1.1)

Though historical masonry structures are capable of accommodating high compressive forces, they are weak in tension. The intricate cross section systems of Gothic cathedrals are arranged so that the acting loads due to self-weight, arch thrust and wind are transmitted into the foundations primarily via compression-stressed building components – the system of flying buttresses (Fig. D 1.2). Investigations of these structures reveal that medieval master builders were likely aware at least qualitatively of the basic stresses. In many cases where large tensile forces existed which could not be taken up via compression elements, iron tie rods were employed (Fig D 1.5). However, because of the difficult and expensive manufacture and processing of iron, its use was limited to specialised constructions.

D 1.3

D 1.4

D 1.5

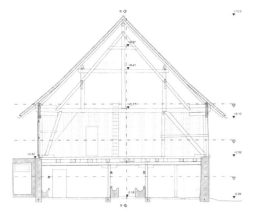

D 1.6

D 1.7

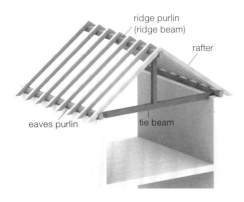

ridge purlin
(ridge beam)

rafter

eaves purlin

tie beam

D 1.8

D 1.9

Empiricism and tradition

A further characteristic of historical structures is that their design and the dimensioning of their parts are typically rooted in artisanal traditions and experiences. The filigree, upward-striving stone skeletons of Gothic cathedrals were created despite the fact that their builders would have been unable to formulate the essential principles of statics and mechanics. Instead, the chosen dimensions of the structural elements are based on simple rules of thumb and are often derived from the main building dimensions or from basic geometric figures. Empirical values dominated the design of the structures; rules arose from established practice and were not scientifically derived. Another typical feature of the older building types is that they are often of mixed construction. Various different roof structures, for example, can be interpreted as both purlin and rafter roofs (Fig. D 1.6); the actual path of load transfer cannot be readily traced without a detailed assessment of, say, the rigidity at the nodes. The introduction of patents for particular construction methods and the eventual development of comprehensive standards and mandatory, nationally applicable regulations mark the transition from the historical structures of the pre-industrial age to the new age of building in the second half of the 19th century.

Typical Elements of Historical Structures

Historical structures are predominantly constructions of timber and stone, where the latter also includes brick. In general, most structural systems can be traced back to two basic subtypes: flexural beam and strut frame structures.

Flexural beams

Flexural beams are simple elements that are designed so that under self-weight, no horizontal force components are produced at the supports, which serve primarily to ensure that vertical loads are accommodated.

In stone construction, the use of flexural beams is constrained by the limited (bending and) tensile stiffness of the material. Large spans are thus not possible; however, flexural beams have enabled the successful creation of sublime structures such as the classic temples of Greek antiquity (Fig. D 1.7). While bending-stressed elements in later stone constructions are usually limited to small-scale architectural elements such as architraves over doors and windows, flexural beam constructs are common in timber construction. Every timber beam ceiling and every girder can be assigned to this type; in roof frames, the rafters as well as the purlins (rafter girders) are bending-stressed elements (Figs. D 1.8, D 1.9).

Strut frame structures

In contrast, strut frame structures are composed of at least two elements joined in such a way that they support one another. The simplest possible strut frame combination, or "couple", comprises two diagonal elements. Under self-weight, furthermore, normal forces parallel to the component directions place the two members under compressive but not flexural stresses. At the ridge, at which the two elements are connected by a hinge, horizontal forces arise that cancel each other out. The bases of the members not only transmit the vertical forces from self-weight and live loads, but the supports are also "driven apart" by outward-acting horizontal thrust forces. [1]

Timber construction

The most common strut frame structure in historical timber construction is the triangular rafter truss in rafter and collar beam roofs (Fig. D 1.11). The bases of the strut couple – i.e. of the rafters – are usually con-

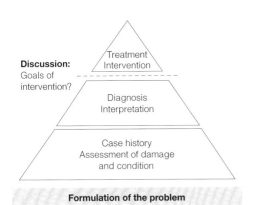

Discussion:
Goals of
intervention?

Treatment
Intervention

Diagnosis
Interpretation

Case history
Assessment of damage
and condition

Formulation of the problem

D 1.10

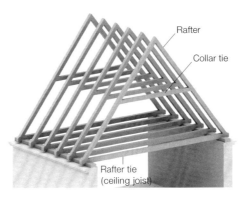

Rafter

Collar tie

Rafter tie
(ceiling joist)

D 1.11

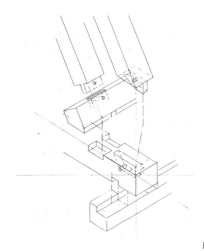

D 1.12

nected via a tension element (e.g. a tie beam or cross tie) such that the horizontal forces there are short-circuited and the walls beneath are subject only to vertical loads. The main challenge in this construction is the point at which the tensile forces are discharged from the rafter base to the tie beam. This joint, the heel, is frequently damaged by penetrating moisture (Figs. D 1.12, D 1.13). More intricate strut frames with multiple interconnected strut ties, often supplemented with vertical tension members from which joists are suspended, are found in all large pitched roofs as well as in historical timber bridges, and also occasionally in the reinforcement of ceiling constructions and in timber scaffolding and timber frame walls.

Stone construction
In stone structures, simple strut frames composed of two individual elements leaned against each other are fairly rare, since the required rod-shaped work pieces

D 1.6   Roof construction open to interpretation: rafter roof with girders or unusually steep purlin roof? Cross section of a historical agricultural building in Ruhpolding, now part of the Glentleiten Open Air Museum (DE)

D 1.7   Stone architrave as a flexural beam over the columns at the Temple of Athena, Paestum (IT)

D 1.8   Schematic representation of a simple purlin roof: rafters, purlins and connecting beams are continuous flexural beams.

D 1.9   Typical purlin roof construction with rafters, purlins and connecting beams as flexural elements; historical agricultural building from Rottach-Egern, now part of the Glentleiten Open Air Museum (DE)

D 1.10   Foundation of the assessment method: three-step process: Case history – Diagnosis – Treatment

D 1.11   Schematic representation of a simple rafter roof with a tier of collar ties. This is a simple strutted frame.

D 1.12   Characteristic heel of a rafter roof, assembly diagram; formerly Antoniterkirche, now Kinderlehrkirche Church, Memmingen (DE)

D 1.13   Typical damage found at the heel points of a rafter roof: Moisture penetration destroying the end of the tie beam.

are very difficult to manufacture. Instead, many individual small stone units were arranged in such a way that here, too, only compressive stresses parallel to the element direction, with as little bending or tension as possible, occur in the overall cross section of the structure. In short: the stones are assembled in the form of an arch. In arches and the more complicated vaults derived from them, tie beams or additional bracing such as flying buttresses, abutments or pilasters take up the horizontal forces generated at the supports.

Responsible Treatment of Historically Listed Constructions

Historical monuments convey important information on many subjects and make associated discoveries possible. They are not only a testament to past events, historical ideas of form and the social fabric of their time, but their material substance also reveals information about manufacturing processes and joining techniques. For these reasons, an overarching responsibility exists to preserve this substance. A form-conserving reconstruction would stand as witness of our time and of our interpretation of the past.

The preservation of historical structures, in particular, is often initially met with certain reservations – on first site inspections, a jovial "If we were to calculate this today, it would collapse immediately" or "That doesn't compute!" are known to be heard. Indeed, the basic structural behaviour of historical constructions is not always immediately apparent, firstly because there is a lack of familiarity with the compositions, but also because the structures one encounters are not easily classifiable into any one specific system. The interpretive ambiguity of the often unspecified structural systems poses one of the greatest challenges to their analysis, but presents an opportunity at

the same time. To certify the structure, it is enough to find one solution among the numerous conceivable load transfer variants in order to confirm the load-bearing capacity of the old building [2].

The counterpart to the basic doubts regarding the computability of historical constructions is the question as to why preservation measures are even necessary: "It's held up all this time – why do we have to do something now?" Of course it is indeed the case that the structures in question have proven their structural stability and longevity over centuries. An overly optimistic reliance on their longevity, however, overlooks the fact that the buildings still standing today merely allow one to make statements about the past, but do not allow one to draw conclusions about the future.

The path to restoration
Historical structures in their existing state are initially "black boxes". Occasionally, design and sometimes even implementation plans exist for more recent objects, but even then, it should not be assumed that the implementation was done according to plan. Older buildings often lack any construction plans whatsoever.
In order for the examination of a historical structure, the subsequent development of

D 1.13

D 1.14

D 1.15

D 1.16

conservation plans and the choice of suitable restoration interventions to be successful, it is critical that the object and its special characteristics are fully understood – only what is known can be preserved. A comparison with a visit to a doctor is quite apt: without a case history (taking stock of condition and recording damage) there can be no diagnosis (analysis of the sources of damage); without a diagnosis, there can be no treatment (restoration) (fig. D 1.10) [3]. When dealing with historical structures, the case history encompasses not only the creation of precise, accurate surveys but also a careful examination of the object's past, a knowledge of the building materials, their characteristics and joining methods as well as the thorough mapping of all phenomena that can be interpreted as damage.
Though the treatment is arrived at directly through the diagnosis, it is possible for several different therapeutic approaches to be based on a particular diagnosis. The interventions arrived at may differ signifi-

cantly from one another depending on how cost, function, visual requirements or a maximal preservation of substance are prioritised. Therefore, in a responsible approach to conservation work, any presentation of recommendations must be preceded by a clear statement of goals. These discussions should involve not only the building client, but also representatives of the historical monuments authorities, regulatory agencies and other disciplines and trade unions relevant to the task. The clarification of the boundary conditions for the desired end result can be a critical factor in the success of a monument-worthy restoration of the structure: what initial load estimates should be chosen? Is it absolutely necessary for a roof framework that was originally designed for wood shingles, for example, to be outfitted now with tiles? Should the initial load estimate for a historical banquet hall really be set at 5 kN/m² as dictated by DIN EN 1991-1-1:2010-12, or can the estimate be lowered given the

limitations on the hall's use?
For historical constructions, particularly in the repair of localised damage to the building substance, there are many established techniques available that must be weighed according to their respective aims. In selecting the appropriate specific repair method, many factors are taken into consideration, including the extent of the damage, its loading in the context of the overall structure, the importance of the element in terms of historical listing, the intended appearance after the work is completed, questions of economics and craftsmanship and the sustainability of the repair as well as that of the resources used. Though the ultimate decision necessarily lies with the client, the planner nevertheless bears the responsibility for presenting a series of options along with their advantages and drawbacks. A simple evaluation matrix can be used to facilitate the identification and discussion of options and document the path to the final decision.

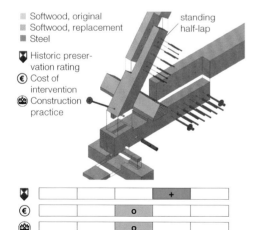

Intervention 1	Tie beam inserted from the front, existing timber notched
Installation conditions	Freely accessible
Historic preservation rating	Intervention minimised
Cost of intervention / economics	Average repair costs per implementation detail
Construction practice	Moderate, some difficulty due to confined space

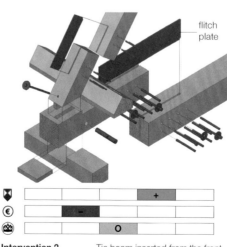

Intervention 2	Tie beam inserted from the front, with flitch plates
Installation conditions	Freely accessible
Historic preservation rating	Intervention minimised
Cost of intervention / economics	Tendency toward high repair costs per implementation detail
Construction practice	Moderate, some difficulty due to confined space

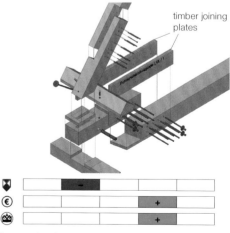

Intervention 3	Tie beam inserted from side, one piece, two timber joining plates
Installation conditions	Freely accessible
Historic preservation rating	Intervention requires additional tampering with original material
Cost of intervention / economics	Tendency toward low repair costs
Construction practice	Good, improved access through infringement on original material

D 1.17

Legend (Intervention 1):
- Softwood, original
- Softwood, replacement
- Steel
- Historic preservation rating
- € Cost of intervention
- Construction practice

standing half-lap

flitch plate

timber joining plates

Monuments are never owned outright, but are simultaneously held in trust for future generations (Fig. D 1.17).

Restoration Strategies for Maximum Preservation of Existing Substance

In the assessment of an historical structure, planners must distinguish between two categories of defect and/or damage: either the construction features fundamental structural flaws and/or localised damage to the substance impacts the effectiveness of an individual load-bearing member. While material damage to individual building components can be documented during a careful initial inspection, not all basic structural flaws can be phenomenologically ascertained. Masonry, for example, can fail suddenly without indicating any conspicuous material damage beforehand (Fig D 1.14). Localised material damage can be related to structural overloads and/or be caused by other defects in construction. The development of cracks and deformations in masonry is usually an indication of a disruption in the load transfer pathways. Salt efflorescence and disintegration, on the other hand, can be traced back to physical and construction-related causes. In timber constructions, gaping joints, breaks or obvious deformations indicate structural problems. Rot, however, results from unintended moisture incursions. Defects in construction could, in turn, be the root cause of comprehensive structural issues. Constant penetration of moisture into masonry leads to a loss of cohesion in the mortar and can significantly lower the compressive strength of the construction. The bottom edge of a roof that has been damaged by rot due to poorly sealed eaves is no longer capable of supporting the horizontal forces that are generated at the bases of the rafters. The base gives way, leading to

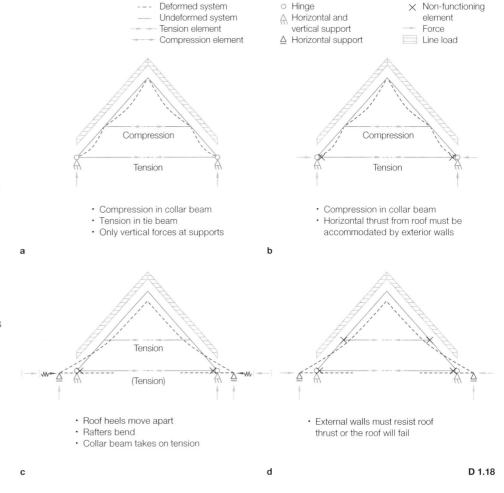

- - - Deformed system
——— Undeformed system
→—→ Tension element
→——→ Compression element
○ Hinge
⩑ Horizontal and vertical support
△ Horizontal support
✕ Non-functioning element
→ Force
▭ Line load

a
Compression
Tension
· Compression in collar beam
· Tension in tie beam
· Only vertical forces at supports

b
Compression
Tension
· Compression in collar beam
· Horizontal thrust from roof must be accommodated by exterior walls

c
Tension
(Tension)
· Roof heels move apart
· Rafters bend
· Collar beam takes on tension

d
· External walls must resist roof thrust or the roof will fail

D 1.18

D 1.14 The sudden failure of a masonry structure under self-weight led to the 1902 collapse of St Mark's Campanile in Venice (IT).
D 1.15 Filling the cracked vault masonry by injection. Stabilisation work at Mainz Cathedral, based on plans by Georg Rüth, 1920–1925
D 1.16 Reinforcement of roof girders through bilateral flanges
D 1.17 Various options for the historically appropriate repair of a typical roof heel detail (damage to the cross tie at the node and at the base of the rafter) with evaluation matrices weighing the historic conservation rating, economic factors and construction practice.

D 1.18 Mechanism of damage and deformation in a rafter roof with damage to the roof heel and/or the tie beam
a Tie beam in place and intact
b Roof heel defective, tie beam defective or absent → outer walls must take up horizontal forces
c Roof heel defective, tie beam defective or absent → outer walls cannot withstand horizontal forces, i.e. give way to the roof thrust
d Roof heel defective, tie beam defective or absent → outer walls cannot withstand horizontal forces → the connection between collar beam and rafter fails

D 1.19

D 1.20

D 1.21

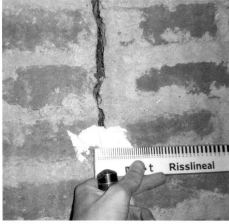

D 1.22

deformations of the roof cross section (Fig. D 1.18 b, c, d, p. 105).

The various damage modes require a differentiated approach. If a thorough structural inspection concludes unequivocally that the entire structure is at risk despite the fact that all individual members are intact, a reinforcement is necessarily in order. Depending on the circumstances, it is possible either to add supplemental bracing constructions that can take up significant loads or to strengthen individual structural members. For example, masonry can be shored up through grouting and reinforcing elements (Fig. D 1.15, p. 104), and timber beams can be spliced (Fig D 1.16, p. 104). Reinforcing individual members is not far from supplementing a subsidiary system. The stabilisation of a masonry wall by needling may still be viewed as a strengthening of the existing substance, but the addition of an anchoring system, in contrast, already represents a significant alteration of the structure. Material damage or overload requires different interventions (Fig. D 1.23). The following options exist for the case of localised damage to a component of the structure:

- Exchange: the entire damaged element is exchanged for a new one of the same type.
- Repair: work is done on the element at the site of the damage. Repair work is always associated with the heterogenisation of the existing element, in which additional nodes and/or connections are created. This in turn can have negative impacts on the load-bearing capacity and may make additional reinforcements necessary.
- Supplementation: the damaged element is rendered inoperable and secured so that no further damage should be expected to occur. Its function in the structural system is taken over by a newly added element.

If a structural element is shown to be overloaded, the approach options are a little different:

- Replacement: the overloaded element is replaced with a member of the same shape but with greater load-bearing capacity.
- Reinforcement: the overloaded element retains its structural function but is reinforced by the addition of stiffening elements (e.g. flitches).
- Supplementation: the overloaded element is rendered inoperable and its load-bearing function is taken over by a newly added structural element.

The complete replacement of parts of a structural system by identically shaped but more stable elements must be viewed critically in the context of historical restoration, since the procedure runs counter to the requisite preservation of as much of the existing substance as possible. English art historian John Ruskin (1819–1900), one of the fathers of modern historical conservation, addressed this concern: "Better a crutch than a lost leg" [4].

Within the supplementation option there are wide-ranging possible actions to take; the appearance and construction of the new structural member can be chosen subjectively in coordination with the other project participants. From the point of view of historical conservation, it is desirable that new building components be incorporated in such a way that their addition remains legible but they do not stand out as foreign bodies – a true challenge for the designer! Another possibility is a partial supplementation, in which the existing elements continue to form substantial portions of the structure but are relieved of their loads through additions (Fig. D 1.20).

In day-to-day practice, repair and/or reinforcement represent the most common option. For this, numerous established solutions using different materials and

D 1.19 Supplemental structure for the support of the domed timber tower of the Maria Loreto parish church, Ramsau (DE)
D 1.20 Stabilisation and reinforcement of beams by partial supplementation through a new girder placed in the floor cavity. Prelate's building, former abbey, Raitenhaslach (DE)
D 1.21 Various repairs adapted to the respective damage conditions of the rafters, with a standing half-lap (left) and a flitch plate (right); formerly Antoniterkirche, now Kinderlehrkirche Church, Memmingen (DE)
D 1.22 Simple monitoring of cracks with a plaster

reference mark and a crack width ruler
D 1.23 Various restoration interventions
   a Stabilisation of the vault in the central nave, former abbey church at Gars am Inn (DE)
   b Stabilisation of the roof framework and hall ceiling, Schloss Ortenburg in Passau (DE)
   c Reinforcement of the roof structure, Wagnerhäusl from Oberratting, now Bauernhausmuseum Amerang (DE)
   d Stabilisation and reinforcement of the roof structure, Basilica of Sts. Peter and Paul, Dillingen an der Donau (DE)

Notes:
[1] Barthel, Rainer; Kayser, Christian: "Sprengwerke und Hängewerke." In: Von Kienlin, Alexander (ed.): *Holztragwerke der Antike. Byzas 11.* Publication of the German Archaeological Institute in Istanbul. Istanbul 2011, p. 39ff.
[2] Heyman, Jacques: *The Stone Skeleton: Structural Engineering of Masonry.* Cambridge 1997
[3] Pieper, Klaus: *Sicherung historischer Bauten.* Munich 1983
[4] Ruskin, John: *The Seven Lamps of Architecture.* London 1849, p. 244
[5] Mader, Gerd Thomas: *Angewandte Bauforschung.* Materialien aus dem Institut für Baugeschichte, Kunstgeschichte, Restaurierung mit Architektur-museum, Technical University of Munich, Department of Architecture. Darmstadt 2005

constructions are available. In the typical example case of a beam that has either broken due to overloading or has been damaged by rot, the beam can be spliced or secured with a flitch plate inserted into a slit in the timber. Localised damage can be addressed by partial replacement using traditional joinery. In addition to the afore-mentioned options, half-lap joints can be used to form the connection to the original components (Fig. D 1.21).

If it cannot be established whether the source of damage is ongoing, it is possible – as long as any danger to traffic or stability is ruled out – to implement a monitoring routine (Fig. D 1.22). This is a much less expensive option than restoration work, and may shed light not only on the basic need for intervention but also on the type of restoration measures required: are com-prehensive measures for the removal of the source of damage necessary, or is it sufficient merely to remove the symptoms left behind by a now-defunct mechanism? It is important to take into account that a conclusive monitoring process should be kept in place over several years, thus requiring a certain amount of patience on the part of planners and building clients.

Specialist for the Protection of Historical Monuments – A Job Advertisement

The inspection and restoration of historical structures confront the planner with spe-cial challenges [5]. Ideally, planners have superior mastery over contemporary stan-dards and regulations and possess well-grounded knowledge of historical structures and historical architectural context. The ability to collaborate effectively with members of other specialised disciplines and to be open in discussions is as necessary as the will-ingness to keep learning throughout one's lifetime. One should not shrink from the dirt

in old attics, should be able to explain com-plex interrelationships clearly even to lay-men, and must be ready to take economic factors into account in one's plans. Would anyone respond to such a job advertise-ment? And, as if that weren't enough, per-sons engaged in work on historical struc-tures must always keep in mind that they are acting in service to something: the star here is not the planner, but the object itself. The monument is there to last – historical conservation merely serves to ensure that it does – because the history of construction begins yesterday and must not be allowed to end today.

a

c

b

d

D 1.23

Bridges with Extreme Spans

Jan Akkermann

Functionality and Form

The form and structure of bridges are highly correlated with their functionality. Bridges span obstacles (e.g. valleys, rivers, transportation routes) while simultaneously functioning as a means of transfer themselves (e.g. as roads, railways, pedestrian and bicycle paths).

When building bridges, the following factors must be considered [1]:
• Topography and geology
• Environment and sustainability
• Economic viability
• Administrative procedures
• Sociocultural context

The selection of suitable building materials and methods occurs in close connection with the criteria named above and the chosen structural typology. The technological opportunities of the digital age and the improvements in building with steel and concrete have opened up new pathways in bridge construction. Founded on the basic structural principles of tensile, compressive and bending stresses, forms can be refined and complex geometries realised.

Material

Contemporary materials provide new design options in bridge construction, in terms of both strength as well as connection technology. Modern steel structures typically employ high-strength S 355 steel in welded constructions. Heavy-duty individual elements are made with very high-strength S 460 steel. Complex geometries also partially comprise cast building components. Concretes with greater strength of up to C 80 are currently undergoing application testing. High-strength wires with a tensile strength of 1,770 N/mm^2 provide a proven material from which bridge cables and tendons can be produced.

In addition to strength, a critical factor of materials is their longevity. Bridges are often exposed to extreme climatic conditions. Adverse experiences with structures of the post-war era confirm the importance of this requirement. Apart from appropriate concrete formulations and corrosion protection coatings, maintenance management becomes extremely important. Modern large-span bridges feature inspection access points and targeted maintenance programmes [2]. Steel elements are protected by active systems such as cathodic corrosion protection and dehumidifying aggregates.

The bridge equipment (for example, bearings, expansion joints and railings) is likewise designed for maximum longevity and scheduled replacements are planned for the end of the components' service life. Increasingly, in a bid to avoid the need for the latter, integral or semi-integral bridges (that is, bridges with few or no bearings) are being developed in which the constraints due to temperature and subsidence must be particularly considered in the structural design.

Implementation

The construction of complex bridges requires complicated auxiliary structures that necessitate their own intensive structural design. Possible construction methods and the bridge design are thus mutually dependent:
• Constructions in the cantilever method, i.e. successive horizontal construction additions at the forward end of the structure which are generally overhanging, require a balancing of the building conditions with the structural form. In some cases, additional guying is necessary (applications: girder bridges, arch bridges, cable-stayed bridges).
• In the incremental launching method, in

D 2.1 Cross section with localised transverse reinforcement, Kocher Viaduct BAB 6 in Geislingen am Kocher (DE) 1979, Fritz Leonhardt
D 2.2 Kocher Viaduct BAB 6 in Geislingen am Kocher (DE) 1979, Fritz Leonhardt

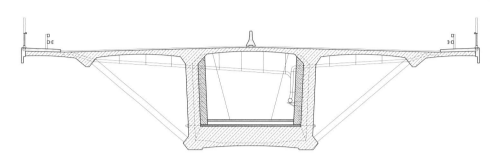

which bridge segments are prefabricated at one or both bridge abutments and then successively attached and pushed over the piers, the bridge underside must be level. The spans must be such that they can be managed by the temporarily cantilevered forward sections during the launching process (application: girder bridges).
- Prefabricated (partial) segments and building components can be lifted in or floated in over water if the conditions allow (applications: suspension and cable-stayed bridges, sometimes girder bridges).
- Vertical or slightly slanted building components are built using climbing formwork (applications: bridge piers, pylons).
- Foundation types depend on the foundation conditions as well as the support loads, and therefore on the spans.

Design

Bridges with extreme spans in particular are structures that can be seen from afar. As landmarks they are expressions of building culture (Fig. D 2.2). Only a cooperative effort by structural engineers, architects and landscape designers can vouchsafe the creation of high-quality and sustainable bridge structures.

Example Typologies

Traditionally, bridges can be classified into types by their structural behaviour in response to compressive, tensile and/or bending stresses.

Bending
Even though the interplay of bending moment and transverse and normal forces make flexurally stressed structures the most statically complex type, to date they

nevertheless represent the most common structural form of bridges. The usually straight-line geometry of the transportation route to be conveyed and the regulation-determined cross sections of the carriageways favour the straightest-possible design, with a lower limit on the radii of curvature for route and gradient. While transportation services have strict guidelines for rail and vehicular traffic, the choices of geometries for pedestrian and bicycle bridges are far less restrictive. Nevertheless, even here designers must take into account the demands of accessibility and traffic safety when determining maximum inclines and minimum radii. In addition, deformation and stiffness requirements arising from fitness for purpose and driving dynamics must be met. In general, the deck beam is thus usually designed as a bending-resistant girder structure.

The efficiency of girder bridges with regard to deformation and structural behaviour is determined by reconciling the height of the structure, the material distribution over the cross section and the span length. To facili-

tate a cost-effective construction process, for example in the incremental launch or cantilever construction method of steel and reinforced concrete bridges, constant-depth or lightly haunched beams and uniform spans are preferred because they can be manufactured in series.

In the case of the Kocher Viaduct, whose bridge piers of up to 178 m height were the tallest in the world until 2004, this principle was perfected for 138-m long free spans. The hollow box girder cross section with a cantilevered slab (deck width of 31 m including both cantilevers) and a uniform height of 6.50 m was built in just three years using the cantilever construction method with jacked formwork girders. The box girder walls, which in some places are only 50 cm thick, attest to the optimisation during that time of prestressed concrete construction. In 2016, basic repairs of the structure were completed. With the help of up-to-date computer simulations of the original force flows, it was possible to adapt the now historically listed structure to modern-day loads merely by installing minimally invasive

D 2.3 Largest girder span in the world, new Shibanpo
Bridge, Chongqing (CN) 2006, T. Y. Lin Inter-
national Group
    a Section showing spans
    b View
D 2.4 Ikitsuki Bridge connecting the islands of Ikitsuki
and Hirado (JP) 1991, Nagasaki Prefectural
Road Public Corporation
D 2.5 Kienlesbergbrücke, Ulm (DE) 2018, Knight
Architects, Krebs+Kiefer Ingenieure
    a Pedestrian and bicycle path along the
       longitudinal beam
    b Elevation and span lengths (north-south
       longitudinal beam)
    c Asymmetrical cross section of axis 50
    d View

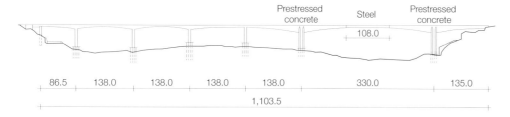

				Prestressed concrete	Steel	Prestressed concrete	
					108.0		
86.5	138.0	138.0	138.0	138.0	330.0		135.0

1,103.5

a

b   **D 2.3**

D 2.4

built-in components in the box girder
and replacing the bearings (Fig. D 2.1,
p. 109) [3].
Haunching the cross section, i.e. enlarging
the height of the superstructure in the vicinity of the supports, makes possible a cost-
effective lengthening of the spans to about
50 times the structural height. In this way,
girder bridges with single spans of up to
330 m are created, as seen for example
in the new Shibanpo Bridge in Chongqing
(Fig. D 2.3 b). Thanks to a mixed construction with a central hollow box girder segment of steel, it was possible to double the
span of the neighbouring old bridge over
the Yangtze, built in 1980 (Fig. D 2.3 a).
The opening-up of flexural beam structures
into trusses (usually of steel) has been
established since the era of industrialisation
in the 19th century. Currently, steel truss
bridges usually feature a trough-shaped
cross section with the traffic deck on the
inside. This allows the structural height of
the truss to be fully exploited and guaran-
tees high structural stiffness, for example
for rail traffic. An well-known example is the
Ikitsuki Bridge in Japan, built in 1991, with a
main span length of 400 m (Fig. D 2.4). The
top chord of the truss is cambered upwards
over the intermediate supports and thus
forms the bending moment curve of a three-
span girder.
In principle, even non-uniform span lengths
and complex ground plan geometries
may be carried out with girder bridges,
which leads to special structural forms.
The structure of the Kienlesbergbrücke in
Ulm (Fig. D 2.5 d), a bridge for the tramway
and for pedestrian and bicycle paths that
was designed to span the railway triangle
of Ulm's main station, derives its form above
all from the non-uniformity of its slightly
curved footprint as well as the highly varied
placement of the piers [4]. Both were prede-
termined by the constraints, the routing
of the tram rails on the bridge and the positions of the spanned railway lines below it.

a

The design of the bridge responds to this extreme heterogeneity with a steel structure that is asymmetrical in its cross section as well as along its length (Fig. D 2.5 c). The wave form of the longitudinal girders accommodates the moment stresses of the five-span beam, the spans of which vary from 33.90 m to 74.50 m (Fig. D 2.5 b). The inner longitudinal girder is subject to greater stresses because the pedestrian and bicycle path runs along only one side of the bridge and therefore has a greater static height. In order to lend this especially tall (5.90-m high) section a more transparent appearance, the steel box girders, hermetically welded to protect against corrosion, are arranged with slanted struts to form what is known as a Vierendeel (or rigid frame) truss (Fig. C 1.118, p. 92; Fig. D 2.5 a). The longitudinal offset of the waves is a consequence of the fact that the axes of the piers are constrained by the underlying tracks to run diagonal to the bridge axis. The bridge design is inhomogeneous yet reflects the flow of the forces. Thanks to modern steel welding techniques during prefabrication and on site, it was successfully implemented using the incremental launch method. The high-strength S 460 structural steel piers are thus welded rigidly to the superstructure and thereby stabilise the semi-integral construction.

Compression

In the early years of civil engineering, building materials limited to compressive stresses (primarily natural stone and brick) led bridge structures from antiquity on to take on a variety of arch shapes. Only the introduction of steel trusses in the mid 1800s, as well as reinforced and prestressed concrete in the early 20th century, allowed for the development of significant spans. In contrast to historical arch bridges with solid filled-in spandrels between the roadway on the top surface and the abutments (springers) at the arch ends, the bridge decks of

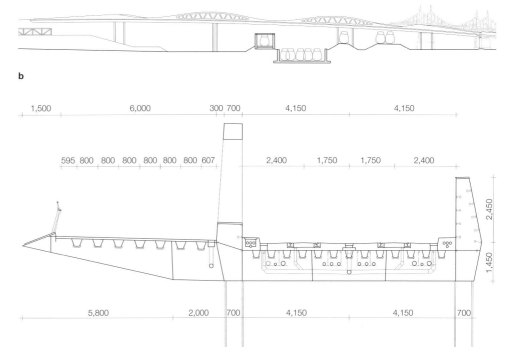

b

c

d

D 2.6 Titan RT suspended rope bridge, Rappbode Dam, Oberharz am Brocken (DE) 2017, Aste Weisssteiner
D 2.7 Almonte railway bridge, near Cáceres (ES) 2016, Arenas & Asociados, IDOM
   a Section, scale 1:8,000
   b Schematic view of arch underside,1:4,000
   c Arch cross sections, scale 1:1,000
   d View
D 2.8 Lupu Bridge, Shanghai (CN) 2003, Shanghai Municipal Engineering Design Institute
D 2.9 Dreiländerbrücke (Three Countries Bridge), Weil am Rhein (DE) 2007, Dietmar Feichtinger Architectes
   a Elevation and bridge layout, 1:2,500
   b Cross section details, scale 1:75
   c View

D 2.6

today, in the form of flexural beams, are relieved of loading by uprights on the arches in order to save on self-weight. Thus, the flatter the arch, the greater the horizontal forces acting on the springers. While these horizontal forces are carried off by the abutments in arches with elevated roadways, suspended decks located below the arches can short-circuit the forces, so to speak (arch-supported beam).

The Almonte railway bridge, built for the Lisbon-Madrid high-speed rail line, crosses the Alcántara reservoir with an arch span of 384 m (Fig. D 2.7 d) [5]. For reasons of aerodynamics the reinforced concrete arch is slightly chamfered, giving it an octagonal cross section; for stability it is splayed at the abutments (Fig. D 2.7 c). The construction of the arch proceeded from the abutments using the cantilever method with stay cables running from support pylons on the bridge piers. The topside deck of the high-speed rail line is a conventional prestressed concrete hollow box girder that was built above the closed arch by means of a formwork carriage.

With most modern arch bridges, steel arches are used – especially in the case of suspended decks. The 100-m high Lupu Bridge in Shanghai, to date the largest bridge of this kind with compact steel arches, crosses the Huangpu River with a span length of 550 m (Fig. D 2.8); its splayed arches are connected to one another via transverse beams for stability. An orthotropic steel plate – a grid composed of primary and secondary beams – forms the deck of the bridge, beneath which a 46-m high clearance for ships remains. Since the deck beam lies above the springers, the horizontal forces on the springers are taken up by the overhanging arch segments on both sides. While the portion of the deck beam beneath the arches is suspended by steel cables, the sections outside the arches rest on piers. 118 steel piers with diameters of 0.90 m and heights

996

| 36 | 45 | 45 | 45 | 45 | 45 | 384 | 45 | 45 | 45 | 45 | 45 | 45 | 45 | 36 |

| 45 | 42 | 42 | 42 | 42 | 42 | 42 | 42 | 45 |

a

b

| 19.00 | 10.94 | 6.48 | 6.00 | 6.48 | 10.94 | 19.00 |

6.90   6.90

c

d   **D 2.7**

D 2.8

of 65 m carry the great structural loads into the critical subsoil of the river delta. The principle of a short-circuited deck beam extended out beyond the springers was also used in the Dreiländerbrücke (Three Countries Bridge) in Weil am Rhein. Thanks to its span length of 229 m over the Rhine River, it is currently the longest pedestrian and bicycle bridge in the world (Fig. D 2.9 c). The very flat arch has a rise of only 20 m and consists of one upright element and an element that is asymmetrically canted toward it (Fig. D 2.9 a, b). The horizontal springer forces that this generates at right angles to the arch axis are short-circuited via a shaft at the abutments in order to ensure a statically determinate support. Despite its extreme slenderness, in a real experiment involving more than 800 people it gave no indication of a tendency to oscillate [6].

Tension

While building components under compression are limited in material strength as well as stability, tension elements can be structurally fully exploited. The most efficient structural use therefore necessitates a tension-resistant material. Such material used in the case of suspension bridges allows for the transfer of vertical loads from self-weight and usage over a horizontal distance. This stipulates a sufficient ratio between the sag of the suspension cable and the distance between the endpoints of the curve in order to avoid extreme horizontal tensile forces.

With the rope bridge, the archetype of the suspension bridge, the roadway follows the rope curvature. Modern applications of this are generally limited to footbridges, preferably in natural settings. The Titan RT, a rope suspension bridge which spans 458.50 m, is one of the longest in the world. Running parallel to the dam wall of the Rappbode Dam in the Harz mountains, the 1.20-m wide footbridge is an attraction

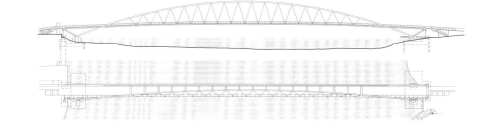

a

1 North arch
2 South arch, steel tube
3 Transverse tie
4 Open spiral strand suspension
5 North longitudinal girder

6 South longitudinal girder, steel tube
7 Transverse beam, bottom chord of footbridge
8 Trapezoidal puncheon cover plate
9 Puncheon
10 Railing

b

c

D 2.9

D 2.10

D 2.11

that draws hikers and adventure tourists (Fig. D 2.6, p. 112). The walkway, which possesses no inherent rigidity, is suspended from the four main 65-mm diameter bearer cables, which are anchored 27 m deep into solid rock. The bridge is stabilised against wind-induced swaying by two lateral bracing cables of opposing curvature beneath the bridge.

With suspension bridges, pylons typically supply the necessary sag of the suspension cables by redirecting them. The bridge deck is geometrically decoupled from the catenary curve of the cables and maintains its connection to them via hangers. The flexural stiffness of the deck beam, which behaves like a continuous flexural beam with short spans, equalises non-uniform loads and stabilises the bridge against wind forces. The suspension cables are

anchored to the ground via abutment piers at the end of the bridge. For almost 100 years, this structural concept has made the creation of some of the greatest spans in the world possible. To date, the Akashi Kaikyo Bridge in Japan, built in 1998, holds the world record with a 1,991-m span between its pylons; this record will presumably be broken in 2022 by the 2,023-m span of the Çanakkale 1915 Bridge across the Dardanelles in Turkey. The 1,624-m span of the Great Belt Bridge connects the Danish islands of Funen and Zealand. Since the main bridge lies in the middle of the Baltic Sea, its structural concept is especially apparent (Fig. D 2.10). Two reinforced concrete pylons 281 m in height, of which 254 m is above the water, redirect the two main cable bundles. Two A-shaped trestles, placed on floated-in cais-

sons with footprints of 121.50 × 54.50 m, anchor the suspension cables in the ground. In the centre of the bridge, the suspension cables impinge on the deck beam, a steel hollow box girder, below which the ship clearance is 70 m. This arrangement achieves a cable sag of approximately one tenth of the span, which is considered a cost-effective use of the cable materials. A significant load on suspension bridges is the wind, in response to which the deck beam is equipped with an aerodynamic cross section.

The idea of combining the curving main cables and the vertical hangers to establish a direct connection between deck beam and pylon was first floated in the 19th century. However, the stayed-cable bridge structure did not establish itself until the second half of the 20th century. The advantage of this construction type is that an appropriate arrangement of the cables allows for direct transfer of the horizontal cable forces through the deck beam, obviating the need for the expensive and complicated anchoring of the main cables. However, an anchoring cable to the bridge abutments is usually required for stabilisation and in order to accommodate asymmetrical loads. Much as with girder bridges, the self-stabilising system ensures that essentially only vertical

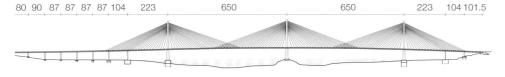

80 90   87 87 87 87 104   223   650   650   223   104 101.5

a

b

D 2.12

D 2.10 Great Belt Bridge, Funen / Zealand (DK) 1998, COWI, Ramboll
D 2.11 Russky Bridge, Vladivostok (RU) 2012, SIC Mostovik
D 2.12 Queensferry Crossing over the Firth of Forth in Scotland, near Edinburgh (GB) 2017, Arup, Jacobs Engineering
        a Cable layout
        b View
D 2.13 Ortenau Bridge, Lahr (DE) 2018, Henchion + Reuter, EiSat
        a Cross section, mid-span area
        b View
D 2.14 Yavuz Sultan Selim Bridge, near Istanbul (TR) 2016, Michel Virlogeux, Jean-François Klein
D 2.15 Sunniberg Bridge, Klosters (CH) 1998, Christian Menn, Dialma Jakob Bänziger

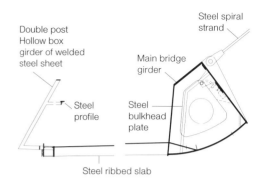

Double post
Hollow box girder of welded steel sheet
Steel profile
Steel ribbed slab
Main bridge girder
Steel bulkhead plate
Steel spiral strand

a

loads of a significant magnitude occur at the supports. The efficiency of the direct suspension of the deck beam, which here, too, features flexural stiffness, drops rapidly with increasing distance from the pylon due to the flatly inclined cables. Firstly, for geometric reasons the horizontal components of the cable forces become ever greater; and secondly, the self-weight of the cables causes them to take on an increasing sag.

The greatest free span achieved worldwide is the 1,104-m distance between the pylons of the Russky Bridge in Vladivostok (Fig. D 2.11). The harp-like cable pairs arranged along the height of the pylon support the deck beam to the middle of the bridge.

The Queensferry Crossing in Scotland compensates for the negative effect of the flat stay cables by overlapping them at midspan (Fig. D 2.12). The middle of the three pylons segmenting the bridge into two main spans of 650 m each was successfully stabilised through the cable layout and did not require a back stay (Fig. D 2.12a) [7]. Using the historical example of the 1883 Brooklyn Bridge in New York, planners are once again adopting hybrid suspension and cable-stayed bridge concepts. In the middle third of the Yavuz Sultan Selim Bridge, designed for both motor vehicle and rail transit over the Bosphorus, hangers at the inner edge of the roadway, directly adjacent to the central railway track, connect the suspension cables with the bridge deck (Fig. D 2.14) [8]. To stabilise the main span of 1,408 m – the largest in the world for a railway bridge – additional stay cables were fastened on both outside edges of the deck over the first third of the span. In this way, overly shallow-angle stay cables were avoided.

When the route has a curved layout, pylons are usually placed outside of the bridge axis and slanted to ensure an efficient transfer of compression forces. This stylistically

pleasing construction is often employed for pedestrian bridges that contribute to landscape or urban design. It is featured in the Ortenau Footbridge in Lahr, which spans about 120 m (Fig. D 2.13b). The curvature-induced torsional moment generated in the beam, which has a box girder cross section and a one-sided deck plate cantilever, is centred by stay cables attached eccentrically to the transverse cross section of the bridge (Fig. D 2.13a). Two guy cables stabilise the sculptural leaning pylon. Another hybrid form can be found in the so-called extradosed bridges, in which continuous girder bridges are stayed by external tendons above the intermediate supports. Though this construction type appears at first glance to be a cable-stayed bridge, the difference is that its vertical load transfer incorporates a significant flexural component. The stay cables serve primarily to relieve the support moments. A prominent example is the Sunniberg Bridge in Klosters, where it was possible to realise both a curvature in the bridge plan but also very slender deck plates (Fig. D 2.15) [9].

Notes:
[1] Mehlhorn, Gerhard; Curbach, Manfred (eds.): *Handbuch Brücken*. Wiesbaden 2015
[2] Kracke, Ernst-August; Lodde, Klaus: *Leitfaden Straßenbrücken: Entwurf, Baudurchführung, Erhaltung*. Bauingenieur-Praxis. Berlin 2011
[3] Angelmaier, Volkhard: "Baudenkmal vor dem Abbruch bewahrt – Ertüchtigung der Kochertalbrücke Geislingen." In: *Bundesingenieurkammer: Ingenieurbaukunst 2017*. Berlin 2016, p. 110–117
[4] Akkermann, Jan; Halaczek, Bartlomiej: "Kienlesbergbrücke Ulm." In: *structure 3*, 2018, p. 20–25
[5] Beade-Pereda, Héctor: Almonte HRS Viaduct, 2020 hectorbeade.com/bridge/almonte-hsr-viaduct/
[6] Stahlbau Zentrum Schweiz: "Drei Länder – eine Brücke." In: *steeldoc* 03/2008, p. 16–19
[7] Romberg, Martin: "Neue Queensferry Brücke in Schottland." In: *Bautechnik 94*, 02/2017, p. 93–103
[8] Klein, Jean-François: "Third Bosphorus Bridge – A masterpiece of sculptural engineering." *Stahlbau 86*, 02/2017, p. 160–166
[9] Menn, Christian: "Baukultur im Brückenbau." In: *Baukultur* 03/1998, p. 25–29

b   D 2.13

D 2.14

D 2.15

Structures for Tall Buildings

Maria E. Moreyra Garlock

For most people the terms high-rise, skyscraper and tall building are interchangeable. In this chapter, however, the term "tall buildings" will be used, following the definition given by the renowned Chicago-based Council on *Tall Buildings and Urban Habitat (CTBUH)*. But what is the definition of a "tall building"? According to the American National Fire Protection Association (NFPA), a high-rise is defined as a building that is more than 75 feet (22.86 metres or roughly seven storeys) in height, a measure relevant to firefighters seeking access from the outside [1]. On the other hand, the CTBUH states that "there is no absolute definition of what constitutes a 'tall building;' the definition is subjective, considered against one or more of the following categories…" [2]. These categories, which are explained further on the CTBUH website, are:

- height relative to surroundings
- proportion
- embracing technologies relevant to tall buildings
- supertall (300+ metres) and megatall (600+ metres) buildings.

In terms of structural design, the last two categories have particular relevance, since for these the building height necessitates structural design considerations and innovations.

Historical Development of the Tall Building

The concept of tall structures has been around since the time of the great pyramids and is even represented in the Old Testament account of the Tower of Babel. But it was not until the late 1800s that these tall buildings were "engineered" – meaning that their construction was no longer a product of a trial-and-error method drawing on the aid of simple mathematical principles, but rather one based on structural calculations. David Billington [3], who based some of his arguments on the scholarship of Carl Condit [4], traced the origins of the modern tall building to Chicago following the great fire of 1871. This fire burned about nine square kilometres of the city to the ground. Thanks to its location in the Midwest on the shore of one of the Great Lakes, Chicago had grown since the 1840s into a railway hub and a centre of commerce. Buildings had been built at a furious pace without much regard to fire protection. Thus the wood and iron infrastructure, which had almost no resistance to fire, was highly vulnerable. After the Great Fire, enormous sums were invested in the reconstruction of this booming economic powerhouse.

Chicago now became an experimental architectural playing field, and the timely and novel invention of the elevator made the erection of even taller structures possible. The architects whose new style came to characterise the city were known as the First Chicago School, the most notable representatives of which included William Le Baron Jenney, John Wellborn Root and Louis Sullivan. The basic foundation of the new building style was the steel skeleton (Fig. D 3.1). This allowed for larger windows and dematerialised the outer walls so that more light could enter the space. The fact that, thanks to the steel framework, these walls no longer needed to fulfil a load-bearing function presented the architects with completely new design opportunities. The dematerialisation of the outer walls is reminiscent of the style of Gothic cathedrals. Billington [5] and Conduit [6] also take the view that the architects of the First Chicago School were influenced by the Gothic cathedral and by the teachings and writings of Eugene Viollet-le-Duc. The novel heights and expression of vertical-

D 3.1

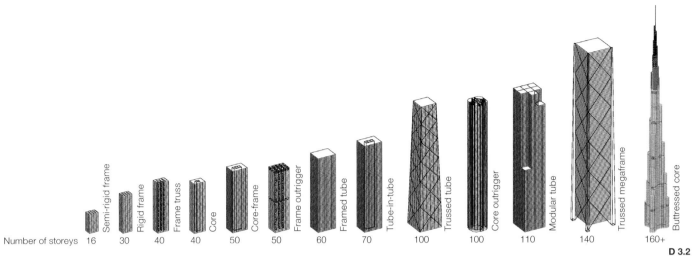

Number of storeys — Semi-rigid frame 16 | Rigid frame 30 | Frame truss 40 | Core 40 | Core-frame 50 | Frame outrigger 50 | Framed tube 60 | Tube-in-tube 70 | Trussed tube 100 | Core outrigger 100 | Modular tube 110 | Trussed megaframe 140 | Buttressed core 160+

D 3.2

ity are further points in common. Gothic cathedrals were the tall buildings of their time and express the spirit, the style and the economic state of a community. Structural innovations such as the ribbed vault and the flying buttress were the developments that made the completely new heights and the large windows and openings of Gothic cathedrals possible at all.

While the invention of the elevator permitted the vertical expansion of tall buildings, there were no major innovations in structural systems – the means by which buildings carry gravitational and lateral loads to the foundations. Billington notes that "for 16-storey buildings the engineering stimulus was too slight to call forth any major imaginative structural art" [7]. The design of such buildings was still determined primarily by gravity, not by wind or seismic loads.

With increasing height, the horizontal loads such as those due to wind or earthquakes begin to control the design of a tall building. For supertall buildings, the upper storeys' lateral displacement and transverse accelerations become significant influencers in the structural system selection. However, the optimal design solutions for wind loads are often unsuited to seismic loading. For example, adding stiffness to the building lowers the dynamic wind forces, but also reduces the building's ability to accommodate seismic forces. Ductility is an important consideration for seismic design since it is assumed that the material will yield permanently in a large earthquake. At the same time, the structure must be stiff enough to resist wind loads. Given the complex inter-relationships that arise when lateral forces control the design of a building, innovations in structural engineering became essential not only for stability, but also for efficiency and economic reasons.

Tall Building Innovations of the 20th Century

Structural engineer Fazlur Khan is arguably one of the greatest minds among tall building designers of the 20th century. He published numerous works on his projects and ideas, which today facilitate a scientific analysis of his structures and shed light on his design philosophy. A comprehensive bibliography of his writings can be found in a monograph published by his daughter, Yasmin Khan [8]. Further prominent engineers and pioneers of this field include Leslie E. Robertson [9] and William F. ("Bill") Baker [10].

Khan began his career working at the Chicago-based architecture firm Skidmore, Owings and Merrill (SOM), where he developed innovative structures for tall buildings in collaboration with architects Bruce Graham and Myron Goldsmith. In his 1953 master's thesis, Goldsmith made the following analogy about bridges: as the span gets longer, the engineer must seek different structural systems. For example, a span of 30 metres can be bridged with a truss, but a span of 1,000 metres will require a completely different structural system such as a sus-

pension bridge. The same concept can be applied to tall buildings: different heights require different structural systems to carry the vertical and horizontal loads efficiently (Fig. D 3.2). Stacked rigid frames can only be used for heights up to about 30 storeys. Anything taller will require very long beams and columns, and more effective structural systems should be considered. The cost drivers of added height are not vertical loads so much as the lateral wind loads, since wind pressure grows with increasing height (Fig. D 3.3). This rise in cost due to wind is what Khan referred to as "premium for height". The "ideal system" is one in which the increase in cost with an increasing number of storeys is controlled entirely by vertical load – as though the building were protected by a glass dome. The cost increase for traditional structures, however, follows the dashed line in Fig. D 3.3, which shows that the cost of

D 3.1 Wainwright Building, St. Louis, Missouri (US) 1891, Louis Sullivan
D 3.2 Tall building structural systems and their efficiency limit by number of storeys
D 3.3 Fazlur Khan's depiction of the unit cost of tall buildings as a function of height

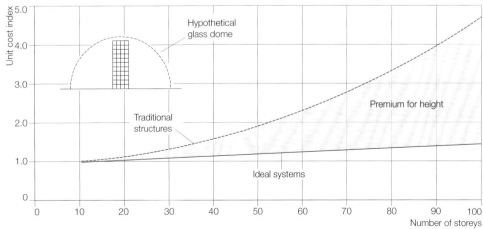

D 3.3

D 3.4

D 3.5

a building rises precipitously with the number of storeys due to of wind forces.

To overcome this height-related explosive cost increase, innovations in structural systems were needed. When Khan began his design of the Brunswick Building in 1961, he recognised that the closely spaced columns on the perimeter would naturally contribute to resisting lateral loads (Fig. D 3.7, p. 120). It had been assumed up until this point that only the walls surrounding the interior core of the structure (the shear walls, or inner "tube") would carry lateral loads. This concept of the perimeter frame that could transmit horizontal and vertical loads was refined in the DeWitt Chestnut apartment building. The 42-storey building, completed in 1964, features a perimeter column spacing of less than 1.70 metres (Fig. D 3.4). The structural system of closely spaced columns can be thought of as a concrete tube, comprising the four outer walls with holes punched in it for windows. If the columns are close together, the tubular structure on the perimeter is stiff and strong enough to carry the wind loads. This "framed tube" structural system (Fig. D 3.2, p. 117), made possible taller buildings without the need for interior columns or shear walls. Further, the example of the DeWitt Chestnut showed that the framed tube was both structure and architectural element – meaning that the structure informs the aesthetics of the building.

The idea of visually expressing the structure in tall buildings was not appreciated by everyone. For example, when the John Hancock Center (now renamed 875 North Michigan Avenue) in Chicago was completed in 1970, one critic called it "an ugly steel-braced colossus" [11] (Fig. D 3.5). Such criticism is evocative of the Eiffel Tower, which was fiercely disparaged as

"monstrous" and "ridiculous" by notable artists in its own day [12]. Nevertheless, both the John Hancock Center and the Eiffel Tower are now symbols of innovative concepts designed to express how the structure carries the wind load. The structural system of the John Hancock Center is known as a "trussed tube" (Fig. D 3.2, p. 117). The idea was developed by Khan and Goldsmith while they were advising graduate students at the Illinois Institute of Technology. With this system, the columns and diagonal struts on the perimeter carry all of the wind load and a large portion of the vertical load. The diagonal elements allow for a local redistribution of the column forces such that all columns on any given floor are of the same size. The column sizes are greatest directly above the foundations and decrease with every storey in height.

The Bank of China Tower in Hong Kong, a product of a collaboration between the structural engineer Leslie E. Robertson and the architect I. M. Pei, has a similar appearance to the John Hancock Center (Fig. D 3.6). While the Bank of China Tower highlights the corner columns and diagonals, unlike the John Hancock Center it does not express all the major structural elements such as the perimeter columns and ties. This is not to point out that one version is better than the other, but merely to illustrate different means of expressing structure in tall buildings. Structurally, these buildings represent different systems, although they both use a perimeter brace. The John Hancock Center is a "trussed tube", while the Bank of China Tower is a "trussed megaframe" (Fig. D 3.2, p. 117).

The concept of a trussed megaframe is based on transferring the loads from the perimeter columns to the megadiagonal at the exact point where the columns rest on the diagonal. The megadiagonals in turn transfer this load to the megacolumns at the building corners. In this way, all of the loads end up being carried by the corner megacolumns. The forces can be redirected in such a way by playing with the axial stiffness of each element. For example, at the column-diagonal interface, the column below the megadiagonal is much less rigid than the one above. Furthermore, the megadiagonal has a very large axial stiffness. Since the force follows the path of greatest stiffness, the vertical load from the column resting on the diagonal is transferred into the megadiagonal.

The structural form of the Bank of China Tower is very efficient and economical. Despite its great height and exposure to strong winds, the construction costs came in under budget. The success of this structural system is based not only on the construction itself but also on a material innovation – a composite of steel and concrete. The megadiagonals are concrete-filled steel tubes, and the megacolumns comprise several steel columns which are connected to the steel diagonals and then encased in concrete in groups. Only the combination of concrete and steel made this cost-effective construction with the requisite strength and stiffness possible. The concept of directing the forces through the form and stiffness of the elements is the basis for the principle encapsulated in the expression "function follows form".

Function Follows Form

Billington put forward a thesis stating that the best examples of successful structural designs – structural art, i.e. the art of the engineer – are characterised by efficiency, economy and elegance [13]. He writes that "the first principle of structural art is that the form controls the forces. In general terms, this means that function follows form and

not the reverse, which had been so appealing as a principle to writers on building in the nineteenth century" [14]. Using the example of the Eiffel Tower, he explains what effect the form has on acting wind loads. The 'transparency' of the structural frame, plus the narrowing of the form, reduce the impact of the wind on the structure. In turn, the forces induced by the wind on the structure also influence the form: the wider the legs of the Eiffel Tower are spread apart, the smaller the forces in the legs become. There is a similar situation in the world's tallest building, the Burj Khalifa, built in 2010 in Dubai. Here, the height is so extraordinary that the dynamic effects of the wind needed to be carefully considered. The form of the tower is designed to "confuse the wind" so that wind vortices do not have a chance to develop [15]. In other words, the form heavily influences how the structure functions under wind loads.

Another application of the principle that forces can be controlled through form is found in the redistribution of column loads into the more widely spaced columns at street level. As mentioned earlier in the case of the Bank of China, forces follow the path of greatest stiffness, which means that the flow of forces can be controlled by creating a rigid path. The framed tube structural system is based on closely spaced columns on the building perimeter. At the ground floor, however, the column spacing must be increased for functional reasons. The loads must therefore be distributed to the more widely spaced column grid before they reach the ground floor level.

D 3.4 DeWitt Chestnut Apartment Building, Chicago (US) 1965, SOM, Fazlur Khan, Bruce Graham
D 3.5 John Hancock Center (now 875 North Michigan Avenue), Chicago (US) 1970, Bruce Graham, Fazlur Khan, SOM
D 3.6 Bank of China Tower, Hong Kong (HK) 1990, Leslie E. Robertson, I. M. Pei

Figures D 3.7 to D 3.10 (p. 120f.) compare two means of achieving this transfer: a direct method and a gradual method, the latter of which is based on controlling the forces through the stiffness of the structure. In the Brunswick building (1965) in Chicago, also designed by Khan, the load transfer takes place via a high beam (Fig. D 3.7, p. 120). A further innovation by Khan is featured in the Two Shell Plaza in Houston, built in 1972 (Fig. D 3.8, p. 120). Here, a series of haunched beams sitting on top of one another are employed to transmit the forces. A haunched beam has a greater depth in the vicinity of the supports than at

D 3.6

120

a

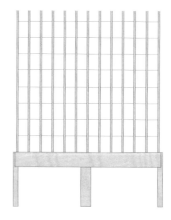

b   D 3.7

D 3.7 Brunswick Building, Chicago (US) 1965, SOM,
Fazlur Khan, Bruce Graham
a Street view
b Direct column load transfer through
deep beam
D 3.8 Two Shell Plaza, Houston (US) 1972, Fazlur
Khan, Bruce Graham
a Street view
b Gradual column load transfer through
haunched beams
D 3.9 IBM Building, Seattle (US) 1964, Minoru
Yamasaki
a Direct column load transfer through arches
b Street view
D 3.10 Marine Midland Plaza (also Five Star Bank
Plaza, One HSBC Plaza), Rochester (US) 1970,
SOM, Fazlur Khan, Bruce Graham
a Gradual column load transfer through
arch action
b Street view

its centre. The beams closest to the ground floor have the deepest haunch and therefore the greatest stiffness. With every storey the haunch decreases, until eventually it is no longer discernible. Figure D 3.9 illustrates the direct arch load transfer in the IBM Building in Seattle (1964), while the load transfer in the Marine Midland Plaza occurs gradually (Fig. D 3.10). Figures D 3.7 through D 3.10 (p. 120f.) also clearly demonstrate how different structural solutions lead to different visual results.

21st Century Approaches and Considerations

The 20th century was exceptionally rich in innovations for tall buildings. Constraints imposed by the site as well as a wish to create more open public spaces and avoid urban canyons motivated engineers to develop ideas for building tall and narrow structures. The fundamental principles upon which engineering is based will not – cannot – change. However, the 21st century has ushered in a few technological advances that have made the implementation of previously unthinkable designs, forms, and heights possible. Most of these

technological advances can be attributed to the efficiency and precision of modern computers and software, but new, higher-strength materials and the use of mass dampers to ameliorate unsettling lateral accelerations have also made significant contributions.

However, engineers should avoid using powerful computer-based structural analysis tools as a first step in the conceptual phase of a design. It is better to use simple formulas and basic principles as an initial guide. These basic tools and the simplification of their intellectual approach enable designers to develop an in-depth understanding of the structural behaviour. It is also critical to use these simple analyses to validate the complex and voluminous results produced by the computer. Otherwise students and newly minted engineers might tend to place too much faith in complex computer programs without scrutinising the results to verify that they make sense, or fail to fully understand the fundamental behaviour of the structure.

Computers can, however, be used to optimise the structural design and weigh the relative considerations of efficiency and economy (since the structure that requires

the least amount of material may be much more expensive to build). Optimisation must also find the balance between elegance and sustainability, taking into account sociocultural and environmental considerations as well as the building context. With so many parameters in play, it is crucial to allow the 'human' factor leeway in choosing the best design. While computers can optimise efficiency and structural behaviour, a holistic evaluation based on knowledge, experience and subjective judgments of aesthetics can only be performed by humans. Further, optimisation in tall buildings encompasses more than just the dimensioning of building components; it also refers to the search for the proper form – to topology optimisation. Selecting the right form, the right geometry and the right structural system has the greatest impact on the quality of a design. The interdisciplinary boundary between architecture and structural engineering lies precisely where the structure, as optimised by the engineer, takes on a significant visual expression.

Today's computer programs make possible the analysis and design of complex geometries and unimaginable heights. It is no longer a question of "can we do it?" but rather "should we do it?" The answer to that question must consider the impact on society and the environment. The 21st century brought sustainability as a design goal and the LEED rating system, developed in 1998 by the U.S. Green Building Council, into focus. The LEED system provides "a framework for healthy, highly efficient, and cost-saving green buildings. LEED certification [or another equivalent certification such as BREEAM, DGNB, etc.] is a globally recognised symbol of sustainability achievement and leadership" [16]. Most projects of this century include LEED certification as a design goal. In general, tall buildings in urban communities have a more positive

a

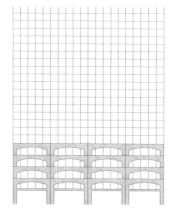

b   D 3.8

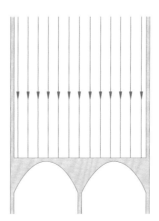

a

b

D 3.9

Notes:
[1] *NFPA 101: Life Safety Code.* National Fire Protection Association. Quincy 2009.
[2] "CTBUH Height Criteria", ctbuh.org/resource/height (accessed December 31, 2019)
[3] Billington, David P.: *The Tower and the Bridge: The New Art of Structural Engineering.* Princeton 1985
[4] Condit, Carl: *The Chicago School of Architecture: A History of Commercial and Public Buildings in the Chicago Area, 1875–1925.* Chicago 1964
[5] see note 3
[6] see note 4
[7] see note 3, p. 100
[8] Khan, Yasmin Sabina: *Engineering Architecture: The Vision of Fazlur R. Khan.* New York 2004
[9] Robertson, Leslie E.: *The Structure of Design: An Engineer's Extraordinary Life in Architecture.* New York 2017
[10] Schittich, Christian (ed.): *SOM Structural Engineering.* Munich 2015
[11] In: *Modern Marvels: John Hancock Center.* DVD. Directed by Emily Lau. History Channel / New Video. New York 2008
[12] see note 3, p. 61
[13] see note 3, p. 5
[14] see note 3, p. 87
[15] see note 10, p. 55
[16] usgbc.org/leed/why-leed (accessed on February 15, 2020)
[17] e.g. IMMERSIFY by Supple

impact on the environment than do smaller buildings in rural or suburban communities. Their residents can rely on mass transit rather than driving to work in their own car and then leaving it in a car park; multiple buildings can be linked so that they share energy resources; and tall buildings have a larger volume-to-surface ratio than single-family houses, so their indoor heating and cooling are less sensitive to the influence of the outdoor climate. However, tall buildings require larger column, beam and wall sizes than lower-height buildings with the same footprint. It is therefore critical to optimise their form and structural elements.

The construction of a tall building is a cooperative effort involving many disciplines, requiring detailed and careful co-ordination between numerous members of the design team. The disciplines involved include architecture, structural engineering, vertical transportation, electrical engineering, mechanical engineering, IT, plumbing, facade design, lighting, fire safety and acoustic engineering, geotechnical engineering and building maintenance. A substantial part of the ground floor area is claimed by public access spaces and building services. The trick is to optimise these such that sufficient quality floor area remains for the building client to lease – an important criterium that is critical to the financial viability of all tall buildings. The 21st century has brought about tools that make it possible through 3D modelling to deliver better real-time information about the size and positioning requirements for all supply and waste removal components. One such tool is Building Information Modeling (BIM). The virtual reality interface integrated into these tools enables a full immersion into the digital design and the confirmation of multidisciplinary coordination before the building is built. Using relevant programs, several members of the design team can 'walk' through the

virtual space, simultaneously and from all over the world [17]. These in-the-model meetings allow real-time observation and permit participants to manipulate objects to obtain detailed information. The high level of coordination and precision in decision-making makes it possible to identify and solve potential conflicts early on, ultimately resulting in greater efficiency and quality.

From the First Chicago School designs of the late 1800s until today, tall buildings have played an important role in communities and in the quality of life of their occupants. Since more than half of the world's population now lives in urban areas and the population density in these areas will likely continue to increase, the need for efficient, economical and sustainable tall buildings is greater than ever. The best examples of successful tall building design have been those that were created in a strong synergistic collaboration between architect and structural engineer. Equipped with the latest tools, today's design teams are more prepared than ever to overcome the challenges of tall building design. The future of urban centres is in good hands.

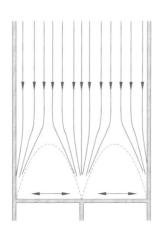

a

b

D 3.10

Shells and Gridshells for Long-span Roofs

Sigrid Adriaenssens

Basic Principles and Context

A sheet of paper held out flat cannot support its own weight and flops down (Fig. D 4.1). However, if it is slightly curved, the same sheet becomes stiff and can now also hold a number of paperclips. Shells like the canopy of Toyo Ito's Meiso no Mori funeral hall act in the same way (Fig. D 4.3).

Mode of function and classification

Shell structures are slender curved structural surfaces that can span distances in the order of 10 to 80 m without internal columns or other supports. Slender in this context means that the ratio of the shell's thickness to its radius of curvature is smaller than 1/10. They carry their own weight and external loading, such as snow or wind loads, through their small thickness to the foundations. Figure D 4.2 illustrates an abstraction of a part of a shell surface. The diagram shows how shells carry loads through axial (N_x, N_y) or in-plane (N_{xy}, N_{yx}) and transverse (Q_x, Q_y) shear forces and through bending (M_x, M_y) and torsional (M_{xy}, M_{yx}) moments. When properly designed, shells resist external loading solely through membrane action – that is in-plane axial and shear forces. Membrane action is the most efficient way for a shell to carry loading because its cross section is then equally stressed and used to its full potential. However, shells often carry external loading through a combination of membrane and bending action; their cross section is then not equally stressed.

The following classifications may be helpful in understanding different shell typologies. In the strict structural sense of the word, prestressed technical textile structures, sometimes simply called "membranes", are also shells, since they exhibit membrane behaviour and only resist loading through tensile stresses. However, these types of lightweight systems more properly fall within the scope of the chapter "Membranes and Air-Inflated Structures" (p. 130ff.). The first thing which typically comes to mind when thinking of shells is continuous smooth shell surfaces. Continuous shells can either be rigid or flexible. A rigid continuous shell such as the reinforced concrete canopy of Meiso no Mori barely deforms under loading (Fig. D 4.3), while a flexible shell can undergo large deformations. A flexible shell is sometimes also called a "compliant" shell. These types of shells have not yet found many applications in architecture but hold

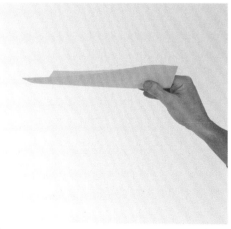

a   b   D 4.1

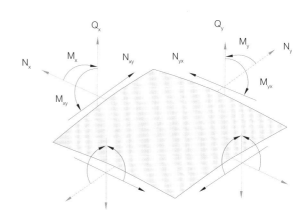

D 4.2

promise as architectural adaptive facade systems. However, they are also outside the scope of this chapter.

In contrast to the continuous shell, this section discusses the faceted shell and the gridshell, also sometimes called a lattice or reticulated shell (Fig. D 4.4). A gridshell is basically a shell with the material arranged in linear elements in a grid. There are two distinct types of gridshells: the elastic or bending-active ones and the pre-bent ones. The elastic or bending-active shells are formed from a flat flexible grid which is bent and twisted into shape during construction to arrive at a curved surface. This surface is then rigidified, for example, through joint connections or shear bracing and edge beams. The gridshell enclosing the Helsinki Zoo lookout tower offers a good example (Fig. D 4.4). Pre-bent gridshells such as the cupola over the Dutch National Maritime Museum (see built example, p. 234), in contrast, are built in their curved form from either straight (segmented shell) or bent individual members. Finally, a faceted shell, sometimes referred to as a plate shell, such as at the Landesgartenschau Exhibition Hall shown in Fig. D 4.5 (p. 124), is a shell consisting of plates connected together to form a curved surface.

D 4.3

D 4.1 A sheet of paper cannot support its own weight (**a**), unless it is curved (**b**).
D 4.2 Shell element with internal loading actions.
D 4.3 Undulating concrete shell of the Meiso no Mori Funeral Hall, Kakamigahara (JP) 2006, Toyo Ito & Associates, Mutsuro Sasaki
D 4.4 Bending-active gridshell enclosing the stairs of Helsinki zoo lookout tower (FI) 2002, Ville Hara Architect, Finnforest Merk, Wood Studio Workshop

D 4.4

Importance for the 21st century

Shells have many inherent qualities that make them ideal for dealing with some of the challenges that 21st century society faces. In particular, they offer a solution for tackling scarcity of natural resources and extreme hazards. Because they are slender, they require less construction material and have a lower mass (and thus a smaller carbon footprint) compared to other large-span structures. Additionally, shells are indeterminate large-span structures that distribute any applied loading throughout their entire surface. Because the loading is shared by the entire surface, shell structures are very resilient. If one part of the shell fails, the loading is redistributed to other intact parts. This means that there are many different paths for the flow of forces through the shell. This inherent shell characteristic is beneficial when resisting extreme loading. In the United States, for example, shells have been proven to withstand hurricanes and tornadoes while other buildings around them collapse (Fig. D 4.7). As a consequence of their low carbon footprint and their capacity to resist extreme loading, shells are architectural building forms that can address the structural challenges associated with society's desire for resilient and sustainable urban environment.

Origin and current interest

Although stone and earthen domes (*tholoi*) have been around since the fifth or sixth millennium BCE, thin engineered shells appeared at the beginning of the 20th century. The impetus for their arrival was the advent of new construction materials (such as reinforced concrete) and analysis techniques such as the theory of shells developed by Augustus E. H. Love in 1888. The 20th century saw a whole gamut of shell master builders who developed novel form finding, analysis and construction methods. The following list of shell builders is in no way exhaustive but gives an idea of the wealth of shell design, building and research activities of that period. Heinz Isler worked solely with physical plaster models for the design and analysis of his reinforced concrete shells. Frei Otto developed hanging chain models to find the perfect shape for elastic gridshells, such as the Mannheim Multihalle (1975). Félix Candela exploited the ruled surface geometry of the hyperbolic paraboloid to develop a construction method based on straight wooden poles, and in doing so generated cost-effective formwork for a curved shell. Their reinforced concrete and wooden (grid)shells still stand today as testament to the ingenuity of these master builders. Today novel digital form finding and computer numerically controled (CNC) and additive fabrication and construction methods, new materials (such as ultra-high-performance concrete) and the influence of blob architecture by e.g. Greg Lynn, Zaha Hadid, Patrik Schumacher, Shigeru Ban and Toyo Ito have catapulted shells back into the spotlight and made them a regular feature of contemporary architectural discourse.

Challenges and Contemporary Solutions

Design and analysis methods, fabrication and construction processes and suitable materials form the basis of modern solutions for the challenges of shell construction.

Design and analysis methods

Since well-designed shells are thin, it is of key importance that the designer generates the best possible structural form for the

a   b   D 4.5

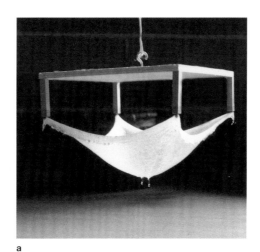

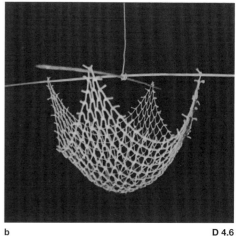

a

b D 4.6

shell. It is not because a surface is curved that it therefore behaves as a good shell. In other words, not all curved forms are structurally efficient shells. From a structural perspective it is appropriate to characterise shells as being either sculptural, analytical or form found in their geometry. Only the analytical and form-found (sometimes also called force-modelled shells) can exhibit membrane action under external loading and are thus structurally preferred.

Sculptural forms

Thanks to the wide availability of digital modelling tools, some designers have motivated the basis for their curved surface design projects on aesthetic considerations with the objective to achieve scenographic effects. This sculptural design intent can be lauded for its ingenuity of visual form, but not for its consideration of structural logic. Unfortunately, the structural solutions necessary to make these sculptural shapes possible typically rely on large amounts of material. The curved surfaces in Frank Gehry's projects, for example, express visual intent but are mostly disconnected from structural considerations. These sculptural forms do not behave like – and thus are not – structural shells.

Analytical shells

Geometry is a tool that has been used since antiquity for the development of architectural forms. These forms (which include the sphere, the cylinder and the hyperbolic paraboloid) are thus limited by the rules imposed by analytical geometry and the designer's imagination. Surfaces of revolution, translational surfaces, and scale-trans surfaces lend themselves excellently to shell action and discretisation into sub-elements. In this context, the work of Joerg Schlaich and Hans Schober on steel gridshells, clad with planar glass, was innovative.

Form-found or force-modelled shells

Of all traditional structural design parameters, a shell's form mostly defines whether the shell will be stable, safe and sufficiently stiff. The important design challenge thus lies in the determination of a three-dimensional form that exhibits membrane action under the shell's self-weight. A number of physical and numerical form-finding approaches exist to aid the designer in finding that three-dimensional form. Physical form-finding techniques are based on inverted funicular hanging models, such as the ones pioneered by Antonio Gaudi and Heinz Isler (Fig. D 4.6). The numerical form-

finding approaches can be classified into three categories:
- stiffness matrix methods (such as finite element method)
- geometric stiffness methods (which are material-independent and include the force density method as well as thrust network analysis)
- dynamic equilibrium methods (which solve a dynamic equilibrium problem to arrive at a steady-state equilibrium and include dynamic relaxation and particle spring approaches).

Once the designer has defined the right shell form either using analytical methods or form-finding approaches, this geometry now has to be materialised and verified for strength, stiffness and stability under all possible loading combinations due to dead and live loads. In particular, shells need to be checked for buckling, an instability phenomenon that can occur in compressed, slender systems (such as shells).

Fabrication and construction methods

Thin shell structures can define architectural forms and resist loads efficiently at the same time. Yet the labour and materials involved in the installation of their formwork and shoring need to be of high quality and

D 4.5 Faceted shell made out of timber plates, Landesgartenschau Exhibition Hall (state garden show) Schwäbisch Gmünd (DE) 2014, ICD/ ITKE/IIGS Institut, University of Stuttgart
 a External view
 b Interior
D 4.6 Hanging cloth and net models were Heinz Isler's tools for generating shell forms
D 4.7 An intact continuous dome amongst the rubble of surrounding houses at Pensacola Beach, Florida (US) after hurricane Dennis in 2005.

D 4.7

D 4.8

are therefore often hand-crafted and thus costly. Engineers, architects and other building professionals are of the opinion that this high construction cost is the main obstacle to the larger adoption of shells in the construction sector today. The formwork and shoring also generate a considerable amount of construction waste. In a bid to become more cost-effective, recently new construction approaches have been pursued that reuse formwork or use repetition of several identical elements and achieve economies of scale. A recently developed new construction method is to build concrete shells from planar concrete plates

using flexible pressurised membranes. During the construction process, the concrete plates are lifted with the aid of pneumatic formwork into the desired curved geometry and the plates are then joined (Fig. D 4.10). Once the shell is complete, the formwork is deflated and removed, after which it can be reused. Other pneumatic formwork approaches have been used in combination with shotcreting techniques or pouring concrete onto the deflated membranes before it is pressurised.

Another interesting shell construction technique is the one employed in 2010 in the construction of the Teshima Art Museum

shell, that used dirt (or sometimes called earth mounds) abundantly available on sites, as temporary formwork (Fig. D 4.9a). Upon the shell's completion, the dirt was excavated and removed (Fig. D 4.9b). Another construction strategy is to build large formwork based on repetitive units which can be lowered, removed and reused.

Elastic gridshells need an entirely different construction process. Their slender grid elements must be bent and twisted into the final desired shell geometry. Traditionally, this process has been achieved by lifting or pushing the grid up at various points with

1 Ventilation duct
2 Openings in the shell
3 Conveyor belt for transport of excavated soil
4 Rough-terrain crane for further soil removal

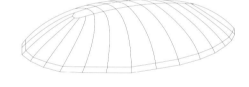

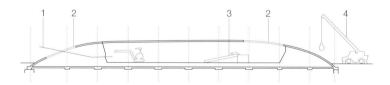

a

a

b   D 4.9

b   D 4.10

a

b

D 4.11

external cranes or internal props. The gridshell of the Weald and Downland Living Museum is a trellis of hinged laths, that was deformed using gravity and strategically positioned shoring (Fig. D 4.12).

The fabrication and construction of shells is challenging due to their complex geometry and their slenderness. These complex geometries or their formwork can be partly constructed off-site. For example, the high-performance concrete shells for a railway station in Calgary were cast on steel moulds in the controlled environment of an off-site laboratory (Fig. D 4.11 a). The precision of the cast had to be very high as the shells

are only 20-mm thick. The shell's size was determined by the transport limitations from the lab to the site. Once they had been cured and pretreated, the shells were trucked to site and lifted by crane onto to their supports (Fig. D 4.11 b).

Materials

Materialising curved surfaces has always been a challenge. Either the construction elements are planar (such as glass, plywood, bricks or steel plates) and need to be segmented into meshes and assembled into a curved geometry. Or the construction material is fluid such as concrete,

for example, and must be cast on formwork. Or it is strong and flexible, such as thin bamboo or fibre-reinforced plastic (FRP) rods (Fig. D 4.8), and can be flexed and twisted into the elastic gridshell's shape.

Recently there has been renewed interest in unconventional building materials with a low carbon imprint that lend themselves well to shell construction. The layered shell of the Rwanda Cricket Stadium consists of low-strength tiles, made on site of local soil by labourers (Fig. D 4.14, p. 126). The soil is strengthened with cement and the bricks do not require firing.

D 4.8 A grid of curved fibreglass-reinforced rods clad with a PVC-coated fabric; temporary structure for the renovation of the Créteil Cathedral, Créteil (FR) 2013, T/E/S/S & Thinkshell

D 4.9 Teshima Art Museum, Teshima (JP) 2010, Office of Ryue Nishizawa, Yusuke Ohi, Rei Naito
   a Section. An earth mound served as temporary formwork for the shell.
   b View

D 4.10 Concrete shell constructed using the Pneumatic Forming of Hardened Concrete (PFHC) method, test structure erected in Kärnten (AT) 2015, Benjamin Kromoser, Johann Kollegger, TU Wien
   a Conceptual diagram of the optimised formwork geometry, in the pressurised and original state as a planar panel before "inflation"
   b Execution with the subsequently cut-out areas

D 4.11 Shawnessy Light Rail Transit (LRT) Station, Calgary (CA) 2004, Stantec Architecture, CPV Group Architects & Engineers
   a Casting of ultra-high-performance concrete shell elements onto steel moulds at the plant
   b On-site construction

D 4.12 Gridshell at the Weald and Downland Living Museum, Singleton (GB) 2002, Edward Cullinan Architects, Buro Happold
   a Actively bending of the flexible yet strong grid of the gridshell using shoring and gravity
   b Close-up of the node clamp that allows for sliding of the laths during construction
   c Interior view

a

b

c

D 4.12

a   b   D 4.13

Emerging Design, Fabrication and Construction Approaches

Current cutting-edge research and design focuses on further exploiting the exceptional structural qualities of shells and on leveraging digital, CNC and additive technologies to enhance their design, fabrication and construction.

From a structural perspective, geometric features in the shell geometry such as corrugations, folds and dimples can beneficially alter its structural behaviour by locally increasing its stiffness. For example, recent research has shown how such corrugations can positively alter the shell's response under earthquake loading and greatly alleviate structural damage.

CNC and additive processes are not only being used to fabricate and construct shells, but more importantly they are defining a whole new form language for shells that was previously unthinkable. For the BUGA Wood Pavilion fabrication, an off-site robotic platform was developed for the assembly and milling of the pavilion's wood segments (Fig. D 4.15). These segments were trucked to the site and put together with sub-millimetre precision like a giant three-dimensional puzzle.

Knitted formwork, made on an industrial knitting machine, served as permanent formwork for the KnitCandela concrete shell sculpture (Fig. D 4.16). The machine produced the double-layer textile formwork in long strips. Upon arrival on site, the strips were joined and tensioned over a wooden frame. The knitted formwork was subsequently sprayed with cement and concrete, staying in place after it cured, contributing to the sculpture's visual appeal.

The shape and topology of the Trabeculae Pavilion shell was obtained by successively stacking high-resistance polymer material, with each layer resting on the previous

a   b   D 4.14

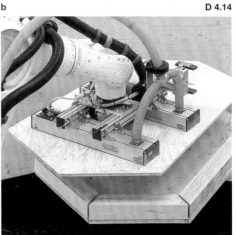

a   b   D 4.15

one, using 3D printing (Fig. D 4.13). The combination of the optimised topology and the lightweight material resulted in a shell with a mass of only 6 to 10 kg/m².

Outlook for Large-span (Grid)shells

More than ever, large-span lightweight (grid)shell structures can contribute to solving some of society's most pressing challenges linked to limited natural resources and increasing numbers of intense man-made and natural hazards. Because of their slenderness and curved geometry, shells can have a low carbon footprint and inherent structural properties of high stiffness and low mass which are beneficial to resisting extreme loading. The untapped potential of these (grid)shell structures comes to the fore for today's construction industry when these typologies are viewed in the context of other emerging innovations such as carbon-neutral materials and CNC and digital design, fabrication and construction technologies.

D 4.13 Trabeculae Pavilion, Milan (IT) 2017, Roberto Naboni, Anja Kunić, Luca Breseghello
   a Perspective view
   b Close-up of 3D-printed high-resistance polymer cells
D 4.14 Rwanda Cricket Stadium, Kigali (RW) 2017, Light Earth Designs
   a Vault structures
   b Unfired tiles made of local clay
D 4.15 BUGA Wood Pavilion, National Garden Show Heilbronn (DE) 2019, ICD / ITKE Institut, University of Stuttgart
   a Perspective view
   b Robotic off-site assembly and fabrication of wood segments
D 4.16 KnitCandela sculpture, MUAC, Mexico City (MX) 2018, Block Research Group, ETH Zurich, Zaha Hadid Architects Computation and Design Group with Architecture Extrapolated
   a Industrial knitting machine manufacturing the formwork
   b Permanent knitted formwork left in place
   c View of the realised sculpture

c

Membrane and Air-inflated Structures

Lars Schiemann

Membrane structures – beginning with simple tents and sails made of natural fibres – have a tradition that goes back many thousands of years. Thanks to the developments in construction with modern synthetics since the mid-1900s, as well as the use of polymeric materials in the manufacture of durable textile membranes and plastic films, membranes have become an established construction type. Used as lightweight building shells, structural membranes and pneumatic cushions differ markedly from other constructions in terms of design, function, structure and building physics.

Definitions, Construction Methods and Design Types

Both mechanically and pneumatically prestressed membrane structures must fulfil the following criteria as load-bearing constructions [1]:
- Slenderness: the thickness is negligible in comparison to the area dimensions.
- Support: the surface edges are flexibly or rigidly supported.
- Loading: under loading, only tensile forces are produced within the surface.
- Prestressing: the surface is prestressed within its plane.
- Curvature: the surface should, wherever possible, be doubly curved in space.
- Materials: the chosen material must be suited to the purpose.
- Incline: the surfaces must be sufficiently slanted.

Membrane structures can be divided into two main types (Fig. D 5.1 and D 5.2). Differentiated by their prestressing (mechanical or pneumatic) and the predominant form of their curvature (synclastic or anticlastic), membrane structures may feature one or multiple layers.

Mechanically prestressed textile membrane structures

The stability of single-layer membrane structures is generated by mechanical prestressing. During assembly, in order to attach the membrane to the substructure at the edges, the membrane must be mechanically pretensioned. In the pretensioned state, the membrane geometries exhibit anticlastic curvatures – that is, curvatures in opposite senses along the two main stress directions of the surface (Fig. D 5.1). The standard materials used for mechanically prestressed structural membranes are PVC-coated polyester textiles and PTFE or silicon-coated fibreglass textiles as well as polymer films of ethylene tetrafluoroethylene (ETFE).

Pneumatically prestressed cushion structures

The membrane layers of pneumatically prestressed cushion structures are pretensioned through internal pressure, which may be either positive or negative. These multilayered pneumatic structures form predominantly synclastically curved surfaces – that is, surfaces curved in the same sense along the two main stress directions (Fig. D 5.2). Most pneumatically prestressed membrane structures are made of ETFE films. Depending on the number of film layers and the form taken by the middle layer, ETFE film cushions can be classified into six main types (Fig. D 5.3).

The nominal internal pressure of ETFE film cushions is approximately 250–400 Pa, which can be raised to a maximum pressure of about 800–1,000 Pa for higher loading. The individual construction types of the cushions vary significantly in their load-bearing behaviour as well as in their physical properties. The middle film layers serve to form a multi-chambered system with improved thermal insulation characteristics. The use of thermally decoupled clamping profiles and separate film layers at the attachments makes a further significant reduction of the heat transmission coefficient possible. In the process of load transfer, curved middle film layers may be considered as semi-bearing, thus increasing the realisable spans of the air cushions.

Historical Development

The pretensioned membrane structures and pneumatically prestressed cushion structures discussed in the following sections have had a marked impact on the historical development of membrane construction.

Mechanically prestressed membrane structures

Textile constructions of natural fibres, which are considered the precursors of today's polymer membrane structures, were already being built many thousands of years ago. These structures can be considered load-bearing only in a limited sense and do not fulfil the criteria defined earlier for structural membranes. They were used exclusively as shelters for protection against rain and sun. As purely technical structures, these temporary membrane constructs are not architecture.

Only the research done on lightweight structures by Frei Otto in the middle of the 20th century opened up new perspectives on membrane construction and laid the foundation for modern membrane architecture. His membrane structures, such as the four-point canopy of the music pavilion at the National Garden Show in Kassel in 1955

D 5.1 Mechanically pretensioned membrane with anticlastic curvature, single-layer system
D 5.2 Pneumatically pretensioned cushion with primarily synclastic curvature, multilayered system
D 5.3 Constructions of pneumatic film cushions

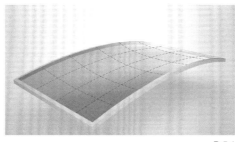

D 5.1

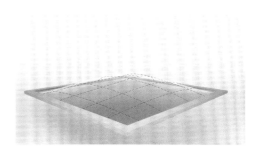

D 5.2

Construction	Type of pneumatic film cushion
1. Single-chamber cushion, single-layered with rigid base	
2. Single-chamber cushion, double-layered	
3. Double-chambered cushion, triple-layered, flat middle layer	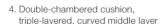
4. Double-chambered cushion, triple-layered, curved middle layer	
5. Multi-chamber cushion, four-layered, curved middle layers	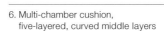
6. Multi-chamber cushion, five-layered, curved middle layers	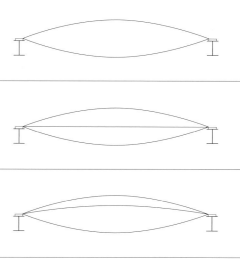

D 5.3

D 5.4

D 5.5

D 5.6

or the Tanzbrunnen at the National Garden Show in Cologne in 1957 (Fig. 14, p. 10; B 1.41, p. 54), are among the most influential lightweight and membrane structures in post-war history [2].

In the following years, the research and development of new materials, more efficient structural systems and new form-finding methods not only made possible the construction of greater spans, but also broadened the range of design, functional and service applications. The membrane constructions for the 1972 Summer Olympics in Munich represented a ground-breaking achievement in its day. Today's state-of-the-art knowledge of membrane architecture and fundamental construction methods is based mostly on the discoveries and research of that time.

The subsequent years saw a steady optimisation of membrane construction in terms of both design and structural considerations. Over the last three decades, innumerable stadium and hall roofs have been created by combining membranes with efficient primary structures such as spoked-wheel systems. One of the prototypes for this building method is the membrane roof of the Mercedes Benz Arena in Stuttgart, erected in 1993 in the course of reconstruction work on the arena.

Towards the end of the 1990s, there was an increase in the creation of building envelopes of structural membranes that were supposed to exhibit multifunctional properties. Among these are acoustically and thermally insulated multilayered textile membrane structures such as the Theater im Hamburger Hafen from 1994 or the community centre in Puchheim near Munich, built in 1999 (Fig. D 5.4). Since the turn of the millennium, transparent ETFE films have also been employed as mechanically pretensioned membranes. An important example is the prestressed ETFE film roof of the HDI Arena in Hanover by Schulitz + Partner, which was built in 2005 and covers approximately 10,000 m² (Fig. D 5.5).

One of the most ambitious membrane structures of recent decades in terms of assembly and execution was the 246-m-high ThyssenKrupp test tower in Rottweil, built in 2019. The reinforced concrete tube, designed for the development and testing of a new generation of elevators, is enveloped in a scrim of PTFE fibreglass, which was installed using a specially built assembly platform that could be moved to heights of over 200 m.

Pneumatically prestressed cushion structures

The first architectural use of pneumatically prestressed constructions dates back to the second half of the 20th century. The development of gas-proof synthetic materials that could withstand the necessary pretensioning of the membranes and maintain lasting pressure differences across membrane layers enabled the construction of load-bearing air-inflated structures. At first, PVC-coated polyester textiles were the materials most often employed. However, the fluoropolymer material ETFE (ethylene tetrafluoroethylene) proved seminal for the development of pneumatic systems when it was introduced to the market in 1970 [3]. Since the 1990s, air cushion structures have predominantly been made of the translucent films. The following projects set trends in architectural and construction history for pneumatically prestressed cushion structures:

The pneumatic radomes of the aerospace engineer Walter Bird, developed in the mid-20th century as a non-metallic protective shell for the sensitive radar systems of the US military, represent one of the first instances of air-supported constructions. Another is the 1963/64 radome in Raisting am Ammersee, according to a design by Hans Maurer.

D 5.7

Visionary concepts, such as Richard Buckminster Fuller's idea of an air dome over Manhattan, arrived at in 1960 together with Ewald Bubner, Kenzo Tange and Ove Arup, or the so-called Arctic City of 1971, adopted the structural principles of pneumatic constructs for architectural applications over the following years.

The pneumatic structures built at the Osaka 1970 World Expo were of great significance to further improvements in their practical implementation. Milestones of this construction type included the arch-shaped Fuji Group Pavilion by Yutaka Murata and Mamoru Kawaguchi, comprising 16 air-inflated tubes 4 m in diameter and 78 m long, and the US Pavilion by Davis, Brody & Associates, a cable-net reinforced pneumatic construct spanning an area of about 142 × 83 m. Despite these impressive temporary structures, the building type could not gain a foothold in the architecture of the 1970s [4].

A new development in pneumatic construction was introduced in 1982 with the mangrove hall at Arnhem Zoo. The cable-supported ETFE film cushions with spans of 3 m are considered one of the first permanent and large-area pneumatic film roofs.

The 1990s saw an increased use of ETFE film air cushions in building envelopes for both functional and purely stylistic reasons. The canopy of the Jungle House for big cats at Hellabrunn Zoo in Munich represents a significant step in their further development (Fig. D 5.7). This project marks the first time that 64 air-filled ETFE film cushions with spans of 2 m were attached to a cable net with anticlastic curvature.

In an innovation shown at the Duales System Deutschland AG pavilion at the 2000 Hanover Expo, which was clad in triple-layer air-filled panels, light transmission through the outer film membrane is controlled through pneumatically regulated

sun protection. To facilitate this, the outer and inner film layers were printed with alternating patterns [5].

The size of the greenhouses at the Eden Project near St Austell in Cornwall, built in 2000 by Nicholas Grimshaw, exceeded that of all of the pneumatic structures that had been realised at that time (Fig. D 5.8). The steel geodesic domes, with radii ranging between 18 and 65 m, consist of hexagons 5 to 11 m in diameter that are spanned by cable-supported ETFE film cushions.

A project that proved decisive in establishing pneumatic cushion structures in architecture is the Allianz Arena in Munich by Herzog & de Meuron, built in 2005. The stadium shell has a surface area of about 66,500 m² and is composed of 2,784 diamond-shaped ETFE cushions up to

4.6 × 17 m in size (Fig. D 5.6) [6]. What sets the stadium apart is its unusual form and the implementation of its construction and structure, as well as its use of the film cushions as light sources.

Of note with respect to the solar energy production capability of facade systems

D 5.4 Community centre, Puchheim (DE) 1999, Peter Lanz with Benno Bauer, Mayr Ludescher Partner
D 5.5 HDI Arena, Hanover (DE) 2005, Schulitz + Partner, RFR Ingenieure
D 5.6 Allianz Arena, Munich (DE) 2005, Herzog & de Meuron, Arup, concept and structural design of the air cushion: Engineering + Design, Linke und Moritz
D 5.7 Jungle House, Hellabrunn Zoo, Munich (DE) 1995, Herbert Kochta, Schlaich Bergermann Partner (sbp), IPL
D 5.8 Eden Project, St Austell, Cornwall (GB) 2000, Nicholas Grimshaw, Anthony Hunt Associates

D 5.8

are the pneumatic film roofs of the carport at the Munich waste management authority, designed by Ackermann Architekten in 2011. This marks the first occasion on which flexible photovoltaic (PV) films were installed on a large scale as the middle layer of triple-layer ETFE air cushions for the purpose of solar energy generation.

The approximately 240-m long and 35-m wide timber gridshell of the Swatch Headquarters in Biel by Shigeru Ban, built in 2019, showcases the potential of computer-assisted tools for the design and production of modular building shells comprising multifunctional roof and facade elements (Fig. D 5.9). The various facade modules, composed among other things of glass, ETFE film and photovoltaic elements, differ in function, size and structural execution. This complexity could be resolved only through the use of digital tools during the design phase, form finding process, structural analysis and manufacture [7].

Load-bearing Characteristics – Form and Structure

Mechanically and pneumatically pre-stressed structural membranes belong to the category of tensile-stressed lightweight long-span structures. In every case, the membrane surfaces are stabilised by an imposed pretensioned state. The implementation of doubly curved membrane surfaces optimises this stabilisation effect and allows for a significant reduction in the membrane loading.

Form finding
Unlike for freely designed forms, form finding for structural membranes occurs in an iterative process according to structural laws which stem from the property of membranes that all loads are transmitted exclusively by tensile stresses.

The initially defined and implemented pre-stressed state of the surfaces, influenced by given boundary conditions and, where applicable, external loading, results in the generation of appropriate structural forms. The surfaces of mechanically and pneumatically prestressed membranes can therefore be calculated using static and structural laws and are always founded on physical principles. Form finding of surfaces is done using experimental and numerical methods.

Load-bearing characteristics
Mechanically and pneumatically pre-stressed structural membranes exhibit exceptionally benign and positive load-bearing characteristics which are largely determined by their curvature. The load transfers and thereby the forces F on the membrane result from the ratio between the radii of curvature r of the membrane surface and the associated load q. For the case of a pneumatic foil construction with an internal pressure p_i, this relationship is nicely illustrated through Barlow's formula:

$$F = r \cdot p_i$$

According to Barlow's formula, in the one-dimensional case the film forces F of the loaded membrane can be approximated by the product of the load p_i and the radius of curvature r. In the two-dimensional load transfer of the square cushion (Fig. D 5.10), the forces are broken up to correspond to the two radii of curvature r_1 and r_2:

$$p_i = \frac{F_1}{r_1} + \frac{F_2}{r_2}$$

If the radii are equal and the material responds isotropically, the forces are distributed evenly along the two main structural dimensions.

D 5.9

D 5.9   Swatch Headquarters, Biel (CH) 2019, Shigeru Ban

D 5.10   Pneumatically prestressed double-layered film cushion under internal pressure with two-axis load transfer and radii of curvature r_1 and r_2

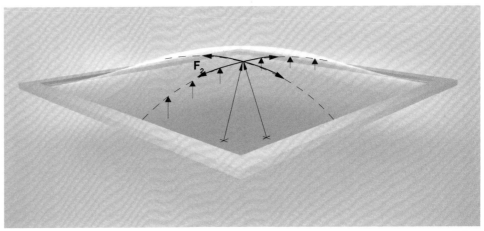

D 5.10

When the load is increased, in this case by raising the internal pressure p_i of the pneumatic cushion, the membrane stretches, the film arc becomes greater and the radius of curvature is concomitantly reduced. Bearing in mind the relationship between curvature and force given by Barlow's formula, this means that an increase in the load does not result in a linear, but rather in a subproportional increase of the membrane forces. The radius of curvature is a function of the material stretch under load. That is to say, load, deformation and internal membrane forces are not linearly dependent on one another. The subproportional relationship among load, deformation and internal membrane forces is what characterises the benign and positive load-bearing response of structural membranes. Because ETFE film constructions stretch more than the comparatively stiffer textile membranes, this positive quality is even more evident in pneumatically prestressed ETFE film cushions.

Challenges and Developments

In the face of global climate change, the steadily growing world population and the increasing worldwide scarcity of resources, the building sector must adopt a more decisive and more active role in protecting the climate. Sustainable and resource-conserving construction means not only minimising the use of materials and the energy consumed in their manufacture, but also reducing energy consumption during the service and dismantling phases of the finished building. Thanks to their properties, membranes employed as building shells for roof and facade systems can contribute significantly to these goals.

Material efficiency

Structural textile and polymer film membranes are among the classic lightweight constructions whose minimal use of ma-

terials and optimised exploitation of those materials make them extraordinarily efficient structural systems. The modest self-weight of the structure positively impacts the energy and ecological balance of the manufacture, transport, assembly, load transfers and disassembly of buildings. In addition, ETFE films are highly recyclable. In contrast to textile membranes, fluoropolymer-based ETFE films are not composite materials and can therefore be recycled and reintroduced into the production process of other materials.

Multifunctionality

As multipurpose systems, complex building shells must increasingly take on many different functions. Among these are acoustic, thermal and fire protection, solar energy generation and radiation and light transmission. Thanks to their material and structural properties, building envelopes of textile membranes or films can fulfil these requirements in many respects. Already, light-transmitting membrane building shells with transparent thermal insulation made of translucent aerogel particles are being created. The use of flexible PV films in ETFE cushion structures also showcases the potential of membrane construction for efficient, energetically optimised building shells.

Their ability to control light and radiation transmission will raise the importance of novel coatings for textile membranes even further, though some coating materials are already available that allow for the targeted absorption or reflection of radiation in defined spectral ranges. Building envelopes are therefore capable of taking on a large bandwidth of building-physical characteristics according to their desired functions.

The considerations presented here clearly show the great potential of membrane construction for efficient roof and facade systems, but they also make clear that

there are significant challenges ahead. For multifunctional membrane structures with material-specific optimisations to coatings and varnishes, it will be important to ensure that the original materials can be recovered from these efficient composites during the recycling process. This will require further technological advances.

The multifunctional demands made of facades and roof systems will also require a more robust modular construction method which makes use of small, distinct units. This small-scale modular technique can be expected to complement the building of long-span structures using membranes in the near future. The modular construction of different individual parts requires the use of digital and numerical tools. Parametric design and automated fabrication allow for all project participants to arrive at a much more timely internal consensus based on a shared digitised data structure. The most recent complex projects demonstrate that membrane construction, with its long evolutionary history from simple tents and sails made of natural fibres all the way to today's polymer-based structures, is also fully equipped to meet these technological challenges.

Notes
[1] Moritz, Karsten; Schiemann, Lars: "Structural Design Concepts." In: Moritz, Karsten; Schiemann, Lars: Skriptum Master Program for Membrane Structures, Chapter 1, Basics of Structural Design, 2007, p. 1.32
[2] Knippers, Jan; Cremers, Jan; Gabler, Markus; Lienhard, Julian: *Atlas Kunststoffe + Membranen*, 1st edition, Munich 2010, p. 17 and 19
[3] Moritz, Karsten: "ETFE-Folie als Tragelement", Dissertation, Technical University of Munich, Chair of Structural Design, Munich, 2007
[4] Knippers, Jan; Cremers, Jan; Gabler, Markus; Lienhard, Julian: *Atlas Kunststoffe + Membranen*, 1st edition, Munich 2010, p. 17 and 19
[5] see note [3]
[6] Moritz, Karsten: "Die Stadionhülle der Allianz Arena – Bauweise der ETFE-Folienpneus". In: *Detail* 09/2005, p. 977
[7] Blumer-Lehmann AG: "Losgröße 1 für die Holzgitterträger." 2019. lehmann-gruppe.ch/holzbau/free-form/swatch.html (accessed 10 November 2019)

Mobile, Convertible and Adaptive Structures

Jonas Schikore

In some instances, the modifiability of constructions turns out to be a very advantageous characteristic. Even though mobility and adaptability represent special challenges for designers, there are already numerous existing construction strategies for modifiable structures.

If the location of a structure can be changed, it is referred to as a mobile structure. "Relocatable building" is a standard term coined to describe buildings that are designed to be repeatedly constructed and disassembled [1]. Convertible structures can reversibly change their geometry and can thus be adapted to suit the needs of their users or to facilitate transport. Adaptive structures, as described below, are even capable of autonomous responses to changing influences. These three qualities are not mutually exclusive.

Mobile Structures

Mobile architecture, which includes constructions such as tents and yurts, is as old as building itself. Evidence for prefinished transportable stones can be found as far back as antiquity [2]. At the beginning of the 16th century, Leonardo da Vinci designed a demountable timber frame construction for the hunting excursions of the French royal court. During the days of colonial expansion, there was increasing demand for transportable, predominantly military shelters. In 1830, John Manning developed a "portable cottage for emigrants", a simple timber frame construction of prefabricated elements, for transport abroad [3].

Mobile structures can be grouped into three main categories:

- structures that change their location in their entirety (e.g. motor homes / RVs, tiny houses, mobile homes)
- structures that are transported as prefinished sub-assemblies and put together at their new locations (e.g. container buildings)
- structures that are broken down into their components for transportation (e.g. modular systems, marquees).

These constructive strategies may also be combined [4]. Some of the characteristics of the various mobile constructions are given in the following paragraphs.

Structures that can be transported whole without assembly or disassembly are limited in size. This is based on the technical difficulty of moving a large structural mass and

D 6.2

D 6.3

on the geometrical limitations of the transport routes. Ships and house boats represent an exception to this rule, as they can sometimes take on considerable dimensions. Apart from the fixed transportation specification, there are no requirements placed on these constructions that do not also apply to immovable structures. Modular buildings differ in terms of their size, but must undergo a commensurate assembly process. The individual sub-assemblies are usually designed for a single configuration. For example, if containers are to be stacked crosswise instead of directly on top of one another, the designer must plan for the appropriate reinforcements (Fig. D 6.1). Structures based on modular systems can be significantly compacted for transport and are especially adaptable. However, they often require difficult mounting and dismounting processes and a well-trained assembly team. If different configurations of the building components are desired, the force conditions must be individually assessed. Modular systems frequently have their own technical regulations, significantly simplifying the structural assessment. Thanks to their lightweight and packable characteristics, textile membranes, cables and cable nets are especially well-suited for

large-span mobile structures. Figure D 6.2 is a picture of the largest mobile event hall in the world. The internal forces of open structural systems are short-circuited over the building site. For example, tent constructions can be anchored in the ground. Self-contained systems omit this ground anchoring. In these cases, the membrane is often installed as a secondary structure, for which traditional constructions such as frames, arches, trusses or gridshells provide the primary structure [5]. In general, a distinction is drawn between systems that are mechanically prestressed (e.g. tents) and pneumatically prestressed (e.g. air-inflated structures). Air-inflated structures use air – that is to say, an on-site resource – as the bearing medium (Fig. D 6.3).

Convertible Structures

There are some indications, though rare, of the existence of convertible structures in antiquity in the form of foldable umbrellas, gatherable tent hides, awnings, street canopies and drawbridges. The awnings of the Roman theatres (*vela, velarium*) are considered very large convertible roof constructions, though there

is no incontrovertible evidence for this. In general, convertible structures are classified as internally or externally convertible, depending on whether it is their inner structure (e.g. walls, floors) or their outer envelope that can be modified [6]. Convertible roofs and building shells can be adapted to changing climatic influences, while bridges or internally convertible structures may be modified to accommodate different usage scenarios with the associated geometrical constraints.

The most basic mechanisms of convertible structures can be grouped into three main classes (rigid, elastic and soft) and their appropriate subclasses. Some of these subclasses, which may be combined, are shown in Fig. D 6.4. Rigid mechanisms are widespread and easy to control, but occasionally feature complex and high-maintenance hinged components. Elastic and soft mechanisms depend on their material, but often represent an easily imple-

D 6.1 Myggen/Mosquito, container building, Oslo (NO) 2013, mmw arkitekter
D 6.2 Mobile event hall Valhalla, 2000, Rudi Enos
D 6.3 Mobile air-inflated structure, AIRtec Tragluft-hallen UG
D 6.4 Main and subclasses of convertible structure mechanisms

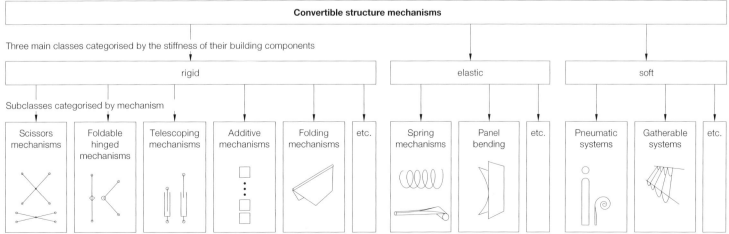

D 6.4

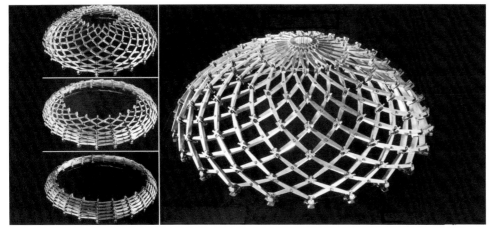

D 6.5

	Direction of motion			
	parallel	central	circular	peripheral
Fixed support structures — pushing				
Fixed support structures — folding				
Membranes / **Movable support structures** — pushing				
Movable support structures — folding				
Movable support structures — rotating				
Rigid support structures — pushing				
Rigid support structures — folding				
Rigid support structures — rotating				

D 6.6

mented, materially homogenous solution [7]. Scissor mechanisms were studied and refined in the 1960s and 70s primarily by Emilio P. Piñero and then, beginning in the 1990s, by Chuck Hoberman. Starting with the basic scissor types (linear, angled and polar), scissor chains with parallel, central or circular motion can be generated. Figure D 6.5 presents the study of a spatially unfolding dome.

Building components called actuators or controlling elements are what set the mechanism in motion. Usually these are run by an electromechanical or hydraulic power source. More specialised options for achieving changes in geometry are a current research topic. These include, for example, piezoelectric actuators, which cause material to expand in response to an electric potential.

The motility of convertible systems is frequently at odds with their load-bearing requirements. The latter necessitates the stiffening or locking of the system for different loading conditions [8]. The locking mechanism can be integrated into the actuator element or placed at another location. Often, the structure is mechanically blocked at a target position, which can be ensured through a latch or the addition of building components or by the extension of cables or membranes to their full target length. The reversible stiffening of elastic or soft mechanisms at the material level is theoretically conceivable, but has not yet been constructively implemented.

Convertible roofs can be classified according to their construction type and direction of motion (Fig. D 6.6).

The main applications of convertible roofs are found in sports and assembly venues, courtyards and street sections. They are especially well-suited to these uses since the mass to be moved is modest and the flexibility of the material makes it easy to stow. For economic and practical reasons, PVC-coated textiles are most often employed. Aramid and PTFE textiles as well as textiles of organic fibres are also technically possible, whereas fibreglass textiles are essentially ruled out for any folding applications [9]. A membrane roof that can be gathered at its centre is pictured in Fig. D 6.7.

Rigid structures are composed of elements that are themselves stable and whose geometries are exactly coordinated with one another. The necessary dimensional precision for this as compared to textile solutions can lead to associated cost increases. However, there are also advantages in the construction of a thermally isolated building shell. Dynamic motile forces play a greater role in the design because of the greater self-weight. When designing The Shed, a New York cultural centre with a convertible building shell, the architects included constructive responses to both factors in their design by encasing the movable but rigid structure with lightweight, highly insulated foil cushions (Fig. D 6.9; see also Built Example on p. 237ff.).

Facades, too, can be convertible. Common drapes, blinds and windows are basically already convertible parts of the building envelope. In larger facade elements, reconciling the motility and the transfer of self-weight and wind loads with the primary

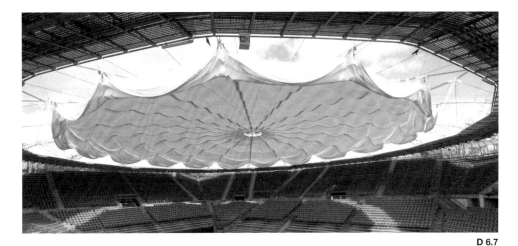

D 6.7

a   b   D 6.8

D 6.9

D 6.5 Iris Dome, model of a spatially unfolding dome using multiaxial hinged connections, movable supports and angled scissor elements, by Chuck Hoberman

D 6.6 Classification of convertible roofs according to construction type and direction of motion

D 6.7 Convertible membrane roof, Am Rothenbaum Tennis Stadium, Hamburg (DE) 1997, Schweger und Partner, 2019 membrane restoration: Alfred Rein Ingenieure

D 6.8 The facade can be opened (**a**) or closed (**b**) via controlled elastic deformation of the GFRP louvres. Expo 2012 Pavilion, Yeosu (KR) 2012, SOMA Architecture, Knippers Helbig

D 6.9 The movable building shell can be pushed out to the adjacent open plaza as needed to create an enclosed event space. The Shed cultural centre, New York (US) 2019, Diller Scofidio + Renfro, Rockwell Group, Thornton Tomasetti

D 6.10

D 6.11

structure becomes more challenging. Figure D 6.8 (p. 139) shows a convertible facade based on an elastic mechanism. Through the controlled bending of the 108 large, glass fibre-reinforced polymer louvres, this facade can be opened to admit daylight into the building.

In the Middle Ages, drawbridges aided in the protection of castles and cities. Today, convertible bridges mainly resolve the conflict between intersecting water and land transit routes. In Fig. D 6.12, bridges are illustrated by their type of motion. In choosing a bridge, designers must heed the following criteria:

- complexity of the conversion mechanism
- spatial requirements of the conversion
- changes in the support conditions or support forces
- energy consumption during conversion
- stylistic considerations

The same principle applies to bridges: lightweight constructions are easier to move. Materials such as timber, steel, aluminium or fibre-reinforced polymers are therefore especially well-suited [10]. Convertible bridges are often spectacular structures in which the mode of conversion is incorporated into the aesthetics of the design. Figure D 6.10 shows a suspension-lift bridge in its open state to allow for the passage of ships.

Adaptive Structures

Structures are called adaptive if they are capable of changing their geometric configuration and therefore their physical properties in a controlled fashion [11]. However, the term is occasionally interpreted differently in science. Ultimately,

the main point is the automated adaptation of the structure to external influences. This feature uses similar principles as found in living organisms.

Passive systems react directly to varying influences or stresses. The use of passive mass dampers, i.e. energy-absorbing or tuned plasticising building components, has been established in oscillation-prone buildings for decades.

Active systems require actuators as well as sensors, in addition to an interactive regulation and control process. The research in this field originated with space travel. One of the first studies, done in the 1980s, investigated the automated oscillation damping of an antenna mast [12]. Today, these same principles are being researched for applications in construction.

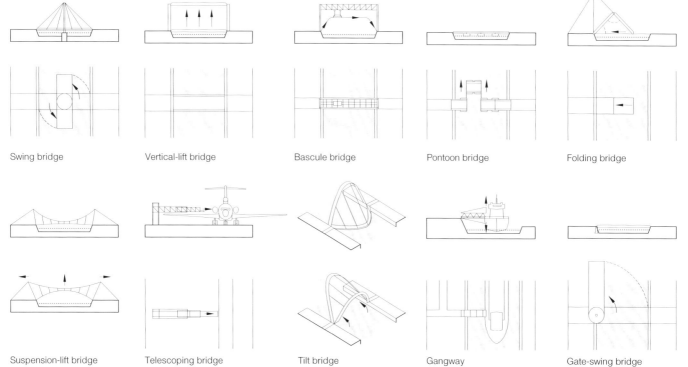

Swing bridge

Vertical-lift bridge

Bascule bridge

Pontoon bridge

Folding bridge

Suspension-lift bridge

Telescoping bridge

Tilt bridge

Gangway

Gate-swing bridge

D 6.12

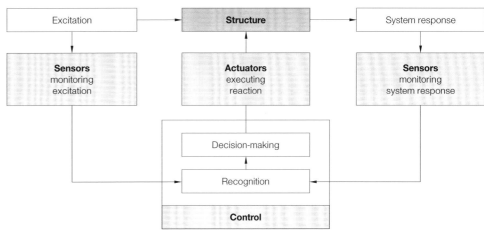

D 6.13

Sensor technology is a basic building block of adaptive structures. It is used to measure changes in external conditions (e.g. wind loads) or in the state of the structural system itself (e.g. structural deformations or stresses) [13]. The recorded quantities are processed in a regulation and control system which then causes the actuators to initiate the appropriate reaction. A schematic representation of the interactions among sensors, actuators and controls is given in Fig. D 6.13.

The development of suitable control methods poses a particular challenge. Numerous far-reaching studies have been done [14]: the prototype of an adaptive cantilevered truss, for example, impressively demonstrates the potential of adaptive structures with regard to slenderness and deformation behaviour. The truss is equipped with sensors and actuators so that any vertical deformations are compensated for by immediate and fully automatic changes in the lengths of the diagonals. Further research is being done to study the energy-saving potential of such structures. The materials used in conventional or passive structures serve not only to vouchsafe load-bearing capacity but also to minimise deformations. The designer of active structures can omit the fraction of the material allotted for the latter function, since deformations are actively countered. The potential for material savings of up to 70 % becomes apparent when the embodied energy of a passive structure is calculated and compared to the energy consumption of an active structure over its service life [15]. The use of adaptive technologies is also being assessed for shell structures. The "Smart Shell" developed at the University of Stuttgart, for example, adjusts the support reactions to conform with the shell loading (Fig. D 6.11) [16]. Thus far, these types of systems have been the subjects of research but have undergone few practical trials.

Opportunities and Challenges

In structural design, various configurations, force conditions and local influences must be taken into account when considering the construction types described above. This requires the development of appropriate safety standards. The construction of reversible mechanisms also requires expertise in mechanical engineering. Advancements in adaptive structures also involve the development of regulation and control software. In order to achieve the hoped-for synergistic effects, interdisciplinary cooperation and suitable design methods are needed.

In addition, the field presents many opportunities with regard to sustainability. Mobile buildings can be reused in different locations. Convertible structures are designed to respond to different use scenarios, and adaptive structures hold promise for significant reductions in material consumption. In nature, mobility, metamorphosis and adaptation are fundamental principles. It makes sense that particular properties and abilities of natural organisms should also be transferrable to architecture. In future, the field of biomimetics could come to have greater influence in such constructions.

Certainly it is safe to assume that mobile, convertible and adaptive structures will play a greater role in architecture in the coming years. Their acceptance is closely tied to a society characterised by rapid progress and globalisation and to its dynamically changing needs. The modifiability of structures broadens the playing field of architectural design in both temporal and spatial dimensions.

D 6.10 Suspension-lift bridge in its open configuration to allow passage of ships, Duisburg (DE) 1999, Schlaich Bergermann Partner (sbp)
D 6.11 Smart Shell adaptive shell structure (DE) 2012, ILEK, University of Stuttgart
D 6.12 Selection of convertible bridge types
D 6.13 Schematic representation of the relationships between sensors, actuators and control elements

Notes:
[1] Rämmler, Benjamin: *Mobile Bauten für die medizinische Versorgung.* Dissertation, TU Berlin 2011, p. 16.
[2] Ludwig, Matthias: *Mobile Architektur. Geschichte und Entwicklung transportabler und modularer Bauten.* Stuttgart 1998, p. 16
[3] *ibid.,* p. 21
[4] Kronenburg, Robert: *Mobile Architektur. Entwurf und Technologie.* Basel 2008
[5] Gengnagel, Christoph: *Mobile Membrankonstruktionen.* Dissertation, TU Munich 2005, p. 154; mediatum.ub.tum.de/doc/601016/ 601016.pdf (accessed 22 Jan 2020)
[6] *Wandelbare Dächer.* Memoranda of the Institute for Lightweight Structures, University of Stuttgart 1972
[7] Howell, Larry L. *et al.*: *Handbook of Compliant Mechanisms.* Chichester 2013
[8] Novacki, Zoran: *Wandelbare lineare Tragsysteme. Analyse und Neuentwicklung.* Dissertation, TU Munich 2014. mediatum.ub.tum.de/doc/ 1223015/1223015.pdf (accessed on 20 Jan 2020)
[9] Sobek, Werner: "Wandelbare Überdachungen aus textilen Werkstoffen." In: 5th International Techtextil Symposium, Frankfurt a. M. 1993, p. 4
[10] Keil, Andreas: *Fußgängerbrücken.* Munich 2013, p. 86
[11] Wada, B. K.; Fanson, J. L.; Crawley, E. F.: "Adaptive Structures." In: *Journal of Intelligent Material Systems and Structures,* 1990, p. 157
[12] Clark, Robert L.; Saunders, William; Gibbs, Gary P.: *Adaptive Structures. Dynamics and Control.* New York 1998, p. 2
[13] Teuffel, Patrick: *Entwerfen adaptiver Strukturen.* Dissertation, University of Stuttgart 2004, p. 13. elib uni-stuttgart.de/bitstream/11682/212/1/ Teuffel_Entwerfen_Adaptiver_Strukturen.pdf (accessed on 20 Jan 2020)
[14] Senatore, Gennaro; Duffour, Philippe; Winslow, Pete: "Synthesis of minimum energy adaptive structures." In: *Structural and Multidisciplinary Optimization 60* (3), 2019, p. 849–877
[15] Senatore, Gennaro; Duffour, Philippe; Winslow, Pete: "Energy and Cost Assessment of Adaptive Structures: Case Studies." In: *Journal of Structural Engineering 144* (8), 2018, p. 04018107-1 to 04018107-23
Senatore, Gennaro; Duffour, Philippe; Winslow, Pete: "Exploring the application domain of adaptive structures." In: *Engineering Structures 167,* 2018, p. 608–628
[16] *ibid.*
[17] ILEK / isys / Rexroth: "Ultraleichtbau steht auf Hydraulik. Adaptive Tragwerke: Revolution für ressourcenschonendes Bauen." ILEK, isys, Rexroth, press release from 16 Apr 2012. architektur.uni-stuttgart.de/fileadmin/user_upload/ Nachrichten/120416_StuttgartSmartShell_PI_lang_ DE.pdf (accessed on 27 Jan 2020)

Potential Offered by New Technologies and Building Materials

Hanaa Dahy

An important quality of architecture is its continual adaptation to the external influences of culture, climate and societal needs. Architects have always strived to develop new concepts, analyse existing problems and find solutions. A continual process of rethinking and improving on established structures happens in order to meet changing demands. In post-war architecture, because of the need to rebuild rapidly and to confront the great housing shortage, there was no discussion about environmental impact or the reuse of building materials after their relatively short service life. The guiding principle of the building industry that is still prevalent today is saddled with a tragic wastefulness. As a result, as much as 50 % of the construction waste in Europe cannot be recycled [1]. Globally, the building sector is responsible for more than 35 % of final energy consumption, almost 40 % of energy-related CO_2 emissions [2] and about 45 % of resource consumption (see "Efficiency and Sustainability of Materials and Structures", p. 150ff.). Since the world's population is expected to increase from seven to almost nine billion people by 2040, the demand for resources will grow exponentially, so that by 2030 the world will need at least 50 % more food, 45 % more energy and 30 % more water – all this, while at the same time environmental conditions are placing new limits on the supply, particularly in connection to climate change [3]. In Europe, concrete and aggregates currently make up the bulk of the building materials that, together with the production of the most emissions-intensive materials such as steel and aluminium, account for most of the greenhouse gas emissions in the construction sector [4]. This problem can no longer be met with an observation period followed by appropriate action, the "cradle to grave" approach, but must be confronted with a paradigm shift. For this reason, the search for sustainable alternatives has now taken on enormous importance.

Increasingly, design processes are focussing on environmentally friendly and bio-based building materials. The BioMat Department of the ITKE (Institute of Building Structures and Structural Design) at the University of Stuttgart is pursuing such an approach under the descriptor "Materials as a Design Tool" [5]. This approach offers architects a certain freedom in design and does not lead – as is typically the case – to a straight-line way of thinking. That is because here, the choice of material is no longer a subordinated step, but rather a fixed part of a circular design process. Aside from an early selection of the materials – especially bio-based materials – the process also includes defining and adapting the material properties, using various form-finding strategies utilising parametric design methods, performing structural analyses and implementing digital fabrication technologies in order to ultimately prefabricate these innovative building components.

One of the main factors of the design process is the maximal exploitation of material performance, which opens up the potential for developing more sophisticated solutions to different architectural challenges. Further optimisation possibilities result from combining the "materials as a design tool" philosophy with the concept of "designing for deconstruction (DfD)", which identifies deconstruction options and considerations. In order to make the process economically and environmentally viable, individual building elements are prefabricated in a conveniently manageable size so that they can be assembled and dismantled quickly without the need for the incorporation of special detailing and connections.

Computer-assisted form finding and various fabrication methods can also contribute to efficiencies in structure and material consumption, which in turn allow for positive life cycle assessments and a reduction of the entire carbon footprint. For this reason,

materials cannot be viewed as constant quantities. Depending on its desired use, the chosen material should be individually refined, fabricated and adapted. It is possible to identify the performance and structural prospects of materials before the design phase by the mechanical testing and computational simulation of prototypes. The fabrication processes of individual materials, such as extrusion, drilling or pouring, for example, also represent an important factor, since they have a significant impact on the material's behaviour and on its geometric variations.

In the following paragraphs, three case studies are analysed in which the previously mentioned design approaches – "materials as a design tool" and "design for deconstruction" – are combined in individualised, project-specific ways. In each case, bio-based materials and materials known as biocomposites determine the design process.

- The first case study used newly developed flexible biocomposite fibreboard panels [6],
- the second, elastic medium density fibreboard (MDF) panels and
- for the third case study, flax-fibre reinforced biocomposites were developed that are sewn and manufactured using a technique known as tailored fibre placement (TFP).

Biocomposites, which are employed in two of the three case studies below, are also referred to as natural fibre-reinforced polymer composites (NFRP) [7]. They are made from two or more main constituent materials, a fibre and a matrix (also known as a binding agent), at least one of which is naturally derived. The use of biocomposites makes it possible to partially replace timber, which takes comparatively long to regenerate and requires considerable conservation measures to ensure a positive life cycle assessment. Aside from timber, biocom-

posites may also contain other lignocellulosic resources, such as the residual agricultural products of annual crops like straw and other natural fibres such as hemp, flax and jute. The advantages of biocomposites lie in their ability to replace some of the classic fibre-reinforced plastics (FRP), principally those of glass fibre (GF) and carbon fibre (CF), with their significant environmental drawbacks. In addition, studies have already been published on improving the fire resistance of other developed biocomposites for their broader applicability in architecture [8]. Most types of straw, for instance, have a naturally high proportion of silicate, which has flame-retardant properties (e.g. rice straw has a 20 % silicate content by weight).

Case Studies

The three case studies presented here were developed in the Department of Bio-based Materials and Materials Cycles in Architecture (BioMat) at the Institute of Building Structures and Structural Design (ITKE: *Institut für Tragkonstruktionen und Konstruktives Entwerfen*) in the Faculty of Architecture and Urban Planning at the University of Stuttgart.

BioMat Pavilion

The BioMat Research Pavilion was the result of a close multidisciplinary collaboration between architecture students and experts from various different disciplines during the 2018 summer semester [9]. The doubly curved shell structure, which was 3.60 m high and spanned an area of 55 m², was erected on the campus of the University of Stuttgart. The modular construction was composed of 121 elements, which had themselves been manufactured from about 350 digitally fabricated segments (Fig. D 7.1–D 7.7, p. 144f.). The lightweight, simply curved elements were assembled to form the doubly curved shell of the modular system. This shell was supported by a structure of three crossing timber beams which carried their self-weight as well as wind loads and transferred them into the ground. The filigree, aesthetic structure could be non-destructively disassembled and subsequently rebuilt in new geometric configurations (Fig. D 7.3, p. 144).

D 7.1   BioMat Pavilion on the campus of the University of Stuttgart (DE) 2018, BioMat at the ITKE / University of Stuttgart
D 7.2   View from below of the filigree structure, BioMat Pavilion

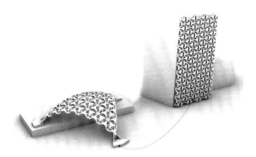

D 7.3

Materials

The pavilion was composed of a segmented shell of timber and biocomposite elements, which were interlaced with one another to form a three-dimensional mesh (Fig. D 7.5). A flexible panel of natural fibres formed the core of each of these biocomposite elements. With the aid of computer numerical control (CNC) guided machines, the panel was shaped according to the specifications of the specially designed computer model and bilaterally reinforced with pre-cut, three-dimensional veneer layers. This process occurred at room temperature in a vacuum pressing bag without thermal or moisture pretreatment. The lamination changed the structure of the flexible core panel, which could be bent into any simply or doubly curved form as desired, into a stiff, curved 3D element – essentially a biocomposite sandwich panel with adjustable mechanical properties. In this way, the originally elastic material could be used as a structural component. Various experiments were done to adapt the reinforcing veneers in order to achieve the optimal behaviour of the materials and their pre-determined target characteristics. Thanks to the optimised orientation of the fibre direction, the use of the veneers resulted in a significant structural improvement of the developed biocomposites.

Fig. D 7.6 shows the quantity and variety of the individual segments, which were sorted into different groups using a clever numbering scheme. Only in their assembled state could they unfold the full effect of the overall system. As previously mentioned, the fibre orientation of the individual segments played a very important role.

Form finding and connection details

A parametric form-finding process made it possible to find the final, implementable

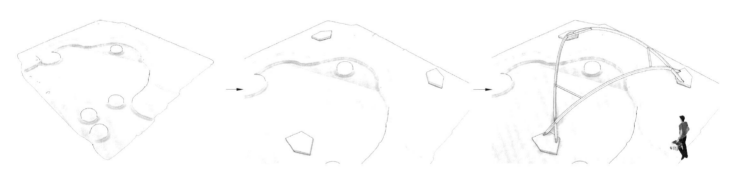

3D laser-scanned photograph (point cloud) of the pavilion site

Exact placement of the foundations, which had to be embedded without drilling, etc.

Erection of the crossing beams

Successive installation

of the four pre-assembled large triangle segments

with temporary scaffolding

D 7.4

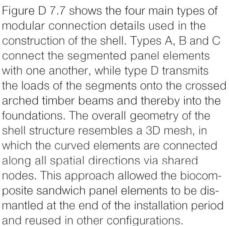

D 7.5

D 7.6

architectural solution that represented an optimised combination of manufacturing conditions, aesthetics and structural capacity. The on-site assembly of the prefabricated components began with the construction of four large triangular segments, which were then sequentially lifted into their correct spatial positions with the aid of temporary scaffolding and finally secured in place (Fig. D 7.4). The 1:1 scale implementation of the structure made it possible to test the entire newly developed system under real operating conditions for a five-month period from August to December of 2018.

Figure D 7.7 shows the four main types of modular connection details used in the construction of the shell. Types A, B and C connect the segmented panel elements with one another, while type D transmits the loads of the segments onto the crossed arched timber beams and thereby into the foundations. The overall geometry of the shell structure resembles a 3D mesh, in which the curved elements are connected along all spatial directions via shared nodes. This approach allowed the biocomposite sandwich panel elements to be dismantled at the end of the installation period and reused in other configurations.

BioMat Biomimetic Pavilion
The bending-active Biomimetic Pavilion of 2018 is based on a special interlocking system inspired by a biological model – diatoms – and translated into the context of

D 7.3 Illustration of different possible geometric configurations of the same building components, BioMat Pavilion
D 7.4 Construction phases of the BioMat Pavilion
D 7.5 One of the connection details of the BioMat Pavilion
D 7.6 The segments were sorted into different groups using a clever numbering scheme, BioMat Pavilion
D 7.7 The four main types of connections, BioMat Pavilion

Type A
1 upper element and 6 legs

Type B
1 lower element and 6 legs

Type C
1 upper and lower element and rod

Type D
edge element and timber beam

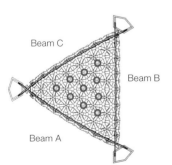

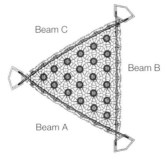

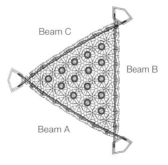

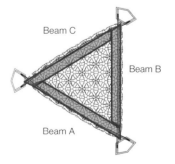

On-site assembly:
connect 6 legs with 1 element
> connection types A and B

On-site assembly:
connect 6 legs with 1 element
> connection types A and B

Pre-assembly:
connect 1 upper and 1 lower element
with a rod
> connection type C

On-site assembly:
connect edge elements
to timber beam
> connection type D

D 7.7

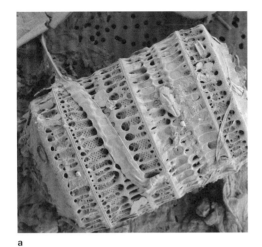

a

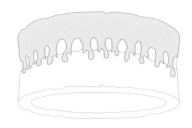

b   D 7.8

lightweight architecture [10]. Some of these algae, which are found throughout the earth's oceans, are single-celled organisms, while others are capable of forming filamentous colonies. The pivotal factor in the design of the pavilion was the particular way in which the latter organisms form vertical connections with one another, in which their spikes, which function as flaps, prevent horizontal displacement. A structural concept inspired by this model was developed for a bio-based material. Intensive analyses of the interlocking structure of the diatoms and work spanning several levels of abstraction made it possible to scale up the principle

mechanism from the microbiological sphere to the macroscopic architectural domain (Fig. D 7.8). The vertical stacking system and the meshing of individual components was translated into an architectural typology, whose modular composition also reduces material consumption. Merely by active bending and by interlocking the long panels, as well as by rigidly attaching the ends into the curved foundations on the ground, it was ultimately possible to erect a doubly curved shell system (Fig. D 7.10). Bending-active construction results in curved structures whose geometry and overall stiffness is a result of the elastic deformation of the

structural elements. Bending can thus be employed to generate variously complex, spatially curved structures from initially straight or planar structural elements. The approach allows for the development of highly efficient structures that are created from short-circuiting the restoring forces – that is, internally stored forces – of the system.

Material

The doubly curved shell structure of the pavilion comprises 6.50-mm thick medium-density fibreboard (MDF) panels of birch. The decisive requirement for the MDF panel was that the material be sufficiently flexible to accommodate the necessary curvature. As it is based on timber, the structure has a high environmental value, especially since the elements can be reused thanks to the specially developed dry joining system. In addition, the panels were fastened to the unanchored, curved timber foundations without screws in order to prevent irreversible deformations. The doubly curved, interlocking shell structure is ultimately a result of active bending alone.

Construction

The goal in the construction of this pavilion was the development of a structure that could be assembled and dismantled rapidly and rebuilt at different locations and on different scales. The stacked connecting system of the biological model led to the design of several uniform, identically constructed elements with toothed edges for subsequent joining. The elements were CNC-milled according to digitally generated patterns and could then be easily transported to the building site for rapid assembly. The construction was carried out in two stages: first, the pieces were laid out flat on the ground and pushed and locked together (Fig. D 7.9a); then the resulting sheet was bent into shape. Finally, the panel ends were attached to the timber foundations (Fig. D 7.9b).

a

b   D 7.9

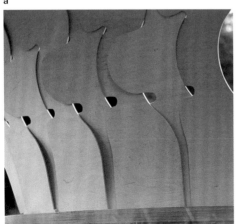

a

b   D 7.10

D 7.11

BioMat Tailored Biocomposite Mock-up

The Tailored Biocomposite Mock-up of 2019 is also the result of a student project [11]. In this one, the goal was to design and create a small canopy (Fig. D 7.11). From the outset it was determined that the technology known as Tailored Fibre Placement (TFP) would be used. TFP is a digitally controlled stitching process that allows for the fabrication of complex textile preforms with precision-placed force-flow oriented natural fibres (Fig. D 7.13, p. 148). In this technique, in contrast to most of the short fibres, the long fibres are incorporated into the binding matrix in a targeted fashion along the main load path direction, so that their tensile strength properties can be fully exploited. The lightweight structure of the 2.25-m high and 1.25-m wide simply curved canopy is the result of an extended form-finding process (Fig. D 7.12). The initial geometrical form was optimised with the aid of special modelling software, after which the geometry with the smallest spread was ultimately chosen [12]. This selected model was then further optimised topologically to reduce the amount of superfluous material and achieve the desired lightness and performance of the form [13]. The parameters produced by

Basic shell optimisation

Topology optimisation of a simply curved canopy

Structure generated through agent-based modelling based on parameters from the previously run topology optimisation

Selection of final design from the generated variants

D 7.8 Biological model for the Biomimetic Pavilion and abstraction
    a *Paralia sulcata* diatom, imaged with a scanning electron microscope
    b Simplification of the stacking system of the biological model
D 7.9 Construction of the Biomimetic Pavilion
    a Simple horizontal stacking effected by pushing the modules together
    b Erection of the pre-assembled pavilion through manual bending and attachment to the curved foundations
D 7.10 Biomimetic Pavilion on the campus of the University of Stuttgart (DE) 2018, BioMat at the ITKE / University of Stuttgart
D 7.11 Tailored Biocomposite Mock-up, Stuttgart (DE) 2019, BioMat at the ITKE / University of Stuttgart
D 7.12 Form finding and design process for the mock-up

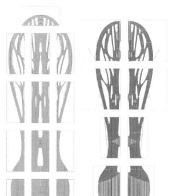

CAD paths of the individual preforms

Detail of the path for the fibre placement (tailoring)

D 7.12

a

b   D 7.13

the topology optimisation were used in the next step as the boundary conditions for the calculations of a so-called agent-based modelling system [14] to simulate the optimal orientation of the fibres. The geometries of the multiple variants of the generated line patterns were reworked and finally the best-suited model was selected. Aesthetic considerations were one of the deciding factors in this step. The line patterns correspond to the force flows and therefore also to the fibre paths in the canopy structure. The entire form-finding process was carried out in collaboration with the Institute of Aircraft Design (IFB: *Institut für Flugzeugbau*) at the University of Stuttgart (Fig. D 7.12, p. 147).

Fibre material
Annually regrowing flax fibres were chosen for this project, since their rapid growth (they can be harvested after approx. 90–100 days) and their properties, which are comparable to those of glass fibres, make them sustainable alternatives to synthetic fibres. Beyond this, the greatest advantage of flax fibres is that their density is significantly lower than that of synthetic fibres of carbon and glass. In addition, they also have sound and vibration-absorbing properties. Added to that is their

high tensile strength and their ready availability in Central Europe.

Manufacture
In order for the TFP embroidery machine to be able to join the predefined fibre patterns into textile preforms, the previously determined 3D form of the canopy was unwound and transferred onto a level surface (Fig. D 7.12, p. 147, D 7.13). Because of the size limitations of the TFP machine, the geometrical template had to be divided up into pieces no greater than 1.00 × 1.40 m. In addition, the TFP preforms for the mock-up structure had four layers. The layers were developed in such a way that they overlap, so that tears at the borders between textile preforms could be avoided. The CAD model generated a predefined path for the embroidery machine for each individual preform layer. This method achieves an accuracy of ±0.3 mm in the placement of the fibres.

After the TFP fabrication of the textile preform pieces came the preparation of the mould. The textile preforms were placed on the mould using a vacuum technique (vacuum-assisted resin transfer moulding, Fig. D 7.14). Most of the fibre composite materials in which such a fibre placement method is used require a counter-mould.

For this mock-up, a reusable mould was created from components of flexible CNC-milled timber. These could be put together repeatedly to form a waffle texture and a series of other shapes, significantly reducing its material consumption when compared to the typical types of moulds. The finished textile preforms were placed onto the mould, impregnated with epoxy resin and then formed and hardened in a closed vacuum-assisted process. After the canopy structure was removed from the timber mould, additional TFP flax strips were attached for further reinforcement. Following the hardening phase, the canopy form received finishing touches, including polishing and coating.

The mock-up is an example of the successful application of the automated TFP technique with long fibres, which allowed for the manufacture of a single-piece canopy without any connections or seams. The method is well-suited for the fabrication of precise shell and panel structures with controlled fibre orientation along the predominant tensile forces. In a follow-up project, the mould that was still needed during the creation of the canopy mock-up was eliminated, with the focus of the research moving instead to the flexural strength of the material [15] (Fig. D 7.15).

a

b

c   D 7.14

a

Conclusions

The case studies presented here not only demonstrate a new aesthetic and architectural use of form, but also the high performance and structural potential of bio-based materials in conjunction with digital fabrication technologies and computer-assisted design methods. The pavilions introduced above showcase different construction and design methods that represent the "materials as a design tool" philosophy of design. The creation of a future-oriented, sustainable architecture should henceforth incorporate newly developed bio-based materials as the basis of every design. This is especially important for the upcoming generation of architects, which will have to contend with alternative materials, digitally controlled fabrication methods and effective life cycles for the buildings of tomorrow. Each case study features a different design approach which focuses on different materials and manufacturing processes. The collaboration with specialists of related disciplines, such as materials engineers, manufacturers, structural engineers and other experts, represents the ideal way to allow these novel ideas to become reality.

D 7.13 Fabrication of the textile preforms
   a Tailored fibre placement using a TFP embroidery machine
   b Structured fibres being brought into the correct position
D 7.14 Fabrication process in three main steps:
   a TFP preforms
   b Mould preparation
   c Vacuum-assisted resin transfer moulding
D 7.15 Fabrication process, Biomimetic NFRP stool, BioMat at the ITKE/University of Stuttgart
   a Prototype
   b Tailored fibre placement
   c Creating form without a mould by knitting
   d Internal perspective of the prototype

Notes:
[1] Eurostat Statistics. https://ec.europa.eu/eurostat/ statistics-explained/images/a/a0/Waste_generation_ by_economic_activities_and_households%2C_ 2014-1.png (accessed 19 Feb 2019)

[2] United Nations Environment Programme 2017. Global Status Report. worldgbc.org/sites/default/ files/UNEP%20188_GABC_en%20%28web%29.pdf (accessed 19 Feb 2019)
[3] United Nations: *Resilient People, Resilient Planet. A Future Worth Choosing.* The Report of the United Nations Secretary-General's High-Level Panel on Global Sustainability. New York 2012
[4] Herczeg, Márton et al.: *Resource efficiency in the building sector.* Final report. Rotterdam 2014
[5] Dahy, Hanaa: "Materials as a Design Tool. Design Philosophy Applied in Three Innovative Research Pavilions Out of Sustainable Building Materials with Controlled End-Of-Life Scenarios." In: *Buildings 9,* 64, 2019
[6] Dahy, Hanaa; Knippers, Jan: "Flexible High-density Fiberboard and Method for Manufacturing the Same." EP3166765A1, 13 Jan 2016. Based on the same patent, as well as WO2016005026A1; CN106604806A; US20170144327, EP2965882 A1.
[7] Dahy, Hanaa: "Natural Fibre-reinforced Polymer Composites (NFRP) Fabricated from Lignocellulosic Fibres for Future Sustainable Architectural Applications, Case Studies: Segmented Shell Construction. Acoustic Panels and Furniture." In: *Sensors 19,* 3, 2019;
Dahy, Hanaa: "Biocomposite materials based on annual natural fibres and biopolymers – Design, fabrication and customized applications in architecture." In: *Construction and Building Materials.* Vol. 147/2017, p. 212ff.
[8] Dahy, Hanaa: "Efficient Fabrication of Sustainable Building Products from Annually Generated Non-Wood Cellulosic Fibres and Bioplastics with Improved Flammability Resistance." *Waste Biomass Valorization 10,* 2019, p. 1167–1175
[9] Dahy, Hanaa et al: "BioMat Pavilion 2018: Development, Fabrication and Erection of a Double Curved Segmented Shell from Biocomposite Elements." In: *Proceedings of the IASS Annual Symposium 2019 – Structural Membranes 2019 Form and Force.* Edited by Lázaro, C.; Bletzinger, K.-U.; Oñate, E., Barcelona 2019, p. 2862ff.;
Dahy, Hanaa; Baszynski, Piotr; Petrš, Jan: "Experimental Biocomposite Pavilion: Segmented Shell Construction – Design, Material Development and Erection." ACADIA Conference, Austin 2019
[10] see note [5]
[11] Dahy, Hanaa; Petrs, Jan; Baszynski, Piotr: "Design and Fabrication of two 1:1 Architectural Demonstrators based on Biocomposites from Annually Renewable Resources Displaying a Future Vision for Sustainable Architecture." London 2020
[12] Rhinoceros plug-ins Grasshopper + Galapagos + Millipede
[13] using Matlab
[14] Coding in progress using Plethora plug-in
[15] Rihaczek, Gabriel et al.: "Curved foldable tailored fiber reinforcements for moldless customized biocomposite structures. Proof of Concept: Biomimetic NFRP Stools." *Polymers* 12(9), 2020

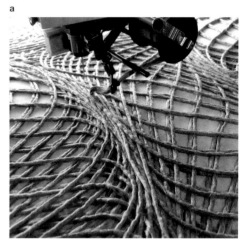

b

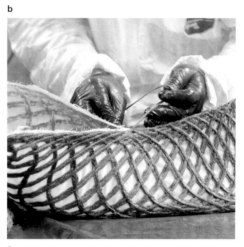

c

d   D 7.15

Efficiency and Sustainability of Materials and Structures

Werner Lang and Patricia Schneider-Marin

Sustainability in the Building Sector

Finding solutions for global challenges such as climate change, environmental destruction, resource competition, demographic changes and urbanisation – and for the associated demands that these place on society – is one of the central tasks of our time. In this effort, the construction industry can play a decisive role, since it is positioned to make significant contributions to lowering CO_2 emissions and reducing resource consumption (e.g. soil, material and water), not to mention adapting our cities, districts and buildings to climate change and to rapidly evolving economic and societal conditions. Currently, about 26 % of the applied final energy in Europe goes into running residential buildings [1]. Almost 40 % of global CO_2 emissions can be traced back to construction and operations in the building sector [2]. In addition, the construction industry is responsible for 50 % of Europe's material consumption [3] and 25–30 % of its waste [4]. In Germany today, about 450 million tonnes (about 5.6 t per capita) of mineral materials such as gravel and sand and more than 15.5 million tonnes (194 kg per capita) of metal (e.g. steel, aluminium and copper) are used every year for the maintenance of buildings and for new construction [5].

Given the current size of the world population's environmental footprint, and given that the earth's biocapacity – i.e. its ability to generate resources and break down harmful contaminants – is already perceptibly overstretched by a factor of more than 1.5, these are alarming numbers. In the context of the exponentially growing world population and the consequences of this growth – equally rapid increases in CO_2 emissions and resource consumption – an immediate readjustment of the building industry to exclusively

sustainable actions is urgently needed. In order to meet the established climate goals, industrialised nations must cut their greenhouse gas emissions by about 80–95 % of their 1990 levels by 2050. According to the EU's Energy Performance of Buildings directive, enacted in 2021, all new buildings in the EU must be built to a lowest-energy standard beginning in 2021. This nearly corresponds to the requirements for zero-energy buildings. It also means not only that the operating energy consumption must be taken into account, but further, that at the material level, the building components and systems used must be as carbon-neutral as possible. Reliable documentation of such carbon neutrality would have to be provided for the entire life cycle of the component.

Aside from the mandatory reduction in CO_2 emissions, the design and implementation process for load-bearing structures in particular should also bear in mind the consumption of resources inherent in their construction, as well as how the materials used impact the earth's ecosystem and human health.

In view of the pressing need for sustainable and therefore environmental as well as health-conscious construction, designers are under particular pressure to use their expertise in the design of holistically optimised structures. Not only must environmental challenges be factored into such a task, but the whole hitherto linear approach must be transformed into an interdisciplinary and iteratively organised design process. This means that the project-specific optimisation potentials must be identified and realised early on. It is the only way to produce structures that achieve their environmental protection targets while also reaching equally important sustainability goals and maintaining sociocultural and economic quality.

D 8.1 Scope, execution and results of a life cycle assessment (author's illustration according to DIN EN ISO 14040:2021-02 / DIN EN 15804:2020-03).

Environmental Impact of Structures

Digital analysis, computation and design tools, ground-breaking fabrication methods and new materials, all of which are already available, can contribute decisively to the exploitation of optimisation potential for minimising negative environmental impacts and resource consumption.

The greatest opportunities to make the changes that result in sustainable structures arise in the early design phases during which the course of a project is set. Gauging and optimising the environmental impact of construction plans and the relevant structures at this early point requires a life cycle perspective as opposed to short-term criteria. In a full life cycle assessment, the material and construction-related energy expenditure and associated environmental impact must be quantified for the extraction of the materials, the manufacture of components and products, transport, construction, maintenance,

eventual deconstruction and disposal or recycling of materials for each individual design approach. Other important considerations are the energy consumption and associated environmental impacts for the operation of the building throughout its life cycle. Depending on building type, building function and energy supply facilities, building operations can heavily dominate the ecological impacts of administrative buildings, for example. In the structural engineering sector, on the other hand, such as in civil engineering and bridge construction or for special structures (stadiums or halls without air conditoning), the environmental impacts are determined primarily by the choice of material and the particular structure type.

Life Cycle Assessment

A design that focuses on life cycle considerations makes it possible to compare and optimise different design approaches and

scenarios with respect to their environmental impact over the entire lifetime of the structure. In this process, the environmental consequences of the construction, operation, maintenance and disposal of the building are ascertained, making a comprehensive evaluation possible already at the design stage.

The basic premise of a life cycle assessment is to quantify all inputs (e.g. material, energy) and outputs (e.g. waste) over the life cycle of a product or service and to use these values to arrive at an environmental impact determination. The general guidelines for performing a life cycle assessment are given in the standards DIN EN ISO 14040:2021-02 and DIN EN ISO 14044:2021-02. According to these, a life cycle assessment is split up into four stages: goal definition and scoping, inventory analysis, impact assessment, and interpretation (Fig. D 8.1). Information on performing life cycle assessments for buildings can be found

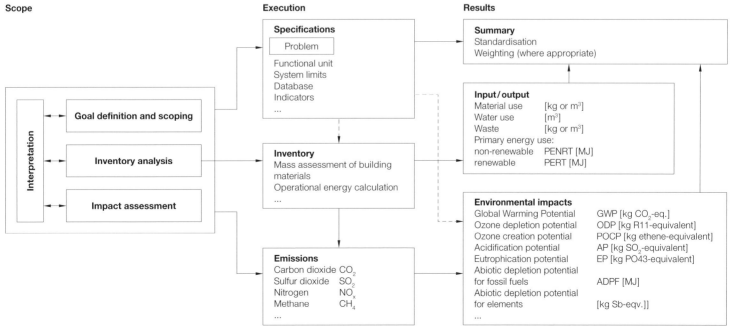

D 8.1

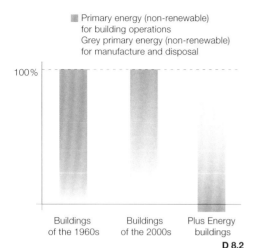

■ Primary energy (non-renewable)
for building operations
Grey primary energy (non-renewable)
for manufacture and disposal

100%

Buildings of the 1960s | Buildings of the 2000s | Plus Energy buildings

D 8.2

in DIN EN 15978: 2012-10 and DIN 15804:2020-03; however, in Germany, specific rules for their actual execution are currently defined only in the certification system of the German Sustainable Building Council (DGNB: *Deutsche Gesellschaft für Nachhaltiges Bauen*) [6] and in the Assessment System for Sustainable Building (BNB: *Bewertungssystem Nachhaltiges Bauen*) [7].

The life cycle stages of a building are subdivided into the production (A 1–3), construction process (A 4–5), use (B 1–7) and end-of-life (C 1–4) stages (Fig. D 8.3). Processes that occur outside the system boundary of the life cycle of a building or structure are assigned to stage D: "Benefits and loads beyond the system boundary". This stage incorporates, for instance, the potentials for the reuse, recovery and recycling of building materials and components. Whether or not this module may be included in the overall tally is disputed. For example, according to the DGNB, stage D is taken into account in the life cycle assessment,

whereas in BNB, stage D values are omitted. Structures are especially critical in the "grey" stages, i.e. all of the stages of the life cycle relevant to materials (all stages except B 6 and B 7). Regarding the energy efficiency of the operational energy use stage (B 6), they play a subordinated role, though they should be evaluated with respect to their potential thermal storage mass on a case-by-case basis. The "replacement" life cycle stage (B 4) is likewise less relevant, since as a rule, the structure of a building is not replaced during the building's lifetime. The main focus in life cycle assessments for structures thus lies in the product/construction process (A) and end-of-life (C, D) stages.

In the context of rising operational energy efficiencies and the growing use of renewable energies, these "grey" life cycle stages become more and more significant to the total energy consumption (Fig. D 8.2). Plus Energy buildings even use up the entire non-renewable primary energy of their life cycle in these early stages. In

the ideal case, this energy expenditure may be compensated for by the generation of renewable energy during their operational use stage.

However, life cycle assessments analyse not only the primary energy demand, but also the environmental impacts of each of the different life cycle stages. Ökobaudat the publicly accessible database of the German Federal Ministry of the Interior and Community (BMI: Bundesministeriums des Innern) for the life cycle assessment of buildings in Germany, lists seven categories of environmental impacts (see Environmental Impact in Fig. D 8.1, p. 151). Both the certification systems DGNB and BNB, as well as numerous life cycle assessment studies, attribute the greatest importance among the environmental impacts of the building sector to the global warming potential (GWP). In terms of the structure, the material that draws particular attention in this regard is reinforced concrete, since the production of cement emits large quantities of CO_2.

Information for Building Assessment

Information on the building life cycle | Supplementary information beyond the life cycle of the building

A1–A3	A4–A5	B1–B7	C1–C4	D
Production	Construction	Use	End-of-Life	Benefits and loads beyond the system boundary

A1	A2	A3	A4	A5	B1	B2	B3	B4	B5	C1	C2	C3	C4	
Raw material supply	Transport	Manufacturing	Transport	Installation	Use	Maintenance	Repair	Replacement	Refurbishment	Deconstruction	Transport	Waste processing	Disposal	Reuse, recovery and recycling potentials

B6 operational energy use

B7 operational water use

D 8.3

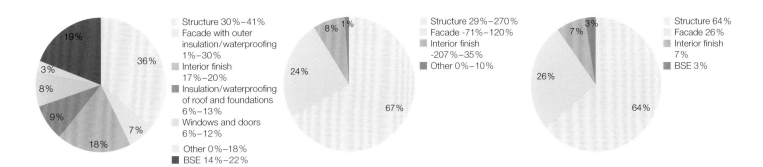

a

b

c   **D 8.4**

The cement industry is responsible for 4–8 % of global CO_2 emissions [8]. Research shows that, for several reasons, structures play a significant role in the life cycle assessments of buildings. The structure represents a large proportion of the building mass, especially if it is a heavy structure of solid building materials. On the other hand, structures generally have a long lifetime of 50 years or more (Fig. D 8.8, p. 154), which has a positive effect on the life cycle assessment. It is important to keep in mind, however, that the structure – depending on the chosen system – has a decisive influence on the functionality of the building, so that structural changes made at a later date are often quite costly and difficult to implement.

A study of newer office buildings identifies the structure as the part of the building that produces an average of 36 % of the "grey" CO_2 emissions. Almost all of this can be chalked up to the manufacturing stage of the building [9]. These and other results of life cycle assessments confirm the structure's role as a significant driver of CO_2 emissions in the building's construction, making it the ideal fulcrum at which to place the largest possible lever for improvement (Fig. D 8.4) [10].

Figures D 8.5 and D 8.6 show a comparison of environmentally relevant structural materials. In this very simplified illustration it is important to keep in mind that a structure composed of a steel or timber skeleton incorporates significantly less material volume than a comparable building of solid reinforced concrete or masonry. Nevertheless, the comparison of possible structural materials makes clear that, with regard to greenhouse gas emissions, timber possesses considerable advantages [11]. This can be explained by the fact that trees sequester carbon as they grow. In contrast, the manufacture of concrete and steel uses fossil fuel sources that produce CO_2 emissions. Depending on the dataset used, the production of 1 m³ of steel profiles generates 19 to 25 times the greenhouse gas emissions as that of 1 m³ of concrete. However, in the case of steel there is a recycling offset to be considered.

The energy consumption of timber creates a less clear-cut picture, since in its "manufacturing stage", wood is assigned a relatively high consumption of renewable primary energy – the portion visible as PERM (primary energy resources used as raw materials) – which it "uses up" in the form of sunlight as it grows. According to Ökobau-

dat, the non-renewable primary energy consumption during the production (stages A1 –A3) of 1 m³ of structural timber is greater than that of 1 m³ of reinforced concrete (C 25/30 with 2 % rebar). Aside from differences in the types of dataset used (generic or average), this is due to the use

D 8.2 Importance of grey energy in the total energy demand of buildings as a function of increasing operational energy efficiency

D 8.3 Life cycle stages of buildings according to DIN EN 15978:2012-10; blue denotes the stages included in the life cycle assessment by DGNB and BNB (without Phase D)

D 8.4 Share of the structure in the total global warming potential (GWP) of buildings based on three studies. The diagrams of the studies shown in a and b report average values, since the data is compiled from several projects. The values in the legends represent the associated ranges. The buildings for which negative values are presented in the results use large quantities of CO_2-sequestering timber in the facade or interior. Since these have negative emissions, the emissions of other building parts can be greater than 100 %.
   a from Design2Eco, see Note 9
   b from Hildebrand, Linda: *Strategic investment of embodied energy during the architectural planning process.* Dissertation, TU Delft 2014
   c from wagnis, see Note 10

D 8.5 Comparison of the global warming potential of structural building materials

D 8.6 Comparison of the renewable and non-renewable primary energy demands of structural building materials

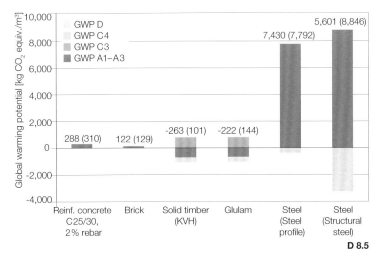

D 8.5

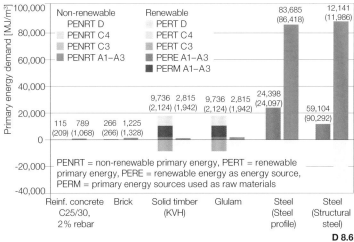

PENRT = non-renewable primary energy, PERT = renewable primary energy, PERE = renewable energy as energy source, PERM = primary energy sources used as raw materials

D 8.6

D 8.7

of fossil fuels during the harvesting of timber from forests as well as in its processing and energy-intensive drying. Not until stage D is energy credit assigned to timber for the energetic reclamation scenario, since in the case of wood, energy can be generated from a renewable resource. The difference between this and fossil fuel energy generation is applied here, so that the overall result is an energy credit. Steel has the highest overall primary energy input (PEI) values, as well, followed by reinforced concrete and bricks, which in turn have somewhat greater values than timber (Fig. D 8.5 and D 8.6).

Designing Sustainable Structures

The design of sustainable structures is determined by numerous factors and requirements. Among these, for example, is the service life, which can be positively impacted by intelligent planning in which possible eventual changes in usage are already addressed during the design phase (Fig. D 8.8). An appropriate flexibility of use can contribute to the extension of a structure's or building's life cycle.

In the context of the design, it is important to consider not only the central requirements

of structural behaviour and costs, but in particular also environmental and health-related factors in line with sustainable actions.

The plans must answer the question of how the construction and the associated material expenditure as well as the maintenance and deconstruction of the structure impact the ecosphere throughout the entire life cycle of the structure. This assessment must weigh the possible criticality of resources on the one hand and the aforementioned environmental impacts on the other. Essential guiding strategies for the conception of sustainable structures are consistency, sufficiency and efficiency.

Consistency: construction with renewable materials

When it comes to the consistency [12], that is, the "eco-effectiveness" of structures in terms of sustainability, the question is how to design structural systems whose environmental impacts at all stages of their life cycles are as positive as possible. In these considerations, the most advantageous structures are those that are made from renewable resources and whose manufacture, construction, maintenance and deconstruction have only slightly negative or – thanks to material-based carbon sequestration – positive environmental impacts. The

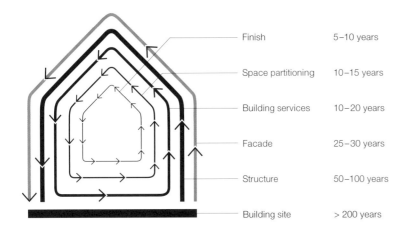

Finish	5–10 years
Space partitioning	10–15 years
Building services	10–20 years
Facade	25–30 years
Structure	50–100 years
Building site	> 200 years

D 8.8

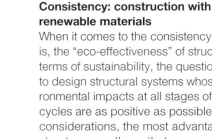

D 8.7   Eighteen-storey timber building, student residence hall in Vancouver (CA) 2017, Acton Ostry Architects, Hermann Kaufmann Architekten
D 8.8   Use categories and their replacement cycles
D 8.9   French National Institute of Agricultural Research, INRA (Institut National de la Recherche Agronomique), Orléans (FR) 2014, Design & Architecture, Nama Architecture
D 8.10 House of straw, Dornbirn (AT) 2014, Georg Bechter Architektur + Design
D 8.11 Administrative building of the Gugler printing plant, Pielach (AT) 1999, Herbert Ablinger, Vedral & Partner, Lehm Ton Erde Baukunst
D 8.12 Church of St Josef, Holzkirchen (DE) 2018, Eberhard Wimmer Architekten, Sailer Stepan & Partner (ssp)
D 8.13 Chapel of Reconciliation, Berlin (DE) 2000, Rudolf Reitermann, Peter Sassenroth

D 8.9

a

b   D 8.10

focus here lies especially on regrowing, i.e. renewable materials such as timber and straw (Figs. D 8.10, D 8.12).

Depending on local availability, traditional renewable raw materials such as timber offer further benefits, such as short transport routes, support of local economies and the preservation of traditional craftsmanship where construction methods have stood the test of time. In addition, the advantage of biogenic building materials is that they cannot become scarce unless they are overused. For non-renewable materials, in contrast, bottlenecks can occur despite the commonly held assumption that they exist in supposedly unlimited abundance. It has already become apparent in the face of the global increase in construction activities that in some parts of the world, the sand needed for production of cement is now a scarce commodity [13].

This is by no means the least reason that speaks for broadening the applications for renewable materials. An example of the growing structural use of timber is the 18-storey student residence building in Vancouver, the structure of which is solid wood (Fig. D 8.7). The building obviated the need for a 2,650 m³ volume of concrete, representing an equivalent CO_2 saving of about 500 t [14].

Sufficiency: modest construction

The strategy of modest construction as it pertains to the design and implementation of structures focuses on how the material and operations-related resource and energy expenditures can be kept to a minimum over the entire life cycle [15]. In buildings, for example, this would involve reducing the floor area required per capita through an intelligent design of the interior spaces without sacrificing quality. When applied to the design and production of structures, the term "sufficiency" can be taken to refer to the extraction and fabrication of building materials at minimal expense. Clay (loam) is a building material that possesses the appropriate favourable characteristics, as it is available in many regions of the earth and has been used for centuries [16]. The preparation and handling of this material requires little energy, especially when it can be extracted and processed locally. In addition, loam has a high thermal and moisture storage capacity and thus exhibits temperature and moisture-regulating properties. These are qualities with positive ramifications for residential construction in particular. Regarding its use as a structural material, there are contemporary examples in which loam is used for the construction of the load-bearing outer walls (Figs. D 8.9, D 8.11, D 8.13).

Straw is another material that is both renewable and highly available locally. In a structural capacity, however, it requires a large area, so that at present it is used primarily for small buildings in rural settings (Fig. D 8.10).

Efficiency: reducing expenditure

Efficiency represents achieving the same goals with less. The aim is to consume as few materials and resources as possible in the creation of a high-performing construction. The focus here lies on the construction-related materials expenditure and the associated environmental impacts over the life cycle. While the financial cost is incorporated into the economic characteristics of a structure, the main consideration in the ecological assessment covers the environmental costs.

The application of the efficiency concept in optimising the sustainability of a structure requires determining which of a set of equally performing design variations exhibits the lowest environmental impact over the entire life cycle. The determining factors include material properties (e.g. renewable/non-renewable) as well as the structural typology (e.g. skeleton construction/cross-wall construction) and its associated material quantities.

D 8.11

D 8.12

D 8.13

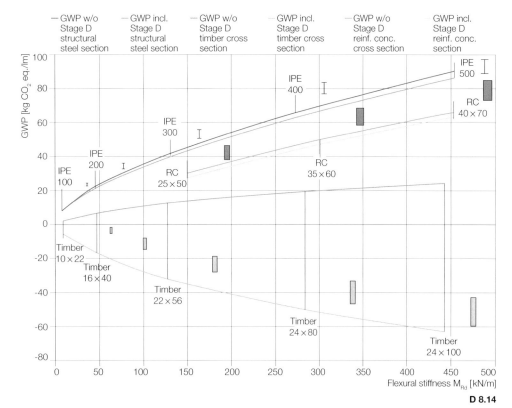

D 8.14

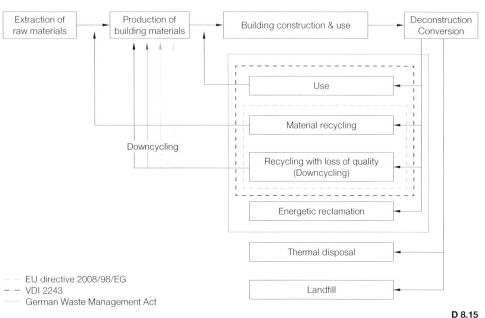

D 8.15

In order to allow for an appropriate comparison of the global warming potentials of structural materials, material cross sections of the same flexural load-bearing capacity are investigated. As an example, various beams of reinforced concrete, steel and timber were given cross-sectional dimensions according to their flexural strength [17]. The dimensions are freely chosen and represent conventional beam cross sections, assuming typical material classes. Figure D 8.14 shows the greenhouse gas emissions corresponding to the different cross sections as a function of their bending strength M_{Rd}, with and without the inclusion of Stage D, as established by Ökobaudat (2019-III). This illustrates that the steel beam consistently exhibits the highest greenhouse gas emissions, while the timber beam has the lowest. Important aspects of the comparison between different structural component materials and their global warming potential are the shape of the cross section and the material strength, since a given structural function requires much less steel, for example, than timber. For this reason, the emissions are closer together than for a pure material comparison (Fig. D 8.5, p. 153). This graph offers starting values which should be verified on a case-by-case basis, since in practice dimensioning is often determined by a combination of several loads, in addition to further performance criteria (beam depth, fire safety, etc.).

In general, timber exhibits very positive properties in comparison to steel and reinforced concrete in this respect, as well. In those cases where steel or reinforced concrete are nevertheless chosen, the amount of material employed should be minimised in pursuit of increased efficiency. Pioneers such as Buckminster Fuller and Frei Otto demonstrated very early on that optimising structures through a highly efficient use of materials can result in aesthetically elegant structures and buildings. The 1972

D 8.16

Olympic buildings in Munich (Fig. 15, p. 10, Fig. C 1.79, p. 84) or the 1975 Mannheim Multihalle (Fig. B 1.25, p. 48) are outstanding examples of an optimised use of materials that can also be found in other structural typologies such as bridges and highrises.

Recycling-optimised construction

Together with the sustainability principles explained above – consistency, sufficiency and efficiency – the recycling of building materials, components or structural systems offers a very effective option for the reduction of environmental impact. There are different recycling levels (Fig. D 8.15), among which the immediate reuse of building components or structural systems represents the most efficient version from an environmental perspective. This type of reuse is already found in contemporary relocatable buildings, which are dismantleable, temporary, usually very lightweight buildings used in industry as well as for large-scale performances and as recreational and sports venues. Similarly, in general the bearing components in timber panel and steel skeleton construction are also suitable for reuse.

An important prerequisite for the reusability of structures is the use of detachable connections such as screw or plug-in connections, so that the components can be disassembled without damage (Fig. D 8.16). In the pursuit of recycling-optimised design (Design for Disassembly), suitable connections must be incorporated already at the design and detail planning stages (Figs. D 8.18, D 8.19, p. 158f.).

The second level in the recycling hierarchy is material recycling. Single-origin separation of the materials used allows the recycled substance to be recovered immediately as an alternative raw material, also called secondary material. From an environmental perspective, this is also a valuable recovery option for building materials, since the material is reintroduced into the material loop after use.

Steel is very well-suited for recycling and already reaches recycling percentages of over 90 %, so that a large proportion of structural steel can be produced from steel scrap [18]. For example, the Environmental Product Declaration (EPD) for structural steel states that 74 % of the raw material required for manufacture is secondary steel, 11 % of structural steel is reused and 88 % recycled [19]. On the other hand, manufacturing the steel requires high energy expenditure in the form of electricity.

In timber construction, untreated structural timber components can generally be reused. Nevertheless, in practice it has been found that when a structure is deconstructed, the timber used in it is typically processed into engineered wood products. The reason for this is usually the fact that the cross sections and lengths of the components are not generally suited for the construction of a new structure. As a source material for the manufacture of engineered wood products, untreated reclaimed timber has the advantage of being thoroughly seasoned.

Demolition concrete can also be recycled, as long as it does not contain hazardous substances. This is often the case in Germany, with about 78 % of generated construction waste is recycled [20]. However, in recycled concrete only the aggregates are from recycled materials. The cement base, which is the most energy-intensive component of concrete, must still be made from primary materials. Most of the aggregate made from demolition concrete is used in road beds, which is an example of downcycling, the third level of the recycling hierarchy. Even building materials whose use in construction is limited due to a lack of information about

D 8.14   Global warming potential (CO_2 emissions) of cross sections of different materials (steel (S 235), timber (C24 use class 1), reinforced concrete (C25/30 with approx. 1 % rebar by volume)) as a function of flexural stiffness
D 8.15   Recycling hierarchy with boundaries as defined by different directives
D 8.16   Detachable connections of timber constructions
D 8.17   Tensile-stressed steel construction, Exhibition Hall 26, Hanover (DE) 1996, Thomas Herzog und Partner

D 8.17

D 8.18 NexusHaus, developed for the 2015 US Solar
Decathlon, TU Munich, University of Texas,
Austin, exhibited in Irvine (US)
D 8.19 Elements of NexusHaus and their allocation
to biological or technological loops or to the
service product category

their specific properties can be downcycled
in certain circumstances. They cannot be
reused for their original purpose, however.

Summary

Because the structure generally makes up
a substantial portion of the overall mass of
a building, the choice of material and the
type of construction play an important role
in terms of environmental sustainability. At
the same time, this represents significant
opportunities for minimising resource consumption and energy expenditure as well as
associated CO_2 emissions.
In the design and construction of (environmentally) sustainable structures, it is important to bear in mind the following four points:

- The consistency of a building material is a
critical factor with regard to environmental
impacts such as primary energy input and
global warming potential. A distinction is
made between renewable and non-
renewable materials.
- A similar importance can be ascribed to
sufficiency. In the context of structures,
this relates to building materials such as
loam, for example, that can be extracted
and produced with minimal difficulty and
expense.
- Independent of the choice of material,
efficiency is an essential criterion by
which building materials are employed
in service of slender or lightweight structures. The focus here is on minimising
the amount of material used.
- In the pursuit of environmentally sustainable structures, special attention should
be paid to recycling-oriented design and
construction, so that the building materials used remain in the material loop as
long as possible.

Through the conscious incorporation of
these considerations into the design process and through the selection of building
material and construction type, structural
engineers can influence the ecological
properties of a structure from the very early
stages of planning.
Nevertheless, it is important to consider all
of the environmental impacts in the overall
life cycle assessment, including resource
extraction, energy expenditure and CO_2
emissions during manufacture, operations
and deconstruction as well as any waste
that may arise at the end of the service life
as a result of deconstruction. Yet it is not
only consciousness, but also the use of
relevant tools such as life cycle assessments that are important for arriving at
appropriate decisions for sustainable structures in the very early design stages.

Notes:
[1] "Energy consumption and use by households",
ec.europa.eu/eurostat/de/web/products-eurostat-
news/-/DDN-20200626-1 (accessed 09 Mar 2021)
[2] International Energy Agency (IEA): "Energy-related
CO_2 emissions from buildings", iea.org/topics/
buildings (accessed 09 Mar 2021)
[3] European Commission, "Buildings and construction",
ec.europa.eu/growth/industry/sustainability/built-
environment_en (accessed 09 Mar 2021)
[4] European Commission, "Construction and demolition
waste", ec.europa.eu/environment/topics/waste-
and-recycling/construction-and-demolition-waste_en
(accessed 09 Mar 2021)
[5] Heinrich, Matthias: "Material Flows of the German
Building Sector." In: F. Di Maio *et al.* (eds.): *HISER
International Conference – Advances in Recycling and
Management of Construction and Demolition Waste.*
Delft 2017, p. 302–305
[6] Braune, Anna; Ruiz Durán, Christine; Gantner,
Johannes: *Leitfaden zum Einsatz der Ökobilanzierung.*
Publ. by the Deutsche Gesellschaft für Nachhaltiges
Bauen (DGNB). Stuttgart 2018
[7] "Bilanzierungsregeln für die Erstellung von Öko-
bilanzen". *Bewertungssystem Nachhaltiges Bauen
(BNB), Neubau Büro- und Verwaltungsgebäude,* publ.
by Bundesministerium für Umwelt, Naturschutz und
Reaktorsicherheit, 2015
[8] Andrew, Robbie M.: "Global CO_2 emissions from
cement production." In: *Earth System Science Data 10*
(1), 2018, p. 195–217. DOI: 10.5194/essd-10-195-
2018.
Aylard, Richard; Hawson, Louise; Sprigg, Graham:
*The cement sustainability initiative. Our agenda for
action.* Publ. by the World Business Council for
Sustainable Development. 2002

D 8.18

[9] Schneider-Marin, Patricia *et al.:* Design2Eco, Final Report. *Lebenszyklusbetrachtung im Planungsprozess von Büro- und Verwaltungsgebäuden – Entscheidungsgrundlagen und Optimierungsmöglichkeiten für frühe Planungsphasen.* Stuttgart 2019

[10] e.g. Lang, Werner; Schneider, Patricia: *Gemeinschaftlich nachhaltig bauen.* Forschungsbericht der ökologischen Untersuchung des genossenschaftlichen Wohnungsbauprojektes wagnisART. Publ. by Oberste Baubehörde im Bayerischen Staatsministerium des Innern, für Bau und Verkehr (Materialien zum Wohnungsbau). Munich 2017

[11] see also Saade, Marcella Ruschi Mendes; Guest, Geoffrey; Amor, Ben: "Comparative whole building LCAs: How far are our expectations from the documented evidence?" In: *Building and Environment 167,* 2020, 106449; doi.org/10.1016/j.buildenv. 2019. 106449

[12] "Consistency is the environmentally compatible quality of material flows." Behrendt, Siegfried; Göll, Edgar; Korte, Friederike: Effizienz, Konsistenz, Suffizienz. *Strategieanalytische Betrachtung für eine Green Economy.* Institut für Zukunftsstudien und Technologiebewertung. Berlin 2018, p. 13

[13] Beiser, Vince: *The world in a grain. The story of sand and how it transformed civilization.* First Riverhead trade paperback edition. New York 2018

[14] Kaufmann, Hermann; Krötsch, Stefan; Winter, Stefan: *Manual of Multi-storey Timber Construction.* Munich 2017, p. 166–169

[15] "Sufficiency […] means producing and consuming in a way that respects overall ecological capacity." Fischer, Corinna *et al.:* "Sufficiency: Begriff, Begründung und Potenziale. Mehr als nur weniger." Working Paper. Publ. by Öko-Institut e.V. Freiburg 2013, p. 8

[16] An impressive example of this are the up to eleven-storey mud-brick buildings in Shibam in the Hadhramaut Region in Yemen, from the 16th century. Leiermann, Tom: *Shibam – Leben in Lehmtürmen. Weltkulturerbe im Jemen.* Wiesbaden 2009

[17] Calculations done according to Eurocode for this publication by Jonas Schikore, Frauke Wilken, Professor of Structural Design Rainer Barthel, TU Munich 2020

[18] Hiebel, Markus; Nühlen, Jochen: *Technische, ökonomische, ökologische und gesellschaftliche Faktoren von Stahlschrott (Zukunft Stahlschrott).* Publ. by Fraunhofer-Institut für Umwelt-, Sicherheits- und Energietechnik UMSICHT. Oberhausen 2016. bdsv.org/fileadmin/service/publikationen/Studie_ Fraunhofer_Umsicht.pdf (accessed 22 Jan 2021)

[19] "Feuerverzinkte Baustähle: Offene Walzprofile und Grobbleche". Environmental Product Declaration (EPD) as per ISO 14025 and EN 15804. Publ. by Institut Bauen und Umwelt (IBU) 2018

[20] Schäfer, Berthold; Basten, Michael: *Mineralische Bauabfälle Monitoring 2016. Bericht zum Aufkommen und zum Verbleib mineralischer Bauabfälle im Jahr 2016.* Publ. by Bundesverband Baustoffe – Steine und Erden e.V. Berlin and elsewhere. 2018

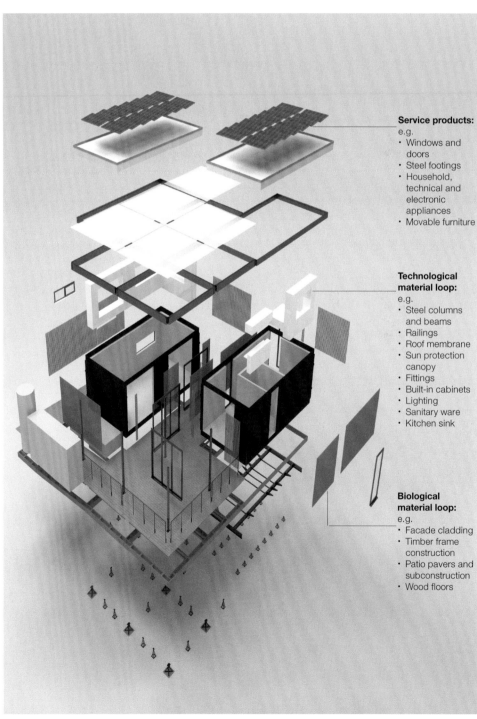

Service products:
e.g.
- Windows and doors
- Steel footings
- Household, technical and electronic appliances
- Movable furniture

Technological material loop:
e.g.
- Steel columns and beams
- Railings
- Roof membrane
- Sun protection canopy
- Fittings
- Built-in cabinets
- Lighting
- Sanitary ware
- Kitchen sink

Biological material loop:
e.g.
- Facade cladding
- Timber frame construction
- Patio pavers and subconstruction
- Wood floors

Built Examples

House on the Hillside

Structure:
Solid timber construction / Cross-laminated timber
slabs and panels
Folded-plate-like load-bearing effect through shear-
resistant connections between slabs and panels

Architects:
Sunder-Plassmann Architekten Stadtplaner,
Utting am Ammersee (DE)

Structural engineering:
TWP Tragwerkplan Ingenieurgesellschaft für das
Bauwesen, Tutzing (DE)

For a long time, solid construction was the domain of mineral building materials like natural stone, brick and concrete. However, in recent years solid timber components have also garnered an increasing market share. Today, high-performance solid cross-laminated timber elements, made by gluing several layers of transversely stacked boards together, are available as both bending-stressed slabs and normally stressed panels.

A spatial structure of wall panels and floor slabs allows a 5-m section of the house to overhang the driveway, despite the fact that large parts of the facade are glazed.

On the south side of the house, the only solid wall element lies along the large bedroom, supported solely at its outermost corner. In order to prevent forward buckling, the wall is held up in part by a floor slab 240 mm thick. Further bearing elements are the 99 and 165-mm thick wall panels extending out onto the cantilevered section on the north facade, as well as the transverse wall panels. An advantageous aspect of the solid timber elements is that, similarly to reinforced concrete, they can resist tensile forces as well as compressive and flexural loads. When compared to the composite material re-

inforced concrete, however, timber is superior when it comes to self-weight, sustainability, climate protection, building physics, processability and recyclability.

The living, dining and kitchen areas of the house are centrally located. Their open-plan arrangement serves as a communal space for the residents. The glazed living room facade as well as the wide panoramic window of the large bedroom offer views of the surrounding open spaces. The extensive green roof ties the house into the landscape. Its loads are accommodated by the cross-laminated timber ceiling slab.

Site map
Scale 1:3,000
Section · Floor plan
Scale 1:200

1 Living and
  dining area
2 Fireplace
3 Kitchen
4 Utilities room
5 Bedroom
6 Office
7 Cloakroom

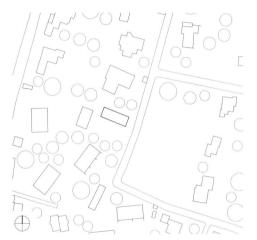

aa

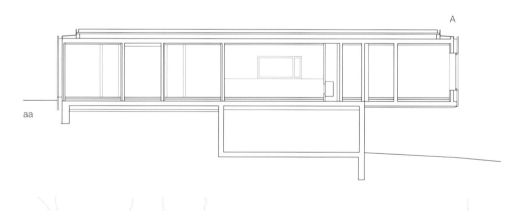

Ground floor

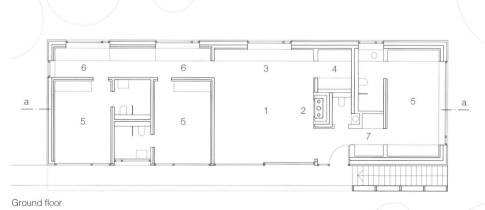

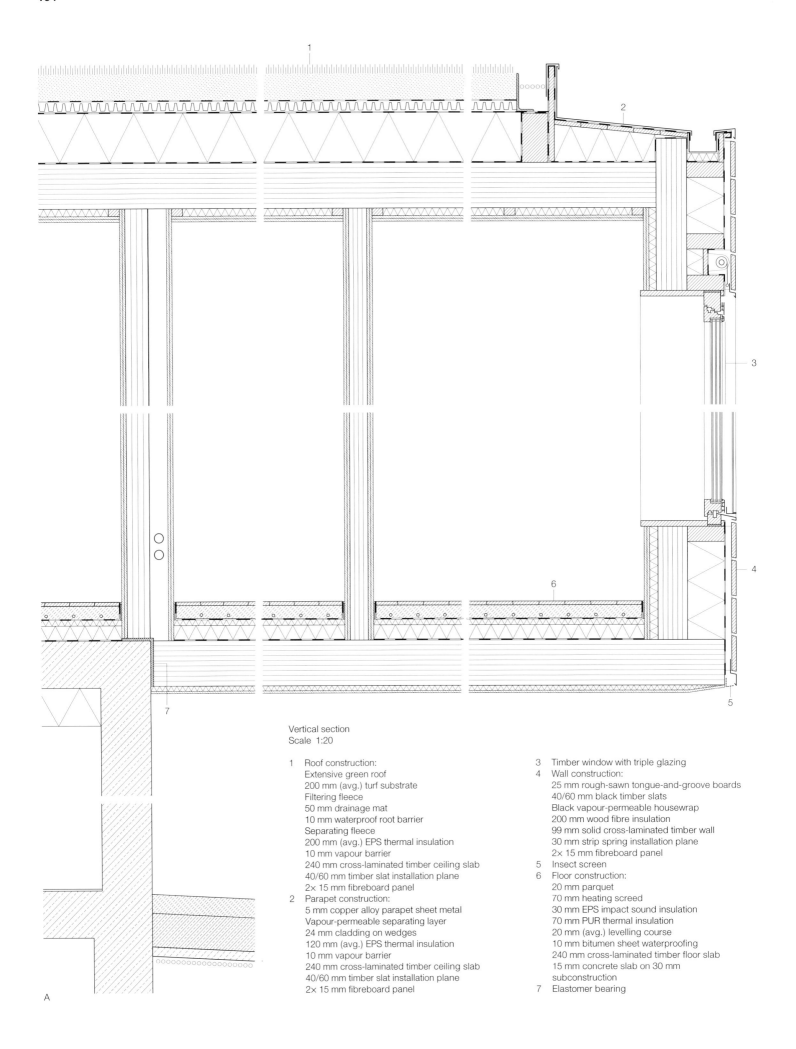

Vertical section
Scale 1:20

1 Roof construction:
   Extensive green roof
   200 mm (avg.) turf substrate
   Filtering fleece
   50 mm drainage mat
   10 mm waterproof root barrier
   Separating fleece
   200 mm (avg.) EPS thermal insulation
   10 mm vapour barrier
   240 mm cross-laminated timber ceiling slab
   40/60 mm timber slat installation plane
   2× 15 mm fibreboard panel
2 Parapet construction:
   5 mm copper alloy parapet sheet metal
   Vapour-permeable separating layer
   24 mm cladding on wedges
   120 mm (avg.) EPS thermal insulation
   10 mm vapour barrier
   240 mm cross-laminated timber ceiling slab
   40/60 mm timber slat installation plane
   2× 15 mm fibreboard panel

3 Timber window with triple glazing
4 Wall construction:
   25 mm rough-sawn tongue-and-groove boards
   40/60 mm black timber slats
   Black vapour-permeable housewrap
   200 mm wood fibre insulation
   99 mm solid cross-laminated timber wall
   30 mm strip spring installation plane
   2× 15 mm fibreboard panel
5 Insect screen
6 Floor construction:
   20 mm parquet
   70 mm heating screed
   30 mm EPS impact sound insulation
   70 mm PUR thermal insulation
   20 mm (avg.) levelling course
   10 mm bitumen sheet waterproofing
   240 mm cross-laminated timber floor slab
   15 mm concrete slab on 30 mm
   subconstruction
7 Elastomer bearing

A

Community Centre in Kist

Structure:
Steel skeleton/compression and
flexural members

Architects:
Atelier Fischer Architekten, Würzburg (DE)

Structural engineering:
Heinz Volz, Höchberg (DE)

A load-bearing skeleton of simple steel sections provides the village community centre in Kist, near Würzburg, with many options for use as a meeting place for citizens and clubs. Since it is only occasionally used to host gatherings, events or parties, it is neither heated nor well insulated. The building was conceived to conform to the ground plan and proportions of an old barn. Sliding glass doors open the 8 × 8 m communal space out toward the village square. Additional rooms such as the kitchen, storage areas and sanitary facilities are located in the preserved, integrated part of the barn, whose historical masonry is of regional lacustrine limestone. An IPE 300 two-span beam forms the long ridge purlin, which rests on three HEB section columns with edge lengths of 140 mm. Rafters spaced at about 2-m intervals support a triple-layered timber slab 51 mm thick, which serves as the roof panel as well as the visible ceiling. At the eaves, the rafters rest on eaves purlins which are supported by steel pillars about every 4 m. Apart from the ridge beam, HEB 140 sections are employed for most of the compression and bending-stressed structural elements. The horizontal loads within the steel structure are carried by wall slabs of framing timbers panelled on both sides with oak boards. In the old portion of the building, this task is performed by the preserved natural stone walls.

The visible, delicate steel frame structure, filled in with glass panes, timber elements and historical masonry, characterises the open appearance of the community centre. The careful joining of the parts of the building creates a harmonious union between the old and new building substance under the large shared gable roof. New construction elements and traditional building complement one another in an exemplary fashion.

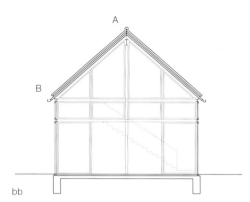

A

B

bb

C

aa

Site map
Scale 1:2,000
Sections · Floor plan
Scale 1:200
Vertical sections
Scale 1:20

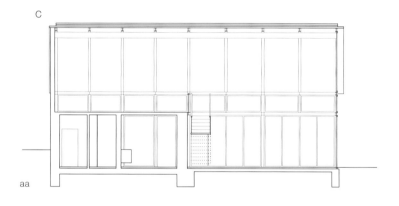

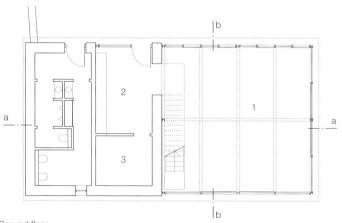

a   a

b

2

3

1

b

Ground floor

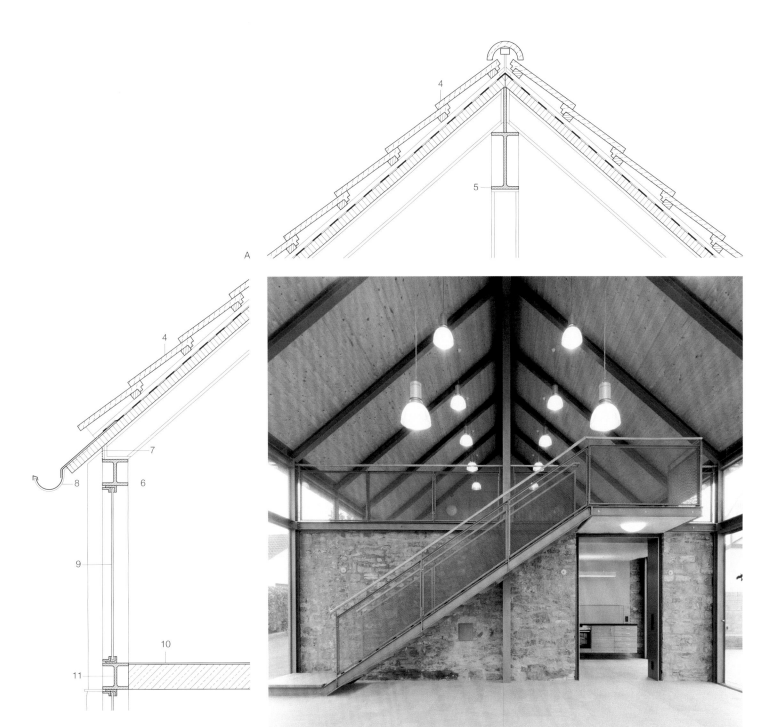

1 Communal area
2 Kitchen
3 Secondary space / storage
4 Roof construction:
  Concrete tile roof covering, grey
  30/50 mm roof battens
  30/50 mm counter battens
  Vapour-permeable underlay
  51 mm three-layer board
  HEB 140 steel profile rafter
5 IPE 300 steel section ridge purlin
6 HEB 140 steel section eaves purlin
7 Insect screen
8 Galvanised steel sheet rain gutter
9 5 mm steel window frame with fixed tempered
  safety glass
10 140 mm reinforced concrete dropped ceiling,
  rendered
11 HEB 140 steel profile girder
12 HEB 140 steel profile column
13 Folded parapet sheet metal
14 240 mm exposed concrete exterior wall

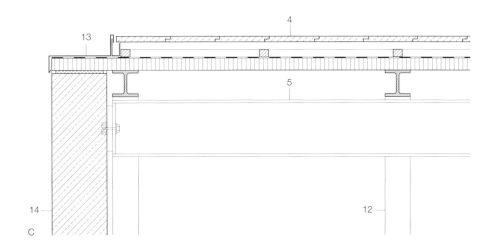

Cowshed in Thankirchen

Structure:
Timber skeleton construction / tension, compression and flexural members

Architects:
Florian Nagler Architekten, Munich (DE)

Structural engineering:
Merz Kley Partner (mkp), Dornbirn (AT)

It is rare that a structure can be as clearly perceived as it is in this cowshed in the foothills of the Upper Bavarian Alps. The framework, featuring a 2.40-m centre-to-centre distance between members, is put together from simple structural elements. The mostly compression-stressed columns and struts and the flexurally stressed beams are of rough-sawn solid timber of grade S 10, felled in the nearby forest belonging to the clients. Both tensile horizontal tie beams are of S 355 round bar steel and have a diameter of 16 mm. Cleats clarify the mechanics of the junctions and nodes. In order to keep the construction costs low,

the architect Florian Nagler, together with the structural engineers and the clients, chose a structure that was simple enough to allow untrained helpers to complete much of the preliminary work such as sizing, cutting and drilling.

The three-bayed building consists of the low resting area on the east side, the central high-ceilinged feed alley and the drive-through passage with the feed tables on the west side. Translucent roller blinds shade the long sides of the barn as needed. Four short wall panels of multilayered boards provide longitudinal reinforcement at both gable ends of the barn. Coupling beams

attached to these panels reduce the buckling length of the tall central columns. In the transverse direction, the intermediate supports fixed to the roof framework carry the horizontal wind loads.

Using the simplest means of construction, the designers succeeded in creating a pleasant atmosphere and a surprisingly differentiated interior effect. The serene staggered arrangement of the structure simultaneously partitions and unifies the three different zones. The use of local softwood contributes to sustainability. Together, the milking shed, an older barn building and this cowshed form a balanced ensemble.

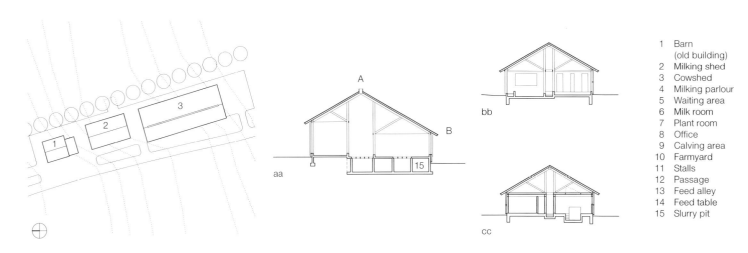

1 Barn
(old building)
2 Milking shed
3 Cowshed
4 Milking parlour
5 Waiting area
6 Milk room
7 Plant room
8 Office
9 Calving area
10 Farmyard
11 Stalls
12 Passage
13 Feed alley
14 Feed table
15 Slurry pit

aa

bb

cc

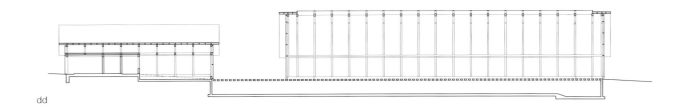

dd

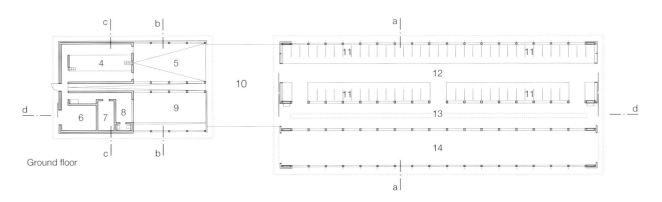

Ground floor

Site map
Scale 1:2,000
Sections · Floor plan
Scale 1:500

1 Galvanised steel sheet coping
2 45/280 mm timber plank
3 50/200 mm ridge cleat
4 500/650/27 mm three-layered spruce
  board ridge connector
5 Roof construction:
  Interlocking tiles
  30/50 mm roof battens
  60/80 mm counter battens
  45 mm tongue-and-groove sheathing,
  panelised
  200/260 mm principal rafter
6 50/200 mm cleat
7 200/260 mm rough-sawn spruce
  interior column
8 200/200 mm strut
9 60/200 mm coupling beam
10 16 mm galvanised steel tie rod

11 80/300 mm coupling beam
12 50/180 mm fascia
13 160/100 mm galvanised steel ∟ angle
14 76.1 Ø/4 mm galvanised steel tube
15 PVC glass fibre mesh sun shades
16 50/80 mm vertical spruce post
17 25/40 mm galvanised steel ⊏ section
  guide rail
  with hard rubber coating
18 200/200 mm facade column
19 80/80 mm ground sill
20 160–200 mm reinforced concrete floor
21 160 mm prefabricated reinforced concrete
  slatted floor
22 Spruce half-round timber threshold
23 24 mm vertical spruce sheathing
24 250 mm reinforced concrete slurry pit
  partition wall

Vertical sections
Scale 1:20

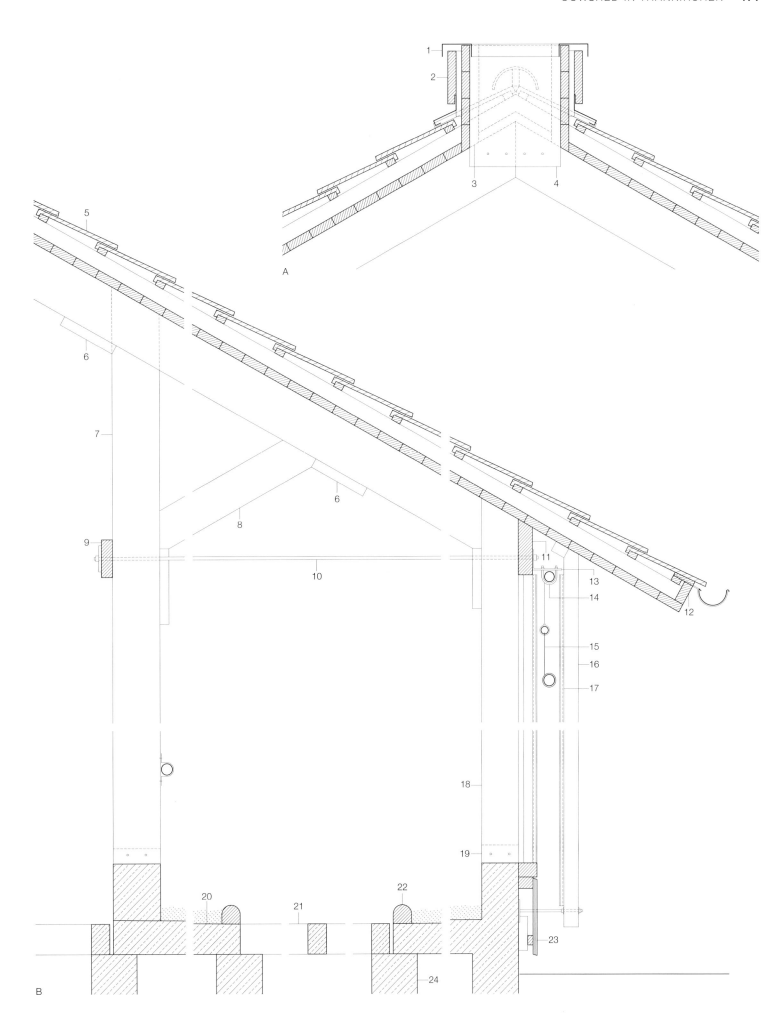

A

B

Sports Hall in Haiming

Structure:
Timber skeleton construction / timber trusses as nail plate
trusses with sloped top chords

Architects:
Almannai Fischer Architekten, Munich (DE)
Ingenieurbüro Harald Fuchshuber, Altötting (DE)

Structural engineering:
HSB Ingenieure, Mehring (DE)

In line with the motto "less is more", many designers have adopted as a guiding principle the achievement of high functionality through comparatively modest means. In a sports hall in Haiming, a small village on the German-Austrian border, an architectural language that merges frugality, restraint and engineering spirit successfully reflects this goal. Proven building approaches such as timber construction, a gable roof, trusses, galvanised truss plates, translucent polycarbonate panels and panelised prefabrication combine to create a structure that ennobles the necessary and transforms it into simple elegance.

Thirty-seven narrow truss plate ties with heights of up to 4 m and top chords inclined at 15° span the 25-m wide sports hall in a narrow grid with 122.5-cm spacing. The ties are supported on the two longitudinal facades by 24-cm thick partially reinforced timber frame elements. The first patent for the galvanised Gang Nail connector plate, which is forced into the unweakened timber beam using compressed air, was issued to the American engineer John Calvin Jureit in 1956. Unlike in this hall, however, these frequently used connector plates are usually employed in concealed areas behind suspended ceilings.

The roof is sheathed with three-layered boards 24 mm thick. Because of their close spacing, the sheathing rests directly on the main trusses without a need for secondary girders. A tremendous reinforced concrete lintel spans the wide but not overly high glazed openings of the long south facade. It is not obvious at first sight, because its profile is subtly matched to the timber framework immediately above. At the gable ends of the hall, two lower side wings with mono-pitched roofs accommodate the changing, equipment and utility rooms. The gymnasium floor lies in a reinforced concrete basin about 1 m below ground level. This allows the large hall to blend more modestly into the village surroundings.

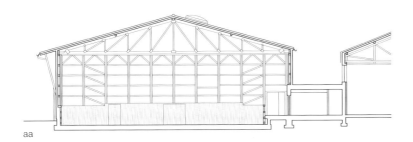

aa

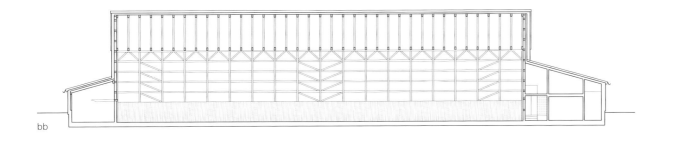

bb

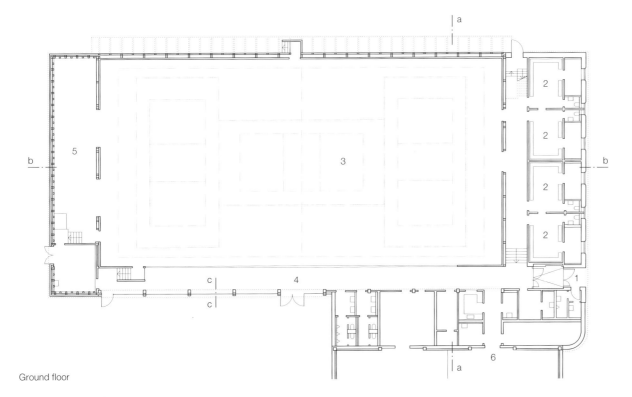

Ground floor

Site map
Scale 1:5,000
Section · Floor plans
Scale 1:400

1 Entrance
2 Changing rooms
3 Sports hall
4 Stand
5 Equipment
6 Gymnasium
   (old building)

Vertical section
Scale 1:20

1 Roof construction:
55 mm (approx.) roofing tiles
40/60 mm roof battens
40/100 mm counter battens
Underlay
120 mm polyiso (PIR) rigid foam thermal
insulation panel
Vapour proofing
24 mm three-layer board
Nail plate roof truss
2 24 mm three-layer board
3 800 × 95 × 60 mm firring
4 635 × 270 mm truss plate
5 465 × 305 mm truss plate
6 Wall construction:
25 mm rough-sawn timber sheathing
40/60 mm battens
30/50 mm counter battens
Facade sheeting
160 mm rock wool thermal insulation
Vapour proofing
28 mm OSB panel
240 mm timber frame element
7 Reinforced concrete window lintel
8 Timber window with triple glazing
9 Sunshade
10 Floor construction:
3.5 mm linoleum athletic surfacing
40 mm elastic athletic flooring
2 mm HDF panel load-distributing layer
30 mm grooved floor heating slab
90 mm XPS thermal insulation
PE film separating layer
28 mm levelling course of fill
PE film separating layer
10 mm bitumen waterproofing sheet
200 mm reinforced ground slab
140 mm XPS pressure-resistant perimeter insulation
50 mm lean concrete blinding layer

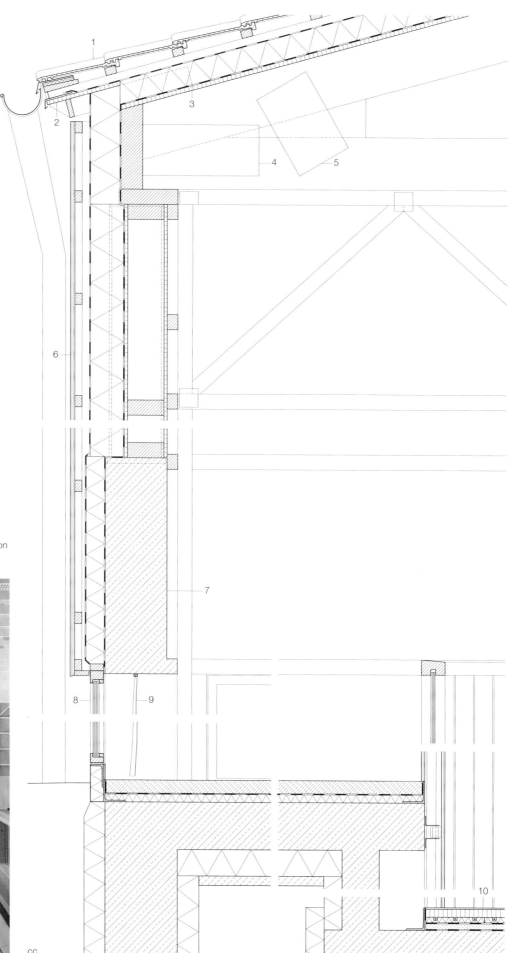

cc

Municipal Library in Bad Vilbel

Structure:
Steel skeleton construction with solid reinforced concrete floors /
two-storey steel trusses

Architects:
Demmel und Hadler Architekten, Munich (DE)

Structural engineering:
Krebs+Kiefer Ingenieure, Darmstadt (DE)

Small settlements and mega-metropolises alike are often near water. The Bad Vilbel public town library is located not just on the banks of the Nidda river, but actually directly above it. With its wide pedestrian and bicycle path, the two-storey bridge building provides an important urban development function by connecting the new town plaza in the south with the Kurpark (spa park) in the north. In addition, the outdoor spaces of the library café offer an attractive venue from which to experience the river area, which has been extensively restored to its natural state.

Three parallel, two-storey steel trusses, each 40 m long and more than 8 m high, span the river. While H sections were used for the top and bottom chords at the levels of the reinforced concrete floor and ceiling, round tubes of 350 mm diameter form the diagonals, which are openly visible within the building. Depending on the loads, sheet metal thicknesses of between 16 and 40 mm were employed.
The steel pavilion is glazed on all sides and rests on square exposed concrete structures on both riverbanks. These accommodate the plant rooms as well as secondary spaces for the library and

café. At the same time, they provide the surface foundations for both bridge ends that are needed due to the ground conditions.
Solar shade slats in the upper storey and setbacks of the south and west facades on the ground floor mitigate the influx of heat in summer. Highly insulated triple glazing reduces heating energy demand during the cold months. Concrete core activation ensures basic cooling and heating. Air channels in the concrete floor also provide an adjustable fresh air supply through displacement ventilation via floor vents near the facades.

Section · Floor plans
Scale 1:400
Site map
Scale 1:4,000

1 Circulation
2 Children's library
3 Lectures
4 Café
5 Open space
6 Office
7 Administration

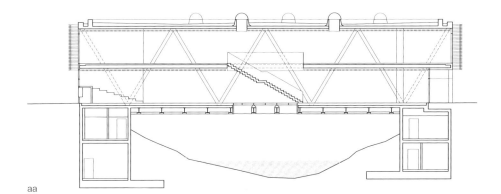

aa

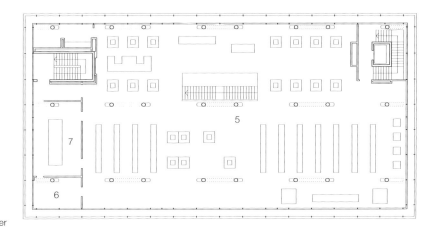

Upper
floor

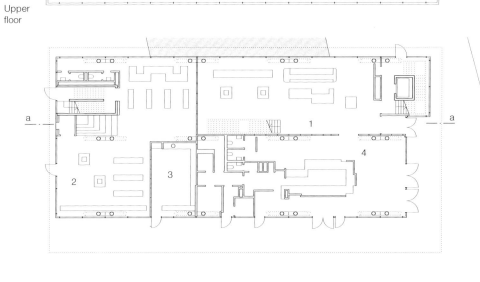

Ground
floor

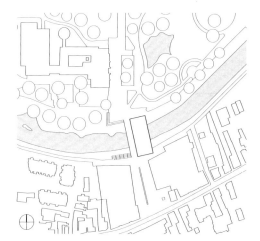

Vertical section
Scale 1:50

1 Roof construction:
extensive green roof
50 mm turf substrate
Filtering fleece
40 mm drainage mat
10 mm waterproof root barrier
Separating fleece
250 mm (avg.) tapered EPS insulation
Vapour proofing
250 mm reinforced concrete slab
2 IPE 800 top chord of truss
3 360 mm ⌀ steel tube truss diagonals
4 Suspended ceiling of timber slats, painted white
5 50 mm superimposed load of pebbles
6 2 mm aluminium parapet coping
7 Fixed galvanised sun protection grating
on 100 × 50 mm hollow section beam
8 2× 8 mm flat bar steel cantilever bracing
9 200 × 30 mm anodised hollow section
aluminium sun protection slats
10 Post & beam facade with triple glazing
11 Galvanised maintenance access grating
12 Underfloor convector
13 Raised floor, multiply coated
14 HEB 360 beam, intermediate floor
15 Aluminium composite ceiling panel
16 Decking of foot and bicycle path:
24 mm Douglas spruce contoured planks
17 Tapered steel beam decking support
18 2 mm aluminium sheet flashing
19 Fire-protection panel cladding
20 IPE 800 bottom chord of truss
21 Steel staircase
22 Domed skylight, double layered
glass-reinforced plastic

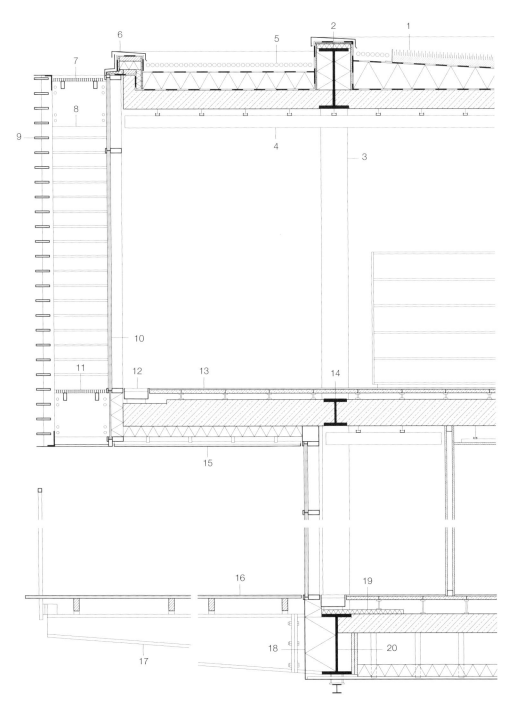

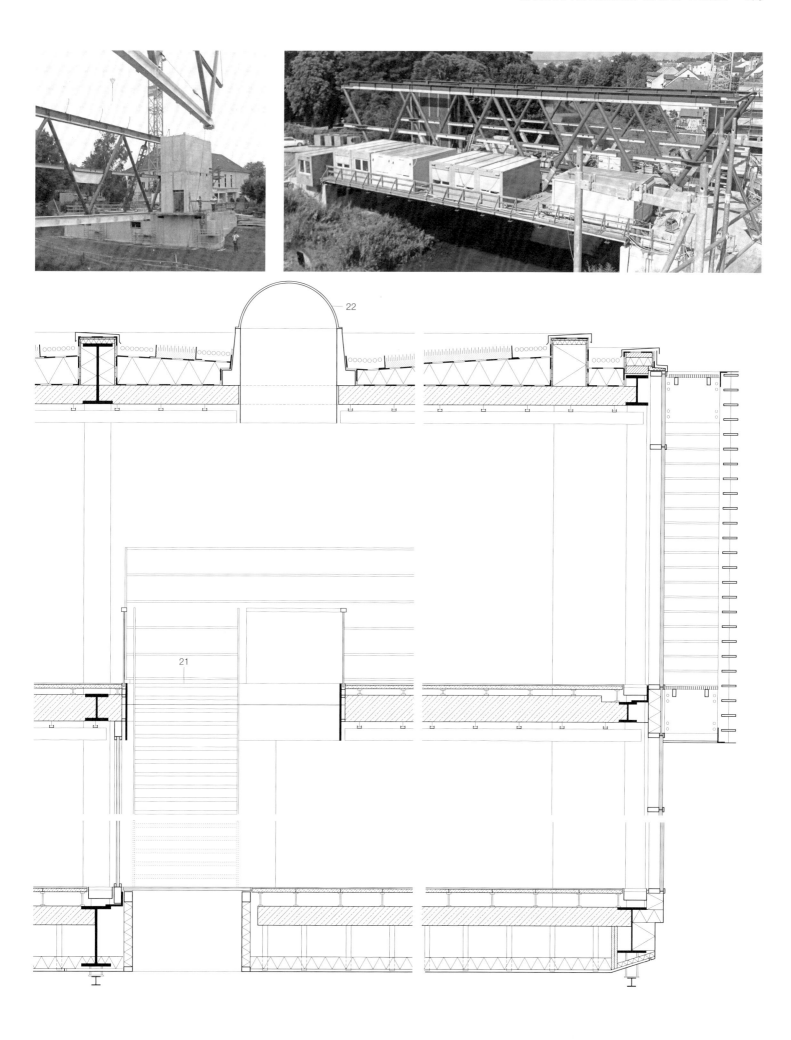

University Cafeteria in Mühlheim an der Ruhr

Structure:
Solid reinforced concrete construction /
storey-height reinforced concrete truss

Architects:
ARGE HHP / ASTOC
HPP Architekten, Düsseldorf (DE)
ASTOC Architects and Planners, Cologne (DE)

Structural engineering:
Schüßler Plan, Düsseldorf (DE)

Next to timber and steel, on rare occasions reinforced concrete is also used as a material for trusses. In the cafeteria building on the campus of Ruhr West University of Applied Sciences, such a truss makes a 10-m cantilever of the upper storey dining hall possible. This overhang creates a versatile, generous and protected outdoor space in the middle of the campus. The space forms the forecourt area in front of the coffee shop on the ground floor. Thanks to the truss, the added construction costs for the column-free space were manageable, since pillars would have been needed along the upper-storey dining hall facade in any case

in order to support the roof. These 40 × 40 cm pillars are now inclined at 60°, with about half of the diagonal members under tension instead of compression.
Reinforced concrete slabs of strength class C 35/45 and 35-cm thickness form the ceilings above the ground floor and the upper storey. Hollow core modules installed in the cantilever reduce the self-weight of the ceilings. The truss is approx. 91 m long, with downward-pointing diagonals at the front corners of the building and highly reinforced nodes. The whole thing, including the top and bottom chords, is made from self-compacting C 50/60 facing concrete. The

heavy-duty columns on the ground floor located directly below the truss supports are of the even higher strength class C 80/95.
On the basis of the computations of the expected deformations, the truss was manufactured with a sufficient camber so that it appears largely undeformed in its installed state and under typical loading. The storey-height glazing of the dining hall, protected by slats, makes the structure of the cantilever evident not only from within, but from the outside as well.

Section · Floor plans
Scale 1:750
Site map
Scale 1:4,000

1	Campus plaza
2	Cafeteria
3	Auditorium
4	Library
5	Institute building
6	Foyer/stairs
7	Coffee shop
8	Coffee shop counter
9	Seminar room
10	Parent/child room
11	Ancillary kitchen spaces
12	Kitchen delivery
13	Dining hall
14	Food counters
15	Dish return
16	Dishwashing area
17	Main kitchen
18	Terrace

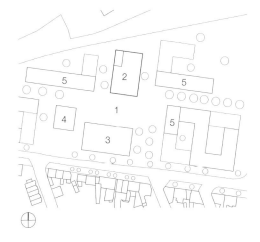

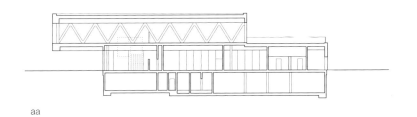

aa

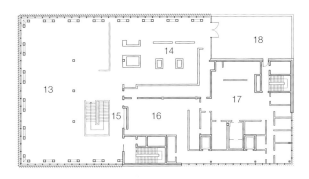

Upper floor

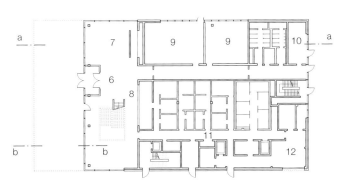

Ground floor

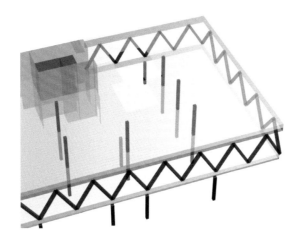

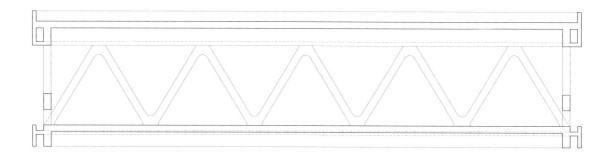

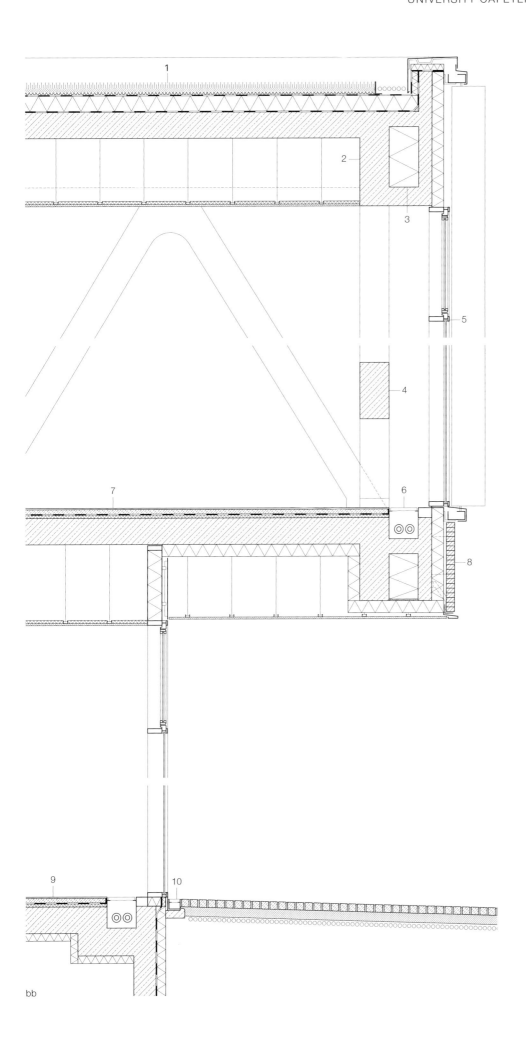

Axonometric view,
no scale given
Truss
Scale 1:200
Vertical section
Scale 1:50

1 Roof construction:
   Extensive green roof
   50 mm turf substrate
   Filtering fleece
   40 mm drainage mat
   10 mm waterproof root barrier
   Separating fleece
   200 mm EPS thermal insulation
   10 mm vapour proofing
   350 mm reinforced concrete
   Acoustic ceiling, perforated plasterboard
   with 18 % perforation, fleece and mineral
   fibre on upper side
2 400 × 250 mm reinforced concrete girder
3 Insulated cavity
4 400 × 400 mm reinforced concrete truss
5 Post & beam facade with double glazing
6 Underfloor convector
7 Upper storey floor construction:
   15 mm wood parquet
   3 mm fleece separating layer
   65 mm cement screed
   20 mm impact sound insulation
   20 mm levelling course
   350 mm reinforced concrete
   160 mm thermal insulation
   15 mm moisture-resistant suspended
   cement panel, primed and painted
8 Slab face cladding:
   115 mm masonry veneer
   40 mm rear ventilation
   160 mm mineral wool thermal insulation
   185 mm reinforced concrete
9 Floor construction ground floor:
   15 mm concrete-look screed
   65 mm cement screed
   Separating layer
   20 mm impact sound insulation
   20 mm levelling course
   350 mm reinforced concrete
   100 mm thermal insulation
10 Facade gutter

bb

Forestry Office in Stadtroda

Structure:
Hybrid timber skeleton and solid reinforced concrete
construction / trussed girders of timber and steel

Architects:
Cornelsen + Seelinger Architekten, Darmstadt (DE)

Structural engineering:
Merz Kley Partner (mkp), Dornbirn (AT)

The concept of environmental sustainability is largely ascribed to Hans Carl von Carlowitz of Freiberg in Saxony. *Sylvicultura oeconomica,* the book he published in 1713, is considered the first scientific work on forest management. It contains formulations of every modern ecological principle of action that is needed to ensure future viability.

It is therefore obvious to build a forestry office using timber. So the designers of the Jena Holzland forestry office employed regional wood species for the structure, facade, claddings and interior finish. Though the building is conceived as a timber construction, other materials supplement the carbon-neutral, renewable raw material in a targeted fashion wherever it is deemed appropriate.

For reasons related to fire safety, durability and building physics, the basement, the access cores and the game cooling chamber were built from reinforced concrete. The ceiling above the ground floor is of a timber-concrete composite, while the upper storey ceiling omits concrete altogether.

In the centrally located open office for the district foresters, trussed girders aid in supporting the roof over the 8.40-m width of the space without the need for columns.

Like the remaining structural timber components of the building, the top chord and the struts are made from extremely load-resistant birchwood laminated veneer timber of strength class GL70; the slender tie beams of the bottom chord, in contrast, are of steel. Partition walls of 120-mm thick cross-laminated timber wall elements serve as transverse reinforcement. Operational carbon neutrality is vouchsafed by a wood pellet stove combined with a photovoltaic array on the roof.

The prize-winning building serves as a model for small office and administrative buildings for municipalities and companies.

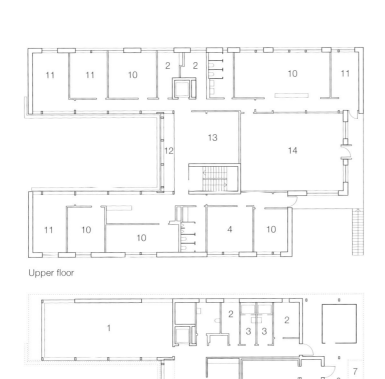

Upper floor

Ground floor

Floor plans · Section	1	Meetings	8	Archive
Scale 1:400	2	Storage	9	Reception
Site plan	3	Showers	10	Offices
Scale 1:4,000	4	Foyer	11	Directors
	5	Maps	12	Air space
	6	Game cooling	13	Kitchenette
		chamber	14	District
	7	Delivery		foresters

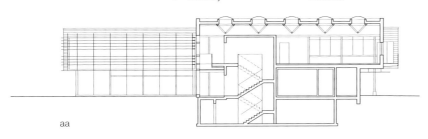

aa

Isometric view of a trussed beam (no scale given)
Vertical sections
Scale 1:20

1 Trussed beam:
  180 × 180 mm top chord, 110 × 110 mm
  compression member
  of beechwood laminated veneer lumber
  20 mm Ø solid steel tension members
2 Domed skylight,
  triple-layered glass-fibre reinforced plastic
3 21 mm engineered spruce panel interior cladding
4 Roof lantern construction:
  FPO synthetic sealing membrane
  190 mm (avg.) tapered insulation
  Vapour proofing
  50 mm beechwood laminated veneer
  lumber ceiling slab, facing quality underside
5 Folded sheet metal parapet coping
6 Roof lantern wall construction:
  24 mm timber planking
  30/35 mm timber battens
  30/50 mm counter battens
  Black underlay
  16 mm timber sheathing
  240 mm thermal insulation
  100 mm solid spruce panel
7 240 × 160 mm frame, beech laminated
  veneer lumber plate
8 Roof construction:
  FPO synthetic sealing membrane
  190 mm (avg.) tapered insulation
  Vapour proofing
  160 mm beechwood laminated veneer lumber
  ceiling slab
  Facing quality underside

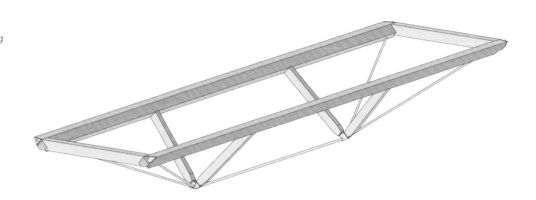

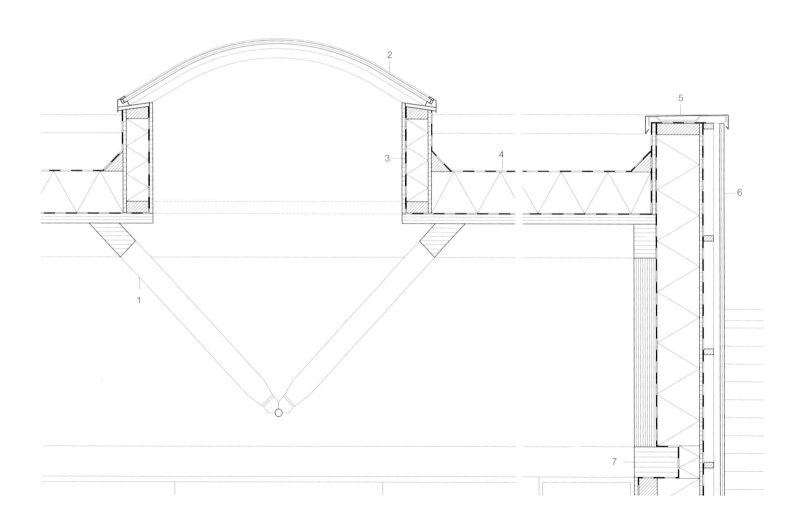

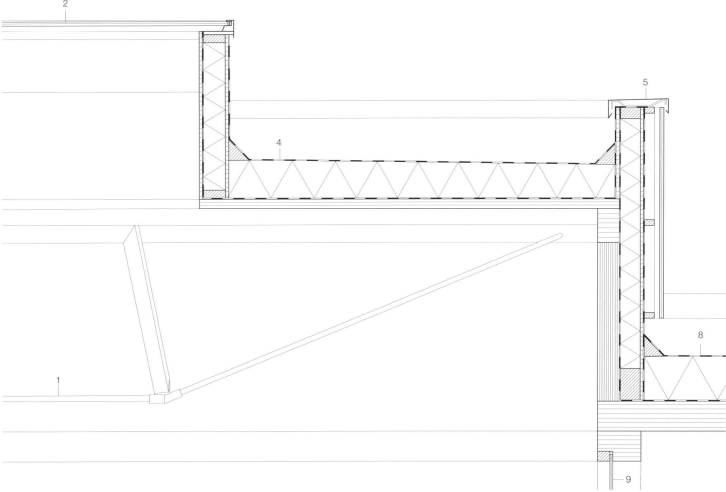

Ice Rink in Hof

Structure:
Steel skeleton construction / trussed beams

Architects:
Die Halle Architekten, Hof (DE)

Structural engineering:
Lauterbach, Franke und Kollegen, Hof (DE)

The first project to be completed as part of the new leisure and sports centre "Am Eisteich" (At the Ice Pond) is an ice rink with a facilities building and entrance pavilion. A steel skeleton roof structure about 72 m long, 40 m wide and more than 10 m high protects the ice surface from the weather. Lenticular trussed beams with a height of up to 3.70 m combine with the columns to form two-hinged frames. At a spacing of 7.50 m, these lend the structure transverse rigidity and at the same time facilitate a simple attachment of the column bases to the reinforced concrete foundation beam.

HEB 450 steel sections were used for the arched compression and bending-stressed top chords. Each trussed beam has eight HEB 240 steel section struts set at 4-m intervals. Two round solid steel rods of 70-mm diameter sufficed for the tensile-stressed bottom chord. The structure is covered with trapezoidal sheet that extends over several spans. Together with coupling purlins and cross-bracing in the plane of the roof, the sheet protects the top chords of the trussed beams from lateral buckling.
Reinforcement in the longitudinal direction is provided on each side by four vertical braces in the top half of the side columns.

Via coupling members, these reduce the buckling tendency of all the columns along their weak axis. Finally, the column bases along the building's long side are rigidly supported by the longitudinal foundation beam. To attenuate sound and reduce the accumulation of condensation, the roof has multiple layers and is lightly insulated.
The two neighbouring buildings, housing the bar, entryway, sanitary and cashier areas as well as changing, recreation, storage and plant rooms are solid constructions of partly core-insulated prefabricated exposed concrete elements.

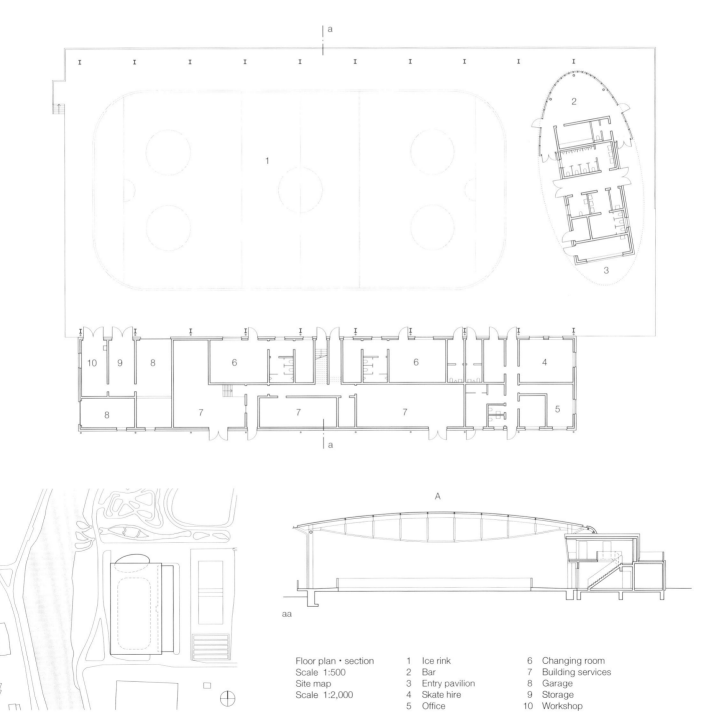

Floor plan · section
Scale 1:500
Site map
Scale 1:2,000

1 Ice rink	6 Changing room
2 Bar	7 Building services
3 Entry pavilion	8 Garage
4 Skate hire	9 Storage
5 Office	10 Workshop

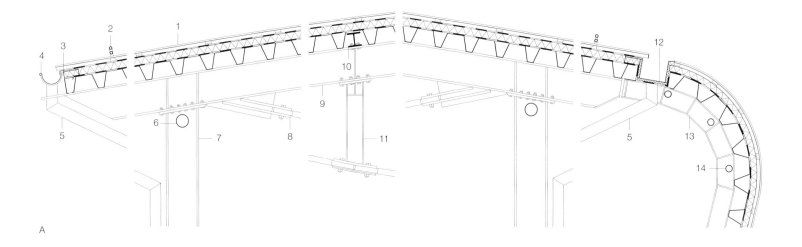

A

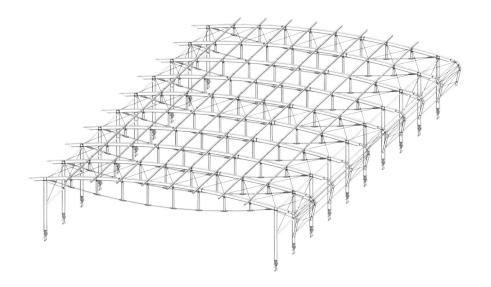

Isometric view of the structure,
No scale given
Vertical section
Scale 1:50

1 Roof construction:
   V65/400 aluminium standing seam
   profile roofing, 1 mm roll-formed
   Galvanised strip metal mounting
   rail, laid diagonally
   Waterproofing
   100 mm packed rock wool
   thermal insulation
   Vapour-proofing
   1.5 mm 200R/840 trapezoidal
   steel sheet
   Steel beam
2 Snow guard
3 1 mm aluminium fascia
4 Galvanised gutter mount
   Plain aluminium half-round gutter
5 3 mm galvanised steel downspout,
   NW 150
6 168 mm Ø steel coupling rod
7 HEB 450 column
8 2× 70 mm solid round steel
   stay cable
9 HEB 450 top chord
10 HEB 180 secondary beam
11 HEB 240 compression member
12 1 mm aluminium integrated gutter
13 Compound beam of HEB 260
   steel sections
14 89 mm Ø steel coupling rod

Sculpture Hall in Neuss

Structure:
Solid reinforced concrete construction /
tensile-stressed suspended timber and steel roof

Architects:
RKW Architektur +, Düsseldorf (DE) with
Thomas Schütte, Düsseldorf (DE)

Structural engineering:
Mayer-Vorfelder und Dinkelacker Ingenieurgesellschaft für Bauwesen, Sindelfingen (DE)

Near the Museum Insel Hombroich in Neuss, the exhibition hall at the Thomas Schütte Stiftung (foundation) offers space for the presentation of contemporary sculpture. The basement, a basin of water-impermeable concrete, provides storage opportunities. An impressive feature of the elliptical hall above is the curved wide-span roof. Its structure is conceived as a suspended construction on short steel columns above the timber-clad reinforced concrete outer walls. As a result, the exhibition space, which has a column-free area of 700 m², varies between 4.50 m and 8 m in height. The roof construction is based on a modified spoked wheel principle. A hollow box girder of steel forms the wheel rim and functions structurally as a compression ring. Hinged into it are 32 tensile-stressed spokes of bent glulam beams. A steel tension ring forms the central hub, which also serves as a central daylight opening. The chosen structural concept has the advantage that the forces present in its most important load-bearing elements are mainly normal forces. A timber pedestal supplies the necessary slope for roof drainage. At the compression ring the roof is supported by 16 thin columns made of round steel tubing. Together with the steel beam of the compression ring, these columns form a stiff frame that rests on the upper edge of the elliptical outer wall. The frame stiffens the roof against horizontal seismic and wind loads. The lightweight timber-and-steel roof construction with its precisely fitted slotted plate connections allowed for a high degree of prefabrication. Cantilevers hinged to the outer part of the roof structure make a wide roof overhang possible. The distinctive sculpture hall is the result of a close collaboration between architects and structural engineers and the designing artist.

Site map
Scale 1:2,000
Sections · Floor plan
Scale 1:400
Isometric view of the structure, no scale given
Vertical section of a node
Scale 1:10

1   Sculpture exhibits
2   Graphics exhibits
3   Secondary rooms
4   Reinforced concrete outer wall, clad in thermally
    treated poplar
5   194 mm ∅ steel tube column
6   60 × 120–740 mm mm spruce glued laminated
    timber console
7   S 355 structural steel slotted plate
8   450 × 250 mm hollow box steel section
    compression ring
9   160 × 480–740 mm main beam, glued
    laminated timber
10 160 × 140 mm squared timber secondary structure

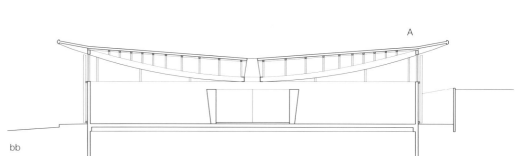

aa

bb

A

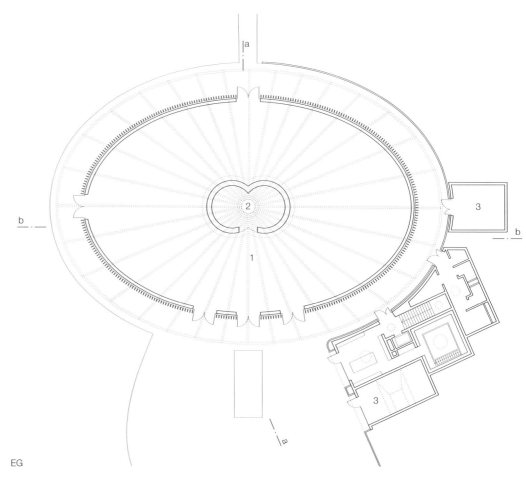

EG

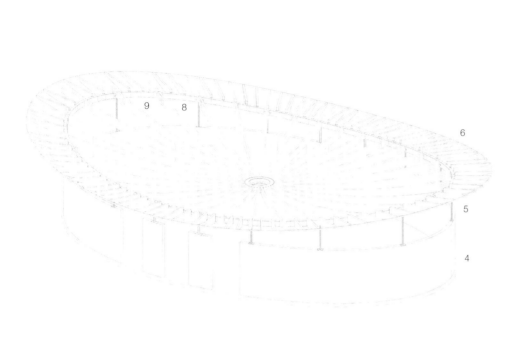

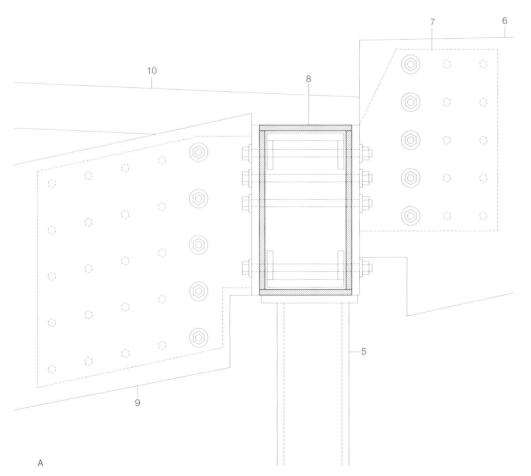

A

Office Building in Hamburg

Structure:
Steel skeleton construction with solid reinforced concrete components /
predominantly compression-stressed arch construction,
floor slabs suspended from tension members

Architects:
BRT Architekten Bothe Richter Teherani, Hamburg (DE)

Structural engineering:
Dr.-Ing. Binnewies, Hamburg (DE)

The structure of the Berliner Bogen (Berlin Arch) office building is a pertinent response by its designers to its special construction site, situated above a water basin near Berliner Tor in Hamburg. The basin is spanned by towering 36-m high parabolic steel arches. Steel vertical tension members, suspended from these 22 two-hinged arches and spaced 2.70 m apart, carry the partial loads of up to seven reinforced concrete floor slabs.

A large glass shell encloses the entire building, which features space for 1,200 workstations. Comb-like platforms around four vertical access cores frame six trapezoid conservatories, which encourage relaxation and provide additional spaces for exhibitions and parties. These buffer zones also supply the offices with light and allow for natural ventilation.

The mainly compression-stressed steel arches comprise an upper tube with a 356-mm diameter and a lower tube with a 194-mm diameter. The two tubes are connected laterally by sheet metal. The component height of an arch is 1.50 m at its crown and decreases toward the hinged supports of cast steel. Sheathing 50 mm thick with an F 90 fire rating encases the suspended columns, which are steel tubes 89 mm in diameter. The 280-mm thick reinforced concrete floor slabs are tempered by incorporated water pipes. This type of thermal concrete activation can be used to cool or heat the building. The central access zone of the building is a self-supporting upright structure. Its loads are transmitted to the undergound floors and provide the needed superimposed load for the water retention basin, which lies below the basement and extends down beyond ground water level.

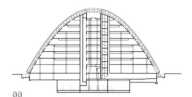

aa

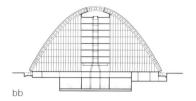

bb

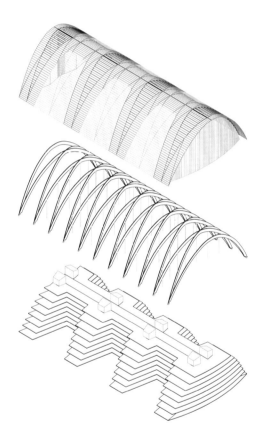

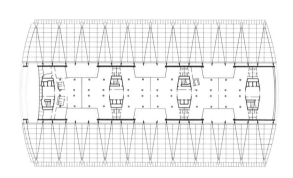

7th floor

Sections / Floor plans
Scale 1:2,000
Exploded view,
no scale given
Site map
Scale 1:5,000

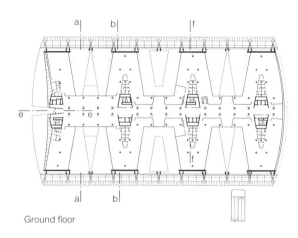

Ground floor

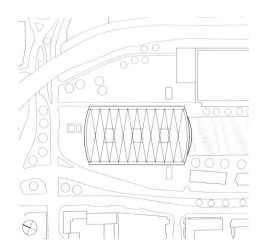

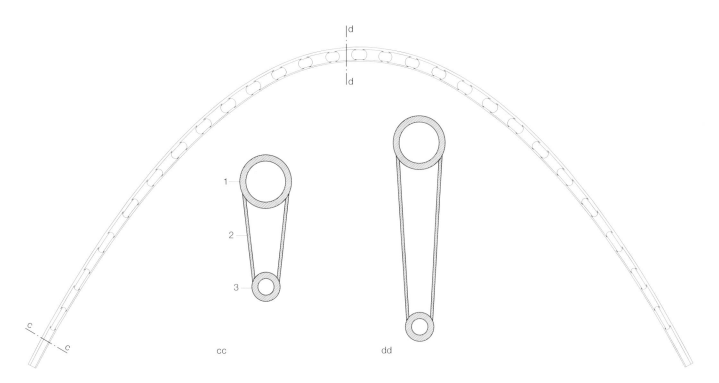

Developed view of the arch beam	1 356 mm Ø upper steel tube
Scale 1:400	2 20 mm steel connecting sheet
Cross sections of the arch beam	3 194 mm Ø lower steel tube
Scale 1:25	4 Glazed roof shell, point-attached
Vertical section of the north facade	5 1,500 mm steel arch at the crown
Scale 1:100	6 178 mm Ø steel tube purlin
	7 300 mm reinforced concrete shell
	8 280 mm reinforced concrete floor slab

9 Double facade construction:
   Point-attached outer glazing
   Slatted construction in the facade cavity
   Sliding glass inner windows
10 Firewall, prefabricated reinforced concrete
   component bonded with Isokorb
11 Glass cladding of walls and ceiling of
   main entrance, point-attached

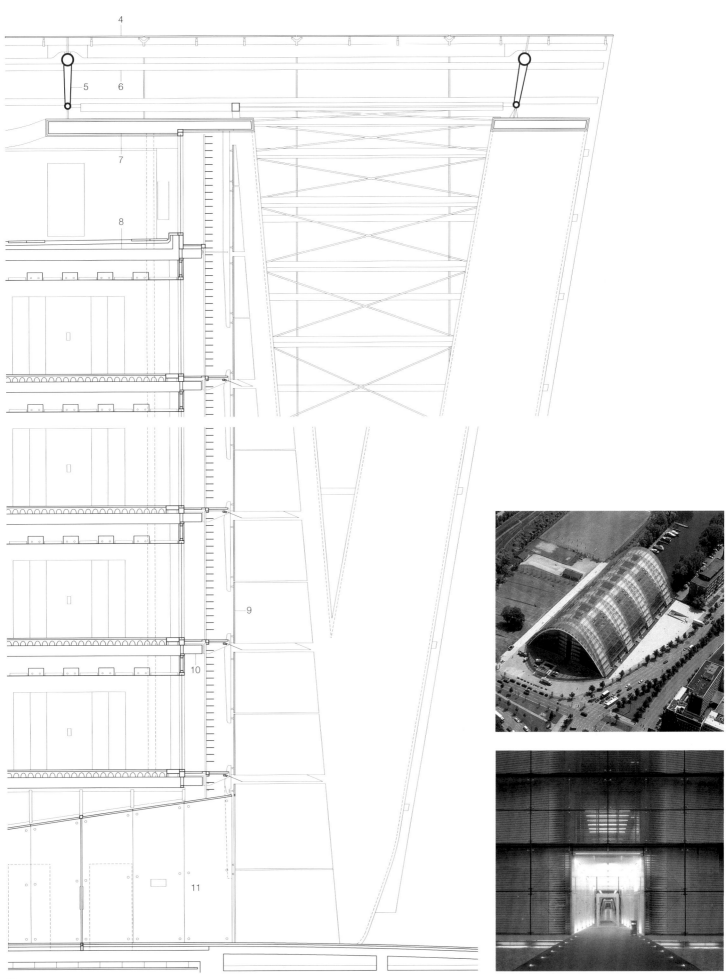

4

5   6

7

8

9

10

11

ee

198

Vertical section
Scale 1:75

1 Galvanised grate roof ventilation exchange
2 356 mm ∅ upper steel tube
3 20 mm steel connecting sheet
4 194 mm ∅ lower steel tube
5 Movable ventilation flaps, facade inspection
   system access
6 Inner facade construction:
   140 mm composite insulating system
   250 mm reinforced concrete shell
   15 mm interior plaster
7 Anchor for facade inspection system
8 Glazed roof shell, point-attached
9 Cast steel cantilevered glass-mounting
   support
10 178 mm ∅ steel tube purlin
11 1,500 mm steel arch at the crown,
   micaceous iron ore coating
12 Concrete core activation
13 Sunshade, externally reversible
14 Rounded shell window with fire-resistant
   VSG G 30 glazing
15 Cast steel two-hinged frame support
16 Checker plate
17 Galvanised grating

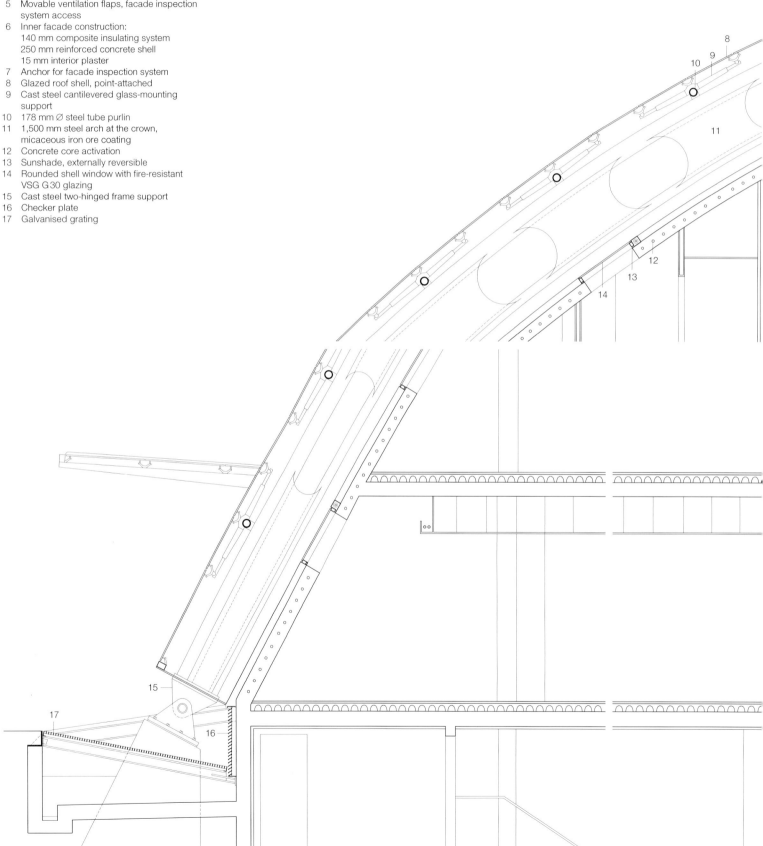

ff

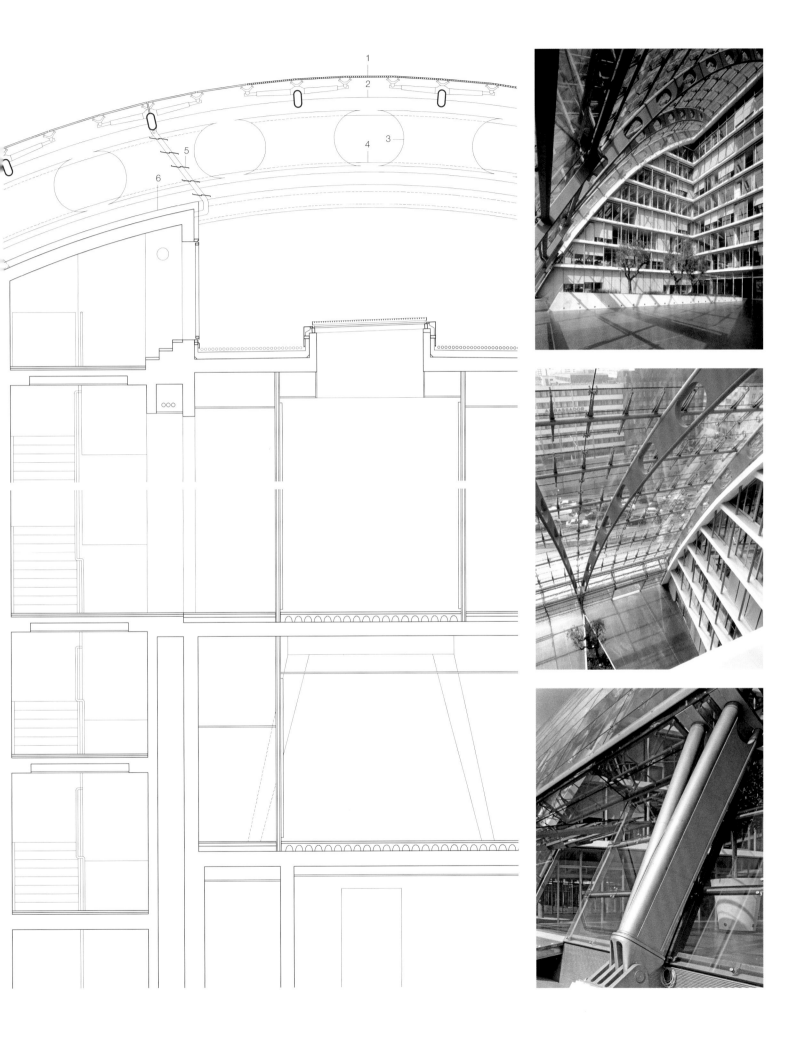

Railway Station in Liège

Structure:
Steel skeleton construction/primarily
compression-stressed arch structure

Architects:
Santiago Calatrava, Zurich (CH)

Structural engineering:
Santiago Calatrava, Zurich (CH)

In spanning large areas, structures subject to normal forces often require less material than bending-stressed structures. For this reason, but also to deliver a clear statement in support of an environmentally appropriate mode of transport, the 39 steel arches over the Liège main railway station are primarily compression-stressed. Their great arcing curve, with a rise of more than 36 m and a span of about 180 m, is visible from afar. The canopies of the terminal hall jut way out over the forecourts on both sides, obviating the need for a facade to protect against the weather and inviting people to enter the public shopping and access passages of the railway station. The 33,000-m² surface of the roof is covered with laminated safety glass panes 23 mm thick. With this impressive steel and glass structure, Calatrava has succeeded in showcasing the Liège railway station as the contemporary update of a long tradition of grand railway terminal halls.

The imposing steel arches themselves are spaced closely together at 1.90-m intervals. The secondary beams of the transparent hall roof were welded to them rigidly. As a result, the entire roof is given a shell-like rigidity. Towards the supports, the arch cross section divides into a top and a bottom chord. The chords merge once again at their ends, which are cantilevered out far beyond the supports. This creates interstitial spaces at both ends of the terminal in which pedestrian bridges 14 m wide cross the tracks, providing a wide connection between the two sides of the station. The steel construction of both pedestrian bridges takes up the combined loads of the individual arches and transmits them to five support points at either end of the terminal. These comprise steel bases, connected to the foundations and hinged in the longitudinal arch direction, which branch out upward into four mighty hollow steel sections.

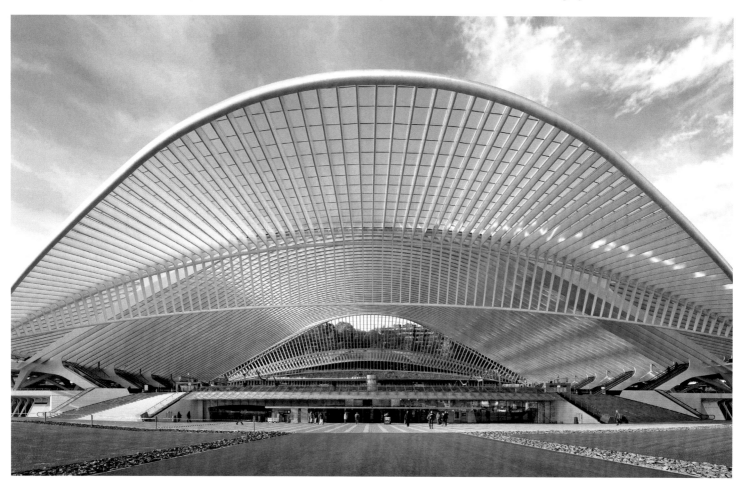

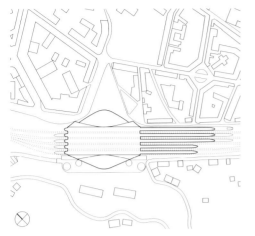

Site map
Scale 1:10,000
Floor plans
Scale 1:2,500

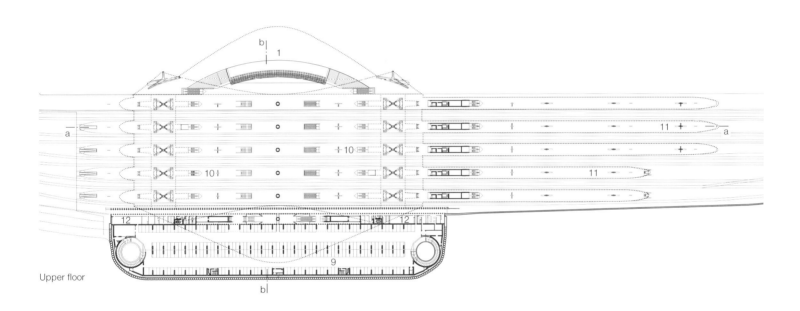

Upper floor

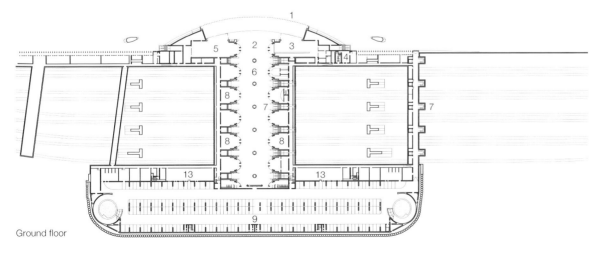

Ground floor

1 Forecourt
2 Entrance
3 Tickets
4 Staff
5 Restaurants
6 Shopping passage
7 Lifts/stairs to
 the platform
8 Shop
9 Parking garage
10 Stairs to the gallery/
 footbridge
11 Platform
12 Lockers
13 Office

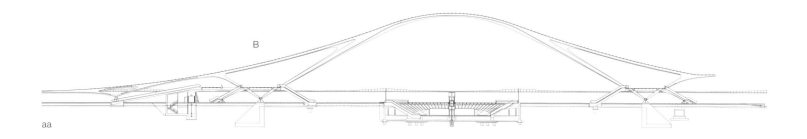

aa

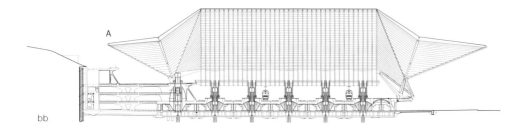

bb

A

Sections
Scale 1:1,500
Section of the steel canopy
Scale 1:250
Details
Scale 1:20

1   660 mm ∅ steel tube
2   22.8 mm laminated safety glass
3   324 mm ∅ steel tube,
    welded to 2× 16 mm bar steel
4   457 mm ∅ steel tube
5   20 mm stainless steel sheet
6   5–10 mm stainless steel sheet
7   159/5.6 mm ∅ steel tube
8   10–25 mm stainless steel sheet
9   159/ 5.6–14.2 mm ∅ steel tube

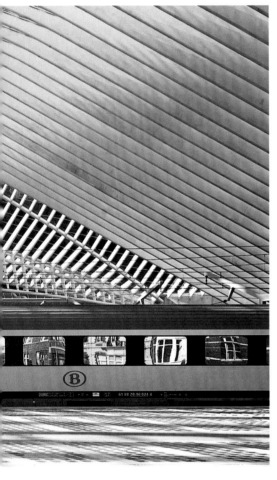

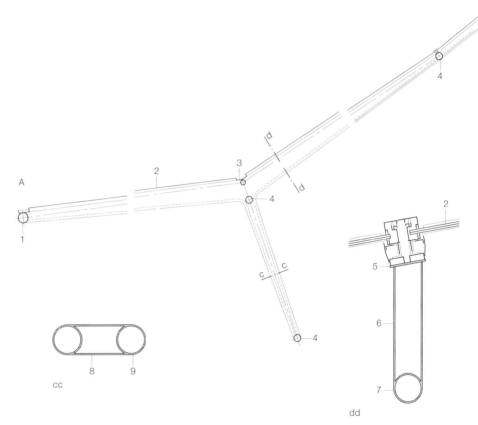

Section of the steel structure
Terminal roof
Scale 1:250
Sections of the supports
Scale 1:100

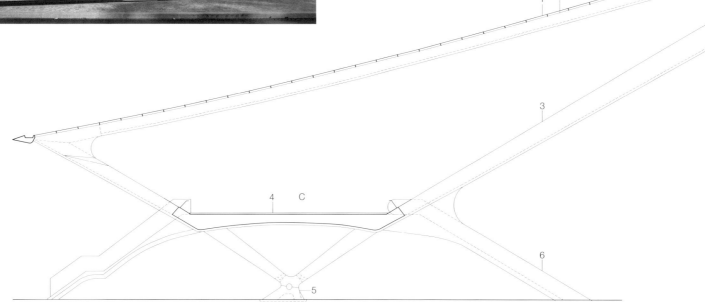

B

1   22.8 mm laminated safety glass
2   Top chord hollow steel section
    267/1,134–1,284 mm welded
    from 267/25 mm ∅ steel tube
    and 15–30 mm steel sheet
3   Bottom chord hollow steel
    section
    267/888–2092 mm welded from
    267/20–50 ∅ steel tube and
    25–40 mm steel sheet
4   Steel pedestrian bridge welded
    from 20–40 mm steel sheet

5   Cast steel support
6   Escalator to the platform
7   40 mm natural stone flooring
    in thin-set mortar
8   Piers welded from 50 mm
    steel sheet
9   460 mm ∅ stainless steel hinge
    bolt in slide bearing
10 Cast steel component fixed
    to foundation with 6 40 mm ∅
    anchor bolts
11 Built-in light fixture

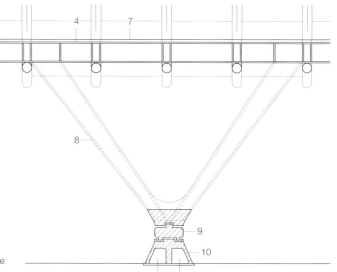

ee

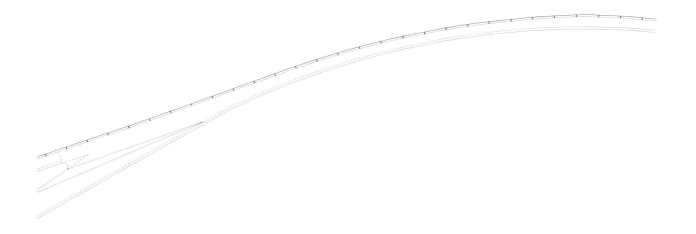

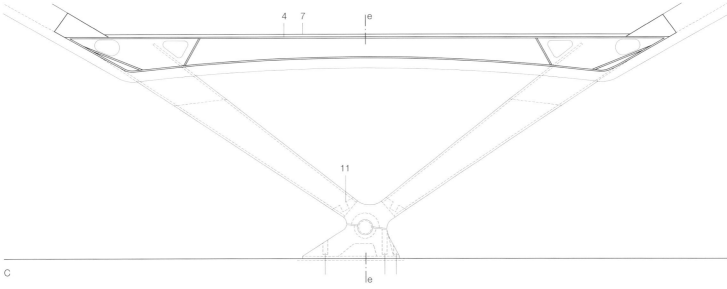

C

Sports Centre in Sargans

Structure:
Timber skeleton construction / frame of glued
laminated timber posts and beams

Architects:
Hildebrand, Zurich (CH)
Ruprecht Architekten, Zurich (CH)

Structural engineering:
WaltGalmarini, Zurich (CH)

Frame structures are characterised by rigid connections between beams and posts. This can aid in controlling the loads on building components, making appropriate use of cross sections and saving material. In addition to vertical loads, frames can also carry horizontal loads in the direction of the frame, thereby contributing to building stiffness. In the quadruple gymnasium of the municipality of Sargans, near Liechtenstein, 40 glulam frames with slender cross sections 140 cm high and 14 cm wide are strung together with a dense axial spacing of 180 cm. They are reinforced by composite timber slabs in the ceiling and walls. The series of frames,

some of which are two storeys high, runs visibly through all parts of the building, which include the equipment room in the north-east as well as the foyer, changing rooms, fitness and gymnastics rooms on the south-west side of the hall. Glued-in threaded rods ensure that the transition between the beams and the 80-cm thick posts exhibits high flexural stiffness. Depending on the structural demands, the wood used for the glued laminated timber of the framework was spruce of varying strength classes. In some areas the engineers relied on ash wood, which has greater load-bearing capacity. One of these areas was the two-storey section on the side of the

building, where the joists of the semi-finished reinforced concrete ceilings feature spans of more than 10 m. Composite anchors familiar from bridge construction made it possible to fashion a hybrid timber-concrete composite system from the concrete slabs and wood frames that was capable of supporting the 15-tonne prefabricated concrete showers. With this sports centre of lightweight timber, the designers succeeded in creating an elegant, filigree appearance within a relatively short construction period and with a high degree of prefabrication, all while making a remarkable contribution to ecology, sustainability and regional value creation.

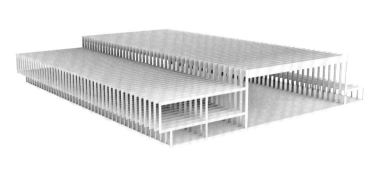

Site map
Scale 1:2,000
Sections · Floor plans
Scale 1:750

1 Entrance
2 Cafeteria
3 Gymnasium
4 Building services
5 Equipment
6 Storage and
  secondary rooms
7 Shower
8 Changing room
9 Office
10 Kitchen
11 Gymnastics room
12 Fitness area
13 Classroom

aa

bb

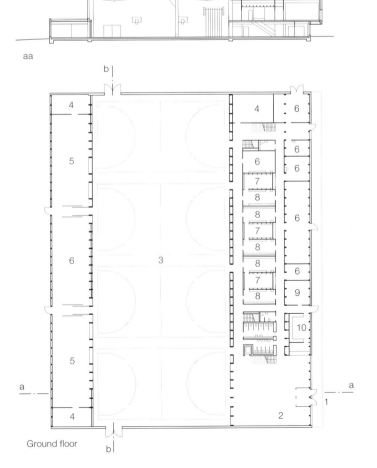

Ground floor

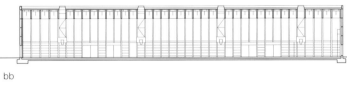

Upper floor

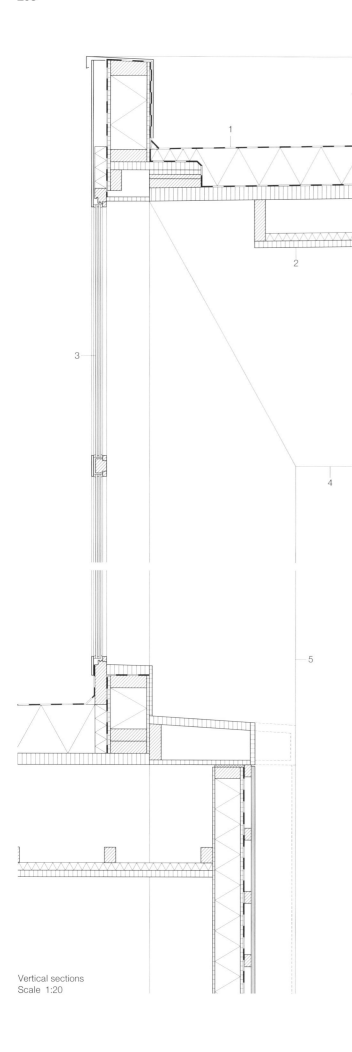

Vertical sections
Scale 1:20

1   Roof construction:
    Bitumen sheet waterproofing,
    double layer
    200–260 mm rock wool
    thermal insulation
    Vapour barrier
    68 mm spruce / fir
    three-layer board
2   35 mm wood wool acoustic panel
    40 mm mineral fibre
    thermal insulation
    60/175 mm squared timber
    subconstruction
3   Insulating glass
4   140/1,400 mm glulam beam
5   140/800 mm glulam post
6   Exterior wall front side:
    120/20 mm rough-sawn
    spruce / fir formwork visibly
    attached with screws
    40 + 10 mm pressure-
    impregnated battens with
    ventilation between
    vapour-permeable facade

    protection
    16 mm MDF panel
    60/200 mm column, rock wool
    thermal insulation between
    15 mm OSB panel,
    panel joints sealed airtight
    40/60 mm battens
    20/120 mm planed
    spruce / fir formwork
7   10/20 mm powder-coated
    flat steel railing
8   140/640 mm glulam beam
9   Floor construction:
    20 mm hardened concrete
    70 mm cement heating screed
    PE film separating layer
    20 mm impact sound insulation
    70 + 50 mm semi-finished
    reinforced concrete ceiling in
    combination with 140/500 mm
    spruce /ash glulam beam
    2× 35 mm rock wool
    thermal insulation
    2× 15 mm gypsum fibreboard

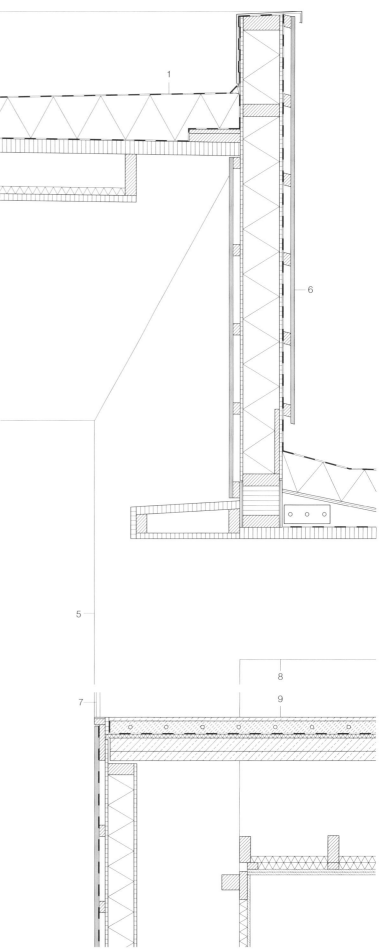

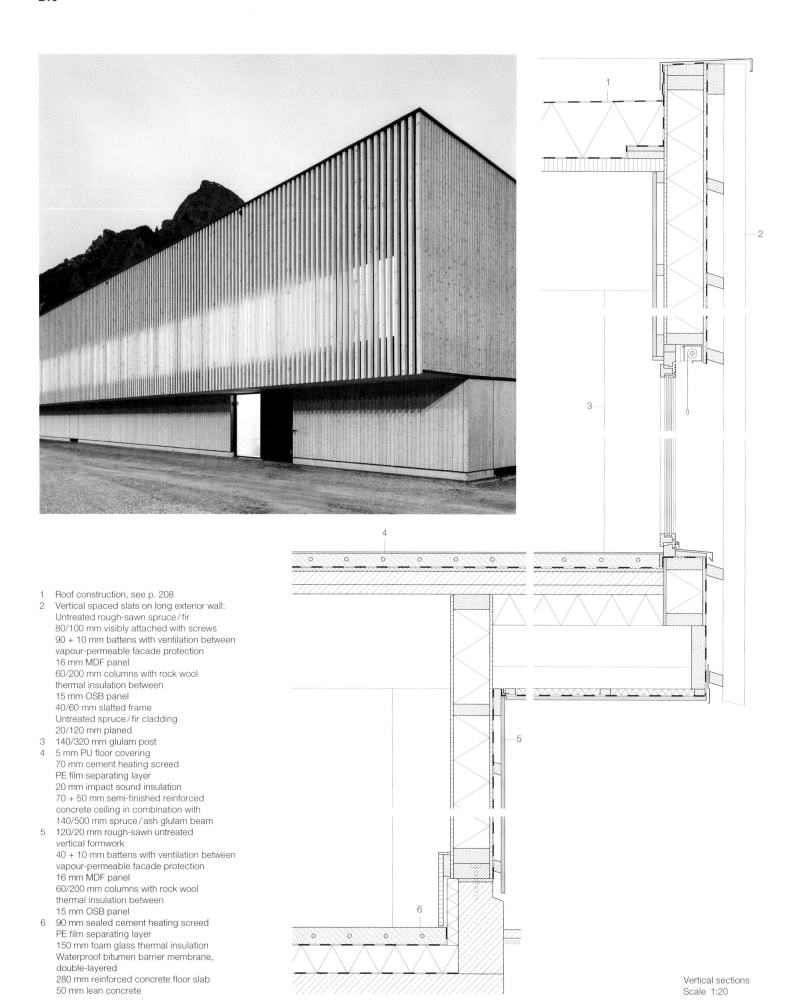

1   Roof construction, see p. 208
2   Vertical spaced slats on long exterior wall:
    Untreated rough-sawn spruce / fir
    80/100 mm visibly attached with screws
    90 + 10 mm battens with ventilation between
    vapour-permeable facade protection
    16 mm MDF panel
    60/200 mm columns with rock wool
    thermal insulation between
    15 mm OSB panel
    40/60 mm slatted frame
    Untreated spruce / fir cladding
    20/120 mm planed
3   140/320 mm glulam post
4   5 mm PU floor covering
    70 mm cement heating screed
    PE film separating layer
    20 mm impact sound insulation
    70 + 50 mm semi-finished reinforced
    concrete ceiling in combination with
    140/500 mm spruce / ash glulam beam
5   120/20 mm rough-sawn untreated
    vertical formwork
    40 + 10 mm battens with ventilation between
    vapour-permeable facade protection
    16 mm MDF panel
    60/200 mm columns with rock wool
    thermal insulation between
    15 mm OSB panel
6   90 mm sealed cement heating screed
    PE film separating layer
    150 mm foam glass thermal insulation
    Waterproof bitumen barrier membrane,
    double-layered
    280 mm reinforced concrete floor slab
    50 mm lean concrete

Vertical sections
Scale 1:20

Railway Terminal in Rotterdam

Structure:
Steel-timber skeleton construction / multi-span steel frame,
secondary beams of glued laminated timber

Architects:
Team CS: Benthem Crouwel Architects, Amsterdam (NL)
MVSA Meyer en Van Schooten Architecten, Amsterdam (NL)
West 8, Rotterdam (NL)

Structural engineering:
Arcadis and Gemeentewerken, Rotterdam (NL)

The structure of the new main railway station in Rotterdam is composed of two very different elements. With a grand formal gesture, the entrance hall of the central station opens out toward the city centre. Concealed behind it in an almost timid manner lies the unassuming, "subtle" terminal hall, almost 250 m long and 160 m wide.
The main structure of this light-flooded platform hall consists of six 145-cm deep hollow box-shaped profiles. They run along the platforms and are connected in a frame-like way to tremendous Y-shaped steel columns. With only few column bases on the platforms, the form of the columns creates many support points for the main girders and thus reduces their free span lengths. At the same time, the frames can carry horizontal loads along the longitudinal direction of the hall. The same formal principle also subtly strengthens the transverse reinforcement. In order for the access to the individual rail platforms to remain unimpeded by columns, the columns near the stairs and escalators bifurcate at their bottoms as well, though this spread is rotated 90° from the other. The clever design of such pillars can contribute to the stiffening of the structure in both directions. Closely spaced slender secondary beams of glued laminated timber, 14 cm wide and 130 cm high, support the hall's glass roof, the surface of which is gently folded for drainage and equipped with printed sun protection and photovoltaic elements. The folded roof construction with its gently inclined bands of double-layered laminated safety glass transitions directly into the north facade. This provides travellers on the platforms with a visual reference to the adjacent neighbourhood.
An extensive shopping passage on the ground floor offers access to the platforms above and connects the city districts on the south and north sides of the railway station.

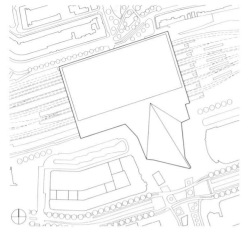

Sections · Floor plans
Scale 1:2,000

1 Terminal hall
2 Information
3 Shops
4 Access to the metro
5 Tickets
6 Pedestrian and
  bicycle bypass
7 Track underpass
8 Platform
9 Commercial area
10 Bus depot
11 Tram station

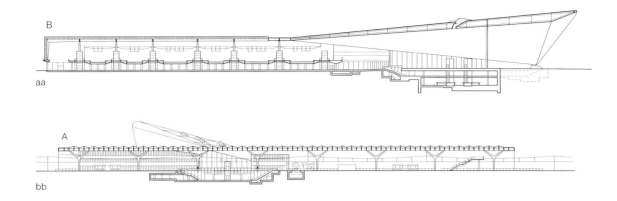

B

aa

A

bb

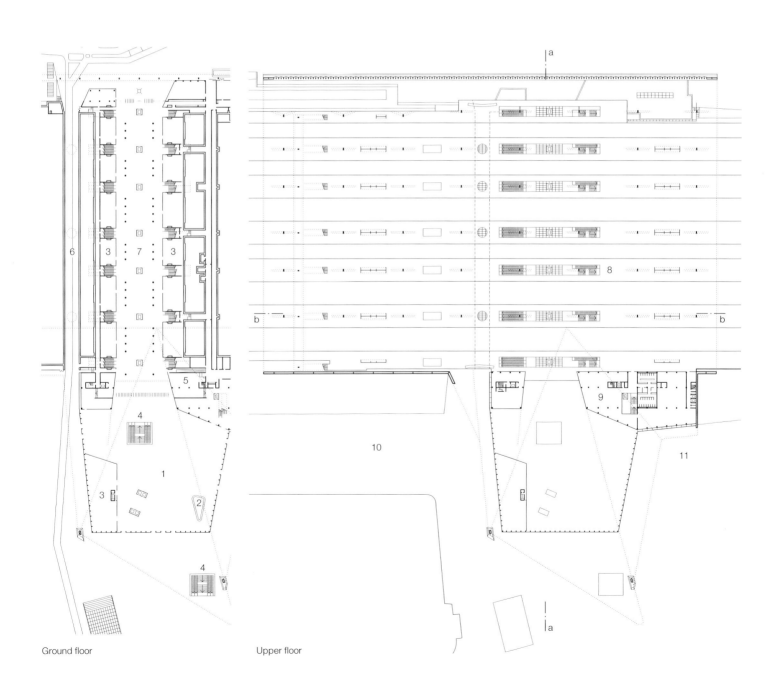

Ground floor   Upper floor

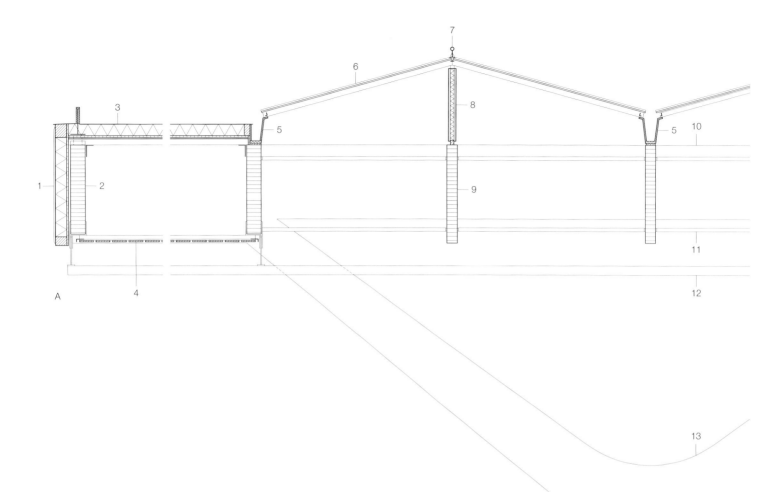

A

Vertical sections
Scale 1:50

1   1 mm aluminium sheet standing
    seam panelling
    150 mm PUR rigid foam
    Bitumen sheet waterproofing
    25 mm laminated veneer
    lumber panel
2   200/1,200 mm glulam beam
3   1 mm aluminium sheet standing
    seam panelling
    150 mm PUR rigid foam
    Bitumen sheet waterproofing
    25 mm laminated veneer
    lumber panel
    100 mm steel trapezoidal sheet
4   20 mm suspended timber
    lath ceiling, butt joints offset
5   Insulated rain gutter
6   Roof covering:
    2× 8 mm laminated safety glass,
    printed with integrated photo-
    voltaic modules, on steel frames
7   Guide rail for cleaning cart
8   100 mm acoustic panel:
    Powder-coated perforated
    steel sheets with mineral wool
    filling between
9   140/1,300 mm glulam secondary
    girder, painted grey
10 380–450/1,450 mm hollow box
    main girder welded from 25 mm
    flat steel
11 30 mm ∅ steel rod
12 Cleaning platform guide rail
13 Hollow box Y column, welded from
    25 mm flat steel

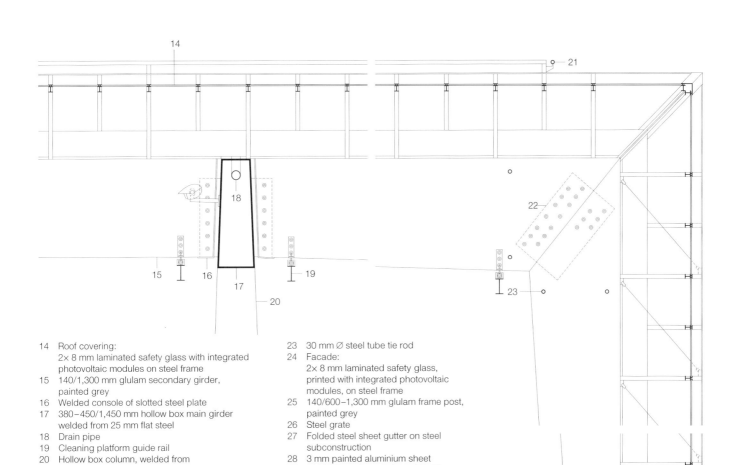

14 Roof covering:
   2× 8 mm laminated safety glass with integrated photovoltaic modules on steel frame
15 140/1,300 mm glulam secondary girder, painted grey
16 Welded console of slotted steel plate
17 380–450/1,450 mm hollow box main girder welded from 25 mm flat steel
18 Drain pipe
19 Cleaning platform guide rail
20 Hollow box column, welded from 25 mm flat steel
21 Guide rail for cleaning cart
22 Slotted steel plate

23 30 mm ∅ steel tube tie rod
24 Facade:
   2× 8 mm laminated safety glass, printed with integrated photovoltaic modules, on steel frame
25 140/600–1,300 mm glulam frame post, painted grey
26 Steel grate
27 Folded steel sheet gutter on steel subconstruction
28 3 mm painted aluminium sheet
29 600/800 mm box girder welded from 25 mm flat steel
30 Steel rolling gate

Technology Centre in Chicago

Structure:
Steel skeleton construction / Vierendeel or rigid frame trusses

Architects:
Barkow Leibinger, Berlin (DE)

Structural engineering:
Knippers Helbig, New York (US) / Berlin (DE)

Hidden behind the description "Smart Factory" is the modern production and presentation building of a Swabian high-tech company, which was opened near the industrial metropolis of Chicago. Digitally networked machines demonstrate the integrated production chain for sheet metal building components to the customers of this machine tool and laser manufacturing firm. The chain runs from order via construction and finishing all the way to delivery. The heart of the complex is a large, column-free showroom covering more than 2,400 m², made possible through eleven Vierendeel trusses up to 3.60 m high, spaced at just under 5-m intervals and spanning about 45 m. The engineers developed the specific form of these trusses taking into account the internal forces due to uniform vertical loading. Because the shear force increases toward the supports and thus generates larger frame moments, the designers reduced the spacing between the vertical struts near the supports. In addition, they increased the width of the members where the frame moments are large. In the centre of the span, the separation of the top and bottom chords becomes greater as a logical consequence of the large bending moments of the simple beams. This creates space for a walkway from which the hall can be viewed from above. The separation of the chords narrows toward the truss ends. Secondary beams connect the top chords with the roof surface of trapezoidal sheet. Upright beams of weather-resistant steel up to 11.50 m long support the glazed post & beam facade. The standard rolled steel profiles, spaced at narrow 1.63-m intervals, take up the wind loads of the internal glazing. Corrugated metal of weather-resistant steel characterises the appearance of the closed facade sections. The discerning choice of materials and the precise detailing lend the structure of this industrial complex an imposing elegance.

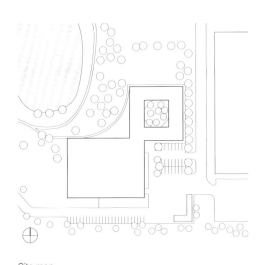

Site map
Scale 1:4,000
Sections · Floor plan
Scale 1:1,000

1 Presentation hall
2 Deliveries
3 Foyer
4 Cafeteria
5 Terrace
6 Office
7 Inner courtyard
8 Auditorium

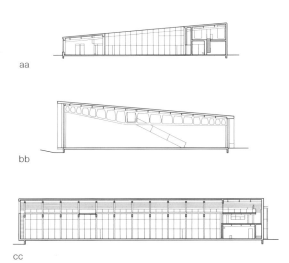

aa

bb

cc

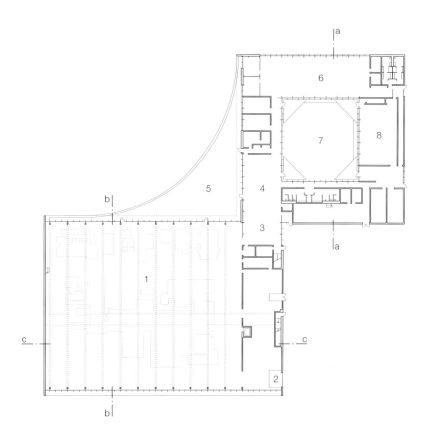

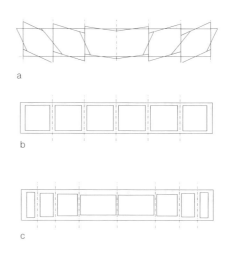

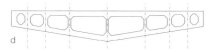

a

b

c

d

Schematic of the development of the truss
a   Localised bending moments
b–d Force-compliant optimisation
     of the truss geometry
Side view of the truss
Scale 1:250
Vertical section
Scale 1:50

A

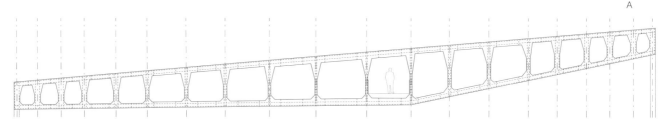

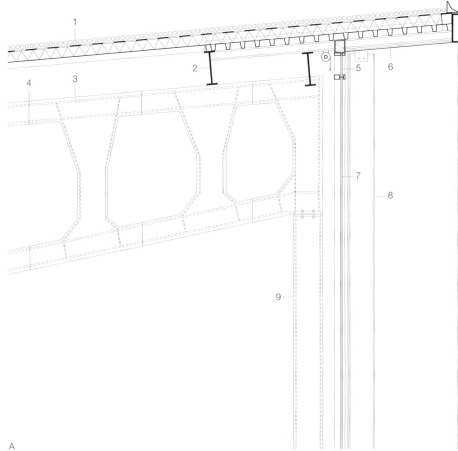

1   Roof construction:
    Pebbles
    Plastic waterproofing membrane
    135 mm thermal insulation
    135 × 85 mm trapezoidal sheet
2   400 × 180 mm steel profile secondary beam
3   Vierendeel truss assembled from welded
    steel plates, painted black
4   Welded seam
5   Black-anodised aluminium thermal
    insulation panel
6   Corrugated weather-resistant structural
    steel cladding, underside of the
    roof overhang
7   Aluminium post & beam facade,
    black-anodised, with double glazing
8   Weather-resistant structural steel facade post
9   Column of welded steel plate, painted black

A

Company Restaurant in Ditzingen

Structure:
Steel-timber skeleton construction/steel beams and columns as
primary structure, timber girder grids as secondary structure

Architects:
Barkow Leibinger, Berlin (DE)

Structural engineering:
Werner Sobek Ingenieure, Stuttgart (DE)

What is immediately striking about this company restaurant for 2,000 employees in the Swabian town of Ditzingen is its unconventional roof construction, which turns a visit to the canteen into a spatial experience. The pentagonal pavilion is glazed all around its perimeter and occasionally follows the contours of the surrounding buildings. Its main floor sits 4 m below the ground surface. This allows the secondary rooms to be concealed underground. A space-defining honeycomb ceiling spans the main room and its mezzanine at a height of up to 9 m. The polygonal cells of varnished glued laminated timber vary in depth and together form the omnidirectional girder grid that acts as the secondary structure. In addition, diagonal steel V or A-shaped columns stiffen the building against horizontal loads. However, all of this does not result in hectic disarray, but rather generates a cheerful atmosphere of self-evident serenity.

The steel beams of the primary structure are welded rectangular hollow profiles. While the widths of the steel profiles remain constant at 300 mm, their heights are adapted to the flow of forces. They vary from 600 mm to 1,500 mm. These hollow box girders are supported by nine groups of columns, positioned in response to the functional constraints as well as the economic aspect, which is predicated on modest steel expenditures for the structure.

The honeycomb texture of the timber girder grid contains different infills. Perforated timber elements serve as acoustic panels. Light fixtures provide artificial illumination. A few of the cells penetrate the roof skin and act as skylights to admit natural daylight. This creates an interplay between lighter and darker surfaces, which lends the ceiling an extra level of plasticity.

1 Main entrance to the
  corporate campus
2 Production /
  development
3 Service centre
4 Company restaurant
5 Sales and
  service centre
6 Connecting tunnel
7 Entrance
8 Restaurant /
  auditorium
9 Food counters
10 Kitchen
11 Storage
12 Deliveries
13 Coffee shop / gallery
14 Terrace
15 Building services
16 Central heating
   system

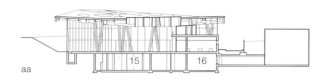

aa

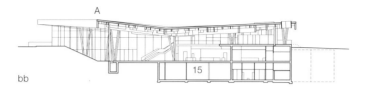

bb

A

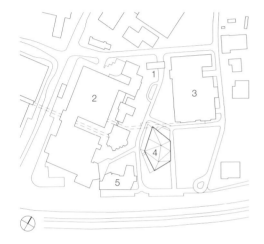

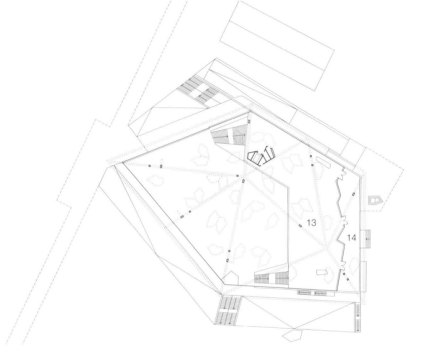

Upper floor

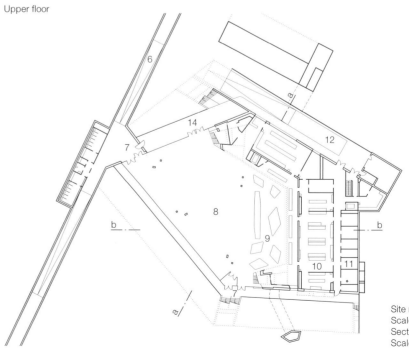

Ground floor

Site map
Scale 1:6,000
Sections · Floor plans
Scale 1:1,000

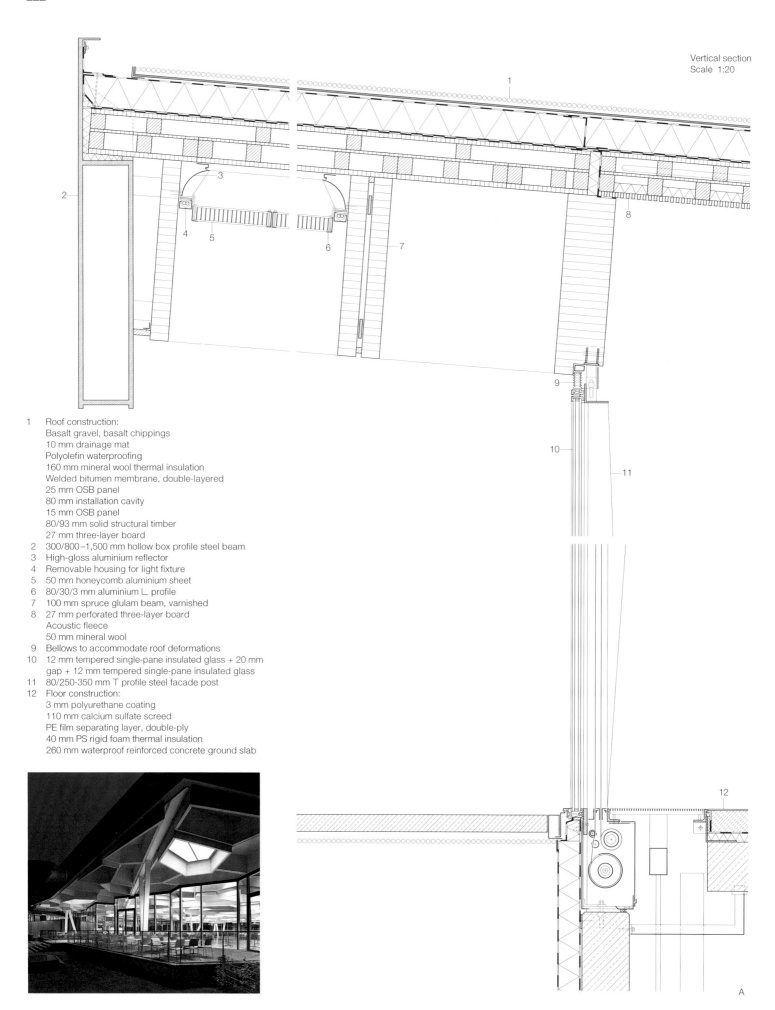

Vertical section
Scale 1:20

1   Roof construction:
    Basalt gravel, basalt chippings
    10 mm drainage mat
    Polyolefin waterproofing
    160 mm mineral wool thermal insulation
    Welded bitumen membrane, double-layered
    25 mm OSB panel
    80 mm installation cavity
    15 mm OSB panel
    80/93 mm solid structural timber
    27 mm three-layer board
2   300/800–1,500 mm hollow box profile steel beam
3   High-gloss aluminium reflector
4   Removable housing for light fixture
5   50 mm honeycomb aluminium sheet
6   80/30/3 mm aluminium L profile
7   100 mm spruce glulam beam, varnished
8   27 mm perforated three-layer board
    Acoustic fleece
    50 mm mineral wool
9   Bellows to accommodate roof deformations
10 12 mm tempered single-pane insulated glass + 20 mm
    gap + 12 mm tempered single-pane insulated glass
11 80/250-350 mm T profile steel facade post
12 Floor construction:
    3 mm polyurethane coating
    110 mm calcium sulfate screed
    PE film separating layer, double-ply
    40 mm PS rigid foam thermal insulation
    260 mm waterproof reinforced concrete ground slab

Vertical section of skylight
Vertical section of structural node
Scale 1:20

1 10 mm tempered single-pane insulated glass + 16 mm gap + 16 mm laminated safety glass, $U_g = 1.1$ W/m²K, 8.3 % slope
2 60/60 mm ⊘ steel section, around perimeter
3 3 mm aluminium sheet flashing
4 2×100 mm spruce glulam beams, connected with gusset plates and bolts, separated by a 30 mm gap
5 Roof construction, see p. 222
6 Bolts welded to steel beam
7 100 mm slotted spruce glulam beam
8 Gusset plate welded rigidly to steel beam
9 300/800–1,500 mm hollow box profile steel beam, painted white
10 30 mm spruce board, attached to glulam beam via angle brackets

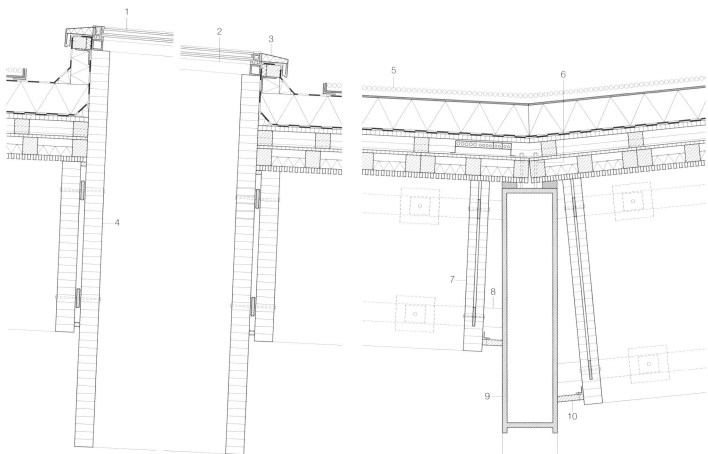

Sports Hall in Chiasso

Structure:
Solid reinforced concrete construction/prestressed girder grid
on four V-shaped columns

Architects:
Baserga Mozzetti Architetti, Muralto (CH)

Structural engineering:
Ingegneri Pedrazzini Guidotti, Lugano (CH)

Girder grids are counted among the non-directional structures. Their use is appropriate when the spans in both directions are similar in length. Manufacturing them using timber or steel is quite cumbersome because of the many nodes. Using concrete, on the other hand, the girder grid can be produced with far less difficulty.
For the dual gymnasium of the cantonal vocational and trade school in the town of Chiasso in Ticino, architects and engineers collaborated closely to develop such a girder grid of prestressed reinforced concrete. The monumental appearance of the hall springs from the exciting contrast between weight and lightness. With apparent ease, only four V-shaped pairs of columns lift the solid-looking roof construction up high. They provide an almost unencumbered view into the square hall, the bottom half of which is below ground. Below the 2.40-m glass facade, which runs all the way around the gymnasium perimeter, the walls are clad in larch. Because of the high groundwater level, the basement construction is waterproof concrete tanking with reinforced joists supporting the hall floor. The building is accessed on the glassed-in gallery level. A staircase with generous head space connects the gallery with the gymnasium level below. The four pairs of columns carry four vertical concrete slabs on which the girder grid is supported. The roof structure is formed from a grid of 14 prestressed reinforced concrete beams with a centre-to-centre spacing of 4 m. Horizontal forces are taken up by the concrete slabs, which combine at the corners with the double columns to act as a rigid frame. In order to avoid a visible anchoring of the tensioning cables, the girder grid was poured and prestressed on a temporary support frame. Only then were the lateral structural wall slabs lifted into place over the columns.

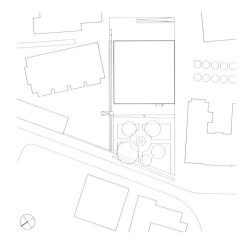

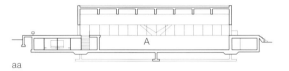

aa

Site map
Scale 1:2,000
Section · Floor plans
Scale 1:800
Vertical section
Scale 1:20

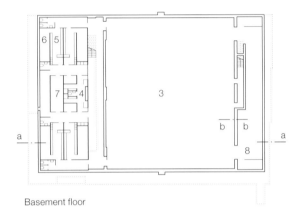

Basement floor

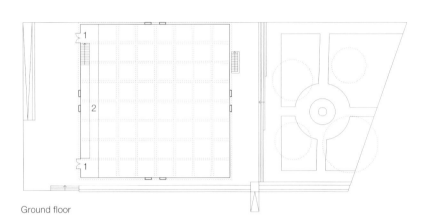

Ground floor

1   Entrance
2   Gallery
3   Gymnasium
4   Instructor changing room
5   Student changing room
6   Shower
7   Building services
8   Equipment
9   Roof construction:
    Approx. 50 mm pebble drainage layer
    Protective coating
    Synthetic waterproofing sheet
    200 mm thermal insulation
    Vapour barrier
    180 mm reinforced concrete ceiling slab
    1,080/350 mm prestressed reinforced
    concrete girder
10 Parapet wall construction:
    400 mm exposed concrete
    140 mm thermal insulation with vertical lathing
    Vapour barrier
    50 mm thermal insulation with horizontal lathing
    35 mm acoustic panel
11 Basement wall construction:
    250 mm reinforced concrete
    120 mm thermal insulation with vertical lathing
    Vapour barrier
    30 mm thermal insulation with horizontal lathing
    120 mm cavity for heating elements and
    vertical lathing
    100 mm larch cladding
12 Basement floor construction:
    15 mm polyurethane coating
    80 mm cement screed
    PE film separating layer
    80 mm thermal insulation
    3.5 mm waterproofing
    250 mm waterproof reinforced concrete
    ground slab
    50 mm lean concrete

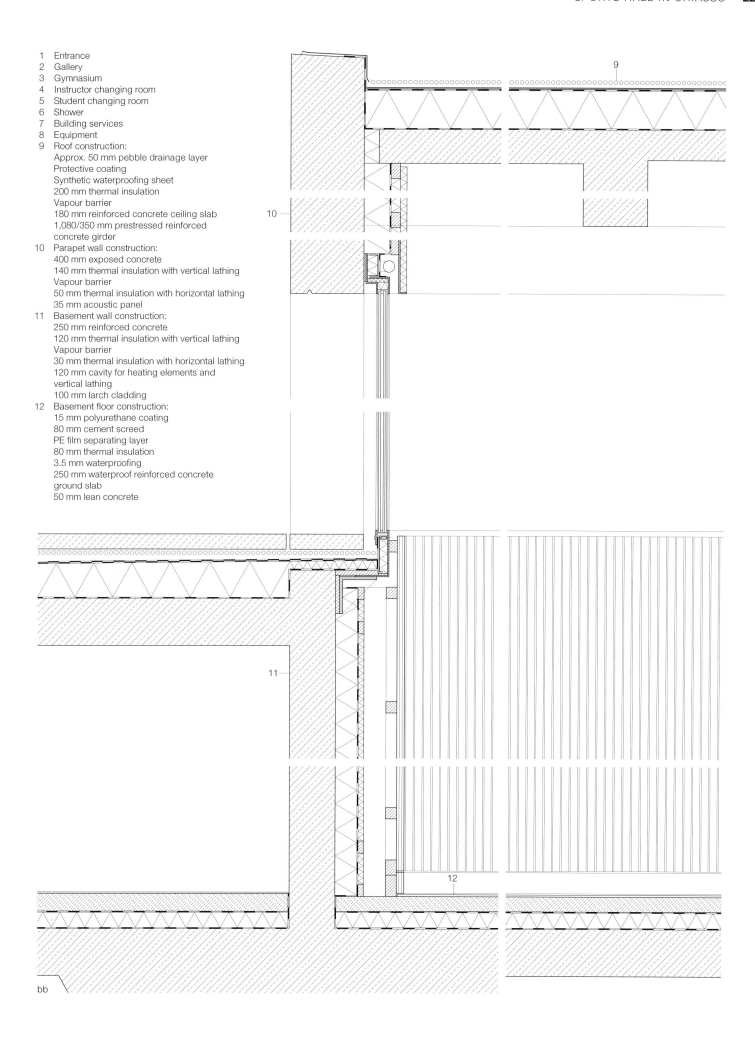

bb

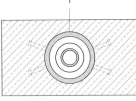

cc

Cross section, perspective
of composite structure
Scale 1:20
Positioning of the
prestressed cables
Roof girder/exterior wall
Scale 1:200

1 270 mm Ø steel tube with
   hollow interior used for
   rain pipe or electrical wiring,
   encased in reinforced
   concrete
2 Stay
3 Connection reinforcement for
   reinforced concrete wall slab
4 Rain pipe

5 Roof girder
6 116 mm Ø steel tension cable
   in jacket tube
7 91 mm Ø steel tension cable
   in jacket tube
8 Lateral anchoring of tension cable
9 Reinforced concrete wall slab
10 73 mm Ø steel tension cable in
   jacket tube

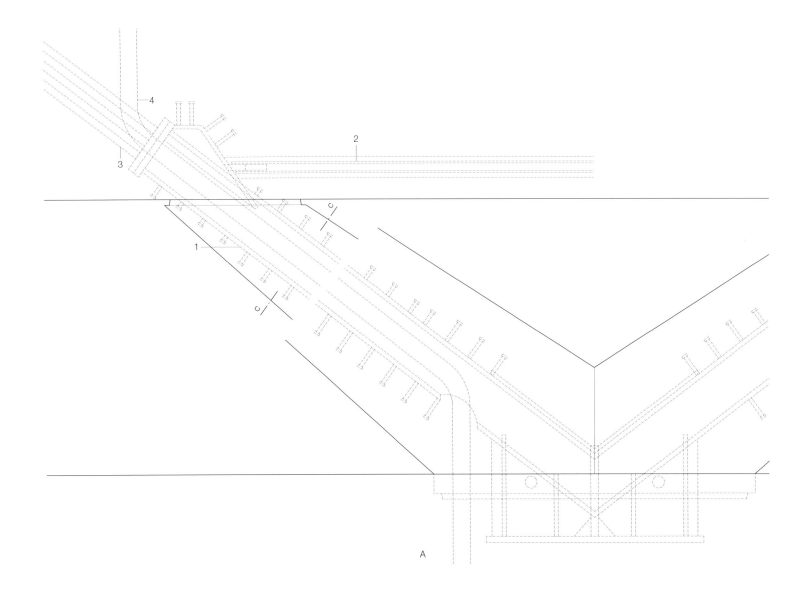

A

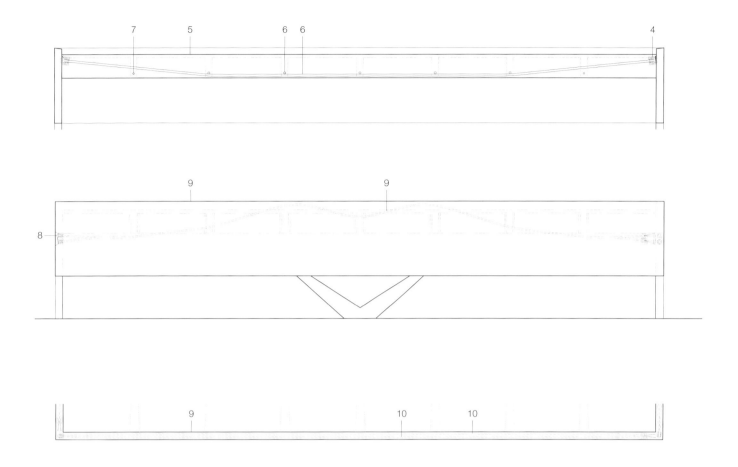

Multipurpose Building in Valencia

Structure:
Steel skeleton construction/space frame

Architects:
Gradolí & Sanz Arquitectes with Carmen Martínez, Valencia (ES)

Structural engineering:
Valter Valenciana de Estructuras, Valencia (ES)

Space frames are usually composed of prefabricated nodes and members. Just like girder grids, they are counted among the non-directional structures. In the early 1940s, the engineer Max Mengeringhausen made decisive contributions to this light-weight and efficient building method with the development of his *MEngeringhausen ROhrbauweise* (tubular construction method) – or MERO for short.
The Escola Gavina offers its pupils a very wide-ranging programme. In support of this, a multipurpose building was added to round out the campus. Its sober shape represents a formal link with the cuboid neighbouring

school buildings from the 1980s. In addition to its main function as a sports hall, the new building also features spaces for musical performances, theatre productions and meetings. A music room as well as a classroom for psychomotor activity are available to the students as permanent facilities.
The character-defining steel space frame of the roof juts out more than 3 m and over-hangs the forecourt like a floating canopy. Shimmering green plastic slats of recycled material cover the facade, forming an additional plane at the front and complementing the truss of the cantilever. They ensure

glare-free use of the hall despite the large glass surfaces of the upper storey. Triangular skylights partially fitted to the open fields of the truss supply additional lighting. Reflecting panels that project vertically into the hall direct and scatter the incoming light. On the ground floor, sliding walls with ceramic panels can be opened to the outdoor sports ground. The colourful glass fillings of the perforated ceramic bricks filter the light and suffuse the interior with a cheerful atmosphere. Thanks to the delicate load-bearing structure and surfaces, the architects have succeeded in creating a surprisingly harmonious unity.

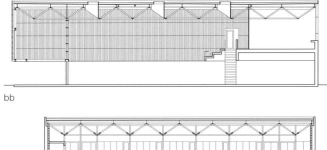

bb

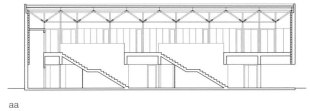

aa

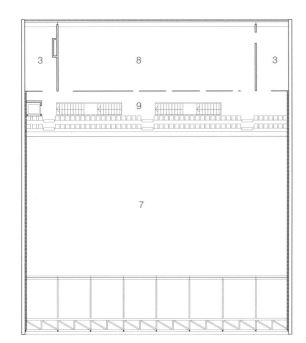

Upper floor

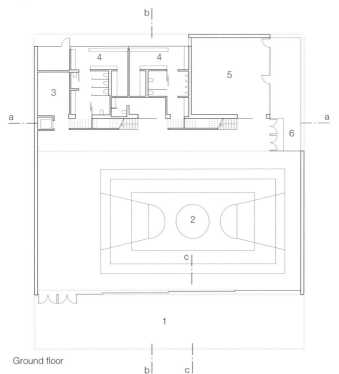

Ground floor

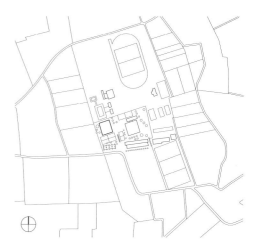

Site map
Scale 1:10,000
Sections · Floor plans
Scale 1:400

1   Covered forecourt area
2   Gymnasium
3   Storage
4   Changing room
5   Music room
6   Main entrance
7   Airspace
8   Psychomotor activities
9   Stands

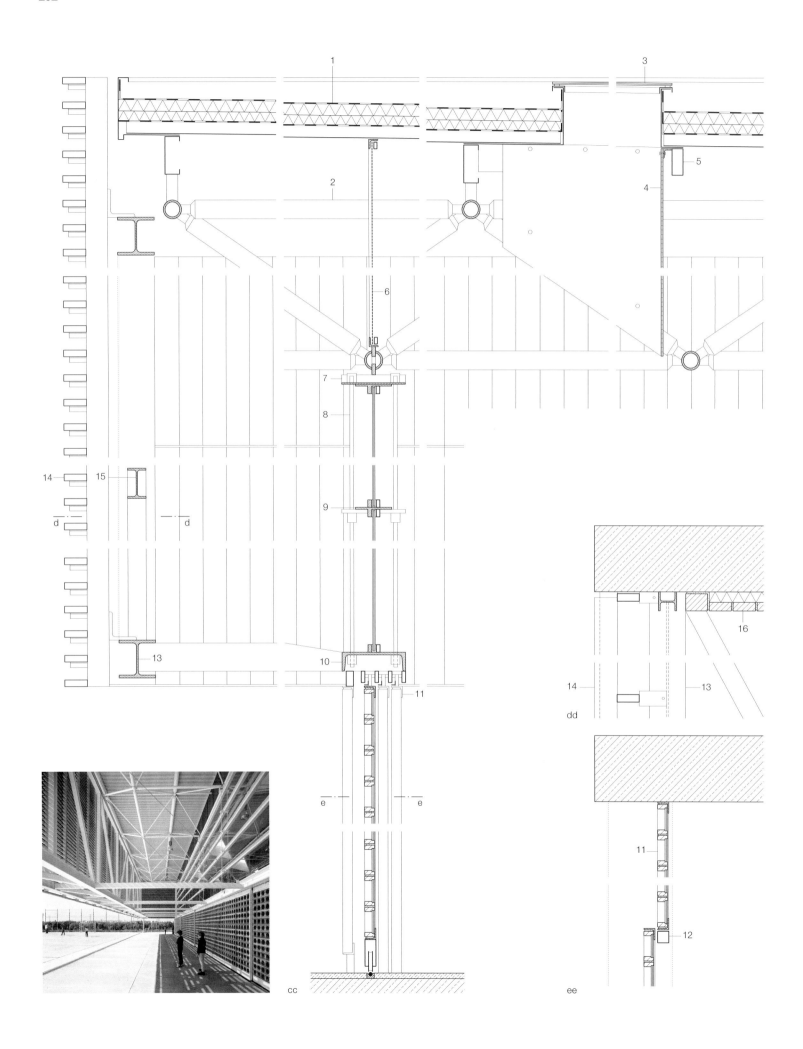

Vertical section · Horizontal sections
Scale 1:20

1   Roof construction:
    Reinforced asphalt waterproofing,
    double-layered
    110 mm rock wool thermal insulation
    geotextile
    67 mm steel trapezoidal sheet,
    perforated and painted
    200 mm steel ⌷ profile, sloped
    due to supports
2   75–219 mm steel tube truss
    members, painted, with 80 mm
    ball node connector
3   2× 6 mm LSG skylight on 1 mm
    folded stainless steel sheet frame
4   10 mm HPL panel sun reflector
5   140/60 mm ⍁ steel section

    skylight reinforcement
6   Ventilation grid in a frame of
    50/50 mm L and 20/40 mm ⍁
    steel profiles
7   100/50 mm UPN steel profiles for
    the suspension of tension member
8   20 mm steel tension member
    with jacketed threading
9   200/40 mm steel T profile with
    2× 6 mm LSG and
    40/20 mm ⍁ hollow steel section
10 UPN 350 steel profile suspended
    from tension member
11 Sliding element:
    60/20 mm ⍁ hollow steel section
    guide rail

    60/60 mm steel L profile frame
    158/158/55 mm ceramic element
    with 2× 3 mm LSG
12 60/60 mm ⍁ hollow steel post
13 Horizontal truss of HEB 200 steel
    profiles and
    150/100 mm ⍁ hollow steel sections
14 125/35 mm recycled plastic
    30/30 mm steel T profile console
    120/40 mm steel ⍁ tube
15 Truss of HEB 200, HEB 160
16 90/120 mm halved horizontal
    coring brick
    100/100 mm steel L profile supports
    55 mm rock wool thermal insulation
    350 mm reinforced concrete

Roof over Inner Courtyard in Amsterdam

Structure:
Glazed steel lattice dome

Architects:
Ney & Partners, Brussels (BE)

Structural engineering:
Ney & Partners, Brussels (BE)

Astonishing spans can be achieved using filigree, doubly curved steel and glass constructions. This is made possible through their shell-like load-bearing behaviour. In the past, key figures such as Frei Otto, Jörg Schlaich and Hans Schober imparted great momentum to this lightweight construction technique.

The building housing the Dutch National Maritime Museum in Amsterdam was formerly a warehouse on the IJ. In the course of restoration work, its 1,024 m² inner courtyard was covered with a shallow transparent dome. Despite a base side length of 34.30 m, the Ney & Partners design calls for a lattice

shell height of only 5 m. This way, the dome does not rise above the existing roofs of the historically listed building. Apart from its load-bearing function, the construction also stylistically references seafaring. The arrangement of its members represents a simplified version of the compass rose found on antique maritime maps.

The solid steel sections are subject mainly to normal forces. They are 40 or 60-mm wide and have depths ranging from 100 to 180 mm. The steel components of strength class S355, together with the edge beams of S460 steel, weigh a total of 148 tonnes. The 1,016 glass panes with areas of up to

5.40 m² add another 62 tonnes. In order to prevent damage, the panes were installed only after the prefabricated steel structure had had a chance to settle. The entire loads of the courtyard roof are transferred into the foundations through the existing courtyard facades. Most of the 868 welded nodes of the dome are constructed as hollow cylinders with diameters of 160 mm and a 40-mm side wall thickness. At night, the many nodes that are outfitted with LED lights create a simulation of a starry sky. During the day, however, the delicate lattice shell impresses with the ephemeral appearance of its construction.

Section • Top view of roof
Scale 1:600
Site map
Scale 1:4,000

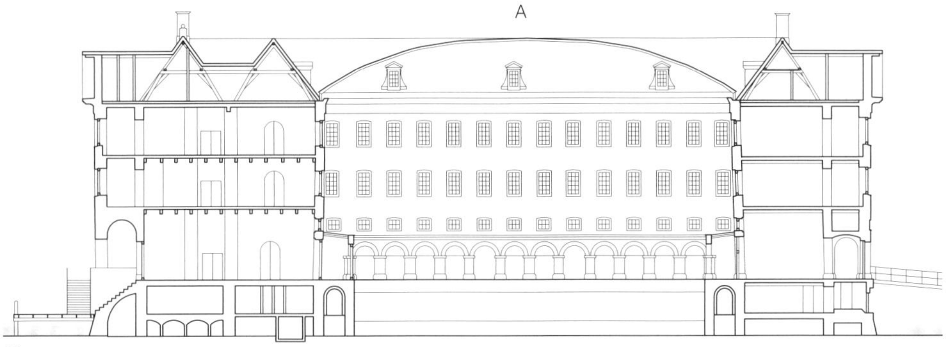

A

aa

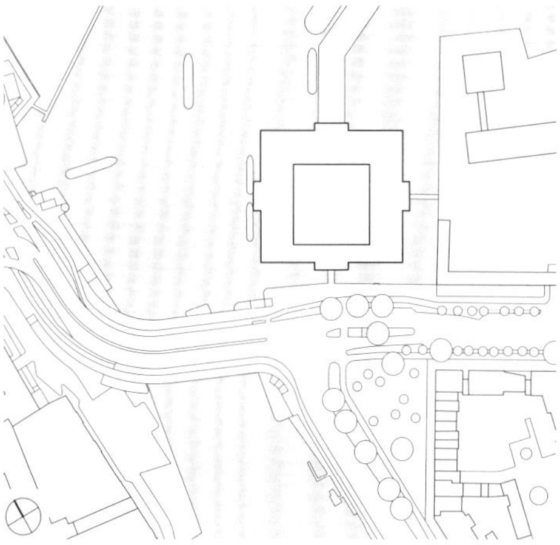

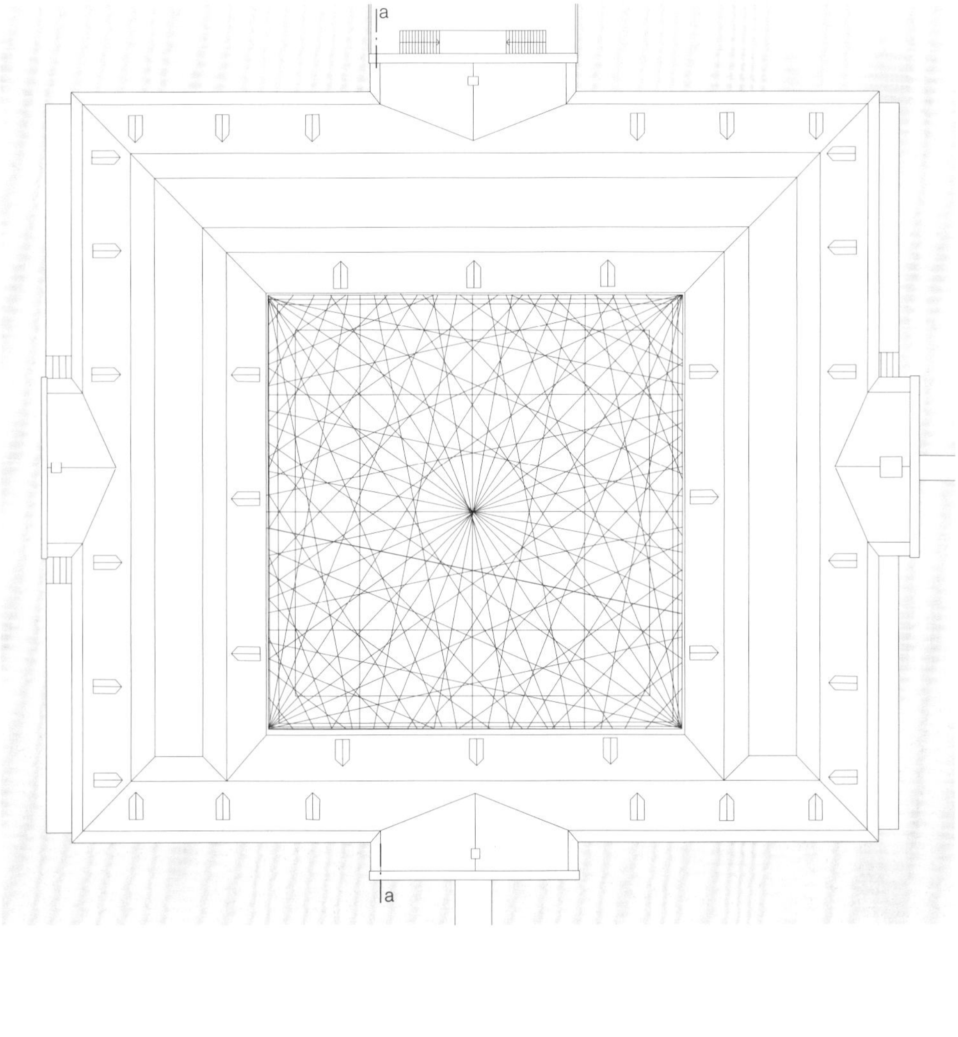

a

a

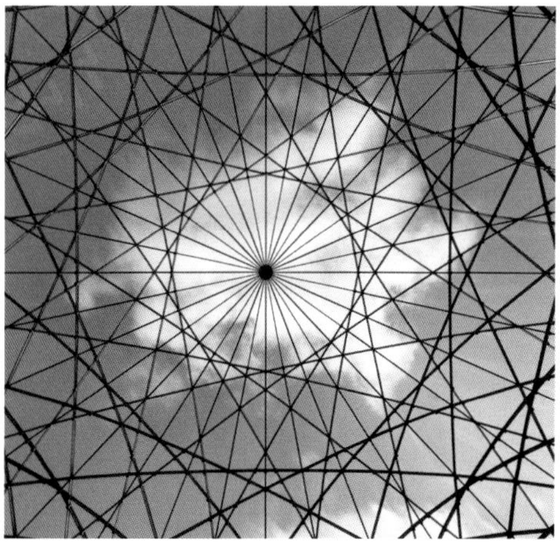

Axonometric view of a node (no scale given)
Section, view of hub
Scale 1:10

1 Attachment anchor for roof cleaning
2 Hinge, rotatable by 360°
3 Stainless steel console
4 M20 bolted connection, waterproof
5 Positioning block
6 100 mm steel plate hub ring
7 Lighting
8 Double-glazing of roof, mechanically secured
9 Aluminium retaining profile, flexibly supported

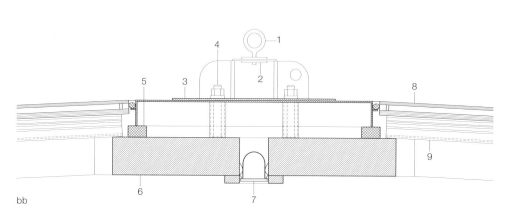

bb

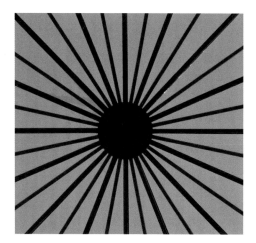

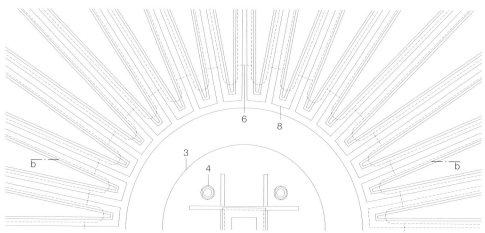

A

Cultural Centre in New York

Structure:
Steel skeleton construction / rollable frame structure, facade with
pneumatically prestressed film cushions

Architects:
Diller Scofidio + Renfro, New York (US)
Rockwell Group, New York (US)

Structural engineering:
Thornton Tomasetti, New York (US)

Directly alongside New York's High Line Park is the new art and cultural centre known as The Shed. The complex is composed of two different building sections.
The fixed main building is of the steel construction typical of New York and encompasses four exhibition and performance levels of various heights which house galleries, rehearsal spaces, a theatre and a creative lab. Steel beams 1.60-m deep span the 30-m wide rooms in the north-south direction. They overhang the side facades by 5 m. In front of the building's eastern end is a 1,720 m² open plaza for concerts, events and performances. It can

be enclosed by the Shed's second section, a telescoping building shell of steel and 148 ETFE film cushions. If the shell is not needed, it can be retracted within five minutes to its parked position over the fixed base building. Parts of the main building's east facade can be opened to link the spaces of both sections.
A diamond-patterned grid framework forms the north and south sides of the movable shell. Roof trusses connect these grids to create a large frame construction. Plenty of room remains between the girder trusses to house the stage technology systems. The 4,000-tonne shell structure rests on a

total of 16 wheels of hardened forged steel and can be moved back and forth along a pair of double-wheel tracks by twelve electromotors. Each of the 16 wheels bears about 250 t of weight on its very small contact surface. The designers chose air-filled three or four-layered ETFE film cushions for the 4,100-m² surface of the facades and roof because they have a low self-weight and good thermal insulation characteristics, and because they exhibit high tolerance to the vibrations resulting from the movement of this mobile building section.

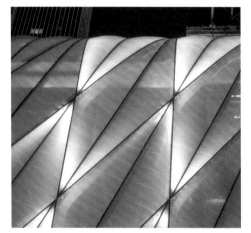

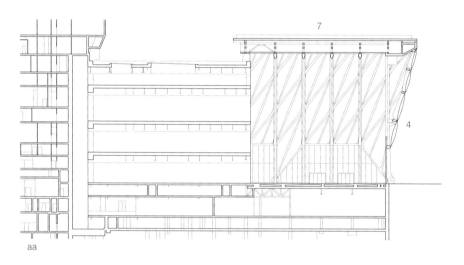

aa

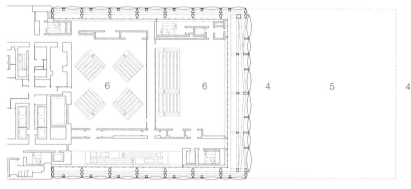

6th floor

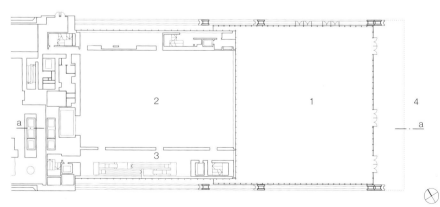

Ground floor

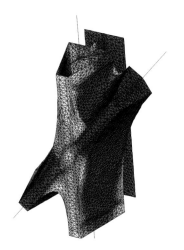

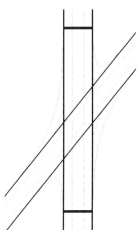

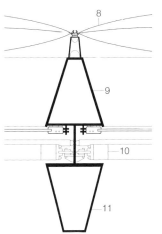

Section · Floor plans
Scale 1:1,000
Distribution of stresses within
a structural node in the
telescoping shell construction
Schematic vertical section
of a steel node
Horizontal section of a
vertical structural element
Scale 1:50
Exploded view of a bogie
assembly with two wheels
(no scale given)
Schematic diagram of the
rack-and-pinion drive with
outriggers (no scale given)

1 Supplementary
   event space
2 Event space
3 Foyer
4 Movable building shell
5 Plaza / open space for
   concerts, etc.
6 Theatre
7 Stage technology area
8 ETFE cushion
9 Primary structure
10 Lift gate
11 Casing for ventilation
    ducts

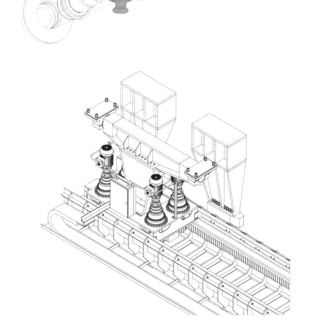

Residential High-rise in Heilbronn

Structure:
Hybrid construction / timber, steel and reinforced concrete
structural elements

Architects:
Kaden + Lager, Berlin (DE)

Structural engineering:
bauart Konstruktions GmbH & Co. KG, Lauterbach (DE)

The 34-m height of this high-rise in Heilbronn makes it the tallest timber high-rise in Germany. By international standards, the height is fairly modest. Currently, a timber high-rise 350-m tall is being planned in Tokyo, though it is not expected to be completed until 2041. By that time, the small tower on the banks of the Neckar River will have already been occupied for 22 years. The building's ten storeys encompass 60 flats as well as communal, commercial and public spaces. Walls, pillars and floors of mostly domestic spruce wood make up the bulk of the structure. Cross-laminated timber (CLT) was used for the floors and walls,

while the columns are of glued laminated timber (glulam). The girders, however, are made from steel. For fire safety reasons, the two-storey plinth and the access core are composed of the non-flammable building material reinforced concrete. And finally, the facade is clad in an elegant skin of matte silver aluminium.

All structural elements are required at a minimum to conform to a fire-resistance rating of F90. This specification is met in part by multi-layered sheathing of fire protection panels. For structurally critical timber components the burn fraction is also decisive, meaning that even after a 90-minute fire, sufficient

load-bearing substance must remain beneath the charred surface to prevent the building from collapsing. In addition, a high-pressure water mist fire protection system can extinguish flames immediately.
The prefabrication of many of the building components allowed for high precision and rapid assembly. The construction time required per storey was only one week.
The cradle-to-cradle principle was consistently employed in the design, which should ensure that separation-by-type deconstruction and extensive recycling of materials will be possible at the end of the high-rise's service life.

Site map
Scale 1:5,000
Sections · Floor plans
Scale 1:1,000

1 Arcade
2 Building entrance
3 Communal kitchen with
  self-service laundry
4 Bicycle storage room
5 Bin room
6 Café
7 Kitchen
8 Flat
9 Sanitary cell fully
  pre-installed in factory

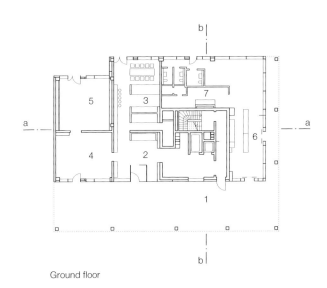

Ground floor

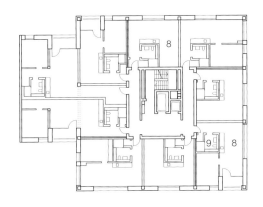

3rd floor

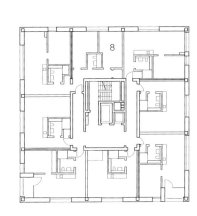

7th floor

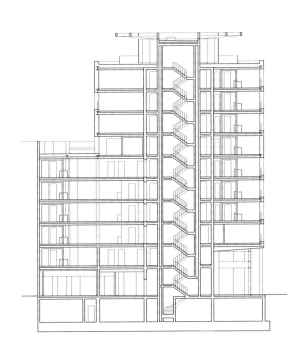

aa

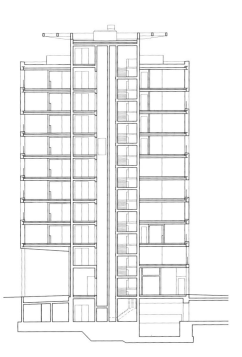

bb

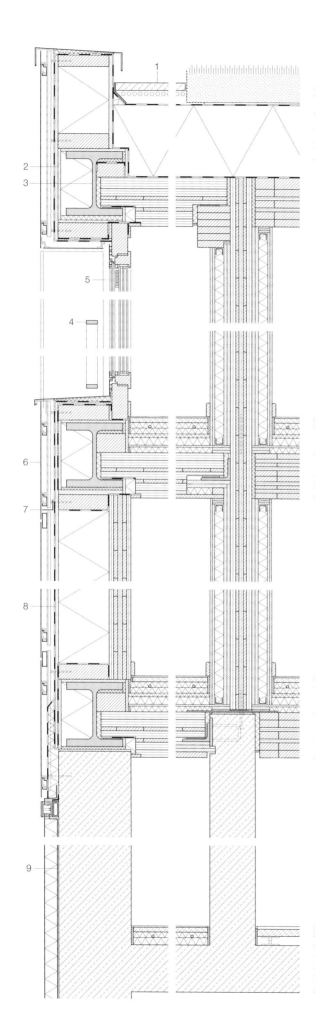

Vertical sections
Scale 1:20

1 Roof construction:
40 mm concrete slab
16–32 mm drainage pebbles
Bitumen sheet waterproofing,
double layer
380 mm foam glass thermal insulation
Vapour barrier
260 mm cross-laminated timber
2 15 mm fire protection panel
3 HEM 300 steel profile
4 20/60 mm flat bar steel railing
5 Composite window:
8 mm tempered single-pane glass in
aluminium frame
20 mm slatted sun shades triple glazing
in timber frame with rabbet ventilation
$U_w \le 1.0$, $g = 0.35$
6 4 mm aluminium sheet cladding,
coated with grey liquid paint
Aluminium joint backing
82 mm rear ventilation spaces interspersed
with top-hat rail subconstruction
7 Steel sheet firewall at storey-height
intervals
8 400/400 mm spruce glued laminated
timber frame element
Windproofing
18 mm plasterboard
280/80 mm timber column interspersed with
280 mm thermal insulation
120 mm spruce cross-laminated timber
9 Plinth storeys:
400/400 mm reinforced concrete wall
10 Terrace construction:
40 mm concrete flags on thin-set points
Drainage layer
Bitumen sheet waterproofing, double layer
120 mm sloped PUR thermal insulation
5 mm temporary seal
240 mm spruce cross-laminated timber
Air-tight film
40 mm mineral fibre thermal insulation
19 mm three-layer board fire protection with
white pigmentation
11 Floor construction:
5 mm linoleum
25 mm dry screed
30 mm floor heating
30 mm honeycomb acoustic insulation
panel with fill
20 mm impact sound insulation
40 mm wood fibre insulation
10 mm smoke-proof plasterboard
fire protection
30 mm space for sprinkler pipes and
lighting wiring
240 mm cross-laminated timber
12 6 mm steel console floor slab support with
acoustic damping strip
13 Smoke-proof joint

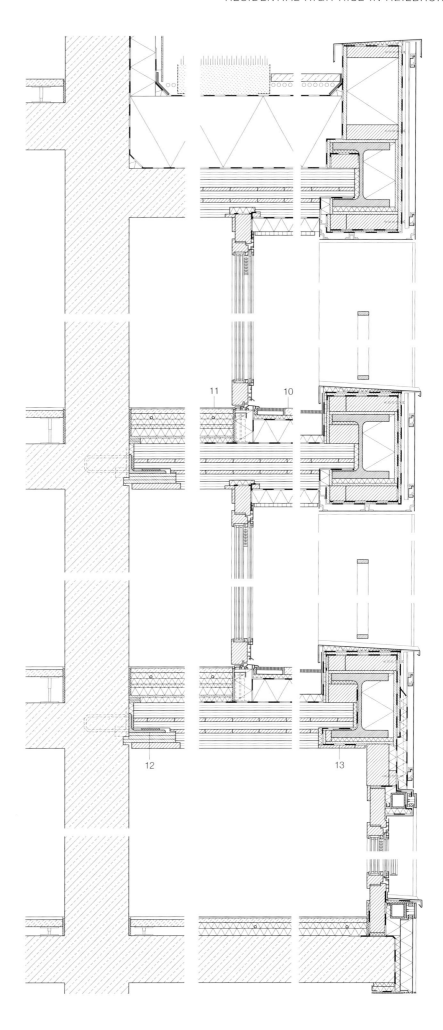

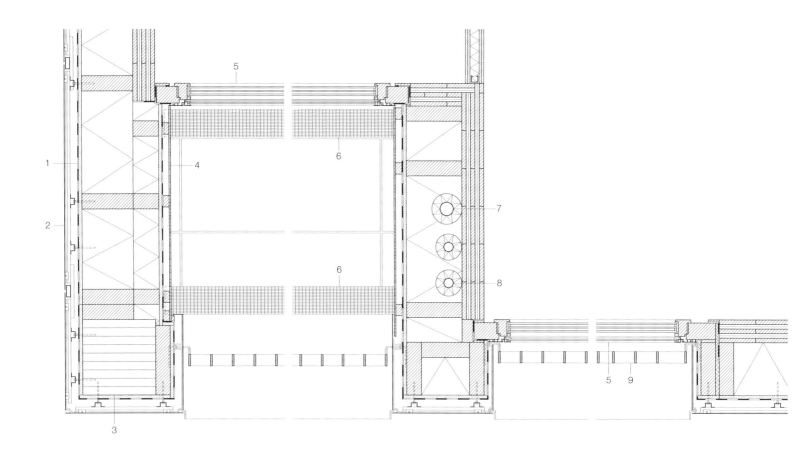

1   Timber frame element:
    Windproofing
    18 mm plasterboard
    280/80 mm timber column
    interspersed with
    280 mm mineral fibre thermal
    insulation
    120 mm spruce cross-laminated
    timber
2   4 mm aluminium sheet cladding
    coated with grey liquid paint
    Aluminium joint backing
    82 mm rear ventilation spaces
    between top-hat rail subconstruction

3   2nd–9th storey
    400/400 mm spruce glulam
    column
4   Doubled timber frame element on
    the inner side of the loggia:
    8 mm grey fibre cement panel
    40 mm battens
    Windproofing
    18 mm plasterboard
    140/80 mm timber column
    interspersed with
    140 mm mineral wool thermal
    insulation
5   Composite window:

    8 mm tempered single-pane glass
    in aluminium frame
    20 mm slatted sun shades
    Triple glazing in timber frame with
    rabbet ventilation, $U_w \leq 1.0$, $g = 0.35$
6   Drainage gutter
7   Insulated downpipes for roof
    drainage
8   DN 50 downpipes for loggia
    drainage and emergency intake
9   20/60 mm flat bar steel railing
10 Plinth levels: ground floor/1st storey
    400/400 mm reinforced concrete
    column

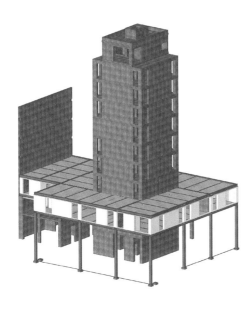

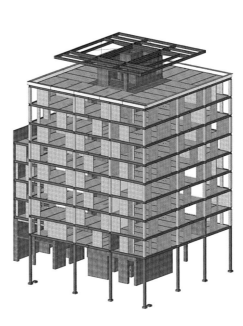

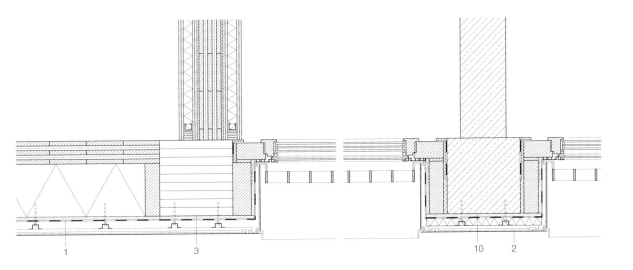

Horizontal section of loggia
Scale 1:20

Steel plates are integrated into the base and top of the timber columns to connect to the steel girders.

The floor panels of cross-laminated timber are notched at the ends where they rest on the steel girders.

The non-structural outer wall timber frame elements are pre-fabricated at the factory.

The outer wall elements are seated on the steel girders between the load-bearing timber columns.

The steel beams concealed within the outer walls at ceiling height minimise deformations.

Inside, HEM 300 sections serve as supports with efficient spans for columns and floor slabs.

Office Skyscraper in Turin

Structure:
Steel skeleton construction with stiffening access core of reinforced concrete

Architects:
Renzo Piano Building Workshop, Genoa (IT)

Structural engineering:
Expedition Engineering, London (GB)

The 166-m tall tower, built in Turin for an Italian banking group by Renzo Piano Building Workshop, rests on a multi-storey foundation. This encompasses parking garages and utility rooms as well as a café and a kindergarten around a sunken inner courtyard. Separated from the ground floor by a gap, the multifunctional auditorium appears to be floating. It can be used for lectures or exhibitions and can accommodate more than 350 people. Above this are 27 office floors, with conference and training spaces incorporated on the north side of the building. A multilevel public pavilion featuring a restaurant, an exhibition space and a roof garden forms the top of the tower, offering breathtaking views.

Aside from the vertical loads, horizontal loads from sources such as wind and earthquakes play a particularly critical role in the structural design of tall buildings. Wind speeds and the associated lever arm increase with height. The load-bearing structure of this office tower was conceived as a stiffening access core of reinforced concrete in addition to a 175-m tall steel skeleton on the east and west facades, consisting of three main pillars and nine horizontal braces stayed with diagonal cables. This allows for flexible, open office floor plans. The pillars have a centre-to-centre spacing of 16.50 m and taper in cross section from 280 × 197 cm at the foundations to just 70 × 60 cm at the top of the tower. Prestressed semi-finished reinforced concrete components form the floor slabs of the office storeys. They are supported on steel girders that are attached to the outer pillars as well as to internally placed columns. A 6.50-m high truss construction comprising high-strength steel plates up to 12 cm in thickness is located on the sixth storey, on the building's maintenance and technology level, to intercept the internal column loads of the 27 office floors above the column-free auditorium. The truss spans 30 m between the six main pillars and the reinforced core.

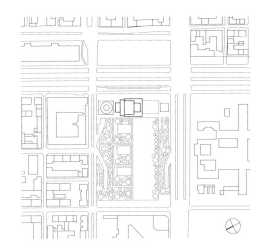

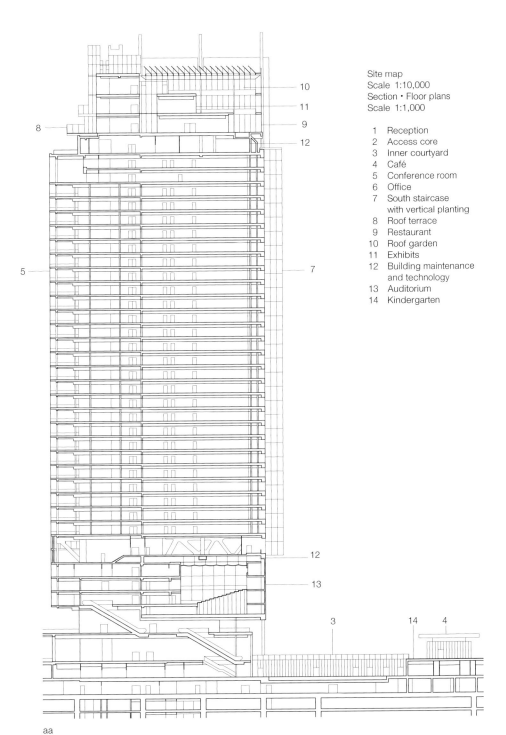

Site map
Scale 1:10,000
Section · Floor plans
Scale 1:1,000

1 Reception
2 Access core
3 Inner courtyard
4 Café
5 Conference room
6 Office
7 South staircase
with vertical planting
8 Roof terrace
9 Restaurant
10 Roof garden
11 Exhibits
12 Building maintenance
and technology
13 Auditorium
14 Kindergarten

aa

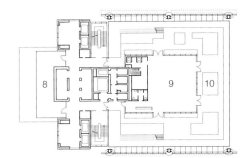

35th floor

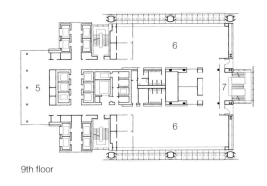

9th floor

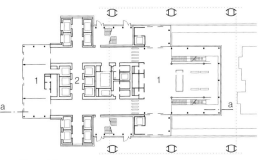

Ground floor

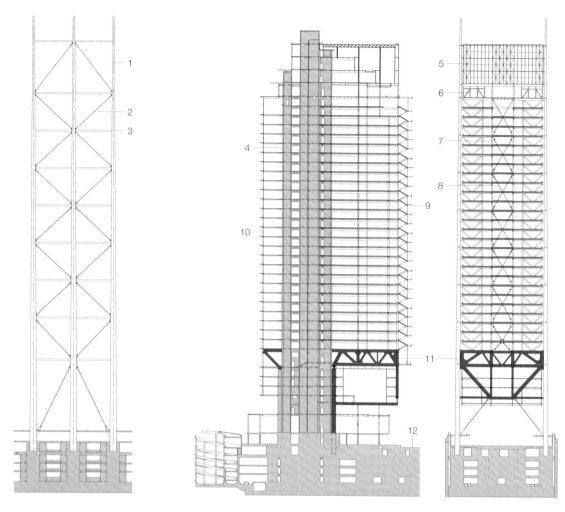

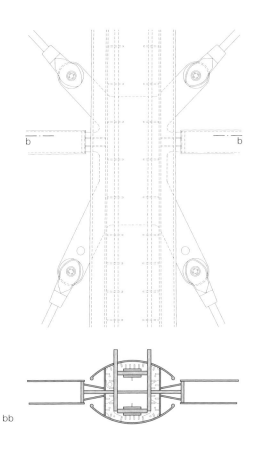

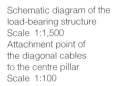

bb

Schematic diagram of the
load-bearing structure
Scale 1:1,500
Attachment point of
the diagonal cables
to the centre pillar
Scale 1:100

1 Main pillar
2 Diagonal stay cables
  on west and east
  sides
3 Horizontal braces to
  transfer loads from
  the outer shell of the
  double facade
4 Reinforced concrete
  core for access
  and accommodation
  of transverse and
  torsional forces
5 Roof pavilion of filigree
  steel sections
6 Truss forming the
  base of the roof
  pavilion
7 Internal columns
8 Diagonal bracing
  of the columns on
  the south side
9 Projecting staircase
  on south side
10 Projecting confer-
  ence rooms on
  north side
11 Truss redirecting
  upper storey loads
  onto the pillars
  and core
12 Reinforced concrete
  foundations

Standards, Guidelines

Physical structures must exhibit stability both as a whole and in their individual parts. At the same time, they must not compromise the load-bearing capacity of neighbouring building sites or of other physical structures.

Another issue that must be avoided is damage done to other parts of the building or to installations or equipment as a result of excessive deformations of the load-bearing structure due to loads that might occur during construction or use.
To comply with these requirements for physical structures, there are technical regulations to be followed.

Throughout Europe, standardised rules known as Eurocodes, pertaining to the basics of structural design, the actions on buildings and to dimensioning in construction, were enacted. These European standards (EN) were developed within the European Committee for Standardisation (CEN) by scientists, engineers and practitioners from member countries.

With the aid of building regulations, the general requirements for physical structures, building products and other facilities and instalments can be put into concrete terms using technical provisions in the context of administrative policies. These specific terms can be arrived at by referring to technical rules based on locality or on other factors, especially
• the design, dimensioning and execution of physical structures and their parts
• characteristics and performance of building products in particular physical structures or their parts
• procedures for determining the performance of a building product that does not bear the CE mark as per construction products regulation
• admissible and non-admissible special uses for building products
• definition of classes and grades that building products should exhibit for particular uses
• requirements for the issuance of a declaration of conformity for non-harmonised products
• information on non-harmonised building products as well as construction methods that require a national technical test certification
• type, contents and form of technical documentation.

In general, the technical rules represent practical information and resources for everyday working practices. They aid in decision-making, provide guidelines for correct technical procedures and/or flesh out the contents of ordinances. Whether or not to use the technical rules is up to the individual. It is only when they are incorporated into laws, ordinances or regulations that they become legally binding (e.g. in building law). Additionally, the liability for individual standards can be determined among the partners to a contract. Because of the unmanageable number of regulations, contradictions between different standards cannot be ruled out. Often standards will contain different quality or requirement levels, so that a blanket statement in contracts stating that all norms are to be complied with is meaningless.

Among the technical regulations are DIN standards, VDI guidelines and rules of technology publications (e.g. Technical Rules for Hazardous Substances (TRGS: *Technische Regeln für Gefahrstoffe*)). Standards are differentiated into product, usage and testing standards. Often they apply only to one specific group of materials or products. In general, the newest version of a standard represents the current state of the art. A new or revised standard is first put up for public enquiry in the form of a draft standard. The origin and scope of a standard can be determined from its designation: DIN plus a number (e.g. DIN 4108) is of primarily national relevance (drafts are denoted by E and preliminary standards by V). The DIN EN plus number designation (e.g. DIN EN 335) indicates the German edition of a European standard which has been adopted without change from the European organisation for standardisation, CEN. The DIN EN ISO

prefix (e.g. DIN EN ISO 13786) reflects national, European and international applicability. Here, a European standard has been developed based on a norm issued by the International Organization for Standardization (ISO) and then adopted as a DIN standard. In DIN ISO designations (e.g. DIN ISO 2424), an ISO standard has been adopted without change as a German national standard.

The following is a selection of standards that reflects the state of the art in structural design as of February 2021.

Basics of Structural Design and Actions on Structures
DIN EN 1990:2010-12 Basis of structural design
DIN EN 1991-1-1:2010-12 Densities, self-weight, imposed loads for buildings
DIN EN 1991-1-2:2010-12 Actions on structures exposed to fire
DIN EN 1991-1-3:2010-12 Snow loads
DIN EN 1991-1-4:2010-12 Wind actions
DIN EN 1991-1-7:2010-12 Accidental actions
DIN EN 1991-3:2010-12 Actions induced by cranes and machinery
DIN EN 1991-4:2010-12 Silos and tanks
ETB directive – Bauteile, die gegen Absturz sichern (Components that prevent falls), June 1985

Physical Structures in Earthworks and Foundations
DIN EN 1997-1:2009-09 General rules
DIN 1054:2010-12 Earthworks and foundations
DIN EN 1536:2010-12 Execution of bored piles
DIN EN 12699:2001-05 Execution of displacement piles
DIN 4123:2013-04 Excavations, foundations and underpinnings in the area of existing buildings
DIN EN 1537:2014-07 Execution of ground anchors
DIN EN 14199:2012-01 Execution of special geotechnical work – Micropiles
DIN EN 12715:2000-10, DIN EN 12716:2019-03 and DIN 4093:2015-11 Execution of special geotechnical work – Grouting, jet grouting and design of strengthened soil – Set up by means of jet grouting, deep mixing or grouting

Physical Structures of Concrete, Reinforced and Prestressed Concrete
DIN EN 1992-1-1:2011-01 Design of concrete structures – General rules and rules for buildings
DIN EN 1992-1-2:2010-12 Structural fire design
DIN EN 206-1:2001-07 and DIN EN 206-9:2010-09 and DIN 1045-2:2008-08 Concrete, reinforced and prestressed concrete structures
DIN EN 13670:2011-03 and DIN 1045-3:2012-03 Execution of concrete structures
DIN 1045-4:2012-02 Prefabricated elements
DIN 1045-100:2017-09: Brick floors
Technical regulation (DIBt) for the maintenance of concrete structures (TR Instandhaltung):2020-05
DAfStb directive – Schutz und Instandsetzung von Betonbauteilen (Protection and maintenance of concrete building components):2001-10
DIN EN 14487-1:2006-03 and DIN EN 14487-2:2007-01 and DIN 18551:2014-08 Sprayed concrete
DIN EN ISO 17660-1:2006-12 and DIN EN ISO 17660-2:2006-12 Welding of reinforcing steel
DIN 4223-101, 102 and 103:2014-12 Application of prefabricated reinforced components of autoclaved aerated concrete
DIN 4213:2015-10 Application in structures of prefabricated components of lightweight aggregate concrete with open structure with structural or non-structural reinforcement
Anforderungen an Planung, Bemessung und Ausführung von nachträglichen Bewehrungsanschlüssen mit eingemörtelten Bewehrungsstäben (Design requirements for supplementary reinforcements with grouted-

in reinforcing rods):2020-05 (see Appendix 1)
DIN EN 1992-4:2019-04 and Anforderungen an Planung, Bemessung und Ausführung von Verankerungen in Beton mit einbetonierten oder nachträglich gesetzten Befestigungsmitteln (Design requirements for the fixing of anchors in concrete with cement or subsequently added fastening methods):2020-05 (see Appendix 2)

Physical Structures in Metal or Composite Construction
Design and Construction of Steel Structures
DIN EN 1993-1-1:2010-12 General rules and rules for buildings
DIN EN 1993-1-2:2010-12 Structural fire design
DIN EN 1993-1-3:2010-12 Supplementary rules for cold-formed members and sheeting
DIN EN 1993-1-4:2015-10 Supplementary rules for stainless steels
DIN EN 1993-1-5:2017-07 Plated structural elements
DIN EN 1993-1-6:2010-12 Strength and stability of shell structures
DIN EN 1993-1-7:2010-12 Plated structures subject to out of plane loading
DIN EN 1993-1-8:2010-12 Design of joints
DIN EN 1993-1-9:2010-12 Fatigue
DIN EN 1993-1-10:2010-12 Material toughness and through-thickness properties
DIN EN 1993-1-11:2010-12 Design of structures with tension components
DIN EN 1993-1-12:2010-12 Additional rules for the extension of EN 1993 up to steel grades S700
DIN EN 1993-3-1:2010-12 Towers and masts
DIN EN 1993-3-2:2010-12 Chimneys
DIN EN 1993-4-1:2017-09 Silos
DIN EN 1993-5:2010-12 Piling
DIN EN 1993-6:2010-12: Crane supporting structures
DIN EN 1090-2:2018-09 Execution of steel structures and aluminium structures

Design and Construction of Composite Steel and Concrete Structures
DIN EN 1994-1-1:2010-12 General rules and rules for buildings
DIN EN 1994-1-2:2010-12 Structural fire design

Design and Construction of Aluminium Structures
DIN EN 1999-1-1:2014-03 General structural rules
DIN EN 1999-1-2:2010-12 Structural fire design
DIN EN 1999-1-3:2011-11 Structures susceptible to fatigue
DIN EN 1999-1-4:2010-05 Cold-formed structural sheeting
DIN EN 1999-1-5:2017-03 Shell structures
DIN EN 1090-3:2019-07 and DIN EN 1090-5:2017-07 Execution of aluminium structures
DIN 4119-1:1979-06 and DIN 4119-2:1980-02 Cylindrical, flat-bottomed, above ground tanks of metallic materials

Timber Structures
DIN EN 1995-1-1:2010-12 Design of timber structures
DIN EN 1995-1-2:2010-12 Structural fire design
DIN EN 1995-2:2010-12 Bridges
DIN EN 1052-10:2012-05 Design of timber structures – Additional provisions
DIN 68800-1:2011-10 and DIN 68800-2:2012-02 Wood preservation

Masonry Structures
DIN EN 1996-1-1:2013-02 General rules for reinforced and unreinforced masonry structures
DIN EN 1996-1-2:2011-04 Structural fire design
DIN EN 1996-2:2010-12 Design considerations, selection of materials and execution of masonry
DIN EN 1996-3:2010-12 Simplified calculation methods for unreinforced masonry structures
DIN 1053-4:2018-05 Prefabricated masonry compound units
Anforderungen an Planung, Bemessung und Ausführung

Bibliography

von Verankerungen in Mauerwerk mit nachträglich gesetzten Befestigungsmitteln (Design requirements for masonry anchors with subsequently placed fastening methods):2020-05 (see Appendix 3)

Glass Constructions
DIN 18008-1:2010-12 Terms and general bases
DIN 18008-2:2010-12 Linearly supported glazings
DIN 18008-3:2013-07 Point fixed glazing
DIN 18008-4:2013-07 Additional requirements for barrier glazing
DIN 18008-5:2013-07 Additional requirements for walk-on glazing
DIN 18008-6:2018-02 Additional requirements for walk-on glazing in case of maintenance procedures and for fall-through glazing

Special Constructions
DIN EN 13084-1:2007-05, DIN EN 13084-2:2007-08, DIN EN 13084-4:2005-12, DIN EN 13084-6:2005-03, DIN EN 13084-8:2005-08 and DIN 1056:2009-01 Free-standing chimneys
DIN 4178:2005-04 Bell towers
DIN V 11535-1:1998-02 Commercial production greenhouses
DIN EN 12812:2008-12 Falsework
DIN EN 12811-1:2004-03 Scaffolds
DIN 4420-1:2004-03 Service scaffolds
DIN 11622-2:2015-09 Silage and liquid manure containers
Richtlinie für Windenergieanlagen; Einwirkungen und Standsicherheitsnachweise für Turm und Gründung (Guidelines for wind turbines; actions and stability certification for tower and foundations), March 2015
Lehmbau Regeln (Rules for mud-brick construction), February 2008 – Lehmbauten für Wohngebäude der Gebäudeklasse 1 und 2 mit höchstens zwei Vollgeschossen (Mud-brick residences of building classes 1 and 2 with at most two full-height storeys)

Physical Structures in Seismically Active Regions
DIN 4149:2005-04 Structures in German earthquake regions

Acknowledgements

We wish to extend our special gratitude to the proven architecture and engineering experts whose thoroughly grounded technical contributions on complex structural problems as well as on the topics of ecology and sustainability have tremendously enriched this manual. They all do research in their areas of specialisation and teach at internationally renowned technical institutes and universities.

Ackermann, Kurt: *Grundlagen für das Entwerfen und Konstruieren.* Stuttgart 1983

Ackermann, Kurt et al.: *Tragwerke in der konstruktiven Architektur,* Stuttgart 1988

Achtziger, Joachim et al.: *Mauerwerk Atlas.* Munich 2001

Adriaenssens, Sigrid et al.: *Shell structures for architecture: form finding and optimization.* London 2014

Adriaenssens, Sigrid et al.: *Shaping Forces: Laurent Ney.* Brussels 2010

Bollinger, Klaus et al.: *Atlas Moderner Stahlbau.* Munich 2011

Carlowitz, Hans Carl von; Hamberger, Joachim (ed.): *Sylvicultura oeconomica oder Haußwirthliche Nachricht und Naturmäßige Anweisung zur Wilden Baum-Zucht.* Munich 2013

Deplazes, Andrea (ed.): *Architektur konstruieren. Vom Rohmaterial zum Bauwerk. Ein Handbuch.* 4th edition. Basel 2013

Egger, Harald et al.: *Tragwerkselemente.* Stuttgart 2003

Engel, Heino: *Tragsysteme.* Stuttgart 2006

Führer, Wilfried: *Der Entwurf von Tragwerken.* Cologne 1995

Fischer, Oliver; Lang, Werner; Winter, Stefan (eds.): *Hybridbau – Holzaußenwände.* Munich 2019

Giebeler, Georg et al.: *Atlas Sanierung.* Munich 2008

Glücklich, Detlef (ed.): *Ökologisches Bauen. Von Grundlagen zu Gesamtkonzepten.* Munich 2005

Grimm, Friedrich B.: *Stahlbau im Detail.* Augsburg 1994

Hegger, Manfred et al.: *Energie Atlas.* Munich 2007

Heinrich, Matthias; Lang, Werner: *Materials Passports – Best Practice: Innovative Solutions for a Transition to a Circular Economy in the Built Environment.* Munich 2019

Herzog, Thomas et al.: *Holzbau Atlas.* Munich 2003

Herzog, Thomas; Lang, Werner; Krippner, Roland: *Fassaden Atlas.* 3rd revised and expanded edition. Munich 2020

Holschemacher, Klaus: *Entwurfs- und Konstruktionstafeln für Architekten.* 7th edition. Berlin 2015

Hugues, Theodor; Steiger, Ludwig; Weber, Johann: *Naturwerkstein: Gesteinsarten, Details, Beispiele.* Munich 2002

Joedicke, Jürgen: *Schalenbau, Konstruktion und Gestaltung.* Stuttgart 1962

Kaufmann, Hermann; Nerdinger, Winfried et al.: *Bauen mit Holz: Wege in die Zukunft.* Munich 2011

Kaufmann, Hermann; Krötsch, Stefan; Winter, Stefan: *Manual of Multistorey Timber Construction.* 2nd edition. Munich 2018

Kind-Barkauskas, Friedbert et al.: *Beton Atlas.* Munich 2009

Knippers, Jan et al.: *Atlas Kunststoffe und Membranen.* Munich 2010

Kolb, Josef: *Systembau mit Holz.* Zurich 1992

Krauss, Franz et al.: *Grundlagen der Tragwerklehre 1.* Cologne 2014

Krauss, Franz et al.: *Grundlagen der Tragwerklehre 2.* Cologne 2011

Krauss, Franz et al.: *Tabellen zur Tragwerklehre.* Cologne 2014

Kuff, Paul et al.: *Tragwerke als Elemente der Gebäude- und Innenraumgestaltung.* Wiesbaden 2001

Kurrer, Karl-Eugen: *Geschichte der Baustatik.* Berlin 2016

Lang, Werner; Hellstern, Cornelia (eds.): *Visionäre und Alltagshelden. Ingenieure – Bauen – Zukunft.* Munich 2017

Leicher, Gottfried W. et al.: *Tragwerkslehre: in Beispielen und Zeichnungen.* 5th edition. Cologne 2021

Lückmann, Rudolf: *Holzbau. Konstruktion – Bauphysik – Projekte.* Kissing 2014

Meissner, Irene; Möller, Eberhard: *Frei Otto – forschen, bauen, inspirieren.* Munich 2015

Meistermann, Alfred: *Tragsysteme.* Basel 2007

Mensinger, Martin et al.: *Nachhaltiges Bauen mit Stahl: Ökologie.* Munich 2009

Möller, Eberhard: *Die Konstruktion in der Architekturtheorie.* Munich 2011

Neufert, Ernst et al.: *Bauentwurfslehre: Grundlagen, Normen, Vorschriften.* 42nd edition. Wiesbaden 2019

Nikolay, Helmut: *Einführung in die statische Berechnung von Bauwerken.* Cologne 2020

Otto, Frei: *Das hängende Dach.* Bauwelt Verlag. Berlin 1954, reprint dva 1990

Peck, Martin (ed.): *Atlas Moderner Betonbau.* Munich 2013

Polónyi, Stefan: *... mit zaghafter Konsequenz.* Bauwelt Fundamente 81. Braunschweig/Wiesbaden 1987

Polónyi, Stefan et al: *Architektur und Tragwerk.* Berlin 2003

Reguvis Fachmedien (publ.): *Schneider – Bautabellen für Ingenieure.* 24th revised edition. Cologne 2020

Salvadori, Mario: *Tragwerk und Architektur.* Braunschweig 1977

Schulitz, Helmut C. et al.: *Stahlbau Atlas.* Munich/Basel 1999

Siegel, Curt: *Strukturformen der modernen Architektur.* Munich 1960

Staffa, Michael: *Tragwerkslehre.* Berlin 2014

Stahlbau Kalender. Berlin, annual publication

Steiger, Ludwig: *Basics Holzbau.* Basel 2013

Stiglat, Klaus: *Bauingenieure und ihr Werk.* Berlin 2004

Vismann, Ulrich (ed.): *Wendehorst Bautechnische Zahlentafeln.* 36th edition. Wiesbaden 2018

Widjaja, Eddy: *Baustatik – einfach und anschaulich.* Berlin 2010

Picture Credits

The authors and the publisher would like to extend their sincere thanks to everyone who contributed to the production of this book by providing images, granting permission to reproduce their work and supplying other information. All of the drawings in this book were custom-created by the publisher. The authors and their staff created those graphics and tables for which no other source is credited. Photographs for which no photographer is credited are architectural or work photos or come from the archives of Detail magazine.

Despite intensive efforts, we have been unable to identify the copyright holders of some images. However, their claim to the copyright remains unaffected. In these cases, we ask to be notified. The numbers refer to the figure numbers.

Introduction

Part A – Fundamentals

Part B – Structural Elements

Part C – Structural Systems

Part D – Complex Structures

Historical Structures

Bridges with Extreme Spans

Structures for Tall Buildings

Shells and Gridshells for Long-span Roofs

D 4.7   By uncredited photographer for the National Weather Service, Mobile/Pensacola Weather Forecast Office – http://www.srh.noaa.gov/mob/cgi-bin/imageview.php?dir=/0705Dennis&file=100_0587.jpg http://www.srh.noaa.gov/mob/0705Dennis/survey_images.shtml, Public Domain, https://commons.wikimedia.org/w/index.php?curid=2205908

D 4.8   TESS/Thinkshell
D 4.9b   Kentaro Ohno/flickr
D 4.10b Christoph Panzer
D 4.11a Lafarge
D 4.11b Stantec Architecture Ltd.
D 4.12   Copyright of and licensed by the Green Oak Carpentry Company Ltd for single use
D 4.13   Gabriele Seghizzi
D 4.14   Light Earth Designs
D 4.15   ICD/ITKE University of Stuttgart
D 4.16a Lex Reiter
D 4.16b Maria Verhulst
D 4.16c Angelica Ibarra/angelica.today

Membrane and Air-inflated Structures
D 5.1, D 5.2   Schiemann, Lars: *Tragverhalten von ETFE-Folien unter biaxialer Beanspruchung.* Chair of Structural Design, Dissertation. Technical University of Munich 2009, p. 119
D 5.3   Moritz, Karsten; Schiemann, Lars: "Structural Design Concepts." In: Moritz, Karsten; Schiemann, Lars: *Skriptum Master Program for Membrane Structures,* Chpt. 6, Construction, 2019, p. 6.11
D 5.4–D 5.6   Lars Schiemann
D 5.7   Eberhard Möller
D 5.8   Stefan Robanus
D 5.9   SWATCH LTD. 2020
D 5.10   see D 5.1, p. 131

Mobile, Convertible and Adaptive Structures
D 6.1   Nils Petter Dale/mmw.no
D 6.2   Rudi Enos
D 6.3   AIRtec Traglufthallen UG Augsburg
D 6.4   from Novacki, Zoran: *Wandelbare lineare Tragsysteme. Analyse und Neuentwicklung.* Dissertation, TU Munich 2014
D 6.5   Chuck Hoberman fonds, Canadian Centre for Architecture, Gift of Chuck Hoberman © Hoberman Associates
D 6.6   from IL, University of Stuttgart (ed.): *Wandelbare Dächer.* Stuttgart 1972
D 6.7   Alfred Rein Ingenieure GmbH
D 6.8   soma
D 6.9   Iwan Baan
D 6.10   HG Esch
D 6.11   Bosch Rexroth
D 6.12   from Mike Schlaich, Ursula Baus: *Fußgängerbrücken.* Basel/Boston/Berlin 2007, p. 194f.
D 6.13   from Teuffel, Patrick: *Entwerfen adaptiver Strukturen.* Dissertation, University of Stuttgart 2004, p. 12.

Potentials of New Technologies and Building Materials
D 7.1–D 7.7   BioMat/ITKE University of Stuttgart
D 7.8a   by Jmpost – University of Tasmania Scanning Electron Microscope, CC BY-SA 3.0, https://commons.wikimedia.org/w/index.php?curid=19586796
D 7.8b   Arzum Coban und Viktorya Ivanova; BioMat/ITKE – University of Stuttgart
D 7.9–D 7.15   BioMat/ITKE – University of Stuttgart

Efficiency and Sustainability of Materials and Structures
D 8.1   authors' representation according to DIN EN ISO 14040:2021-02/DIN EN 15804:2020-03
D 8.2   authors' illustration, Werner Lang and Patricia Schneider-Marin
D 8.3   according to DIN EN 15978:2012-10

D 8.4a   authors' illustration, data from Design2Eco, Final Report. *Lebenszyklusbetrachtung im Planungsprozess von Büro- und Verwaltungsgebäuden – Entscheidungsgrundlagen und Optimierungsmöglichkeiten für frühe Planungsphasen.* Stuttgart 2019
D 8.4b   authors' illustration, data from Hildebrand, Linda: *Strategic investment of embodied energy during the architectural planning process.* Dissertation, TU Delft 2014
D 8.4c   authors' illustration, data from Lang, Werner; Schneider, Patricia: *Gemeinschaftlich nachhaltig bauen. Forschungsbericht der ökologischen Untersuchung des genossenschaftlichen Wohnungsbauprojektes wagnisART.* Publ. by Oberste Baubehörde im Bayerischen Staatsministerium des Innern, für Bau und Verkehr (Materialien zum Wohnungsbau). Munich 2017
D 8.5, D 8.6   authors' illustration, Werner Lang and Patricia Schneider-Marin
D 8.7   KK Law; naturally:wood
D 8.8   authors' illustration, as per Brand, Stewart: *How Buildings Learn.* New York 1994
D 8.9   photoarchitecture.com
D 8.10   Georg Bechter Architektur + Design
D 8.11   Bruno Klomfar
D 8.12   Werner Lang
D 8.13   Reinhard Görner
D 8.14   authors' illustration, calculations done according to Eurocode by Schikore, Jonas; Wilken, Frauke, Professor of Structural Design Rainer Barthel, TU Munich 2020
D 8.15   from Brenner, Valentin: *Recyclinggerechtes Konstruieren: Konzepte für eine abfallfreie Konstruktionsweise im Bauwesen.* Stuttgart 2010, p. 15
D 8.16a inholz GmbH
D 8.16b Holzbau Willibald Longin GmbH
D 8.17   Thomas Haase
D 8.18   Thomas Kelsey/U.S. Department of Energy, Solar Decathlon, 2015.
D 8.19   Simone Matschi

Part E – Built Examples

p. 160   David Franck
p. 162, 163   Christina Kratzenberg
p. 165, 167   Thomas Nutt
p. 165, 166   Atelier Fischer Architekten
p. 168   Florian Holzherr
p. 170   Florian Nagler
p. 172–175   Sebastian Schels
p. 176–178   Jörg Hempel
p. 179   Demmel und Hadler
p. 180, 181, 182 top   Christa Lachenmaier/© HPP/ASTOC
p. 182 bottom   Schüßler-Plan
p. 184–187   Thomas Eicken
p. 188, 189   Ralph Böttig/© Die Halle Architekten
p. 190   Matthias Scheffler/© Die Halle Architekten
p. 191–193 diagrams   Thomas Schütte/© VG Bild-Kunst, Bonn 2021
p. 191   Markus Pietrek/Thomas Schütte/© VG Bild-Kunst, Bonn 2021
p. 192   Nic Tenwiggenhorn/© VG Bild-Kunst, Bonn 2021/Thomas Schütte/© VG Bild-Kunst, Bonn 2021
p. 193 top, centre top, bottom   Krogmann Ing.-Holzbau/Thomas Schütte/© VG Bild-Kunst, Bonn 2021
p. 193 centre bottom   RKW Architektur +
p. 194–196   Jörg Hempel
p. 197 top   Matthias Friedel

p. 197 bottom   Jörg Hempel
p. 198, 199   Jörg Hempel
p. 200   Ralph Richter
p. 201–205   Palladium
p. 206–210   Roman Keller
p. 211, 212   Jannes Linders
p. 214   Frank Kaltenbach
p. 215   Jannes Linders
p. 216, 219 top   Hall + Merrick Photographers
p. 217, 218 bottom   Simon Menges
p. 218 top   McShane Construction
p. 219 bottom   Simon Menges
p. 220, 223   Christian Richters
p. 222   Amy Barkow | Barkow Photo
p. 224   David Franck, Ostfildern
p. 225, 226, 229   Filippo Simonetti
p. 228   Baserga Mozzetti Architetti
p. 230–233   Mariela Apollonio
p. 234   BRS Building Systems
p. 235, 236   Jean-Luc Deru
p. 237, 238 bottom   Iwan Baan
p. 238 top   Wade Zimmerman
p. 238 centre   Timothy Schenck
p. 239 centre   Hardesty + Hanover
p. 239 top right   Timothy Schenck
p. 239 centre right   Brett Beyer
p. 239 bottom right   Iwan Baan
p. 240, 242   Bernd Borchardt
p. 245   Züblin Timber
p. 246, 248, 249 top   Enrico Cano
p. 249 bottom   Michel Denancé

Subject Index

Authors

Eberhard Möller
Born in 1970, Prof. Dr.-Ing. Architect

1991–1996 studied architecture at Technical University of Munich (TUM)
1996–1997 Master's programme in Historical Conservation at the Universidad Politécnica de Madrid
1994–2000 studied civil engineering at TUM, worked at architecture and engineering firms
Since 2001 member of the Bayerische Architektenkammer (Chamber of Architects)
Since 2001 independent work as an architect and civil engineer
2004–2011 research associate at the Architekturmuseum and at the Chair of Structural Design, TUM
2009 founded TWP Tragwerkplan Ingenieurgesellschaft für das Bauwesen mbH with Stefan Müller
2010 lectureship at the Coburg University of Applied Sciences and Arts, Department of Design
2011 earned doctorate at TUM
Since 2011 professor at the Faculty of Architecture and Civil Engineering at Karlsruhe University of Applied Sciences
2019 research semester at Princeton University, New Jersey

Sigrid Adriaenssens
Born in 1973, Associate Professor

2000 earned doctorate at the University of Bath
2002–2003 project engineer at Jane Wernick Associates, London
2003–2006 chief engineer at Ney and Partners, Brussels
2006–2009 lecturer at Vrije Universiteit Brussel and Sint-Lucas School of Architecture, Brussels and Ghent
2009–2016 Assistant Professor of Civil and Environmental Engineering at Princeton University, New Jersey
Since 2009 head of the research group Form Finding Lab at Princeton University, New Jersey
Since 2014 co-chair of Working Group 5 "Concrete Roof Shells" of the International Association of Shell and Spatial Structures
Since 2015 co-editor of the *International Journal of Space Structures*
Since 2016 associate professor at Princeton University
2019–2023 chair of the Aesthetics in Design Committee of the American Society of Civil Engineers (ASCE)
2021 Fellow of the ASCE, Structural Engineering Institute

Jan Akkermann
Born in 1969, Prof. Dr.-Ing.

1989–1994 studied civil engineering
1994–2000 research associate at the University of Karlsruhe (TH)
2000 earned doctorate at the University of(Karlsruhe (TH)
Since 2000 Krebs + Kiefer Ingenieure
Since 2007 managing partner at Krebs + Kiefer Ingenieure
Member of the board of the Deutscher Beton- und Bautechnik-Verein e. V.
Member of VBI, AIV, BÜV and PIANC
Since 2012 Professor of Structural Engineering – Infrastructure Preservation at Karlsruhe University of Applied Sciences
2020 Deutscher Ingenieurbaupreis (German Structural Engineering Prize)

Hanaa Dahy
Born in 1980, Jun. Prof. Dr.-Ing. M.Eng. Architect

2003–2006 studied Architectural Engineering in Cairo, earned Master's degree
Since 2003 freelance work as an architect in Cairo
2003–2009 associate professor at the Faculty of Engineering, Ain Shams University and at the Arab Academy for Science, Technology & Maritime Transport, Cairo

2009–2016 research associate at the Institute of Building Structures and Structural Design (ITKE), University of Stuttgart
2010–2014 earned doctorate at the University of Stuttgart
Since 2016 assistant professor at the ITKE, University of Stuttgart and founder of the Department of Biobased Materials and Materials Cycles in Architecture (BioMat)
Since 2017 member of the Architektenkammer Baden-Württemberg (Chamber of Architects)
Since 2020 Associate Professor in the Technical Faculty of IT and Design at Aalborg University, Copenhagen
WS 2020–2021 visiting professor, Nuremberg Institute of Technology

Maria E. Moreyra Garlock
Born in 1969, Professor

1991 Bachelor's degree in civil engineering, Lehigh University, Bethlehem, Pennsylvania
1993 Master's degree in civil engineering, Cornell University, Ithaca, New York
1993–1997 consulting engineer at Leslie E. Robertson Associates, R.L.L.P, New York
Since 1997 New York State Professional Engineering License
2002 earned doctorate at Lehigh University, Bethlehem, Pennsylvania
2003–2011 Assistant Professor of Civil and Environmental Engineering at Princeton University, New Jersey
2011–2017 Associate Professor of Civil and Environmental Engineering at Princeton University, New Jersey
Since 2017 Professor of Civil and Environmental Engineering at Princeton University, New Jersey
Since 2017 Fellow of the American Society of Civil Engineers (ASCE), Structural Engineering Institute
Since 2018 Head of Forbes Residential College, Princeton University, New Jersey

Christian Kayser
Born in 1980, Dr.-Ing.

1999–2004 studied architecture at TUM and the University of Bath (2001–2002)
2003 + 2004 architectural historian on the Diokaisaria / Olba campaigns (German Research Foundation (DFG) project)
Since 2004 project manager at the engineering firm Barthel & Maus Beratende Ingenieure, Munich
Since 2012 managing director at Barthel & Maus, Munich
2005–2010 Dissertation under Prof. R. Barthel, TUM
2008–2011 academic advisor at the Chair of Structural Design, Prof. R. Barthel, TUM
Since 2013 lecturer on the Technical Analysis of Historic Monuments at TUM
Since 2014 lecturer at Ludwig Maximilian University, Munich
Since 2013 lecturer at the Propstei Johannesberg, Fulda
Since 2020 managing partner at Kayser + Böttges, Barthel + Maus, Ingenieure und Architekten GmbH

Werner Lang
Born in 1961, Prof. Dr.-Ing. M. Arch. II (UCLA)

1982–1988 studied architecture at TUM and at the Architectural Association in London (1985 / 86)
1988–1990 Fulbright Scholar at the University of California, Los Angeles (UCLA)
1990 M. Arch. II (UCLA)
1990–1994 worked with the architecture firm Kurt Ackermann + Partner, Munich
Since 1993 member of the Bayerische Architektenkammer (Bavarian Chamber of Architects)
1994–2001 research assistant at the Chair for Building Technology, Prof. Dr. Thomas Herzog, TUM
2000 earned doctorate at TUM
2001–2006 architecture firm Werner Lang, Munich

2001–2007 lecturer for special topics in facade design and building materials sciences, Faculty of Architecture, TUM
2006 founded the architecture firm Lang Hugger Rampp GmbH Architekten, Munich
2008 – 2010 Associate Professor of Architecture and Sustainable Design, University of Texas at Austin School of Architecture (UTSOA)
2009–2010 Director of the Center for Sustainable Development at UTSoA
Since 2010 Professor of Energy Efficient and Sustainable Design and Building and Director of the Centre for Sustainable Building, Department of Civil, Geo and Environmental Engineering, TUM
Since 2010 Director of the Oskar von Miller Forum, Munich

Lars Schiemann
Born in 1973, Prof. Dr.-Ing.

1993–2000 studied civil engineering at the University of Karlsruhe and at TUM
2000–2002 employed at the engineering firm Mayr I Ludescher I Partner, Munich / Stuttgart
2001–2008 research assistant at the Chair for Structural Design, Prof. Dr.-Ing R. Barthel, TUM
Since 2006 lecturer in the Membrane Structures Master's programme at the Institute of Membrane and Shell Technologies IMS e. V.
2007–2012 employed at engineering firm Engineering + Design Linke und Moritz GbR, Rosenheim
Since 2009 consulting engineer, member of the Bayerische Ingenieurekammer – Bau (Bavarian Chamber of Engineers)
Since 2009 consulting engineer, engineering firm Mayr I Ludescher I Partner, Munich / Stuttgart
Since 2009 lecturer on Membrane Structures, TUM
2010 earned doctorate at TUM
2012–2015 Professor for Structural Design, Beuth Hochschule für Technik, Berlin
Since 2015 Professor of Structural Design at Munich University of Applied Sciences

Jonas Schikore
Born in 1986, MSc. Civil engineer

2006–2013 studied civil engineering at TUM
Since 2012 independent work with a focus on lightweight and membrane construction
2015–2016 structural engineer, engineering firm LEICHT Structural engineering and specialist consulting GmbH, Rosenheim
Since 2016 academic advisor at the TUM Chair of Structural Design (Prof. Dr.-Ing. Rainer Barthel)
Since 2016 lecturer at TUM
Since 2016 (projected completion late 2021) graduate doctoral programme at TUM – research on lightweight construction and bending-active mechanisms
Work and research with digital parametric design tools for geometric and mechanical modelling

Patricia Schneider-Marin
Born in 1973, Dipl.-Ing. Architect

1993–2000 studied architecture at TUM, EPFL and the University of Stuttgart, graduated
2000–2009 employed at the firms House and Robertson Architects, Coop Himmelb(l)au und Gehry Partners, Los Angeles
2009 founded own architectural office in Munich
Since 2010 research associate at the Chair of Energy Efficient and Sustainable Design and Building, TUM
2011 founded ±e Bürogemeinschaft für energieeffizientes Bauen
Since 8/2021 Associate Professor of Life Cycle Assessment and Environmental Systems Analysis at the Norwegian University of Science and Technology (NTNU), Trondheim